Writing and Reporting the News as a Story

Series Editor: Jeanne Zalesky
Series Editorial Assistant: Brian Mickelson
Marketing Manager: Susan Czajkowski
Production Editor: Michael Granger
Editorial Production Service: Marty Tenney, Modern Graphics, Inc.
Composition Buyer: Linda Cox
Manufacturing Buyer: JoAnne Sweeney
Electronic Composition: Modern Graphics, Inc.
Interior Design: Carol Somberg
Photo Researcher: PoYee Oster
Cover Designer: Kristina Mose-Libon

For related titles and support materials, visit our online catalog at www.ablongman.com.

ISBN 13: 978-0-205-44001-6
ISBN 10: 0-205-44001-0

Library of Congress Cataloging-in-Publication Data

Lloyd, Robert
Writing and reporting the news as a story / Robert Lloyd, Glenn Guzzo.
p. cm.
Includes bibliographical references and index.
ISBN-13: 978-0-205-44001-6
ISBN-10: 0-205-44001-0
1. Journalism—Authorship. 2. Reporters and reporting. I. Guzzo, Glenn.
II. Title.
PN4783.L59 2009
808'.06607—dc22

2007049367

Printed in the United States of America
10 9 8 7 6 5 4 3 2 1 RRD–VA 11 10 09 08

Credits appear on page 391, which constitutes an extension of the copyright page.

Writing and Reporting the News as a Story

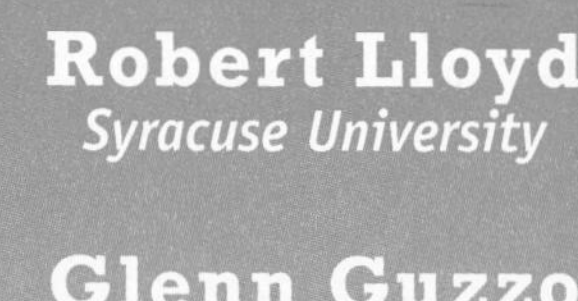

Robert Lloyd
Syracuse University

Glenn Guzzo

Boston New York San Francisco
Mexico City Montreal Toronto London Madrid Munich Paris
Hong Kong Singapore Tokyo Cape Town Sydney

DEDICATION

To Donna and Scheherazade,
Whose beauty is equaled only by their grace in enduring the special demands on a journalist and an author.

To Carla,
Whose mystery dances unfettered along the Wasatch horizon,
And Dominic,
Whose spirit inspires thanksgiving for the Onondaga wind.

Brief Contents

CHAPTER 1 Why Journalism Matters 1
CHAPTER 2 What Is News? 19
CHAPTER 3 Writing Leads 36
CHAPTER 4 Writing Simply 54
CHAPTER 5 How To Structure a News Story 74
CHAPTER 6 Interviewing Well 94
CHAPTER 7 Using Quotations Well 113
CHAPTER 8 Writing News about Crime 128
CHAPTER 9 Writing about Victims of Crimes 150
CHAPTER 10 Writing about Disasters 168
CHAPTER 11 How to Write News from Speeches, Press Conferences and Press Releases 186
CHAPTER 12 Writing the Meeting Story 204
CHAPTER 13 Writing Nontraditional Leads 219
CHAPTER 14 Obituaries: What You Do When Someone Dies 236
CHAPTER 15 Writing Profiles 253
CHAPTER 16 Features 272
CHAPTER 17 Ending Stories Well 289
CHAPTER 18 Writing and Reporting Online 304
CHAPTER 19 An Ethical Approach to Journalism 320
CHAPTER 20 Diversity as Ethics 336
CHAPTER 21 What Journalists Need to Know about the Law 353
CHAPTER 22 How to Land Your First Job (and Your First Promotion) 367

Contents

Preface xxix

CHAPTER 1

Why Journalism Matters 1

A Journalist's Role 2

ADVANCED TIP **What is a Journalist's Role?** 4

Journalism Matters 4

Journalists Give Information Unavailable from Other Sources 5

WIRED AND WIRELESS/WEB 6

Journalism Gives People a Sense of Community 7

ADVANCED TIP **A Journalist's Impact** 8

Journalism Helps the Democracy 8

Talent Showcase: **STEVE COLL** 10

Journalism Questions Institutions 12

Journalism Exposes Wrongs 14

ADVANCED TIP **Some Recent Stories Unearthed by Journalists** 15

Journalism Can Change the Way We Live 15

IN CONCLUSION 17

TOOLKIT 17

EXERCISE 1 17

EXERCISE 2 18

EXERCISE 3 18

CHAPTER 2

What Is News? 19

Guidelines 20
Against the Tide 21
What's Changed, What's Different 21

THE ART OF STORYTELLING 22

ADVANCED TIP What Is Currency 24

Ticket to the Backstage 24
People, People, People 26
Context 27

Talent Showcase: PAUL MOORE 28

ADVANCED TIP Traditional Elements of News Judgment 30

Conflict 30

HOW TO Show Context 30

Timeliness 32

WIRED AND WIRELESS/WEB 32

That's Just Weird 33
The Crowd 33

IN CONCLUSION 34
EXERCISE 1 34
EXERCISE 2 34
EXERCISE 3 34

CHAPTER 3

Writing Leads 36

Leads Play a Critical Role 37
Traditional Lead 38
How to Begin: The Essence 40

HOW TO Write a Lead 40

How to Write the First Sentence 40
Use Simple Language 41

THE ART OF STORYTELLING / A 21ST CENTURY APPRECIATION OF THE INVERTED PYRAMID 42

Clarity Works 48

Concrete Words 48

ADVANCED TIP **What Experienced Writers Say about Leads** 49

Shorter Is Better 49

WIRED AND WIRELESS/WEB 50

Analyzing Some Leads 51

IN CONCLUSION 52
TOOLKIT 52
EXERCISE 1 52
EXERCISE 2 53

CHAPTER 4
Writing Simply 54

1. Keep One Idea to Each Sentence 55

THE ART OF STORYTELLING 56

2. Use Fewer Adjectives and Adverbs 61
3. Omit Needless Words 62
4. Avoid Overusing Prepositions 62
5. Keep Number to a Minimum 63
6. Avoid Proper Names Close Together 64
7. Put Verbs as Close to the Subject as Possible 65
8. Avoid Using Not 66
9. Avoid Repetitive Phrases 66
10. Write with Anglo-Saxon Words 66

WIRED AND WIRELESS/TV 68

Talent Showcase: RON HUTCHESON 69

IN CONCLUSION 70
TOOLKIT 71
EXERCISE 1 71
EXERCISE 2 71
EXERCISE 3 72
EXERCISE 4 72
EXERCISE 5 72
EXERCISE 6 73

CHAPTER 5

How To Structure a News Story 74

Techniques Before, During and After Writing 75

HOW TO **Write a News Story** 76

The Essential Nut Graph 77

Talent Showcase: **ROY WENZL** 78

WIRED AND WIRELESS/NARRATIVE WRITING AND THE WEB 81

Writing Effective Nut Graphs 83

The Trend Nut Graph 83

The Counter-Trend Nut Graph 83

The Timing Nut Graph (Two Variations) 83

The Counter-Intuitive Nut Graph 83

The Analytical Nut Graph 84

Narrative Techniques 84

THE ART OF STORYTELLING 86

Support the Lead 88

Self-Editing 89

Pace 89

Redundancy 90

Extraneous Information 91

EXERCISE 1 92

EXERCISE 2 92

EXERCISE 3 92

CHAPTER 6

Interviewing Well 94

Preparation 95

THE ART OF STORYTELLING 96

HOW TO **Tell If a Source Is Being Evasive** 97

Rapport with Sources 98

WIRED AND WIRELESS/INTERVIEWING WITH E-MAIL 99

Interview Integrity 100

WIRED AND WIRELESS/TV 100

Talent Showcase: BILL MARIMOW 102

Interviewing Techniques 104
Ask Questions When You Already Know the Answer 105
But Leave Yourself Open to Surprise 105
Insist on Answers, Not Merely Responses 106
The Power of Silence 106

ADVANCED TIP The Ultrasensitive Source 106

Seek Descriptive Answers 107
Above All, Don't Leave the Interview Confused 107
Taking Notes and Recording Interviews 107
Anonymous Sources 109

IN CONCLUSION 110
TOOLKIT 111
EXERCISE 1 111
EXERCISE 2 111
EXERCISE 3 111

CHAPTER 7
Using Quotations Well 113

Whom To Quote 115
What Quotes to Use 115

ADVANCED TIP Use Quotes Wisely 115

THE ART OF STORYTELLING 116

ADVANCED TIP When to Paraphrase 119

How to Quote Them 120
Quality Trumps Quantity 121
Structuring Quotes 122

WIRED AND WIRELESS/QUOTES CAN BE DECEITFUL 123

Ethical Quoting 124

IN CONCLUSION 125
EXERCISE 1 126
EXERCISE 2 126
EXERCISE 3 127

CHAPTER 8
Writing News about Crime 128

Why Crime Stories Are So Popular 129
Crime Is a Personal Story 129
ADVANCED TIP Criminal Justice Timeline (State Felonies) 130
Crime Is a People Story 130
Crime Is a Community Story 130
Crime Is a Trend Story 131
Crime Is a Political Story 131
Crime Never Ceases to Amaze 131
THE ART OF STORYTELLING 132
Crime Is an Enterprise Story 134
Crime Story Essentials 135
ADVANCED TIP Knowing Your Way around Court 135
Writing the Incident Story 136
Identity Issues 138
HOW TO Avoid Rookie Mistakes 139
Talent Showcase: MICHAEL CONNELLY 140
Writing Accident Stories 142
Writing Fire Stories 143
Case Study A CRIME REPORTER ON HER BEAT 144
Report More, Write Less 146

IN CONCLUSION 147
TOOLKIT 147
EXERCISE 1 148
EXERCISE 2 148

CHAPTER 9
Writing about Victims of Crimes 150

Why Talk To Victims 152
Filling in the Puzzle 152
How To Approach Victims 153
THE ART OF STORYTELLING 154
HOW TO Approach Victims 157

The Whippy Dip 158
ADVANCED TIP Why Journalists Talk to the Victims 159
Elements of a Victim's Story 159
Talent Showcase: TINA GRIEGO 160
Writing the Victim's Side 162
What To Ask 163
WIRED AND WIRELESS/WEB 164
A Last Example 165

IN CONCLUSION 166
EXERCISE 166

CHAPTER 10
Writing about Disasters 168

Breaking News 169
HOW TO Organize a Story on Disasters 170
WIRED AND WIRELESS/WEB 172
How Eyewitnesses Can Help Tell the Story 174
Daily Enterprise 175
THE ART OF STORYTELLING 176
ADVANCED TIP Covering 9/11 180
Enterprise: Start with Stakeholders 181
Resisting Distractions 181
Public Service Journalism 182
Pulitzer Prize Examples 183

IN CONCLUSION 183
TOOLKIT 184
EXERCISE 1 184
EXERCISE 2 185

CHAPTER 11

How to Write News from Speeches, Press Conferences and Press Releases 186

Speeches 187

THE ART OF STORYTELLING 190

Press Conferences 192

WIRED AND WIRELESS/WEB 194

Press Conference Tips from Veterans 194

HOW TO Use Websites 196

Writing the Story: Press Conferences and Speeches 196

Press Releases 198

ADVANCED TIP Online Exchanges 199

Talent Showcase: DIEDTRA HENDERSON 200

IN CONCLUSION 202

EXERCISE 1 202

EXERCISE 2 203

CHAPTER 12

Writing the Meeting Story 204

ADVANCED TIP What's Missing? 206

Avoiding a Journalistic Dead End 206

Reporting the Meeting Story: Get Ahead of the Curve 206

Writing Clearly: Know the Language of Government, Then Translate It 207

THE ART OF STORYTELLING 208

Dull, But Important 210

Writing the Meeting Story 211

The One-Issue Story 211

The Pros and Cons of Each Lead 212

ADVANCED TIP A Matter of Time 212

ADVANCED TIP Jargon Is Your Enemy 214

Numbers as Context 214

The Roundup Story 214

Talent Showcase: JANE VON BERGEN 215

IN CONCLUSION 217

EXERCISE 1 217

EXERCISE 2 218

CHAPTER 13

Writing Nontraditional Leads 219

Reporting Entertaining Leads 220

Storytelling 221

ADVANCED TIP Think Storytelling 222

Anecdotes 223

THE ART OF STORYTELLING 224

Situationers 226

ADVANCED TIP Nontraditional Leads 227

Roundup 228

Intriguing Statement 229

Talent Showcase: GAYLE REAVES 230

Change in Direction 232

ADVANCED TIP Impact of a Weak Lead 233

Humor 233

IN CONCLUSION 234

EXERCISE 1 234

EXERCISE 2 235

EXERCISE 3 235

CHAPTER 14

Obituaries: What You Do When Someone Dies 236

Why Obituaries Matter 238

ADVANCED TIP **The Past Is Prologue** 238

Life Stories vs. Paid Obits 239

THE ART OF STORYTELLING 240

ADVANCED TIP **Celebrate a Life** 242

How To Write Life Stories 242

HOW TO **Write Life Stories** 243

Talent Showcase: **ALANA BARANICK** 244

How To Talk To the Bereaved 245
Develop an Eye for the Common 247
Always Check 248
Look for the Unusual 249

IN CONCLUSION 250
TOOLKIT 250
EXERCISE 1 251
EXERCISE 2 252

CHAPTER 15

Writing Profiles 253

Choosing the Right Person 254
Well-known vs. The Unknown 255

ADVANCED TIP **Who Makes a Good Profile Subject** 255

WIRED AND WIRELESS/WEB 256

News Peg 257

THE ART OF STORYTELLING 258

Capturing the Essence 260
An Example of Capturing the Essence 261
Conflict 262
Change 262

ADVANCED TIP **Before You Write a Profile, Answer These Questions** 263

Writing the Profile 263
Have You Interviewed Enough? 263

Talent Showcase: KATHERINE BOO 264

What Is Your Best Beginning? 266
Have You Justified Why You Should Write This Profile? 267
When Do You Give the Person's Background? 268
Have You Identified the Best Moments? 268
Do You Have an Ending? 269

IN CONCLUSION 269
TOOLKIT 270
EXERCISE 270

CHAPTER 16

Features 272

What Is a Feature? 273

ADVANCED TIP What Is a Feature? 273

Time Element 274
Organization 274
Feature Leads 275

Talent Showcase: TOM HALLMAN 276

Reconstruction Leads 278

ADVANCED TIP Features vs. Breaking News 278

Intriguing Statement 279

THE ART OF STORYTELLING 280

The Middle 282
Chronology 283
How To Use Chronology 283

ADVANCED TIP Chronology Is Your Friend 283

WIRED AND WIRELESS/WEB 284

Present, Past, Future 285
Endings 286

IN CONCLUSION 287
TOOLKIT 287
EXERCISE 1 287
EXERCISE 2 288

CHAPTER 17

Ending Stories Well 289

Why Endings Matter 290

ADVANCED TIP Characteristics of Strong Endings 290

Echo the Lead 291

HOW TO Echo the Lead 291

An Example of an Echo 291

THE ART OF STORYTELLING 292

Other Examples of Echoes 295
The Kicker Quote 296

ADVANCED TIP Don't Overuse Kicker Quotes 296

Some Kickers that Work 297

Talent Showcase: BARRY SIEGEL 298

Being Careful, Fair 298

Wrap-up Scene 300

IN CONCLUSION 302

EXERCISE 1 302

EXERCISE 2 303

CHAPTER 18

Writing and Reporting Online 304

Like a Wire Service 306

Think with Visuals 307

THE ART OF STORYTELLING 308

Breaking News 310

Talent Showcase: JIM AMOSS 312

What About Voice? 313

ADVANCED TIP Top Newspaper Websites 315

Driven By Numbers 315

What Beginning Journalists Should Know 316

IN CONCLUSION 317

EXERCISE 1 317

EXERCISE 2 319

EXERCISE 3 319

CHAPTER 19

An Ethical Approach to Journalism 320

ADVANCED TIP Principles of Journalistic Independence and Professional Conduct 321

Don't Accept Anything of Value from Anybody 322

Resist Alliances that Suggest Conflicts of Interest 322

ADVANCED TIP Should Sports Reporters Vote for the Heisman? 323

THE ART OF STORYTELLING 324

Do Your Own Work 326

Don't Deceive Your Audience or Your Sources 327

ADVANCED TIP Be Aboveboard 328

When In Doubt, Ask 328

WIRED AND WIRELESS/WEB 329

Disclosure Is Preventive Medicine 329

ADVANCED TIP Facts or Truth? 329

Talent Showcase: GREG MOORE 330

What Journalists Can Do 332

IN CONCLUSION 333

TOOLKIT 333

EXERCISE 1 333

EXERCISE 2 333

EXERCISE 3 335

CHAPTER 20

Diversity as Ethics 336

ADVANCED TIP What about the Photographs? 337

True Newsroom Diversity 338

ADVANCED TIP The Voice of Diversity 339

Diversity Improves Content 341

THE ART OF STORYTELLING 342

ADVANCED TIP Not Just Race and Gender 346

Talent Showcase: MARJIE LUNDSTROM 347

IN CONCLUSION 350
TOOLKIT 351
EXERCISE 1 351
EXERCISE 2 352
EXERCISE 3 352

CHAPTER 21

Libel: What Journalists Need to Know about the Law 353

Limits of Speech and Print 354
What Is Libel 355

ADVANCED TIP What Is Libel? 356

ADVANCED TIP What the Plaintiff Must Prove in Libel Cases? 356

Defenses 357

ADVANCED TIP Defending Libel 357

Public Official, Public Figure 358

ADVANCED TIP Landmark Case 360

The Chiquita Case 361
Wen Ho Lee 362
Privacy 362

WIRED AND WIRELESS/WEB 363

What Journalists Are Allowed to Print 364

IN CONCLUSION 365
EXERCISE 1 365
EXERCISE 2 365
EXERCISE 3 366

CHAPTER 22

How to Land Your First Job (and Your First Promotion) 367

Your Search 368
Cast Your Net Wide 368
Set Realistic Expectations 368

WIRED AND WIRELESS/WEB 369

Your Application 369
Cover Letter 369
Résumé 370
Published Work 370

ADVANCED TIP **Advice for Résumés** 370

THE ART OF STORYTELLING 371

ADVANCED TIP **How Many Clips?** 372

Your Interview 372
Your Job 373
Demands of the Job 373
Proving Yourself 373
Performance 374
Attitude 374

IN CONCLUSION 374

INDEX 375
PHOTO CREDITS 391

List of Features

Advanced Tip

A Journalist's Impact 8

Some Recent Stories Unearthed by Journalists 15

What Is Currency 24

Traditional Elements of News Judgment 30

What Experienced Writers Say about Leads 49

The Ultrasensitive Source 106

Use Quotes Wisely 115

When to Paraphrase 119

Criminal Justice Timeline (State Felonies) 130

Knowing Your Way around Court 135

Why Journalists Talk to the Victims 159

Covering 9/11 180

Online Exchanges 199

What's Missing? 206

A Matter of Time 212

Jargon Is Your Enemy 214

Think Storytelling 222

Nontraditional Leads 227

Impact of a Weak Lead 233

The Past Is Prologue 238

Celebrate a Life 242

Who Makes a Good Profile Subject 255

Before You Write a Profile, Answer These Questions 263

What Is a Feature? 273

Features vs. Breaking News 278

Chronology Is Your Friend 283

Characteristics of Strong Endings 290

Don't Overuse Kicker Quotes 296

Top Newspaper Websites (unique visitors in millions) as of November, 2006 315

Principles of Journalistic Independence and Professional Conduct 321

Should Sports Reporters Vote for the Heisman? 323

Be Aboveboard 328

Facts or Truth? 329

What about the Photographs? 337

The Voice of Diversity 339

Not Just Race and Gender 346

What Is Libel? 356

What the Plaintiff Must Prove in Libel Cases? 356

Defending Libel 357

Landmark Case 360

Advice for Résumés 370

How Many Clips? 372

How To

Show Context 30

Write a Lead 40

Write a News Story 76

Tell If a Source Is Being Evasive 97

Avoid Rookie Mistakes 139

Approach Victims 157

Organize a Story on Disasters 170

Use Websites 196

Write Life Stories 243

Echo the Lead 291

The Art of Storytelling

The Art of Storytelling 22

The Art of Storytelling/A 21st Century Appreciation of the Inverted Pyrmid 42

The Art of Storytelling 56
The Art of Storytelling 86
The Art of Storytelling 96
The Art of Storytelling 116
The Art of Storytelling 132
The Art of Storytelling 154
The Art of Storytelling 176
The Art of Storytelling 190
The Art of Storytelling 208
The Art of Storytelling 224
The Art of Storytelling 240
The Art of Storytelling 258
The Art of Storytelling 280
The Art of Storytelling 292
The Art of Storytelling 308
The Art of Storytelling 324
The Art of Storytelling 342
The Art of Storytelling 371

Wired and Wireless

Wired and Wireless/Web 6
Wired and Wireless/Web 32
Wired and Wireless/Web 50
Wired and Wireless/Web 68
Wired and Wireless/Narrative Writing and the Web 81
Wired and Wireless/Interviewing with E-mail 99
Wired and Wireless/TV 100
Wired and Wireless/Quotes Can Be Deceitful 123
Wired and Wireless/Web 164
Wired and Wireless/Web 172
Wired and Wireless/TV 194
Wired and Wireless/Web 256
Wired and Wireless/Web 284

Wired and Wireless/Web 329
Wired and Wireless/Web 363
Wired and Wireless/Web 369

Talent Showcase

Steve Coll 10
Paul Moore 28
Ron Hutcheson 69
Roy Wenzl 78
Bill Marimow 102
Michael Connelly 140
Tina Griego 160
Diedtra Henderson 200
Jan Von Bergen 215
Gayle Reaves 230
Alana Baranick 244
Katherine Boo 264
Tom Hallman 276
Barry Siegel 298
Jim Amoss 312
Greg Moore 330
Marjie Lundstrom 347

Preface

The newspaper editor cautioned against a president and his administration who tried to silence the press in the name of national security.

"If the press is muzzled, only the American people will be deceived," he wrote.

The year was 1950, the war was in Korea, the president was Democrat Harry S. Truman and the editor was also a newspaper publisher and owner, John S. Knight.

The anecdote illustrates that, throughout American history and regardless of political party, journalists have had to be independent and courageous to resist power's preference for secrecy.

Knight's wisdom is as relevant today as ever.

Today, the opportunistic forces of secrecy are political, ideological and financial, each with unholy alliances in government. They inflame public fears about terrorism and privacy, then attack the press with uncommon vigor. They prey on public concerns to erode public confidence in the press, but their agenda is to hide from public scrutiny.

The encouraging news: Despite obstructionist federal government, difficult economic times and shallow public approval, the 21st century press has risen to the occasion repeatedly when citizens have needed it most.

When terrorists attacked the World Trade Center Sept. 11, 2001, causing fear among citizens and confusion in the economy, journalists fanned across the globe to answer readers' urgent questions. How could this happen? Is it safe to travel? Why do Muslims hate America? What is it about Afghanistan that makes it a haven for terrorists? Will my son or daughter be going to war? These and hundreds more were answered only by journalists.

When, after years of warnings in the press about vulnerable levees and decaying bridges, Hurricane Katrina destroyed New Orleans in August 2005, journalists disregarded their own safety. They reached victims far in advance of paralyzed federal, state and local bureaucrats. For weeks, journalists in New Orleans, Biloxi, Miss., and elsewhere in Katrina's path threw a lifeline to homeless and nearly hopeless thousands, and to a horrified nation: reliable information and ways to help each other. Journalists made the fate of their own homes and futures secondary to the life-or-death needs of other victims—needs beyond the talent and will of inept public officials.

When the United States invaded Iraq in 2003, journalists worldwide risked their lives to report from battlefields and Iraqi communities. Their words and pictures described a shattered nation struggling to reinvent itself as a democracy amid daily atrocities. By late 2007, the Committee to Protect Journalists reported 124 journalists had been killed on the job—more in those four years than in the much longer Vietnam War. More than a dozen journalists were killed accidentally from U.S. military fire. Iraqi journalists suffered the majority of deaths—most were murdered. Other journalists, including American Jill Carroll, a freelancer for *The Christian Science Monitor*, were abducted (she was held captive for 82 days, then released). More, including ABC News co-anchor Bob Woodruff, suffered serious wounds.

Meanwhile, it was left to journalists to expose the secrets of an American administration in times of a war.

First, news organizations revealed prisoner abuse in Iraq (at Abu Ghraib prison), Afghanistan and Guantanamo Bay, Cuba. The Bush Administration had resisted attempts to limit its authority and acknowledged few boundaries of law, geography or time. It claimed a right to hold prisoners indefinitely, to the end of a vaguely defined war against terrorism that most analysts figured would never end. It insisted it could hold these prisoners without charges or access to legal help and to treat them as it saw fit, without regard to American and international laws against inhumane treatment. In late 2007, news reports indicated that of neearly 800 prisoners once held at Guantanamo, nearly 500 had been released, while only about 10 others had been charged with crimes.

The Washington Post's Dana Priest won a Pulitzer Prize after revealing in 2005 that the Bush Administration had taken this stance a giant step further, by exporting terrorism suspects to secret "black site" prisons in Eastern Europe and elsewhere. This was done, *The Post* reported, without the knowledge of the nations where the suspects were seized and without the knowledge of the U.S. Congress.

Then *The New York Times*' James Risen and Eric Lichtblau won a Pulitzer Prize after revealing in 2005 that the Bush Administration had launched a massive domestic campaign of warrant-less electronic eavesdropping. The administration claimed it had the right to monitor any citizen telephone conversations and to do so without first convincing a judge that a crime was suspected.

It is no exaggeration to say that American citizens would know very little about any of these, including Sept. 11, 2001, and Hurricane Katrina, if not for a free, independent, courageous press.

These are only the highest-profile examples. Every day in every state, journalists fight for enforcement of existing laws involving concealed public records, closed courtrooms and secret meetings of public officials.

Recent events sharpen the point that an independent press, constitutionally empowered to scrutinize government, has always had a dual relationship with government—co-existing for mutual need, but often adversarial. It is true today. It was true in John S. Knight's day. It was true long before that.

Journalists accepting this responsibility keep citizens first in mind. The spirit of reporting we have seen in Iraq and Washington, D.C., is every bit as vital in American communities of every size. Hurricane Katrina was, foremost, a local story. The 9/11 attacks created countless stories of local concern. Short of war, the actions of state legislatures, school boards, police departments, city councils and zoning commissions have more direct impact on readers' lives and their tax dollars than the federal government.

The authors offer this book as a way to encourage and prepare for the satisfying experience of serving communities and democracy while sharpening your skills as reporters and writers.

We offer many voices of experience—ours, as reporters, editors and teachers, and those of some of the most accomplished journalists of this era—so that you may advance your careers with more confidence. We offer many lessons learned on the job so that you may start faster, aim higher and require correction less often.

While today's finest journalists sharpened their skills over years of varied and demanding experience, many professionals have yet to master the writing and reporting techniques shared in this book. It's not that these lessons are too sophisticated for beginning journalists. It's not that the veterans are incapable or miscast. They simply have not been taught in an industry that invests considerably less in training and development than other professions.

In addition to the training gap, cost-cutting in print, broadcast and online news operations contributes to the insecurity of new and veteran journalists. This book emphasizes techniques to make you more secure about your skills and about your place in the ever-evolving Information Age. We aim to supplement the expertise of your classroom instructors and to sharpen the journalism you perform in class and elsewhere. By emphasizing on-the-job experience, we seek to help you prepare for professional success. In all industries, the people best trained for the challenges they are most likely to face are the ones who excel when expectations are highest.

We have kept that foremost in mind as we organized, wrote and designed a book that can be used for years by journalists who choose to excel.

Organization

We chose the number of chapters and their sequence to coincide with the way many journalism classes are taught. But we also have created each chapter to stand alone for those instructors who wish to customize and for those students who wish to explore what their instructors bypass. This makes the book flexible enough to be used by a wide array of classes, yet complete enough for students who want to explore its full depth at different times as their careers evolve.

Writing

We have chosen clear, direct language to share the successful practices of respected news organizations. It's the voice of experience in a quest to remain unambiguous. But we scorn homogeneity. Diversity—in staffing, writing styles and content—is a hallmark of journalistic success. There is seldom a sole correct way to proceed on any story. In many chapters, we offer alternatives, while also warning about the most common ways journalists fall short of reader expectations and their own.

Talent Showcase

We quote outstanding journalists throughout the book. The superb journalists who are showcased individually in chapter sidebars represent diverse backgrounds and talents. What they have in common is the admiration of their peers. Many have won Pulitzer Prizes. Most are frequent visitors to classrooms. Each is a journalist that just about any journalism class would love to have as a guest speaker. We bring them all to you, and they bring priceless gifts—specific reporting and writing tips that have helped set them apart as the best in their craft.

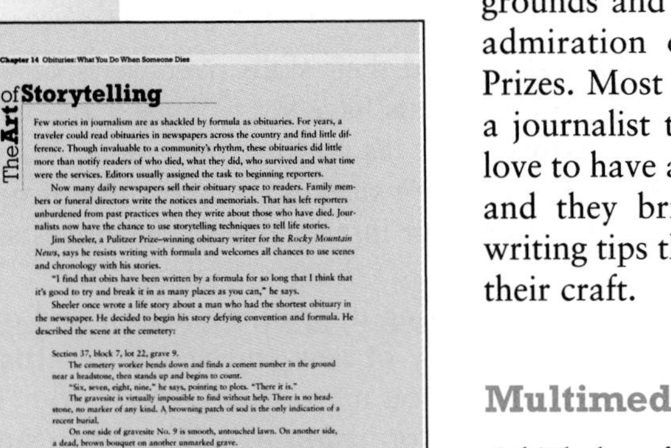

240 Chapter 14 Obituaries: What You Do When Someone Dies

The Art of Storytelling

Few stories in journalism are as shackled by formula as obituaries. For years, a traveler could read obituaries in newspapers across the country and find little difference. Though invaluable to a community's rhythm, these obituaries did little more than notify readers of who died, what they did, who survived and what time were the services. Editors usually assigned the task to beginning reporters.

Now many daily newspapers sell their obituary space to readers. Family members or funeral directors write the notices and memorials. That has left reporters unburdened from past practices when they write about those who have died. Journalists now have the chance to use storytelling techniques to tell life stories.

Jim Sheeler, a Pulitzer Prize–winning obituary writer for the *Rocky Mountain News*, says he resists writing with formula and welcomes all chances to use scenes and chronology with his stories.

"I find that obits have been written by a formula for so long that I think that it's good to try and break it in as many places as you can," he says.

Sheeler once wrote a life story about a man who had the shortest obituary in the newspaper. He decided to begin his story defying convention and formula. He described the scene at the cemetery:

> Section 37, block 7, lot 22, grave 9.
>
> The cemetery worker bends down and finds a cement number in the ground near a headstone, then stands up and begins to count.
>
> "Six, seven, eight, nine," he says, pointing to plots. "There it is."
>
> The gravesite is virtually impossible to find without help. There is no headstone, no marker of any kind. A browning patch of sod is the only indication of a recent burial.
>
> On one side of gravesite No. 9 is smooth, untouched lawn. On another side, a dead, brown bouquet on another unmarked grave.
>
> The man in the new gravesite spent the bulk of his life working in the reflection of some of the city's most powerful people, in a job where he had to look up

with Nicholson in Philadelphia in the mid-1980s. In her book *The Dead Beat*, Marilyn Johnson says editors put Nicholson on the obituary desk as punishment, but he soon made the most of his new assignment, turning his daily stories into an art form. He even won an award from the American Society of Newspaper Editors in 1987 for his obituary work.

"He figured out a way to make the obit

leach into the

200 Chapter 11 How to Write News from Speeches, Press Conferences and Press Releases

Talent Showcase

DIEDTRA HENDERSON

Reporter, *The Boston Globe*

With 200 new e-mailed press releases arriving every day, Diedtra Henderson has to be decisive to the point of being ruthless about when to hit the delete key. After more than a decade of covering health, technology, and science, she has her system down to, well, a science.

Her techniques are instructive to reporters concerned about news judgment and time management and to public-relations agents trying to get a reporter's attention.

The e-mails are not spam. Covering the Federal Drug Administration for *The Boston Globe*, Henderson welcomes the press releases because they often contain sources or alert her to something out of the ordinary.

But those gems are rare. Press releases, which push a single point of view, are not meant to be published, but to trigger further reporting for well-balanced stories. On Henderson's computer, few press releases have a life expectancy of more than a few seconds.

"If there's nothing in the first three to four sentences, it gets deleted. If the topic is something I think I might come back to, it goes into the file for a future story," she says.

Bottom line: Of 200, only five survive for a potential story that day. Twenty achieve dubious, "maybe someday" status and 175 get the computer-version of the guillotine.

Lesson one to press-release writers: Get to the point quickly. "The least helpful are those written in story form and bury the news below the lead," Henderson advises.

She prefers the science press releases from Washington University in St. Louis, which summarizes its items on the first page with a no-nonsense approach. "It's, here's the news. Here's the source. Then they devote no more than one more page to each of those items."

Henderson also finds helpful the approach by the *New England Journal of Medicine*, which sorts its releases in order of newsworthiness, and divides them among those that are of public and political interest and those that are cutting-edge science.

When the reporter-source rapport has been well established, phone calls can be even more efficient.

"I don't need to see a whole press release," Henderson says. "Call me, say there's something going on and here's what's interesting about it. Instead of taking the time to polish a press release, and get your execs to sign off on it, run it by me."

That conversation might go like this:

PR person: "I've got this."

Henderson: "Nope."

"I've got this."

"Nope."

"Well, I've also got this."

"Okay, tell me more."

This efficiency is likelier when everyone understands what is newsworthy. While news judgment is just that—

Reporters should remain skeptical, but not cynical. Don't assume that self-interested research or laudatory press releases are inaccurate or deceptive. Also, those who produce press releases can be reporters' allies.

The Globe's Henderson says that when she's looking for human experience to explain medical issues, "some of the best sources for that are the drug companies.

Multimedia

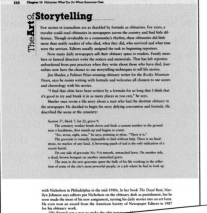

Gil Thelen, former publisher of *The Tampa Tribune* and a veteran editor, says that journalists of the future must be "amphibious," able and willing to excel in print, online and on the air. While this book deliberately emphasizes print skills, it offers numerous examples of how journalists online and on the air can do the job differently, faster, better.

This book is print-oriented for many reasons:

- This is a book about writing and reporting. For those talents (distinguished from visual journalism), more print skills adapt to online and broadcast than vice versa. Therefore, sound training in print journalism is a foundation to build on for success on other media platforms. Walter Cronkite and Bob Schieffer began their careers in print.

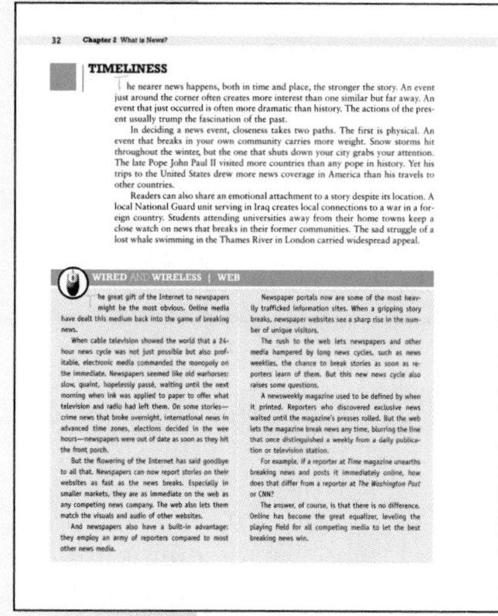

32 Chapter 2 What is News?

TIMELINESS

The nearer news happens, both in time and place, the stronger the story. An event just around the corner often creates more interest than one similar but far away. An event that just occurred is often more dramatic than history. The actions of the present usually trump the fascination of the past.

In deciding a news event, closeness takes two paths. The first is physical. An event that breaks in your own community carries more weight. Snow storms hit throughout the winter, but the one that shuts down your city grabs your attention. The late Pope John Paul II visited more countries than any pope in history. Yet his trips to the United States drew more news coverage in America than his travels to other countries.

Readers can also share an emotional attachment to a story despite its location. A local National Guard unit serving in Iraq creates local connections to a war in a foreign country. Students attending universities away from their home towns keep a close watch on news that breaks in their former communities. The sad struggle of a lost whale swimming in the Thames River in London carried widespread appeal.

WIRED AND WIRELESS | WEB

The great gift of the Internet to newspapers might be the most obvious. Online media have dealt this medium back into the game of breaking news.

When cable television showed the world that a 24-hour news cycle was not just possible but also profitable, electronic media commanded the monopoly on the immediate. Newspapers seemed like old warhorses: slow, quaint, hopelessly passé, waiting until the next morning when ink was applied to paper to offer what television and radio had left them. On some stories—crime news that broke overnight, international news in advanced time zones, elections decided in the wee hours—newspapers were out of date as soon as they hit the front porch.

But the flowering of the Internet has said goodbye to all that. Newspapers can now report stories on their websites as fast as the news breaks. Especially in smaller markets, they are as immediate on the web as any competing news company. The web also lets them match the visuals and audio of other websites.

And newspapers also have a built-in advantage: they employ an army of reporters compared to most other news media.

Newspaper portals now are some of the most heavily trafficked information sites. When a gripping story breaks, newspaper websites see a sharp rise in the number of unique visitors.

The rush to the web lets newspapers and other media hampered by long news cycles, such as news weeklies, the chance to break stories as soon as reporters learn of them. But this new news cycle also raises some questions.

A newsweekly magazine used to be defined by when it printed. Reporters who discovered exclusive news waited until the magazine's presses rolled. But the web lets the magazine break news any time, blurring the line that once distinguished a weekly from a daily publication or television station.

For example, if a reporter at *Time* magazine unearths breaking news and posts it immediately online, how does that differ from a reporter at *The Washington Post* or CNN?

The answer, of course, is that there is no difference. Online has become the great equalizer, leveling the playing field for all competing media to let the best breaking news win.

- While newspapers' imminent demise has been predicted for generations, newspapers still employ the majority of journalists. At least for now, young journalists most likely will begin their careers at a newspaper.
- Newspaper websites are the most-visited news sites in most major metro areas. Journalists performing for the printed newspaper are the most frequent suppliers of news to those sites. Many major newspapers also have television partners. Typically in those relationships, more print journalists appear on the air than broadcast journalists appear in print.
- The result of newsroom reductions in all media is more repackaged news. Most of these stories originate with print journalists, as do the stories that fuel talk shows and blogs.
- "Old media" is the province of the journalism of verification, which is what this textbook teaches.

No industry writes the ballads of its own doom more often—and has more outsiders joining the chorus—than mainstream media. While there is good reason to face the music, a few verses of comfort are not out of tune. No medium has ever died. TV failed to fulfill widespread expectations that it would kill radio or newspapers. Online media, which have done more damage to TV viewership than to newspaper readership, haven't killed anything. Troublesome readership and ratings declines owe more to the inevitable math of dispersing the audience among more media choices. Although the "old media" of newspapers and broadcast TV may have to continue doing with less of everything, they still dominate compared to the audience and advertising revenues for the growth media (radio, cable-TV and online).

This all might change. Up-and-coming journalists might find themselves changing media platforms mid-career. More likely, they will perform several functions for news organizations that use all media.

Regardless, in this Information Age, those who gather, edit and present news and information expertly have great value to a society that demands to be entertained and needs to be informed to self-govern.

Because of its pivotal role in the rise or fall of democracy, journalism is more precious than any one media format. *Journalism* must be preserved, at all costs. There are places on this planet where journalism is impotent or nonexistent. Wherever that is true, other freedoms are scarce, too.

The most promising way to preserve journalism is to keep it vital through continual improvement. That starts with its practitioners. They must be ever sharper—smarter, more talented, more agile, more expert, less gullible. That is why this textbook was written, to pass along knowledge from one generation to the next. Then, the latest generation starts with all of that, adds all that is yet to be learned, and passes it along in turn.

That circle of education, and the will to put it to use, is the secret to extending freedom as a way of life.

Acknowledgments

To all those who surrendered their time and wisdom so selflessly in interviews that were equally thoughtful and inspiring.

To our editors, Jeanne Zalesky and Brian Mickelson, for encouraging our vision, supporting our effort and shining a guiding light on our path.

To Professors Mark Obbie, Roy Gutterman and Joel Kaplan for their gracious assistance on media law, and to Walt Wasilewski for his thoughtful suggestions and improvements.

And to Tim Bunn for his patient feedback on writing, politics and life.

The authors also want to thank the following reviewers of the manuscript: Barbara Bullington, East Carolina University, Neal Haldane, Madonna University; Edward Horowitz, Cleveland State University; Reed Markham, Salt Lake Community College; Patricia G. Newberry, Miami University–Ohio; and Barbara S. Schlichtman, University of Hawaii at Hilo.

Writing and Reporting the News as a Story

CHAPTER 1

Why Journalism Matters

IN THIS CHAPTER, YOU WILL LEARN:

- A journalist performs many important roles in society.
- Journalism matters to a free democracy.
- Journalism can unite a community during times of crises.
- Journalists deliver information unavailable from other sources.
- Journalism exposes wrongs.
- Journalism questions institutions.
- Journalism can change the way we live.

If they wanted these questions answered, the press was going to have to ask them.
Steve Coll, former managing editor, *The Washington Post*

INJURED VETERANS AT WALTER REED ARMY MEDICAL CENTER had complained to their commanders for at least three years. Yes, doctors and nurses treated them well at the Army's top hospital. But when these soldiers suffering from crippling injuries in Iraq and Afghanistan began rehabilitation, their care turned deplorable.

These outpatients lived in rooms and apartments infested with roaches. Moldy walls were collapsing before them. The bureaucracy was numbing. The Army's forms, often overlapping and contradictory, frequently were lost. Even some soldiers awarded Purple Hearts had to prove they had served in Iraq. Some patients fell through the cracks and didn't see therapists for weeks.

When would the Army's leaders hear the complaints from these soldiers who had lost arms and legs fighting for their country?

The Washington Post writers Dana Priest and Anne Hull spent four months investigating the story. Under the Army's radar, they attended meetings, slept on the floor of the apartments, talked to veterans and their spouses. When their stories ran in February 2007, the news shocked both readers and politicians.

Within a few weeks, the White House had fired top administrators at Walter Reed. Congress held hearings. The Army changed its procedures. The president himself learned of the conditions from newspaper accounts. He was not alone.

Most of us discovered this story because journalists told us. Few of us were at Walter Reed to look at the conditions ourselves. Unless we attended the president's briefing, toured the apartments or interviewed the soldiers, we relied on someone else's account.

In fact, most of us trusted what the news media said. We formed our opinions about the hospital and the soldiers based on what journalists reported.

Each day, thousands of significant stories run in newspapers and magazines, on television and radio, through the Internet. These stories tell us about events across the world and just a few blocks from our homes. We learn about new ideas, traffic accidents, scientific breakthroughs, who won ball games, what movies will be released.

We accept much of what we read and see in these reports. Though it sometimes is fashionable to criticize the news media, we know about world and local events from journalists telling us. We believe as fact what they report. We make decisions based on their stories.

A JOURNALIST'S ROLE

Journalists go to events most of us can't possibly attend. They talk to people most will never meet, witness history most will only read about. They tell the important and the trivial in ways that can be highly amusing or simply informative.

Few citizens have the money or time to unearth answers to the issues raised in the public discourse. Even fewer believe it their job to get these answers impartially, as an independent, third party. And still fewer ever feel the standards of absolute accuracy applied to them. Their work isn't held up for all to examine its truthfulness, its fairness, its reliability.

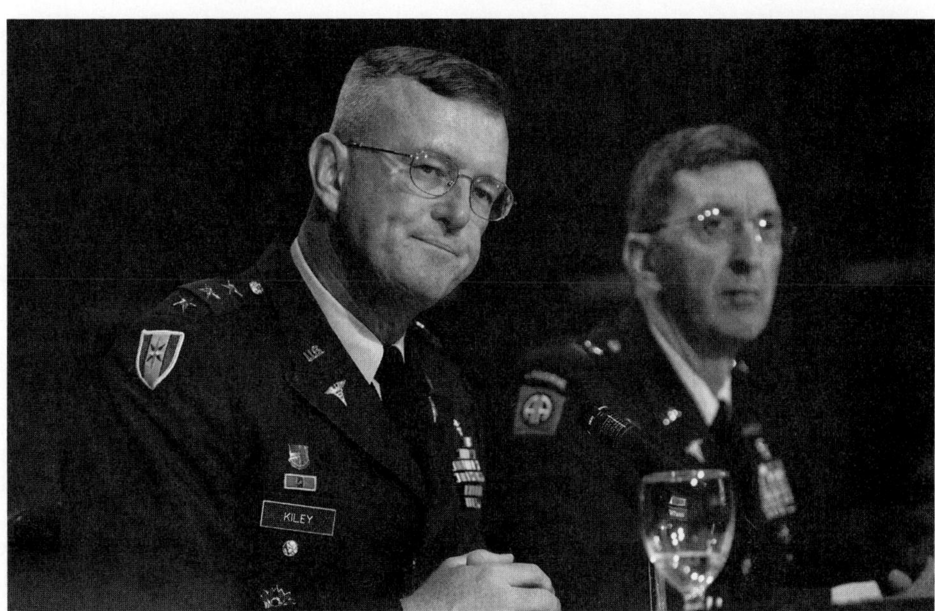

Two *Washington Post* reporters, Dana Priest and Anne Hull, spent four months investigating deplorable conditions for veterans who were outpatients at Walter Reed Army Medical Center. Most of these soldiers, veterans from fighting in Iraq and Afghanistan, lived in substandard housing and fought numbing battles with the Army's bureaucracy to receive outpatient care. Priest's and Hull's reporting prompted Congressional hearings where Lt. Gen. Kevin C. Kiley, army surgeon general (left), and Maj. Gen. George W. Weightman, former commander of Walter Reed (right), were called to testify. Asked during the hearings if they had anything to say to the Walter Reed patients, Weightman turned to a military couple behind him and apologized. Weightman was removed as head of Walter Reed. Kiley retired from the Army shortly after the scandal broke.

But journalists confront all these standards. Their job is to get to the bottom of things. They question how institutions run. They verify the information they gather. They ask difficult questions to understand their stories fully. Their work withstands the scrutiny of those who didn't want it published. Their stories benefit society, change the way groups or governments run, raise uncomfortable subjects, expose uncomfortable practices.

Journalists are truth tellers. They trade in facts. They wield influence only for as long as they are believed. Journalists report accurately so readers can trust the information. The information they deliver must be correct and as close to the truth as they can determine.

They tell us facts as important as who was elected president or whether the Los Angeles Angels (of Anaheim) defeated the Oakland Athletics (in major-league

ADVANCED TIP

What Is a Journalist's Role?

Bill Kovach and Tom Rosenstiel, authors of *The Elements of Journalism,* studied the history, practice and opinions of journalists to say the purpose of journalism is to "provide people with the information they need to be free and self-governing." In their book, they say these principles flow from that purpose.

1. Journalism's first obligation is to the truth.
2. Its first loyalty is to citizens.
3. Its essence is a discipline of verification.
4. Its practitioners must maintain an independence from those they cover.
5. It must serve as an independent monitor of power.
6. It must provide a forum for public criticism and comment.
7. It must make the significant interesting and relevant.
8. It must keep the news in proportion and make it comprehensive.
9. Its practitioners must be allowed to exercise their personal conscience.

baseball). Journalists' stories can show as much fun as how women wearing short skirts cope riding New York's subways or as much sadness as how a family accepts a son's or daughter's death in military service.

They go to war zones to report nations in conflict. They go to Broadway shows to tell us if we should. They go to family reunions, plane crash sites, city council meetings, basketball games, presidential press conferences, traffic snarls, college graduations: any place they believe might interest or be important to their readers or viewers.

Journalists can make the public scratch its head over why they cover one topic and ignore another. Those in power claim distortion of facts and quotes used in the wrong context. The media are blamed for stirring up sleepy ills of society. But don't report the stories, and the issues lie dormant.

Some criticisms have merit. Journalists can make mistakes, misuse quotes, ignore valid stories. Yet most who examine the system of mass media that inform and entertain us, including the courts that judge our laws, usually conclude we fare far better with an aggressive media than an impotent press.

JOURNALISM MATTERS

Journalism matters. Here's why:

- Journalists give people reliable information they could never get from other sources. Reports unearthed by working journalists spur much of the discussion of the day's issues.
- Journalists give readers a sense of community. They tell those who live near each other what is happening in their own surroundings, creating connections with one another.
- Journalists help democracy. They tell citizens their government is running and chronicle the actions of those who run it.
- Journalists question institutions. They ask hard questions about why society and government work the way they do. They point out needed changes.
- Journalists expose wrongs. They question those in power and write about those who feel powerless.

- Journalists can change the way we live. Every day, stories run in newspapers or on television that change public policies or expose someone's need for help.

JOURNALISTS GIVE INFORMATION UNAVAILABLE FROM OTHER SOURCES

When John Kerry ran for president, some fellow Vietnam veterans said he lied about his military record. Kerry, awarded three purple hearts, a silver star and a bronze star, called the group liars themselves. The exchange sparked a classic case of he said/she said, meaning two sides offered opinions at opposite ends.

But who was right? Did Kerry exaggerate his stories to win his medals, and later the presidency? Or did the accusing veterans make up stories just to derail Kerry and re-elect their candidate, George W. Bush? Which side was telling the truth?

The New York Times answered these questions. On Aug. 20 of the election year, *The Times* ran a story that showed naval documents and sworn testimony of sailors backed Kerry's claims. The story also said Kerry's accusers were connected to one of President Bush's top advisers, Karl Rove. The veterans' accusations actually contradicted earlier statements in which some of the veterans had praised Kerry.

The revelation didn't change the outcome of the election, nor squelch the debate. But the story does show that without journalists, an accurate accounting of what happened would have eluded voters. The reporters dug until they discovered the truth of each side's claims.

Much of what we know comes from journalists' reporting. That's true for the way government works, businesses run and institutions act. These groups don't send out press releases when things aren't going their way. In practice, they usually try to put the best face on them. Journalists see whether that spin holds water.

When Hurricane Katrina slammed into the Gulf Coast, flooding New Orleans and wiping out several Mississippi towns, residents who stayed behind suffered for days. Many complained they received little help from government agencies.

Journalists swooped in, especially into New Orleans, and told these victims' stories. Some elderly died unattended in wheelchairs. Residents were forced to sleep on elevated interstate highways. Hotel guests were turned out to fend for themselves. Conditions in the giant Superdome deteriorated to squalor within days.

Many complaints focused on the federal government's slow response. The news reports coming from New Orleans helped spur the government to send help. Even President Bush said the federal government had waited too long. Without the news reports, the government probably would not have admitted its missteps. It almost certainly would not have sent out a press release detailing its mistakes. The journalists showed the public what was happening in New Orleans and told them how their government had performed.

A few months after the United States invaded Iraq, President Bush declared the major fighting in Iraq over, speaking on an aircraft carrier under a sign MISSION

WIRED AND WIRELESS | WEB

When Hurricane Katrina flooded New Orleans and leveled the Mississippi coast, *The New Orleans Times-Picayune* was unable to print a newspaper. But it used its website, nola.com, to give residents up-to-date information, create community bulletin boards and break news vital to the region's safety and security. The paper won two Pulitzer Prizes for its coverage, both in print and online.

When *The Houston Chronicle* covered the long trial of Enron's leader, Ken Lay, the newspaper blogged and updated on its website throughout the day. Reporters discovered an online following. Readers would check the newspaper's portal ritually for information both meaningful and trivial.

When a shooter killed 32 students and professors at Virginia Tech University, information flew through the Internet on e-mail and digital social pages. Students posted video and still photos and became sources for news accounts well ahead of official announcements.

Within a few years after the new century turned, the Internet has rewritten the rules for daily journalists. No longer beholden to artificial news cycles of when presses roll or telecasts air, journalists of all stripes now have the ability to break news in real time. The speed can be breathtaking.

Now anyone who can create a website or offer a blog falls under the constitutional definition of a journalist. They still are miles from those who professionally practice journalism. But the medium has opened horizons to those once hindered by economics.

The impact is noticeable. Though daily journalists' reporting still sets the stage and tenor for the public discourse, online blogging and websites have grown in importance and influence. Politicians pay them heed. Mainstream journalists check them for news nuggets. Readers visit them.

For beginning journalists, however, the technology's awe can tempt them to stray from the prize, which is the content. Those who run websites for a living constantly remind the unschooled that this journalism is the same as before. It is being delivered in different storytelling forms, on new platforms. The web demands sound fundamental journalism, but new storytelling techniques.

ACCOMPLISHED. Yet battles continued and American soldiers kept dying. By June 2003, the toll reached approximately 300.

But these were soldiers. How many Iraqi civilians had died? When reporters went to the Pentagon, they were told that the military keeps track only of soldiers' deaths. After looking, the reporters discovered no agency in the United States government counts civilian deaths. In essence, the civilians didn't count.

So the Associated Press went to work. Journalists examined hospital records throughout Iraq. They looked into cemeteries. They found Iraqi documents. They interviewed doctors, nurses, clerics, families.

In the end, the journalists believed they could verify that about 3,200 Iraqi civilians had died during the first three months of the invasion, easily 10 times more than American soldiers. After that, other groups tried to keep track of how many civilians have died during that war.

Less dramatically, journalists each day report high school sports scores, local government meetings, traffic accidents, ethnic festivals, new business openings: a host of events that seem small by themselves, but added together make up the sum of a community's life. Without reporters telling the public, finding this information would prove difficult.

JOURNALISM GIVES PEOPLE A SENSE OF COMMUNITY

In the spring of 1997, the Red River in North Dakota was swollen from a quick thaw and 100 inches of melting snow. The river began flooding Grand Forks, soon breaking the city's dikes and filling the city with water.

Fires then burned through downtown buildings, including the one housing the newspaper, the *Grand Forks Herald.* Still, the newspaper's staff set up shop at a nearby university and published each day. The paper ran stories and editorials describing the area's effort to beat back the waters.

Since then, the paper's performance has grown into legendary status among those in daily journalism. Many journalists and Grand Forks officials have credited the paper's persistent publishing for keeping the community united and hopeful during the disaster.

The newspaper won the Pulitzer Prize the next year. Judges cited the paper, saying its coverage "helped hold its community together in the wake of flooding, a blizzard and fire."

Journalists tell those who live near each other what is happening in their own surroundings, creating connections with one another. Those stories can stir people to action. The information can help residents take steps to assist victims or solve problems.

Tom Hallman, himself a 2001 Pulitzer Prize winner for the Portland *Oregonian*, won the award for a story about a young boy with a disease that misshaped his face. The boy's disease was similar to one dramatized in a 1980s movie *Mask*. Hallman chronicled the steps taken by the boy, Sam Lightner, and his family as he underwent risky surgery.

After the story ran over several days, Hallman said the *Oregonian* received an outpouring of reader response. To Hallman, the story represents what can happen when journalists tell stories that touch their readers. Those who cared about Sam hailed from varied races, social classes and neighborhoods. They were united, for a few days, around a single story told by a journalist.

"[Journalism] gives meaning to the world," Hallman says. "In this fragmented society, a good story can unite a community in ways that nothing else can.

"It can make someone who lives in the inner city find power in a life lived in a rural area four or five hundred miles across the state. It can make somebody who lives in the same rural area who might have only seen black people on TV read one of my stories about a cleaning lady working her way through college in inner city Portland and be deeply moved enough to write her a letter."

Jay Rosen, a professor at New York University, believes journalists improve their communities when they tell their readers about problems, and then give them avenues to solve those problems. In his 1999 book, *What Are Journalists For?* Rosen says journalists actually can help the areas where they publish.

"The point of having journalists around is not to produce attention," Rosen writes, "but to make our attention more productive. When journalists get done doing what they do, we should find it easier to meet public challenges and get our work done as citizens."

ADVANCED TIP

A Journalist's Impact

Journalists often have to report information that belies popular opinion. Eugene L. Roberts, former executive editor of *The Philadelphia Inquirer,* told the American Society of Newspaper Editors at their April 2001 meeting of such courage from white editors of Southern newspapers during the civil rights era. Often, these editors endured a severe backlash from the white majority.

"Humor, even in the toughest of times, kept the editors afloat. Two of the most courageous editors were father and son, Hodding Carter Jr. and Hodding Carter III, of Mississippi's *Delta Democrat Times*. They never lost their ability to laugh or their sense of outrage at racial injustice, particularly the organized brand pushed by the white citizens' councils.

"After Hodding Carter Jr. wrote an article for *Look* magazine detailing the dangerous menacing spread of a white citizens' council, the article was branded on the floor of the Mississippi House of Representatives as a quote, 'Willful lie by a nigger-loving editor.' And the House then voted to censure Carter. Carter's reply in a front-page editorial was a classic. It said, 'By vote of 89 to 19, the Mississippi House of Representatives has resolved the editor of this newspaper into a liar because of an article I wrote. If this charge were true, it would make me well qualified to serve in that body. It is not true. So to even things up, I hereby resolve by vote of one to nothing that there are 89 liars in the state Legislature. I am hopeful that this fever,' he wrote, 'like Ku Kluxism that arose from the same kind of infection will run its course before too long a time. Meanwhile, those 89 character mobbers can go to hell, collectively or singly, and wait there until I back down. They needn't plan on returning.' "

JOURNALISM HELPS THE DEMOCRACY

Ron Hutcheson, a former White House reporter for McClatchy newspapers, each day attended press briefings or read what other journalists wrote about the administration. He also knew about the many blogs and websites that spun fact with opinion. His job, he said, was to write his stories so readers could trust his reporting.

That role has grown more important because many sources twist facts to suit their politics. For Hutcheson, delivering an unspoiled report to his readers mattered a lot.

"In some ways I think it matters even more because there's so much information available and so much of it is so bad or tainted by deliberate bias . . ." Hutcheson said. "So mainstream media fulfill a vital role of trying to give people information straight.

"I think we can make ourselves even more valuable by sorting through all the information: take all the various bits of information available that are out there and put them in some form that makes sense to people."

Hutcheson's point begs the questions: Why do we even need this information told in a straight way, with no bias? What's wrong with opinion thrown in with facts?

That is free speech, but not journalism. Those who report the news are supposed to give information fairly, no matter whether it fits or disagrees with their views. Whether reporters like or despise the facts of a story should make no difference in how they write the story.

Political scientists and historians agree. This practice of informing the public helps keep a democracy healthy. Citizens of a democracy need to know how their government is behaving. Without journalists to tell them, the free flow of information is left to those with political agendas. The information might be factual. It might not. Who's to say?

That's where journalists step in.

The success of democracies has always depended on the rank and file knowing what those in charge were doing, say Bill Kovach and Tom Rosenstiel in their book, *The Elements of Journalism.*

"Whether one looks back over 300 years, and even 3,000, it is impossible to separate news from community, and over time even more specifically from democratic community," the authors write.

Journalists also play the unglamorous but important role of simply giving voters an accurate account of their government's behavior.

"It used to be we were the only vehicle to tell people what's going on," McClatchy's Hutcheson says. "Now there are so many vehicles that in some way they need somebody who's reliable. That's our biggest challenge: a reliable choice."

Pete Hamill, a longtime New York newspaper journalist, makes this case in his book *News Is a Verb: Journalism at the End of the Twentieth Century.* His highly critical look at how newspapers function in society wraps its argument around the need for newspapers to do their jobs of informing the public.

Hamill focuses on newspapers, but he could also aim his criticisms at other media that give readers, viewers and listeners superficial information. He announces himself as a citizen of the democracy, and as such, he says he needs quality, in-depth information to know how he should critique and vote on his government.

He holds up newspapers here, but he's also talking about all types of journalism.

"Without good newspapers, operating primarily as instruments of knowledge, we cannot truly function as a healthy, continuously evolving democracy," Hamill writes.

"In the age of the ten-second spot, the superficialities of political coverage on television, the sometimes hysterical urgencies of the twenty-four-hour cable news cycle, the blather of talk radio, the unedited paranews of the Internet, newspapers are essential to our political discourse."

Talent Showcase

STEVE COLL ▸

Former managing editor of *The Washington Post* and current writer with *The New Yorker*

In June 2004, the United States military staged an elaborate memorial service to honor a fallen hero: former professional football player Pat Tillman. With his family attending, Tillman was praised as someone so moved by the Sept. 11, 2001, attacks that he had turned his back on million-dollar football contracts to enlist in the Army and protect his country. He was part of the Army Rangers, a special operations unit fighting in Afghanistan. On a barren hill near dusk, his unit had taken enemy fire. He valiantly sacrificed his life.

The only problem with the moving ceremony and wave of tributes was this: They were built on a lie. Tillman had been killed, accidentally, by his own unit through a tragic mixup in communications. Though the Army knew the truth within a few days of Tillman's death, officers still staged the memorial ceremony and waited weeks to quietly tell the family and public. No civilian knew fully what had happened or who was to blame.

Several months later in October, Steve Coll sat in a hotel room in London and pieced together how Pat Tillman had actually died. Coll, then the managing editor for *The Washington Post*, was in England on a different reporting assignment. But he had been investigating Tillman's death for about two months. He had spent much of that time getting military reports through sources and freedom-of-information requests. In the hotel room, he pored over the documents, autopsy reports, the military's investigation.

To help him understand the story, he outlined a detailed chronology, beginning a few weeks before the accident. As he grew closer to Tillman's death, he mapped out what happened in 10-minute increments. He backed up most moments with many sources. At the end of three days, Coll understood, profoundly, that Tillman had died because of his unit's leadership, and that Coll himself had nailed the story.

"I had something you don't usually have, which is I had the goods," said Coll, who has won two Pulitzer Prizes for his reporting. "I had the evidence. I had a really rich documentary trail. . . . It was kind of hard at least in the first or second takes of my reporting for the Army to come to terms with the fact that I really had all these documents.

"But it also gave me a high degree of confidence because basically I had what you would have in a normal court case, really."

Coll's story, published weeks later in his newspaper, showed how Tillman died and how the United States military had lied to the family and then tried to cover up the accident. His story exposed the several versions the military offered to explain the death, and eventually prompted more investigations. Eventually, the Army found that even generals had cooperated in covering up the correct version of events.

For Coll, the story proved again that society often needs reporters to question those in authority and uncover the truth.

"This was one of those times when there really wasn't any other way to redress the problem than through journalism. The family was never going to come close to having the questions they wanted answered but for the intervention of a free press.

"There wasn't an alternative. There was no whistle-blower path. There was no congressional investigation because the politics all lined up in the wrong ways. . . . In this case it was a pretty classic problem for this family [that] if they wanted these questions answered, the press was going to have to ask them."

Coll first learned of the possible coverup through confidential sources. These sources gave him some military documents. They also pointed him to others that he acquired by asking the government through freedom of information requests. But it wasn't until he mapped out in sequential order how Tillman died that he fully understood the story.

"I find that chronology is central to insight in investigative reporting or at least the reporting that I do. I often start with a big mass of complicated material or really complicated subject and start picking at it and feel that I'm bouncing off of it or that I don't really see the whole.

"And then at some point, when I've got enough material to do this, I just force myself to sit still for a few days, and it often takes a few days, and construct a really careful, multiple-sourced chronology. Then often that produces a eureka series of insights into what this is really about."

After writing the chronology, Coll then knew he needed to talk to more people. He tried to contact every soldier who was in Tillman's unit. He visited the bases where they were stationed and knocked on their doors. He tried to explain what he was doing and that he needed their help in understanding fully what had happened in Afghanistan.

Coll said most declined to cooperate, although he understood how they felt.

"For the people who had been there and lived through this, this was a really traumatic, powerful, important event in their lives even though nobody quite knew what they had done. Some of them were now civilians and had come out or had been thrown out of the Army. They killed Pat Tillman. They knew that. Of course they had all decided that it was something that they couldn't change and it was a genuine accident, those that were involved in the actual shooting.

"But then you have the dynamic of why is it always the people at the bottom of the rank chart that take the blame. These guys are not dumb. They get that. They feel scapegoated. They feel resentful. They feel angry. They feel helpless. These are the most powerless people in the military, anyway."

Just after Thanksgiving that year, Coll was preparing to visit Afghanistan and see the spot where Tillman had been shot. Then on a Friday afternoon, he heard some disturbing news: Reporters at the *Los Angeles Times* also were looking into Tillman's death. Coll didn't believe *The Times* reporters had matched the depth of his reporting.

"But I didn't know what they had. This was like a shock. And I thought, 'Well, hell, I'm not going to lose this thing.' "

So Coll scrapped his plans, dropped what he was doing and wrote the story on the spot.

"Fortunately I was still managing editor of the newspaper, so I ordered myself to write it and cleared some space and we decided to go Sunday."

Coll talked the story through with some other editors at *The Post*. Then he stayed up all Friday night writing the story.

"An editor said to me a long time ago when I first started to let chronology be your friend. I'm a narrative-oriented writer and I'm a narrative-oriented reporter and fortunately in this case I had so internalized the story from that long period of constructing. That chronology that I originally did in October is what I put on my desk that Friday night.

"And also chronology was at the heart of the coverup story, was the heart of the management story because once you realized that the documents showed that they possessed overwhelming evidence that he had died from friendly fire within 48 or 72 hours of his death and that this evidence was written down and passed up the chain of command, but they behaved as if they didn't know it for three weeks."

He felt rusty, even though he had been writing off and on since he became managing editor, "but it had been a while since I had that adrenaline-choked fear of deadline pressure."

(continued)

Talent Showcase (continued)

The story ran that Sunday, followed by a second part on Monday. Coll's reporting was quoted in news accounts across the country. The Army, pestered by the family and the media, later reopened the investigation.

The Army's behavior still baffles Coll. Tillman was a visible soldier, and many cared about him through his sports career and his publicized choice to shun football and enlist in the Army. That the Army would offend Tillman's family makes little sense, he said.

"The thing I still don't understand is why they treated the family the way they did. It just seems so cruel and stupid. . . . I don't know. It doesn't make any sense to me to treat any family that way and then to have a situation where you know the stakes are higher than normal in some institutional sense."

Coll worked at *The Post* for more than 15 years then joined *The New Yorker* staff. That same year he won his second Pulitzer Prize, this for his nonfiction book, *Ghost Wars*. As managing editor, he made difficult decisions. He found the Army's delay to publicly state the truth of Tillman's death troubling. That fellow soldiers killed Tillman is upsetting. That the Army lied about it is deeply disturbing.

"You've got to do the right thing. . . . You should be trained to do the hard thing sometimes because it is the right thing.

"And then to have a lapse in judgment of this scale, it still boggles my mind as to what colonel could have reached the rank of colonel and at some point along those two weeks [after Tillman's death], stop and said to himself or had one of his subordinates say to him, 'You know, sir, this may not be the right way to handle this.'

"Even out of self-interest—never mind our moral obligation—just out of pure narrow self-interest, how could you not understand that you were blowing it?"

JOURNALISM QUESTIONS INSTITUTIONS

Just after the new century turned, reporters at *The Boston Globe* were uncovering civil lawsuits against the Boston Archdiocese of the Roman Catholic Church. Some present and former parishioners claimed priests had sexually abused them years earlier.

As part of a routine filing related to the suits, reporters learned that the cardinal knew of allegations against a particular priest. But a judge had sealed the case against the priest. Reporters were unable to unearth more information.

The Globe chose to fight the secrecy. The newspaper spent the next several months asking the court to unseal the suit. The courts finally agreed. Suddenly, the public could see a pattern.

Along with searching other records and documents, the reporters found that church leaders had been putting suspected priests on administrative leave or shuttling them between parishes. Bishops and cardinals had yet to contact police—under Massachusetts law, they didn't have to.

As word of the Boston scandal spread, many parishioners in other states made similar allegations. The picture grew clear: Catholic Church officials across the United States routinely moved priests who were sex offenders to other churches rather than turn them in to authorities. Massachusetts's elected officials changed their laws to require church officials to report the wrongdoings. The cardinal for Boston, Bernard Law, resigned.

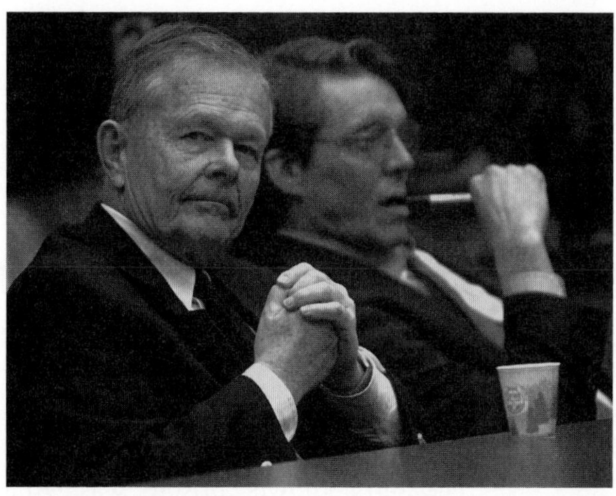

The Boston Globe broke open the Catholic priest scandal, winning a Pulitzer Prize for its reporting, prompted by charges against defrocked priest John Geoghan, left. Geoghan was sent to prison where an inmate later killed him.

The Boston Globe won the Pulitzer Prize for public service in 2003. Reporters at *The Globe* performed one of journalism's most compelling and unpopular roles.

Journalists must question all institutions, even those as large and influential as the Roman Catholic Church. They must question the obvious ones with buildings, such as business, education and government. They must also question the institutions without buildings, societal ones such as social class and racism.

A journalist's job is to ask the uncomfortable questions: Why has this always been? Why can't this be better?

Editors at the afternoon newspaper in Syracuse, the now defunct *Herald-Journal*, once asked New York state legislators for an accounting of how they spent taxpayers' money on themselves. That seemed an easy request. By law, all state budgets were open to public scrutiny. In fact, budgets of all government bodies—federal, county, town, city, courts—are public information.

But because they make the rules, the New York lawmakers had exempted themselves from anyone looking at what assembly members spent on their offices, employee salaries and supplies. Requests from the newspaper to examine the budget met with outright refusal.

Executive Editor Timothy Bunn was appalled, and soon figured out a way to circumvent a legislative body whose spending should be open to the public.

Every dollar the state spends has to go through the comptroller's office. So Bunn assigned two reporters to look at all checks written for items related to the state assembly. The checks were public information, which means all citizens have access to them.

Using the Freedom of Information Act, the reporters spent 18 months requesting these checks, combing through the expenditures, putting them in categories and finding the discrepancies.

They discovered the New York Legislature was one of the most bloated state bodies in the nation. Excess was rampant. Several assembly members had relatives on their payrolls. One member had multiple offices in his district only blocks apart.

The series, called "Secrets of the Chamber"—a few years before the Harry Potter book of a similar name—raised an outcry among readers. The series later won the national Investigative Reporters and Editors competition.

Though state legislators refused to change their practices, the newspaper demonstrated anew that journalists must ask tough questions of those in power, and should refuse to back down despite the roadblocks thrown in their paths.

Journalist Seymour Hersh, writing for *The New Yorker* magazine, helped break the Abu Ghraib prison scandal story. Information about the scandal spread through the mass media, which ran photos such as this one of a hooded and wired Iraqi prisoner.

JOURNALISM EXPOSES WRONGS

In May 2004, *The New Yorker* magazine published a story difficult for many Americans to believe.

Investigative reporter Seymour Hersh, who had won a Pulitzer Prize 34 years earlier, wrote that American soldiers were torturing and abusing Iraqi prisoners. Worse, they were using the same prison the deposed Iraqi leader, Saddam Hussein, himself had used for such acts.

The little-known prison was Abu Ghraib. Soon, photographs of soldiers abusing the prisoners traveled across the Internet. All news media—television, magazines and newspapers—showed the public.

Seeing was believing. Abu Ghraib became synonymous with mistreating prisoners. The scandal prompted an internal investigation and court-martial trials.

Hersh and *The New Yorker* demonstrated one of journalism's great services. Through the mere power of public exposure, journalists can tell the public when its society or government behaves badly.

Reporters of all media have exposed wrongs:

- Television station KHOU in Houston took a phone call from a viewer and found that a defective tire made by Firestone had contributed to the deaths of hundreds.
- *The Willamette Week*, a Portland, Ore., weekly newspaper, published a story detailing the former governor of Oregon's sexual relationship with a 14-year-old babysitter.
- A writer for *Fortune* magazine, Bethany McLean, wrote a straightforward story that questioned how the corporation Enron made money. The story proved prophetic, setting the stage for the energy giant's collapse and one of the largest corporate scandals ever in the United States.
- The *Los Angeles Times* investigated a hospital created years ago to help the disenfranchised residents of southern Los Angeles. The newspaper discovered the hospital was so badly run that many seeking medical treatment were actually made worse, and in some cases, died.

These stories and others don't populate the news each day. Many come after months of digging and combing through public documents. But when they are published, their impact can be dramatic.

ADVANCED TIP

Some Recent Prominent Stories Unearthed by Journalists

Catholic Priests Scandal. *The Boston Globe* won a 2003 Pulitzer Prize for its reporting that began the nationwide uncovering of sexual abuse of children by Roman Catholic priests and a systematic coverup by their superiors.

Abu Ghraib. *The New Yorker* reporter Seymour Hersh, who won a Pulitzer Prize in the 1970s, exposed abuse at a little-known Iraq prison called Abu Ghraib. Once photos of the abuse at the hands of U.S. soldiers hit the Internet, the prison became synonymous with the troubled military campaign in Iraq.

Warrantless wiretapping. James Risen and Eric Lichtblau, reporters from *The New York Times* won a 2006 Pulitzer Prize when they discovered the Bush administration was bypassing a special court and eavesdropping on U.S. citizens without obtaining the necessary search warrants dictated by Congress.

Secret prisons. Dana Priest, a reporter from *The Washington Post* won a 2006 Pulitzer Prize when she discovered the CIA was holding prisoners in a secret prison system that the U.S. government had set up around the world. At the time of the story, almost nothing was known of who the prisoners were, how they were treated, and how long they would remain.

Perhaps the most famous expose is the Watergate scandal of 1972–1974. Two reporters for *The Washington Post*, Bob Woodward and Carl Bernstein, kept reporting that the Nixon administration was trying to cover up a burglary at Democratic headquarters in Washington.

The series of reports filed by the two young reporters helped spark a congressional hearing that eventually led to Nixon's resigning and many in his administration going to jail. Watergate remains a watershed moment in American life, easily one of the nation's worst political scandals.

JOURNALISM CAN CHANGE THE WAY WE LIVE

Every day, stories that run in newspapers or on television change government policies or expose someone's need for help. Sometimes, stories simply describe the human condition, and readers are moved in deep ways.

A few years back, a high school football coach in Ohio let an autistic teenager play with the team. The teenager, whose first name was Jake, didn't actually play, but he suited up and participated to his capacity.

For the season's last game, the coach wanted the boy to go in for the final play. With the opposing coach's cooperation, Jake would take the ball, then go down on one knee. The opposing team wouldn't try to tackle Jake, and the game would end.

But when the time came, the opposing coach had a different idea. He told his team to let Jake run for a touchdown.

When the ball was snapped, Jake was going to take the knee. But players from both teams stopped him. Then they cleared a path and told him to run. Several ran next to him nearly half the field's length until they reached the end zone.

Stories such as those can touch readers, and not just parents of children with disabilities. These stories can change the way readers view those who struggle. The stories also inspire others to copy the example shown them.

Another time, editors picking stories for the front page of the Sunday newspaper in Syracuse, N.Y., were told of one about hunger in the city. It was the Sunday

Figure 1.1 **Journalists Killed in Iraq**

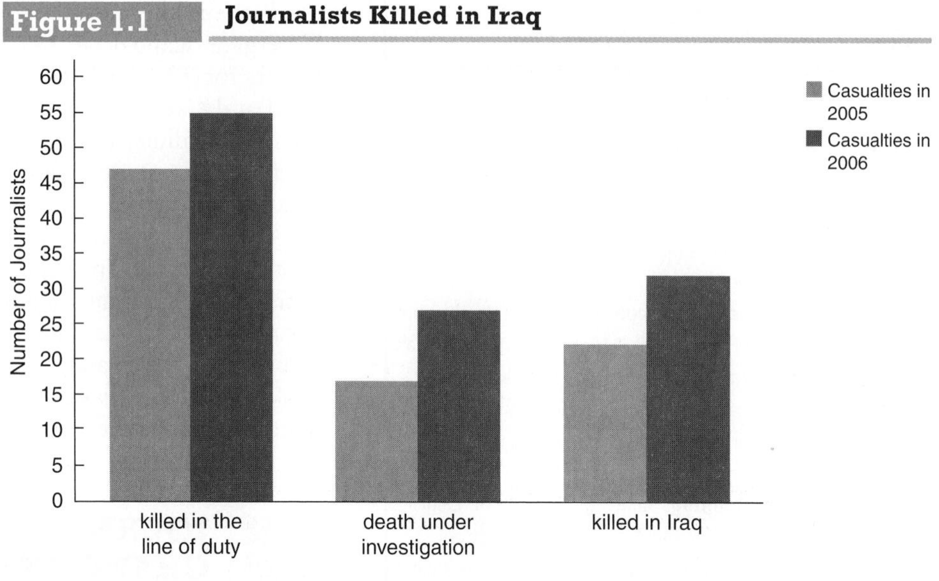

Source: (STATISTICS) Report released by nonprofit group Committee to Protect Journalists. www.journalism.org/node/3405

before Thanksgiving, and the local food pantry had run out of holiday baskets for needy families.

The editors knew this was a strong story, but not the strongest of the day. Still, they believed many families would be without on Thanksgiving. The two editors chose to play the story in the lead position of the Sunday edition.

The response was overwhelming. By Monday morning, residents had flooded the food pantries with calls to donate food. Employees at one area business canceled its traditional company dinner to give away all its food.

After the terrorist attacks of Sept. 11, 2001, *The New York Times* began publishing a remarkable section each day covering the aftermath. One page of this special served as an obituary, of sorts. The paper ran four-to-five-paragraph profiles on those known to have died during the attacks.

The stories were powerful in their simplicity. Though short, they were filled with intimate details of lives lost in the tragedy. Reporters sometimes spent several days tracking down relatives and friends to paint a full picture.

The page grew in popularity among *Times* readers. Even readers who lived far from New York City felt moved. Readers who never met the deceased felt connected to those profiled. *The Times* printed a new page of obituaries each day until the year's end.

The Times won the Pulitzer Prize for its public service of covering the story fully in the special section, and for remembering with dignity those who simply showed up to work that awful day and later became the subjects of a moving story just a few paragraphs long.

IN CONCLUSION

Each day, thousands of journalists go to work at their homes, newsrooms and offices. Much of what they do is routine. Sometimes they write or edit stories that make a splash in their communities. Combined, the exciting and the routine create a flow of ideas that tell people about themselves and their times. And the news can make readers merely smile to themselves, or stir them to action.

TOOL KIT

Some books you might wish to consider:

All the President's Men, by Carl Bernstein and Bob Woodward, Warner Books, New York, 1975.

The Elements of Journalism, by Bill Kovach and Tom Rosenstiel, Three Rivers Press, New York, 2001.

The News About the News, by Leonard Downie Jr. and Robert G. Kaiser, Alfred A. Knopf, New York, 2002.

What Are Journalists For? by Jay Rosen, Yale University Press, New Haven, 1999.

News is a Verb: Journalism at the End of the 20th Century, by Pete Hamill, Ballantine Books, New York, 1998.

EXERCISE 1

Write a one-page discussion paper that answers one of the following questions:

1. How would you learn about who was elected president without the Internet, radio, television, newspapers or magazines?
2. A woman was seriously injured when an off-duty police officer driving drunk crashed into her car. No news media learned of the accident. The district attorney declined to prosecute. If the woman tells the news media, what will be the result?
3. When the Abu Ghraib prison scandal broke, did the news media help the American public by writing about the prisoner abuse and spreading the photos?
4. After Hurricane Katrina, news reporters showed video footage and photographs of victims inside and outside the New Orleans' Superdome. How did publicizing the suffering help or hurt?
5. During an interview when he played for the Philadelphia Eagles, wide receiver Terrell Owens criticized his quarterback, Donovan McNabb. Should the news media have reported Owens' critical comments?

EXERCISE 2

Write a one-page discussion paper about the following:

1. Should a college administration be able to tell a college newspaper what it can print?
2. If your college newspaper didn't cover the women's field hockey team, where else could you find out about the team?
3. If a professor says a racist or sexist remark during class, what good will it do to write a story about it?
4. How could journalism help students who live in dorms feel more connected with those who live off campus?
5. What stories should journalists write that would discuss the most pressing issues to students on your campus?

EXERCISE 3

Go to a news website, read a local newspaper or watch a television broadcast. Explain how the top stories fulfill or fail to fulfill one of journalism's roles discussed in this chapter.

CHAPTER 2

What Is News?

IN THIS CHAPTER, YOU WILL LEARN:

- Why editors in all media make similar news judgments.
- The stronger the news element, the stronger the story.
- What are the elements in judging news.
- News judgment is inexact and debated among journalists and readers.
- Developing news judgment helps beginning reporters understand what makes stories interesting.

Trying to judge the magnitude of events and their scope is what you're trying to do.
Paul Moore, public editor,
The Baltimore Sun

JUST AFTER CHRISTMAS DAY A FEW YEARS AGO, an earthquake created a huge tidal wave that swept over islands and shorelines throughout the Indian Ocean. The tsunami killed at least 250,000, wiping out villages, destroying homes, ruining beaches.

News media across the United States played the story prominently. National broadcasts led with it. Magazines put it on their covers. Newspapers ran it on their front pages. Internet sites updated it for days.

How could this happen?

Why would all those editors working in competing media know which story was No. 1? They didn't talk beforehand. What told them the tsunami would attract the most readers, viewers and unique visitors?

Each day, journalists sift through hundreds of stories, judging them for reader appeal. Journalists rely on time-honored characteristics of storytelling to make their way through the maze of competing interests and reader demands. What story has the most conflict? Which one changes the norm? Which surprises?

At every turn, these editors think about their audiences. Which news that day will their specific readers or viewers want to know?

Answering these questions is the earliest lesson journalists should learn: how to judge a story for its appeal. Knowing what makes news unlocks the secret to writing interesting stories.

News judgment is just that—judgment, not science. Two smart people can disagree about the same item. Yet some stories are obviously compelling. The 9/11 attack drew our interest for weeks, no matter where we lived. The space shuttle that came apart during re-entry saddened many. The controversy in 2000 over who won the election for president held the nation in suspense. Lance Armstrong's struggle against cancer to win the Tour de France bicycling race an unprecedented seven straight years was well known to most Americans.

Those stories, and the tsunami, are easy to decide. Debate rages when the news isn't as obvious. That's when journalists look at the guidelines used for generations to judge what stories will most interest their readers.

GUIDELINES

Editors rely on these mile markers to tell them if a story is appealing:

- If they have learned the real story behind an action or event.
- If the story defies conventional wisdom or will surprise readers.
- If the story is about people well known.
- If the story shows the norm has changed.
- If the story has conflict, and perhaps controversy.
- If the story can show how it touches readers, or if it is the first, last or only of its type.
- If the story is tied to a recent event or has timeliness.
- If the story portrays one of life's odd or bizarre moments.
- If the story appeals to the particular media's readers, viewers or visitors.

AGAINST THE TIDE

A reporter for *The New York Times* once found a woman in Hattiesburg, Miss., who had a remarkable story. The woman, who was African American, had worked washing clothes her entire life. She never married, never vacationed, never spent most of her money.

When the reporter, Pulitzer Prize winner Rick Bragg, caught up with her, she was 87, and had saved $150,000. So she donated the entire amount to a university in Hattiesburg to give scholarships to African-American students.

The story is intriguing for many reasons. But at its heart it describes the human character. The woman's overwhelming selflessness makes the story appealing. She clearly could use the money, and yet gave it all away.

Backed into a corner, humans can respond in remarkable ways. Often those ways defy conventional wisdom. They go against the current of how people typically act. A journalist able to unearth information that confounds conventional wisdom has an interesting story to tell.

For decades in this country, many (mostly white) believed chances to improve class status were open to any who worked hard enough. Each succeeding generation was supposed to improve its lot over the last.

But in the late 1980s, two reporters for the *Philadelphia Inquirer*, Donald Barlett and James Steele, wrote a series of stories that proved this untrue. The series, "America: What Went Wrong," showed how policies of the Reagan administration wounded and shrunk the middle class, shouldering them with higher taxes and fewer ways to advance out of their economic class. They actually had a lesser life than their parents.

Though Barlett and Steele endured heavy criticism, the series rang true with middle America. the *Inquirer* received more than a half million requests for its reprinted series, which was nominated for a Pulitzer Prize. For years, Barlett and Steele were in demand as speakers throughout the country.

Several years ago, child abductions hit record numbers. Or so it seemed. Fueled by the tragic stories of Adam Walsh and others, fear grew about children snatched by strangers from safe neighborhoods. Abducted children's faces appeared on milk cartons. Stories of stolen children ran frequently.

However, *The Denver Post* investigated these abductions. It found that contrary to what many believed, most children in these cases were abducted by relatives or parents involved in custody disputes. The number of children snatched by strangers was quite low. *The Post* won a Pulitzer Prize for that reporting.

WHAT'S CHANGED, WHAT'S DIFFERENT

Hurricane Katrina was all about change. In a blink, the storm changed the way thousands lived along the Gulf Coast. It changed where they slept, where they worked, where their children went to school, what their hometown looked like, how they trusted their governments.

The Art of Storytelling

To explain the No. 1 reason she tried to give her writing vigor, Lisa Pollak starts with the runners-up.

She shunned clichés. She tried to sound conversational. She thought about active verbs. All great lessons, for sure.

But what drove her to write as vividly as possible was the thought that someone might grow tired of her story.

"Vigor is . . . about wanting to hold onto the reader," says Pollak, who won a Pulitzer Prize for feature writing when she was a reporter for *The Baltimore Sun*.

". . . Students are taught that a lead should grab somebody so it keeps them in the story. But I think the whole story is this string that should be pulling the person along. You just can't give up after you've hooked them with the lead. You want the person to finish the story.

"So I think that's what it's more about. It's so easy in newspapers to just read the front and then stop. So my goal would be: I want to write a story that a person is going to read until the end."

The best journalists share Pollak's goal. Good reporters worry often whether their stories are boring their readers. They understand their stories need to move smartly to avoid losing their readers.

How do journalists learn to write with such vigor?

Vigorous writing is the marriage of compelling facts and bare prose. Unexpected information gives energy to sentences. Unadorned writing lets that information carry the story. Vivid images, active language, surprising facts and telling details keep readers interested from start to finish.

Timothy Bunn, the retired deputy executive editor of *The Syracuse Post-Standard*, often called a vapid piece of writing "cotton candy." He complained that when writers relied on their skill at words rather than the hard work of finding interesting information, stories read like cotton candy. They went down sweet, but once done, little substance remained, and even that vanished quickly.

To avoid their stories reading like cotton candy, journalists should remember the following guidelines:

- **Know the story thoroughly.** There's no substitute for fully understanding what you are writing. Unanswered questions leave your writing sounding insecure.

- **Have a core point.** Many writers and editors say being able to state your story's point in one sentence tells them what questions they still need to ask. Knowing your focus opens the way to how you will write your story.
- **Look for telling details.** Even in breaking news stories, details matter. Look for how people talk and act. Watch for actions that show readers emotion and human qualities.
- **Find something interesting.** Intriguing facts create intriguing stories. Pollak said she first understood the importance of reporting when she realized, "It wasn't so much about trying to take the press conference and turn a pretty phrase about it or have the perfect description of the school superintendent and what he looked like. You had to find something interesting going on."
- **Write with urgency.** Besides concrete details, nothing helps your writing more than movement and action. Even writing a story that takes a somber mood can evoke an undertone of urgency.

"I don't think there's such a thing as a bad writer," says Marjie Lundstrom, a writing coach and projects writer at *The Sacramento Bee*. "Ninety-nine percent of the problems happen before they sit down at the keyboard. Most of the time it's a lack of reporting. Even the prettiest writers can't write their way around reporting holes. The logic isn't there, and the reporting isn't there.

"They just can't wait to create and give birth. But they haven't got the goods."

Lundstrom, who won the Pulitzer Prize in 1991 for national reporting, believes this is true for both breaking news stories and those off deadline. Shortcuts in reporting produce anemic writing.

"I know it's possible to over-report," Lundstrom says, "but under-reporting is so much more common."

To let the power of their reporting shine through, journalists should write with clear language. Barry Siegel, a former *Los Angeles Times* reporter and Pulitzer Prize winner, calls that having "faith in the story."

He means that with nonfiction writing, less is more. The best journalists write with a stripped-down, understated tone. The story then becomes the star, not how many pirouettes journalists can perform with their words.

"I believe in details, and to let the theme itself be powerful rather than me verbally pounding the table with it," Siegel says. "So I begin with the idea that I don't want to get in the way of the story. But I want the words to resonate. The fewer you have, the fewer convoluted sentences. Those sentences that are simple can also be very powerful."

ADVANCED TIP
What Is Currency?

According to professor and textbook writer Melvin Mencher, one element of deciding what's news is called "currency." If a subject is being discussed in the media or in society, then stories about that subject carry more news value than they would at other times.

A few years ago, several stories broke about athletes taking steroids. Testimony at a grand jury accused several baseball players of using the drugs. While not illegal, steroids give players who use them an advantage, thus questioning the game's integrity. Congress brought current and former professional baseball players to testify before a committee. Representatives later called baseball officials to testify as well. At that time, any story related to steroid use received more attention, simply because the subject was the topic of conversation.

Currency is temporary. Its news value fluctuates with the public's interest. AIDS, the Internet, immigration, global warming—all have been hot topics at times.

The 9/11 terrorist attacks changed how Americans viewed their safety, their economy, their religion, their world allies and enemies.

The advent of the Internet, the waves of Spanish-speaking immigrants, the conservative drift of the U.S. Supreme Court, the rise of agribusiness, the explosion of professional sports, the emergence of the Chinese economy: All these stories create interest because they have changed the way we communicate, the common language we speak, the laws we obey, our entertainment, the ways we make our livings.

News is change. As life and society move forward, journalists tell their readers about these changes. Answer the easy question of how something is different, and you know whether the event is news: the more dramatic the difference, the more interesting it is to your readers.

Most moments we now consider historic are wrapped around a change: the Iraq conflict, the shuttle disaster, the Kennedy assassination, polio vaccine, women's right to vote. These stories show events that changed the status quo. Disrupting routine life intrigues readers.

Consider change when writing about people. The best profiles show people who have grown from their experiences. All face significant emotional events or life-altering decisions. Those events change a person's character or cause us to live differently. Those changes interest readers.

Journalists who show readers how much something has changed write better stories. Readers are interested in or shocked by the new ways society develops. Change compels readers to keep looking for further details.

TICKET TO THE BACKSTAGE

On election night of 2000, the major four television networks declared early that Democrat candidate Al Gore had carried Florida. Winning that state probably would have elected Gore president.

But soon, all networks had to rescind their early call. The Florida count grew too close. Viewers would have to wait to know who won.

What concerned many about the networks that night was not that they had made the wrong call, but that they all had made the wrong call. If each network was conducting its own research independently, one network might have erred, but not every network.

With the newspapers featuring the tsunami disaster on display, a Muslim volunteer collects donations for the victims of the tsunamis in Asia at a shopping mall in Kuala Lumpur Sunday, January 2, 2005.

Time magazine gave its readers the behind-the-scenes story. It told them what really happened that night, and answered the baffling question of why all four networks could make the same mistake at the same time. To save money, the networks and some newspapers and wire services had pooled their resources, creating the Voter News Service. The new service had miscalculated, thus feeding all the networks the same flawed numbers.

Journalists who make a habit of lifting the curtain to the backstage give their readers interesting stories. Stories that tell how something truly works carry high news value. Readers can't get enough.

This works for a host of stories. When *Houston Chronicle* reporter Mary Flood covered the Enron trial of CEO Kenneth Lay, she answered readers' questions online in a column called, "Ask Mary." She found that many readers wanted to ask an insider such questions as how the federal law of discovery works.

When the United States first invaded Iraq, many reporters spent weeks or months with combat troops. The embedded reporters were given access to tell readers what it was like to live and fight in combat conditions.

Journalists should always strive to get to the backstage. It is in the wings and behind the scenery—not watching the staged production—that they discover the truth and better serve their readers.

PEOPLE, PEOPLE, PEOPLE

A few years ago, an 18-year-old driver in Los Angeles was involved in a minor car accident. No one was hurt. The damages were minimal. No tickets. Case closed—not quite. The driver was actress Lindsay Lohan. A paparazzi photographer had rammed her car to stop her from leaving. Suddenly, an uneventful traffic mishap—out of the hundreds that day—became a news item that ran on television and in magazines and newspapers across the country.

During a break from his strenuous job, a man hunting turned quickly and shot a member of his party. The wounded man went to the hospital but suffered no life-threatening injuries. The sheriff's department investigated, declaring it an accident. Nothing special, except that the shooter was Vice President Dick Cheney, and he waited nearly a day to tell his boss, the president. That story lived for months, becoming the easy target of comedians and late-night talk show hosts.

Once a woman in her 60s who had arrived at the Salt Lake City airport asked a tall black man to carry her suitcases to the car. She apparently thought he was a porter, and when they reached her car, she offered him a tip. He refused, because he was NBA superstar Karl Malone, who had arrived at the airport at the same time. An embarrassing moment for a woman suddenly became an item picked up in sports columns.

Most people keep track of a circle of acquaintances: friends, relatives, neighbors, classmates, co-workers. Add to that another circle of people many have never met but still know their intimate details: the famous.

The well-known of our society have always held our gaze. Those who lead our governments, those who entertain us, those who do the extraordinary, all grow familiar as they act, or act up.

Readers share this interest. When events happen to the well-known, they carry weight when judging whether the story is news. That's why when the pop singer Michael Jackson went to trial charged with molesting a child, his case was elevated from among the many other trials with the same charges. His celebrity status attracted more attention.

Familiar names become news. They take a routine event and turn it into the extraordinary by their mere presence. Sometimes, it's difficult to judge when the well-known's actions are so routine that they are uninteresting.

- When the actress Angelina Jolie flew to Africa with her husband, actor Brad Pitt, to give birth, her travel brought media attention to struggles in that part of the world. It was a clever way to use their celebrity.
- Of all the weddings in Italy one year, perhaps none attracted more attention than the one uniting Tom Cruise and Katie Holmes.
- When the daughter of the president attended college, Chelsea Clinton's stay at Stanford University was chiefly ignored, except when her parents visited.
- When the daughters of another president were caught drinking under-age, the Bush twins' exploits made news. Most of their other activities—the ones that did not violate the law—usually went unreported.

John Edwards and his wife, Elizabeth, who celebrate their anniversary each year at a Wendy's restaurant, were joined by running mate John Kerry and his wife, Teresa Heinz Kerry, shortly after Edwards and Kerry won the Democratic nomination for president in 2004.

- Sen. John Edwards, who ran for vice president in 2004, celebrates his wedding anniversary each year at a Wendy's restaurant, the site of his first anniversary dinner. He and his wife drew little national attention until Democrats nominated him for vice president. Then their anniversary dinner, out of all their previous ones, and all the other routine meals at Wendy's, became part of the national news that day.

People are more interesting to read about than programs and policies. Even finding a person who is obscure but mixed up in an issue will add to a story. Find a better-known person, and the same story creates intrigue.

The American culture is saturated with celebrities. Concerned sociologists and cultural observers complain that we spend too much time paying attention to the well known. These critics worry that the famous too greatly influence impressionable children and teenagers. In addition, journalists have an obligation to report about the well known with fairness. Some stories and photographs fall short of meeting the test for taste and public good.

Still, there's no denying that the actions, significant and small, of famous people interest readers. These actions are worthy of coverage. How much attention depends on their status and what they've done.

CONTEXT

Early in your stories, readers need to know why they should keep reading. They need to see a story's significance, why the reporter bothered to write it in the first place. A new executive editor at *The Fort Worth Star-Telegram* in Texas once promised money to the first reporter who started the second paragraph of a story with "This means that . . ." The editor, now retired Knight Ridder newspaperman Walker Lundy, wanted to give the reader context.

Lundy's request still makes great sense. Context helps a reader see the story's importance. To this day, reporters in all media fail to honor that suggestion. The best journalists, though, always have their readers in mind. They know intuitively that readers look for a reason to stop. These writers take great care to tell readers why they should stay with the story.

Journalists can show context by:

- **First, Last or Only.** When plants close, or politicians quit, or players retire, that's the last time we'll see them in their long-familiar jobs. Being first also

Talent Showcase

PAUL MOORE ▶

Former executive news editor of the *Fort Worth Star-Telegram* and current public editor with *The Baltimore Sun*

On a Friday night early in his career, Paul Moore faced a tough choice. The United States hockey team had just upset the Soviet Union at the Lake Placid Winter Olympics. At the time, Moore picked the stories that ran on the front page of the *Fort Worth Star-Telegram* in Texas, and he sensed this was a big story. But there was an issue.

Hockey wasn't a big sport in Fort Worth. And in those days, sports news almost always ran in the sports section, except for major championships. Rarely did a sports story find its way to the front page.

Yet to Moore, this one seemed different. He listened to his colleagues talk in the newsroom. He thought more about the significance of Americans upsetting their nemesis at the height of the Cold War in a sport the Russians had dominated for years. So Moore decided to redo his front page. This one, he figured, meant more than just a hockey game.

He had an hour before deadline. He picked a photograph that now has grown famous: the U.S. hockey team celebrating its improbable win. He went home that night and then worried about his decision all weekend.

"I came in Monday, wondering, 'Jeez, am I going to be ridiculed for this?'—even though you could start to sense the [excitement] building, and of course, the U.S. won the gold medal two days later," Moore said.

His boss later told him he made one of the best choices ever at the paper.

For Moore, who later picked the front-page stories for the Sunday editions at both the *Philadelphia Inquirer* and *The Baltimore Sun*, news choices are how much an event changes a person or community, and how far the event's lasting effects will reach.

Events with obvious long-range implications, Moore said, carry stronger news content. Journalists should explain to their readers just how broad they stretch and deep they run.

"No one can always ascertain right away when something happens," Moore said, "but trying to judge the magnitude of events and their scope is what you're trying to do."

Moore said news also means how much an event or discovery changes a community. The bigger the change, the stronger the story.

makes history: the first airplane flight, the first landing on the moon, the first woman to run the Boston Marathon.

- **Size Matters.** A hurricane that is the strongest to hit an area, a drug bust that captured the highest street value of narcotics, a month where the least amount of rain has fallen—the largest, and smallest, attract readers' attentions.
- **Part of a Trend.** Even though the phrase "one of a nationwide trend" is overused, a careful writer knows readers will deem the story more significant if the

"The change you're talking about is multi-level when it affects human beings directly or even indirectly. . . . Whether it's hurricanes in Florida or major weather anywhere, that does it on [a] number of levels: human, monetary, political, policy, everything. Those kind of things can have immediate change, those help define the value of news."

Sometimes the media err in their news judgment, Moore says. He believed the Michael Jackson trial a few years ago received too much notice. It was intriguing for the moment, but it changed little and carried too few lasting effects.

"Did Michael Jackson change the climate of this country? Probably not. Did it interest some people? Yes. Did newspapers have a tendency to overplay it? Absolutely. . . . Whereas, you could make the case that the verdict in the O. J. Simpson trial had tremendous implications for the country at large. You could see it at the time. I don't see it with Michael Jackson."

Moore has decided what is news for nearly three decades. He was the executive news editor at the *Fort Worth Star-Telegram*. In Philadelphia, he was the assistant managing editor for news and later assistant managing editor for features. In Baltimore, he recently was the deputy managing editor for news. Moore said his news judgment choices might have met his own sensibilities, but they didn't always please his bosses.

Once, when he worked in Philadelphia at *The Inquirer*, a prominent high school athlete had disappeared. Her mother led a vocal, highly visible campaign to find her daughter.

The *Inquirer* had covered the event, but never made the story the top item of the day. Then, on a Sunday afternoon, police arrested the mother, charging her with killing her daughter, who had been having an affair with her stepfather.

Moore, with the metro editor, decided to run the story stripped across the top of page one. He believed the story carried great interest among his readers. He left work that night convinced the paper had played the story correctly.

When he came to work the next day, his boss questioned his decision. His boss was aghast, saying that Moore and others had lowered the paper's standards to a tabloid. Moore still remembers his boss's words.

"What is this, *The National Enquirer* or the *Philadelphia Inquirer*?" Moore said his boss asked. Still, he doesn't regret running the story where he did.

"I listened to the staff. I listened to my instincts. I still think I was right. But the editor did not," Moore said. "It puts you in those situations again where you often have to make decisions on the best available information you have at the time.

"I would do that again. Today that thing would be even bigger than it was when we did it."

Moore works now as *The Sun*'s public editor. He writes a column about issues his paper faces, especially looking at stories from a reader's perspective. He said if he returned to his old job, he would see news much differently. At the forefront of his thoughts would rest the reader. And he would have to answer these questions: Who is picking up the newspaper, and what do they need?

More than 25 years later, and still tough choices.

writer can show how it fits elsewhere. This can be local—several burglaries in a neighborhood—as well as national.

- **The Future.** How will this story influence the future? Will erecting a fence on the Mexico border hurt diplomacy later? Will a Supreme Court ruling on so-called partial-birth abortion signal an end to *Roe v. Wade*? Offering this insight tells the reader that the story carries significance.

These examples show context. Readers need context to size up whether a story is worth their time.

ADVANCED TIP
Traditional Elements of News Judgment

Journalists and educators through the years have compiled several lists of what makes news. Traditionally, many look at news from this perspective, judging the strength of the story on:

1. **Personality.** Is someone famous?
2. **Impact.** Whom does the story affect?
3. **Timeliness.** How recently did it occur?
4. **Proximity.** How near is it?
5. **Quantity.** How many does it affect?
6. **Human Interest.** Does the story show the human condition?

CONFLICT

All great stories have conflict at their heart. This does not necessarily mean controversy, although that might become part of the story. But it does mean issues unresolved or problems to overcome. Readers long have been addicted to plots in myths, movies and novels that require leading characters to overcome great obstacles.

Journalists routinely cover stories that show conflict. Michael Jordan once tried summoning his youth to play a last time in the NBA. The United States waged war in Iraq and Afghanistan. Nancy Pelosi broke through the glass ceiling of politics to become the first woman Speaker of the House, and third in line for the presidency.

Conflict intrigues readers because most of life is a series of conflicts, subtle and obvious. Readers identify with those who struggle: they have struggled themselves. Writing about people while ignoring the conflict in their lives renders stories impotent.

Sometimes beginning reporters confuse controversy with conflict. Controversy is an obvious conflict. It means opposing sides, arguing over a decision or proposal. When neighbors oppose a local government that wants to build a new landfill near their homes, they have created a controversy: two or more sides disagreeing about the outcome. Two sports teams and their fans disputing a referee's decision is considered a controversial call. This means the disagreement is a quarrel, a dispute.

These disagreements meet the standard for good stories, and many reporters write about disputes. Controversy is fun to read about for a while, but it carries a short shelf life. Quarreling grows tiresome, and readers long for resolutions.

Instead of continually writing about controversy, a reporter should look for stories that answer the questions to the controversy. That is, if the neighbors say the landfill will lower the price of their homes, the reporter should look at other landfills. Did prices of homes drop when that landfill was built? Reporters do their readers no greater good than answering the questions raised during a controversy.

Conflict in any form is intriguing. Readers are attracted to stories that show conflict. The best reporters understand this and make sure their stories have it.

HOW TO
Show Context

- **First, last or only.** How unusual or rare is a story?
- **Size matters.** Is it the largest, smallest?
- **Part of a trend**
- **The future**

Often journalists can disagree about what is the most compelling story. Here is the list of the top stories from 2006 chosen by editors who subscribe to the Associated Press. Next to it are lists from the Pew Research Center for People and the Press, the Tyndall Report (which measures network television newscasts), *Time* magazine and the charitable organization, Doctors Without Borders.

The Associated Press

1. **Iraq.** U.S. death toll nearing 3,000
2. **U.S. Election.** Democrats take over
3. **Nuclear Standoffs.** North Korea, Iran develop nuclear programs
4. **Illegal Immigration.** Efforts at legislation continually collapse
5. **Scandals in Congress.** Several Republican congressmen resign
6. **Saddam Convicted.** Saddam Hussein convicted and sentenced to death
7. **Mideast Fighting.** More than 900 killed during Israeli-Hezbollah fighting in Lebanon
8. **Rumsfeld Resigns.** Defense Secretary Donald Rumsfeld leaves office
9. **Airliner Plot.** Terrorist plot thwarted
10. **Darfur Disaster.** Over 200,000 dead

The Pew Research Center: U.S. News Interest Index

1. High Gasoline Prices
2. Airline Plot
3. WV Miners' Deaths
4. Midterm Election
5. School Shootings
6. N. Korea Nuclear Test
7. Iraq News
8. Immigration Issue
9. Arabs Running U.S. Ports
10. Israel-Hezbollah Conflict

***The Tyndall Report:* 2006 Review**

1. Iraq
2. Israel-Hezbollah Conflict
3. Hurricane Katrina Aftermath
4. Hijacked Jets Kamikaze Attacks
5. Oil, Natural Gas, Gasoline Prices
6. Illegal Immigration Legislation
7. Iraq—Sectarian Violence
8. Risk to War-Zone Journalists
9. Campaign 2006
10. North Korea Nuclear Weapons

***Time* Magazine: Top Ten Underreported Stories—2006**

1. Islamist Takeover in Somalia
2. Tuberculosis Gets Even Scarier
3. Intelligence Community Reforms
4. Congo's Still-ravaged State
5. Civilian Casualties in Iraq
6. Effort to Rebuild Afghanistan
7. Number of Americans Jailed
8. U.S. Troops Willing to Re-enlist
9. Insurgency in India
10. Middle-Class Neighborhoods Shrinking

Doctors Without Borders: Most Underreported Humanitarian Crises of 2006

1. Somalis Trapped by War and Disaster
2. Fleeing Violence in the Central African Republic
3. Increasing Human Toll Taken by Tuberculosis
4. Consequences of Bitter Conflict in Chechnya
5. Civilians Under Fire in Sri Lanka, Assistance Limited
6. Effective Strategies for Treating Malnutrition Not Implemented
7. Congolese Endure Extreme Deprivation and Violence
8. Living in Fear in Colombia
9. Violence Rages in Haiti's Volatile Capital
10. Clashes in Central India

Sources: The Associated Press, *Time* magazine, The Pew Research Center for People and The Press, *The Tyndall Report* and Doctors Without Borders.

TIMELINESS

The nearer news happens, both in time and place, the stronger the story. An event just around the corner often creates more interest than one similar but far away. An event that just occurred is often more dramatic than history. The actions of the present usually trump the fascination of the past.

In deciding a news event, closeness takes two paths. The first is physical. An event that breaks in your own community carries more weight. Snow storms hit throughout the winter, but the one that shuts down your city grabs your attention. The late Pope John Paul II visited more countries than any pope in history. Yet his trips to the United States drew more news coverage in America than his travels to other countries.

Readers can also share an emotional attachment to a story despite its location. A local National Guard unit serving in Iraq creates local connections to a war in a foreign country. Students attending universities away from their home towns keep a close watch on news that breaks in their former communities. The sad struggle of a lost whale swimming in the Thames River in London carried widespread appeal.

WIRED AND WIRELESS | WEB

The great gift of the Internet to newspapers might be the most obvious. Online media have dealt newspapers back into the game of breaking news.

When cable television showed the world that a 24-hour news cycle was not only possible but also profitable, electronic media commanded the monopoly on the immediate. Newspapers seemed like old warhorses: slow, quaint, hopelessly passé, waiting until the next morning when ink was applied to paper to offer what television and radio had left them. On some stories—crime news that broke overnight, international news in advanced time zones, elections decided in the wee hours—newspapers were out of date as soon as they hit the front porch.

But the flowering of the Internet has said goodbye to all that. Newspapers can now report stories on their websites as fast as the news breaks. Especially in smaller markets, they are as immediate on the web as any competing news company. The web also lets them match the visuals and audio of other websites.

And newspapers have a built-in advantage: they employ an army of reporters compared to most other news media.

Newspaper portals now are some of the most heavily trafficked information sites. When a gripping story breaks, newspaper websites see a sharp rise in the number of unique visitors.

The rush to the web lets newspapers and other media hampered by long news cycles, such as news weeklies, the chance to break stories as soon as reporters learn of them. But this new news cycle also raises some questions.

A newsweekly magazine used to be defined by when it printed. Reporters who discovered exclusive news waited until the magazine's presses rolled. But the web lets the magazine break news any time, blurring the line that once distinguished a weekly from a daily publication or television station.

For example, if a reporter at *Time* magazine unearths breaking news and posts it immediately online, how does that differ from a reporter at *The Washington Post* or CNN?

The answer, of course, is there is no difference. Online has become the great equalizer, leveling the playing field for all competing media to let the best breaking news win.

The second path is time. For generations, producers in radio and television have known if they are first on the air, they are beating their competitors. As long as fresh information keeps coming, the story remains newsworthy. Print media had to wait—usually hours, sometimes an entire day—until the next news cycle to give their reports.

Now, the Internet has dealt print journalists back into the game. Through websites, all media can break news as fast as journalists can report it. Print journalists often file first for the web, then write their print version. Offering readers the freshest information makes a news medium necessary.

Journalists also can benefit from the lifespan of nonbreaking news. A story might cover an event in the past, but if readers are unaware, the story is still urgent. New developments in an old case, unearthing a story never before reported: readers are learning this for the first time. The latest information gives these stories a boost.

THAT'S JUST WEIRD

A few years ago in Erie, Pa., a pizza-delivery man went to the address phoned in on an order. When he arrived, two men strung around his neck what they said was an explosive. They gave him a complex set of instructions to follow, which included robbing a bank. They turned on what they said was a timer, and sent him on his way.

The delivery man did rob a bank. But just afterwards, police caught up with him. He was detained in the parking lot of an eyeglass center, the odd-looking device wrapped around his neck. Skeptical police kept their distance. The man shouted his unlikely story to police and begged for their help. They called experts. The bomb squad was minutes away from reaching them.

Then the worst happened. The device exploded. The delivery man died. For years, police believed he had been telling the truth, unusual as it sounded. They have since concluded he was part of the plot all along.

When the bizarre happens, it is compelling. As fiction, such plots would be rejected as implausible. As fact, the details are riveting. Curiosities that defy expected patterns make great reading. If you have an element of the curious in your stories, you will have better stories: The more bizarre, the more interesting.

THE CROWD

Above all, journalists have to know their readers. Readers differ about what they consider news, about what they find interesting. Journalists must develop knowledge and a sense for the topics that will resonate with their audiences.

Reporters and editors weigh that question each time they decide the news. Ultimately, readers have the most influence over how news is covered and displayed.

Often, deciding what is news simply means asking where readers live. What is news for those who live in Decatur, Texas, differs from those who live in Decatur, Ga., or Decatur, Ill. The common denominators among readers in each location tell reporters what their readers will find interesting. But geographic location isn't a foolproof standard.

That's why four newspapers in metropolitan New York City will play up different stories. Editors at each of these papers have a strong sense of who is reading their publications. The readers differ, and therefore so does the news judgment.

IN CONCLUSION

Journalists must develop news sense early in their careers. Knowing what makes interesting reading will guide them throughout. News judgment will save them from pursuing the insignificant. It will compel them to dig for the important. At the heart lies the reader. Readers influence news judgment. All journalists form their stories around what they believe will interest their audience.

EXERCISE 1

Read the front page of your campus or community newspaper, or read the top stories of these papers' online sites. For each story, identify what makes each story news. Explain why these stories would appeal to the audiences of the particular news medium you selected.

EXERCISE 2

Look at the following: Read the synopsis for a story, and answer the questions at the end.

In the past two months, at least five students have been robbed at gunpoint on streets that border your campus. These robberies occur late at night, and usually when the students are walking alone to their off-campus housing. No great amount of money has been stolen. But during the last robbery, a male student was walking to class in the afternoon. Three men took about $100 and also hit him with something he said looked like a long pole. Students have expressed their fear. School administrators are holding several meetings to discuss how to be safe at night. Even the mayor attended one of these meetings.

1. What news points apply to this story?
2. What audience would find this story appealing?
3. How would the story change if someone wrote this for students, or the community at large, or for the alumni newsletter?
4. What angles could a journalist look at to get stories behind the story?

EXERCISE 3

Read the following synopsis for a story and answer the questions.

A student-run television station decided to create a comedy/news program patterned after Jon Stewart's *The Daily Show* and Stephen Colbert's *The Colbert Report*. After a few shows, the students had told jokes that demeaned women, ethnic minorities and homosexuals. The chancellor acted swiftly, canceling the program and shutting down the station. The chancellor then put the station under faculty control. Students, while not supporting the program's bad taste, protested losing control of the station. Famous alumni whose careers started at the station sided with the students. The student newspaper ran letters to the editor for weeks. The vast majority opposed shuttering the station. The chancellor refused to back down. The new station under faculty control is set to open next semester.

5. What news points apply to this story?
6. What good did it do to run stories and letters to the editor?
7. Identify all the points of conflict in the story. Why do they make the story more interesting?
8. What other angles could a journalist pursue to get a deeper story behind the story?

C H A P T E R 3

Writing Leads

IN THIS CHAPTER, YOU WILL LEARN:

- Leads are critical to great news stories.
- Leads must tell readers the story's central point.
- Leads must be written in clear, simple language.
- Leads with fewer words help the reader grasp the story quickly.
- Leads are rooted in facts.

I'm getting at what's the most exciting, what's the most compelling bit of information.

Tasneem Grace Tewogbola, former reporter, *The Post-Standard*

TO FIGURE OUT HER LEADS, Tasneem Grace Tewogbola thought of her family.

"If they would say, 'Hey, how was your day?' I would say, as I'm sitting at the computer, 'What would be the first thing I would use to describe my experiences?' " says the former *Syracuse Post-Standard* reporter.

". . . I'm getting at what's the most exciting, what's the most compelling bit of information. How can I hold my family's attention?"

Tewogbola's (pronounced Tay-wog-bow-lah's) task might have been more difficult than most. Her parents were professional storytellers in the African tradition. She had to think hard, sifting through what she calls the "puzzle of facts and details" to capture her story's essence, hunting for just the right words to make her storytelling parents take notice.

To those who write for a living, Tewogbola's search rings familiar. All veteran journalists know this important lesson: In news stories, the opening is the most critical.

Journalists call the way to begin stories "the lead," and they spend a lot of time trying to make their leads glisten. The best writers think about their leads often. Some spend almost as much energy on writing their beginnings as they do writing the rest of their stories. They can redo their leads several times, polishing, perfecting, working on the rhythm. These writers have learned their stories won't succeed unless their leads do.

LEADS PLAY A CRITICAL ROLE

The first few sentences should tell readers what they're reading. These sentences need to be clear, direct, to the point of the story. They should try to be as simple as the way you would tell a friend about the news.

Leads have many jobs:

- **Essence:** The lead is the first chance a writer has to introduce the reader to the story. It might be the last. The reader needs to have an idea of the story's core point, of what the story is all about.
- **Simplicity:** The need for simplicity can't be stressed too often. The writing can't get in the way. The more difficulty readers have wading through the words, the more likely they will stop reading. Reject writing that draws attention to itself.
- **Clarity:** The lead's main purpose is to lure readers into the story. Readers must understand the story's point before moving on. Clear writing gives readers what they need to keep reading.
- **Concrete, specific:** One time-tested way to lose readers is to use nonspecific language. Phrases that rely on vague terms and euphemisms chase readers away. Help the reader visualize the story.
- **Concise:** Leads that pack extra words must go on diets. Pare the unnecessary. Tight, sleek sentences propel readers to the next paragraph.

TRADITIONAL LEAD

Reporters may start their stories several ways. Especially when writing breaking news, many use a traditional approach. In direct, specific language, this lead telegraphs the story's point immediately. This traditional lead answers the questions: who, what, when, where, why and how. Journalists commonly call these the five W's and H.

A traditional lead usually tries to tell the reader those five W's and H in one sentence. The traditional lead explains to readers the main news points in just a brief space. Writers have but a few words to say what is newsworthy.

This is from Cox News Service:

> Space shuttle Columbia broke apart during re-entry Saturday, sending a streak of fiery debris tumbling from the Texas sky and killing a crew of seven astronauts just minutes before their scheduled landing in Florida.

This lead answers most of the 5 W's and H.

- **Who:** space shuttle Columbia
- **What:** broke apart, killing all seven astronauts
- **When:** Saturday, just before landing
- **Where:** in the sky over Texas
- **Why:** unknown at that time
- **How:** unknown at that time

This lead resembles the first words you would tell a friend about this tragic event: "*Did you hear the shuttle broke up over Texas and all the astronauts died?*" There is some added language to say exactly where it was during re-entry and where it was supposed to land, but the structure of the lead stays familiar. The information is all there.

Look at this lead from *The New York Times* the day after 9/11:

> Hijackers rammed jetliners into each of New York's World Trade Center towers yesterday, toppling both in a hellish storm of ash, glass, smoke and leaping victims, while a third jetliner crashed into the Pentagon in Virginia.

This lead about one of the major events of the past 50 years relies on an uncomplicated approach. Look at how the lead answers the 5 W's and H.

Who: hijackers
What: toppled the two towers
When: yesterday
Where: World Trade Center towers
Why: unknown at that time
How: jetliners

The lesson here is that important stories can be told simply. The traditional lead gives readers information quickly and clearly.

Here are the leads to some historic events. Each conveys a momentous time with few words. Although urgent, many almost seem understated:

Jan. 28, 1986—*The Washington Post*

The space shuttle *Challenger*, carrying six astronauts and schoolteacher Christa McAuliffe, exploded in a burst of fire 74 seconds after liftoff yesterday, killing all seven aboard and stunning a world made witness to the event by television.

Dec. 20, 1998—*The New York Times*

William Jefferson Clinton was impeached on charges of perjury and obstruction of justice today by a divided House of Representatives, which recommended virtually along party lines that the Senate remove the nation's 42d President from office.

Dec. 13, 2000—*USA Today*

WASHINGTON—All but ending Al Gore's hopes of winning the presidency, a divided U.S. Supreme Court said late Tuesday a count of disputed Florida ballots poses "constitutional problems" that can't be resolved before the Electoral College picks the next president.

March 21, 2003—*The Wall Street Journal*

American forces poured across the border into Iraq, as U.S. cruise missiles struck Saddam Hussein's main palace and other targets in Baghdad in an attempt to bring down his regime.

Dec. 26, 2004—*The Associated Press*

The world's most powerful earthquake in 40 years triggered massive tidal waves that slammed into villages and seaside resorts across Asia on Sunday, killing more than 3,300 people in five countries.

Tourists, fishermen, homes and cars were swept away by walls of water up to 20 feet high unleashed by the 8.9-magnitude earthquake, centered off the west coast of the Indonesian island of Sumatra.

HOW TO BEGIN: THE ESSENCE

Before you can write a word, you must know your story's central point. Can you answer the questions: What is this story all about? What makes it newsworthy? What is new, interesting?

This is what veteran reporters do instinctively. They grow so adept at it that often during interviews they recognize their lead immediately. To start thinking this way, remember the lessons of news judgment. The news points in your story will guide how you decide your lead.

When you understand your story's point, you are well on your way to writing a solid lead. This one is from *The Associated Press*:

> A suicide bomber walked calmly into a popular Baghdad kebab restaurant at lunchtime Sunday and killed at least 23 people eating plates of lamb and rice—the deadliest attack in the capital in just over six weeks.

If you ask the news questions, you see immediately why the reporter wrote this lead.

- The deaths, of course, are a dramatic change.
- The immediate conflict of a violent act during what usually is a nonviolent event adds to the tragedy.
- The underlying conflict of two sides at war creates tension.
- The context says this was the worst attack in weeks.
- Twenty-three dying is a large number.
- The story ran the next day, making this story timely.

The writer managed to put all these news points in the lead. Though simple, the lead says this story is important.

HOW TO WRITE THE FIRST SENTENCE

Most writers start their stories with a declarative first sentence. That means the sentence follows a pattern known as S-V-O, or subject-verb-object. "The university raised tuition" follows an S-V-O format. "University" is the subject. "Raised" is the verb. "Tuition" is the object.

This construction forces journalists to write simply and to put action into their sentences. Consider this lead from *The Associated Press*:

HOW TO
Write a Lead

Here are the steps to writing a clear lead:

1. Ask yourself "What is the most interesting point to this story? What would be the first few words or sentences that I would tell a friend or family?"
2. Ask yourself: "What has changed? What is new here? What will grab the reader's attention?"
3. Think "S-V-O," that is, subject-verb-object. How do you tell this information as one sentence that is stated as simply and clearly as possible?
4. With the news points in mind, and the goal to write a simple, declarative sentence at the forefront of your thoughts, write a straightforward sentence.
5. Now self-edit. Look for clarity—is this as simple as possible? Does it capture the essence of this story? Look at your verbs. Can they be stronger? Are they active? Count your words. Is this the most readable? Are all words necessary? Can I make any part of this shorter without losing the meaning?

> The season's first big wintry storm blustered across the Midwest on Friday and closed in on the Northeast, leaving hundreds of thousands without electricity, stranding airline passengers and burying streets in wet, heavy snow.

The lead takes advantage of a vivid subject—the wintry storm—and strong verbs: blustered, stranding, burying. Verbs hold the key to aggressive, active language. Careful writers always write with verbs that have movement.

This lead from *USA Today* shows how a few well-placed action verbs make this writing have more life:

> In a rising wave of rural larceny, thieves are tracking commodity prices to steal everything that grows, plows or sprinkles on the USA's farms.

The verbs "grows," "plows" and "sprinkles" push readers into the next sentence.

As a corollary, write in the active voice. This is not the same as putting action into sentences, but they are related.

Active voice: "The university raised tuition."

The opposite of the active voice is the passive voice.

Passive voice: "Tuition was raised by the university."

"Tuition" has become the subject of the sentence. In this form, the action happens to the subject, or passively. In the earlier form, the subject forces the action, or is active. The active voice usually creates a stronger sentence.

The passive voice uses more words than the active voice. Fewer words give the reader less to digest. The active voice is a better way to write.

Prefer the active voice in almost all sentences. But sometimes you can't avoid the passive voice, especially when what you are writing about has to be the subject of the sentence.

This sentence—"A 2-year-old was shot by a stray bullet"—works better in the passive voice because it lets the writer emphasize the child's age. In general, however, writers should try to write as straightforward, and actively, as possible.

The traditional lead should be a simple sentence, written actively, that tells the story's central point.

USE SIMPLE LANGUAGE

Big words impress someone who doesn't understand that those big words discourage reading. The temptation to use academic or obscure words runs deep with writers who feel a need to show off their vocabularies.

Readers notice. Big words, and complex sentences, are hard to miss. But they usually fail to have the impact the writer hoped. Those who want to call attention to their writing are telling the reader that they are more important than their stories.

Write with easy-to-understand phrases. Big words make stories difficult to read. Opt for shorter, more familiar ones. If you confuse readers, they leave your story to find something new.

The Art of Storytelling

A 21st Century Appreciation of the Inverted Pyramid

Increasingly, today's leading writers advocate storytelling through skillful narrative journalism. The finest newspapers, magazines and websites rely on artful anecdotal leads that draw readers deep into stories. However, no media have abandoned that journalism classic, the inverted pyramid lead.

Like the Great Pyramids in Egypt, the inverted pyramid news lead is ancient (to the minds of many modern journalists), yet durable. Though shunned by some as old-fashioned, it functions frequently and well, even today.

A newswriting structure dating to the 19th century, the inverted pyramid puts the foundation of the news story at the top. Dispensing with suspense, it gives away the plot immediately by putting the most important information first. It requires writers to deliver the Who, What, When, Where, Why and How promptly—as much of it as possible in the first sentence or paragraph. The next most important information follows and so on, so that if a story needs to be shortened on deadline, it can safely be trimmed from the bottom.

Such discipline is invaluable when time is precious, inspiration lacking or facts so powerful that embellishment hinders more than helps.

Figure 3.1 The Inverted Pyramid

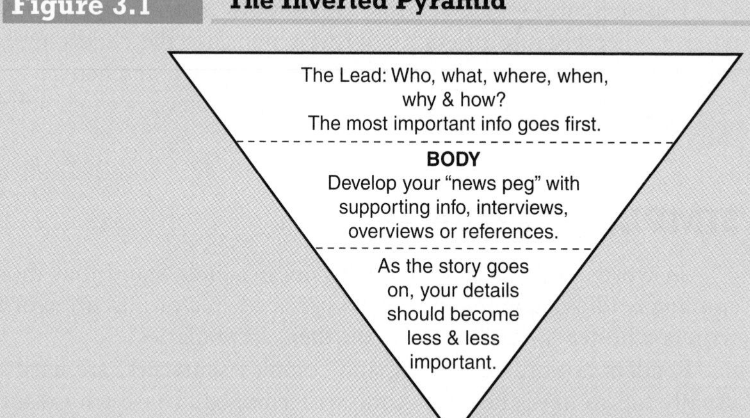

The Lead: Who, what, where, when, why & how? The most important info goes first.
BODY
Develop your "news peg" with supporting info, interviews, overviews or references.
As the story goes on, your details should become less & less important.

Source: www.delawarenationalguard.com/upar/de_uparc_elo5.htm.

Ironically, the more modern the information medium, the more it relies on the venerable inverted pyramid. First wire services, then radio, then television, then Internet news offered up-to-the-minute information. They found nothing did the job faster than the inverted pyramid. All media compete for shrinking attention spans. Nothing delivers the news more economically.

Even as today's newspapers turn increasingly to narrative and other engaging alternatives to the sameness of electronic news, the inverted pyramid is by far the most popular choice for breaking news.

That includes the finest examples of breaking news stories. Almost all of the stories that won the Pulitzer Prize for coverage of breaking news employed the inverted pyramid.

Examine these leads from winners posted at www.pulitzer.org/index.html:

FROM THE *LOS ANGELES TIMES*, Oct. 26, 2003
By Janet Wilson, Lance Pugmire and Monte Morin
Times staff writers

Wildfires driven by winds and high temperatures burned out of control Saturday in the San Bernardino Mountains, triggering firestorms that destroyed more than 200 homes in foothill suburbs and forced the evacuation of thousands of residents from San Bernardino to Rancho Cucamonga.

Stoked by Santa Ana winds that knocked firefighters off their feet and grounded water-dropping helicopters and airplanes, scattered fires covered more than 50,000 acres from Ventura to San Diego counties and raised a ceiling of thick black smoke that spread ash for miles. In all, more than 4,000 firefighters were deployed and more than 13,000 homes threatened.

Two San Bernardino men were reported dead, apparently from heart attacks, Saturday—one as he tried to evacuate and another as he watched his house burn. They were identified as James W. McDermith, 70, and Charles Cunningham, 93. Firefighters searched smoldering homes overnight for residents who might have failed to escape.

Firefighters, who had already labored for days in triple-digit temperatures, faced their gravest challenge Saturday in the foothills of the San Bernardino Mountains just east of the 215 Freeway.

Cyclones of embers tore through the historic San Bernardino neighborhood of Del Rosa, setting dozens of houses ablaze. Flames leapt from building to building along cul-de-sacs on the edge of the foothills, as palm and pine trees exploded in flames. As residents fled, some homeowners ignored the order, wrapped towels over their faces and attempted to save their homes with garden hoses.

(continued)

"Today we have bad news and worse news," San Bernardino County Deputy Fire Chief Dan Worl told a group of fire evacuees. "We just don't have any place to contain this fire."

FROM THE *STAR-LEDGER* of Newark, N.J., Aug. 13, 2004
By Jeff Whelen and John Hassell
Star-Ledger Staff

Gov. James E. McGreevey announced yesterday that he will resign, citing an adulterous affair with a male lover and declaring, "I am a gay American."

"Shamefully, I engaged in an adult consensual affair with another man, which violates my bonds of matrimony," the governor said from the Statehouse as his wife Dina stood, expressionless, at his side. "It was wrong. It was foolish. It was inexcusable."

McGreevey, the state's 51st chief executive and the first to quit under the cloud of scandal, said he will step down Nov. 15 to protect the governor's office from "rumors, false allegations and threats of disclosure."

"I am removing these threats by telling you directly about my sexuality," he said in a blunt six-minute speech that threw the state political scene into turmoil. He added, "I am required . . . to do what is right to correct the consequences of my actions."

FROM THE *HARTFORD COURANT*, March 7, 1998
By John Springer

NEWINGTON—A silent and seething employee went on a bloody rampage at Connecticut Lottery Corp. headquarters Friday, killing four senior lottery officials before committing suicide as police closed in.

Lottery President Otho Brown, 54, and former New Britain Mayor Linda A. Blogoslawski Mlynarczyk, 38, were among the victims of what is believed to be the state's deadliest workplace slaughter.

Also killed were Frederick Rubelmann III of Southington, 40, vice president of lottery operations and administration; and Michael Logan, 33, of Colchester, the agency's information systems director.

The killer used a handgun and a knife. Police identified him as Matthew E. Beck, 35, a state lottery accountant involved in a seven-month dispute with the agency over job duties and pay.

FROM *THE DENVER POST*, April 21, 1999
By Mark Obmascik
Denver Post Staff Writer

JEFFERSON COUNTY—Two students, cloaked in black trench coats and armed with guns and bombs, opened fire Tuesday at Columbine High School, killing as many as 25 people and wounding at least 22 others in the worst school shooting in U.S. history.

> Police found the two suspects shot to death in the library.
>
> The masked shooters first targeted specific victims, especially ethnic minorities and athletes, then randomly sprayed school hallways about 11:30 a.m. with bullets and shotgun blasts, witnesses said. The bloody rampage spanned four hours.
>
> "I saw them shoot a girl because she was praying to God," said Evan Todd, 15, a sophomore. "They shot a black kid. They called him a nigger. They said they didn't like niggers, so they shot him in the face."
>
> School hallways were booby-trapped with at least 12 bombs, some on timers, which still were exploding at 10:45 p.m. One suspect's coat was laced with explosive devices, and undetonated pipe bombs were planted around bodies, police said.
>
> Students described the shooters as part of an outcast group of a dozen or so suburban high school boys known as the Trench Coat Mafia who often wore dark trench coats and had German slogans and swastikas on their clothes. The suspects were identified as Eric Harris, 18, and Dylan Klebold, 17.
>
> The murders came on the 110th anniversary of Adolf Hitler's birth.
>
> "I've heard numbers as high as 25" deaths, said Jefferson County Sheriff John Stone, adding that 17 were confirmed. "When we did make entry into the library, it was a pretty gruesome scene." He called the murders a "suicide mission."

It takes more than shocking facts and a powerful news lead to win a Pulitzer Prize. The winning entries cited above were the lead stories in packages of up to 10 stories that covered the historic events from a wide array of perspectives. But the trend is clear: Each of these newspapers relied on the inverted pyramid to tell the story under their largest headline, even after the event had been announced via electronic media for hours.

More and more, print journalists rely on narrative and other creative writing to differentiate their work. Wire services that fill websites and broadcast reports are published sooner, but they also are nearly homogenous. By late 2005, even the Canadian Broadcasting Company (television) and Bloomberg News (wire service) were encouraging their writers to employ narrative storytelling more often. This is especially prevalent on feature stories and news features with strong human-interest angles. The Associated Press and others were writing alternate leads based on "imagery, narrative devices, perspective or other creative means" on major breaking news as well.

When the news is stranger than fiction and carries astonishingly large implications, when the story is propelled swiftly and compellingly by paragraph after paragraph of jaw-dropping fact, the inverted pyramid often tells the story best. It tells the story rapidly, without distraction. Its five-W discipline protects writers from temptation.

When a story of historic proportion arrives, usually without warning, writers often try to summon unfamiliar powers. They try to write the story of their lives.

(continued)

That is a story they have never written. Too often, it ends up a mess of rookie mistakes committed by experienced journalists.

In *Writer's Toolbox*, Poynter Institute writing coach Roy Peter Clark offers this timeless wisdom: "When the topic is most serious, understate. When the topic is least serious, exaggerate."

In the successful stories above, note the fidelity to Who, What, When, Where, Why and How. Note the order. Who (subject) and What (verb) are superior in rank to When and Where. They are more meaningful, more forceful. Time and location are weaker ways to begin, and should be avoided, unless one of these *is* the news of the day.

In the examples below, the first lead, opening with the Where angle, is the strongest.

> LONDON, England (CNN)—London has defeated European rival Paris to host the 2012 Summer Games, bringing the Olympics back to Britain for the first time in more than half a century.

FROM BBC SPORT

> The 2012 Olympic Games will be held in London, the International Olympic Committee has announced.

The Why and How often are not known at the time of breaking news. Yet, when a famous person commits suicide or is implicated by scandal, readers can't bear to wait to know Why and How. When a killer opens fire in a school, at a post office or at a public event, readers want to know Why as much or more as Who. The answers make powerful follow-up stories on matters of continuing importance. News magazines, which cannot compete with other media on breaking news, thrive by answering the Why and How. *Time* or *Newsweek*, Sunday newspapers and television "I-Teams" typically promise to deliver the "inside story" or to take us "behind the scenes" of major news stories by telling us Why or explaining How. Stories that do this first gain the urgency of breaking news.

Here is an example from *The Associated Press* where the writer could have used fancier-sounding language, but chose words that sound the way we talk.

> Gov. Arnold Schwarzenegger on Monday called a special election for November to try to change the way California spends money, picks its politicians and evaluates its teachers.

Here's why this works:

- **Spends Money:** The writer could have easily written "state expenditures" or "disburses payments." But when couples argue over their bank accounts, they

In any media, the best reporters do not rest until they can answer these questions, even if that takes months. The Pulitzer winners are exemplary in large part because they provide the answers immediately.

Most of the Pulitzer winners have another element in common: context.

We wait only until the second paragraph to read in *The Star-Ledger* that the New Jersey governor was "the state's 51st chief executive and the first to quit under the cloud of scandal . . ." and in *The Hartford Courant* that the government officials were murdered in "what is believed to be the state's deadliest workplace slaughter."

The Denver Post tells us in the opening paragraph that this is "the worst school shooting in U.S. history."

In so doing, these works convey the magnitude of the news—an important virtue in any news story. The bit of extra reporting required for that comes from the same ambition that generates vivid detail and provocative quotes. All make the reader an eyewitness to historic events. They convey motion and propel readers to the next paragraph, and the next.

These compelling stories owe their success to the discipline of the inverted pyramid. Report relentlessly on the Who-What-When-Where-Why-How. Write the strongest, clearest lead that the confidence in your reporting permits. Then make sure that subsequent paragraphs track the lead.

That's recommended practice for any story, including those that will be written as narratives, as features or as dramatic reconstructions of spot news events several days later. The inverted pyramid is more often the format of choice as the story gets bigger and the deadline shorter.

The inverted pyramid is not limited to breaking news. It will work on investigative stories and trend stories, for instance, where the revelations carry nearly the urgency of breaking news. In these cases, however, there is usually much more time to report the human drama that can make for an even more compelling narrative.

rarely discuss each other's habits of disbursing funds. They argue about spending money.

- **Picks its Politicians:** The reporter also could have written about changing "California's electoral process." That would carry the same meaning but risk losing the reader. "Picks its politicians" sounds more the way we would talk in relaxed conversation.
- **Evaluates its Teachers:** Lastly, a bureaucrat would say "secondary instructor performance reviews." But "evaluating teachers" is the way we talk.

All these big phrases would have held the same meaning as the simpler, more common ones. But using the larger ones would weaken the writing.

Consider this lead, also from *The Associated Press*:

> Police unleashed a hail of gunfire yesterday on a car full of unarmed men driving away from a bachelor party at a strip club, killing the groom on his wedding day in a shooting that drew a furious outcry from family members and community leaders.

There are few big words in this lead, and yet the story is compelling, and the meaning is clear.

CLARITY WORKS

One of the best writing professors at Syracuse University, William Glavin believes that readers hate to work. If they run into a confusing sentence, they won't try to figure it out. They will just stop. Make readers work, argues Prof. Glavin, and you lose them.

Veteran journalists follow Glavin's mantra: The writer works so the reader doesn't.

The writer must make sure that the opening sentences flow so easily that the reader meets no resistance getting through them. Note the phrase is "no resistance," not "little resistance."

Readers should be able to glide through the lead as if it were coated with a fine grade of oil. The best stories champion such vivid writing that readers race through the opening paragraphs before they realize they've been reading.

This is from *The Associated Press*:

> A coal mine explosion that may have been sparked by lightning trapped 13 miners about three miles underground, state officials said.

This lead follows the S-V-O structure. While less exciting than some others, perhaps, it gets an A for readers' ability to understand what the story is all about. Its simplicity lets the reader grasp in a moment the story's central point. It also telegraphs in few words that more information lies only paragraphs away. In your career, you might write more enticing leads. But you will grow into a strong writer if many of your leads boast this much clarity.

This lead is from *USA Today*:

> The nation's food banks are scrambling to serve a growing demand for help during the holidays at a time when the government food donations and private cash contributions have fallen.

This lead has to do a lot. It tells not only what is happening but also why it is occurring. But the reader is never lost because the writer took care to make this as easy to understand as possible.

Concrete Words

Often, beginning writers rely on language that is too general. That means the words can apply to many situations and aren't specific enough to hold a reader's attention.

ADVANCED TIP

What Experienced Writers Say about Leads

It has to get you past the I-don't-want-to-read-this.

—Katherine Boo, Pulitzer Prize winner, ASME winner, *The New Yorker* staff writer

I think it's really important that the lead establish the voice and tone of the story. . . . I think that's why sometimes . . . it takes a few tries to get the right sound of the story.

—Lisa Pollak, Pulitzer Prize winner, *The Baltimore Sun*, producer, *This American Life*

For me it has to be the most interesting component, and it's a personal decision. But sometimes when I'm doing the interview or sitting and observing something, it will occur to me that whatever I'm observing is the lead. I think, "OK, so this is it."

—Tasneem Grace Tewogbola, former reporter, *The Post-Standard*

Think: what is this story about, and how am I going to keep it focused on this aspect of what I'm working on?

—Claire Martin, *The Denver Post*

To capture readers, give them enough information that they can form a picture in their minds. They can't do that if the writing is nonspecific. Concrete words let readers see the action. Once those pictures form, readers tend to forget they are reading.

Instead of saying precipitation, write "rain" or "snow" or "sleet"—whatever was falling from the sky. Precipitation can mean any of this weather. But readers can picture what snow looks like.

Instead of saying the snow was falling on "higher elevations," use "hills" or "mountains" or "plateaus." Specific is always better.

Hurricanes hit beaches, not coastal regions. Environmentalists worry about rivers, not waterways. Students live in dorms, not residential facilities. Children play dodge ball, not engage in leisure activities. Readers appreciate words that identify specific action.

This is an example from *The Associated Press*. The writer tried to use language so the reader could picture the lead:

A retired public school teacher so frugal that he bought expired meat and secondhand clothing left $2.1 million for his alma mater, Prairie View A&M—the school's largest gift from a single donor.

Readers can see the teacher buying the expired meat at stores. They can also see the secondhand clothing. This lead would be fine without those images. But by adding them, the writer strengthens this lead.

What also helps this lead is the ironic twist: A person who could afford quality meat and clothes ignored them to save a fortune. Then he chooses to donate this fortune to the place that gave him the tools to earn it. That his gift was the school's largest makes this story that much more intriguing.

SHORTER IS BETTER

Readers understand shorter sentences better than longer ones. Readers' comprehension of facts and detail grow when you give them shorter takes. The fewer the words, the easier to grasp the meaning.

Many newsrooms around the country encourage short sentences for leads. Some even have enforced word counts, making reporters add up how many words they've used to begin their stories.

WIRED AND WIRELESS | WEB

Few media shine as brightly as the Internet when news breaks. Events such as the Virginia Tech shootings, the 9/11 attacks and Hurricane Katrina have shown the power and demand for instant knowledge. News professionals have learned that their readers and viewers rush to websites and expect to find the most recent information.

Flush with urgency, stories that report on the immediate must be understood in an instant. The traditional lead lies at the heart of these quick hits and constant updates.

Though out of fashion in some corners of journalism, the traditional lead has proven a sturdy and lasting way to talk directly to readers or viewers. When big stories break, especially through the Internet, the traditional lead does the heavy lifting.

A casual glance at websites of newspapers, television networks and news magazines reveals breaking news stories sporting these leads. This holds true for both staff-written updates and wire-service reports from the Associated Press.

Why does the newest technology rely on one of the oldest sentence structures? Readers must know quickly what they're reading. In the hands of a skilled writer, the traditional lead cuts through the smoke and fog. It is wound tight. It signals urgency. It works when space or time is limited.

Written well, the lead can carry grace and power. It also forces reporters to understand what is newsworthy. When you write a traditional lead, there's no hiding if you haven't figured out what is the news. You either know, and say it directly, or you don't, and find yourself stuck in vague language.

Often a traditional news lead might read formulaic. The temptation for beginning writers is to skip the traditional lead for less conventional ways to lure the reader into their stories. That idea has some merit, especially for stories other than breaking news.

But as more readers and viewers rely on news websites for their instant updates, the traditional lead will not go away anytime soon. All writers need the skill to write that lead.

While extreme, the point is well taken. Usually, 18–20 words promote the best readability. After 30 words, comprehension from readers begins to drop. Forty words generally become difficult for quick understanding. Sentences that boast 45–50 words generally run too long.

It's not that writers are forbidden to use long sentences or pack content into their writing. Writers also should vary their sentence length throughout their stories to offer their readers variety and pace.

But wordier sentences run the risk of making your reader work too hard.

Here are some differences:

An earthquake shook Japan on Monday, toppling buildings, damaging bridges and buckling roads (13 words).

"Defense Secretary Donald H. Rumsfeld said Sunday he is bracing for even more violence in Iraq and acknowledged that the insurgency "could go on for any number of years" (29 words).

"Terry Schiavo suffered severe irreversible brain damage that left that organ discolored and scarred, shriveled to half its normal size, and damaged in nearly all its regions, including the one responsible for vision, according to an autopsy report released Wednesday" (40 words).

"Iran's newly elected president, Mahmoud Ahmadinejad, said Saturday that he wanted to create a strong Islamic nation and issued a call for unity in his first comments after a landslide victory that left the country's reformist movement virtually powerless and threatened to further complicate relations with the United States" (49 words).

It's not that any of these leads are better or worse than the others. In fact, some longer leads can actually be more powerful as the writer can use a few extra words to add a twist or flavor to the news. But there's little arguing that the longer sentences take more work to get through.

If you want to write longer sentences, you have to take care to avoid losing the reader. The sentences have to read quickly. You can't bog them down with unfamiliar names or difficult concepts. They have to flow freely.

Always think of readers. Think of them as uncertain if they want to continue. Imagine them with a television remote pointed at your story, surfing throughout the vast number of other stories available. At the first hint of confusion, they'll quickly switch. Don't let them bail from your story because you have made the writing difficult.

ANALYZING SOME LEADS

Some leads work well. Some don't. You can take all the points we've looked at and hold them against various leads. Following the guidelines for getting started won't guarantee success. Some leads stick to the rules and don't work. Some break all the rules and read beautifully. However, in general, the guidelines we've discussed can help you write a readable beginning to your stories.

This lead is from *The Chicago Tribune*:

> St. Petersboro University took a first step to cleaning up its athletic program when it fired its athletic director and head basketball coach amid NCAA allegations that it cheated to recruit players to the school, the school's president, James Edwards, announced Monday.

The first issue is the word count. This lead runs 42 words. It needs tightening. The lead also would improve if it grew simpler by following the S-V-O format. The attribution can be slipped in without tacking it on at the sentence's end.

Rewritten, this looks now:

> St. Petersboro University's president fired his athletic director and head basketball coach Monday amid allegations they violated NCAA recruiting rules.

This simplifies the sentence to 20 words without losing the main core of the news.

Here's a lead from *USA Today*:

> Oil prices jumped above $55 a barrel Monday as energy markets were lifted by rising costs for heating oil and an unusual admission by OPEC members that there's not much they can do to alter prices.

This lead starts directly, using an action verb "jumped" that gives this sentence a boost. The sentence also explains clearly why the prices jumped and used familiar language to explain it. The phrase "there's not much they can do" reads quickly. The common words add to the lead's clarity.

Even though the word count here is 35, there's little reason to change this except for two points. One, an editor might have changed "as energy markets were lifted" and substituted "spurred." In that way you save words and add another action verb.

The second is using the word "prices" twice so close together. They are prominent words in the sentence and stick out that near one another.

This now reads:

> Oil jumped above $55 a barrel Monday spurred by rising costs for heating oil and an unusual admission by OPEC members that there's not much they can do to alter prices.

IN CONCLUSION

One final observation: All leads root themselves in fact. You will find no opinion. News writing is all about facts, or what most agree is true. In the shuttle lead, few would argue it was tragic. But by merely describing the events, the writer shows the reader it was tragic. In the 9/11 lead, the writer describes the towers falling and shows the ash and smoke. The facts tell the story. They are a powerful tool in your belt.

Leads are critical. They demand thought and hard work from the reporter. Readers must glide through them with ease. The leads that work are active, packed with content and enticing to the reader.

They don't materialize from thin air. They reflect the story's news value. They tell the reader what the story is about, then help the reader understand the story's significance.

Great leads are clear, to the point and aggressive. The careful writer weeds them of all unnecessary words, all confusing parts. They require effort. Once perfected, they lead the unsuspecting reader to the next paragraph.

TOOL KIT

Some books you might want to consider:

Magazine Editing, by J. T. W. Hubbard, Prentice-Hall Inc., Englewood Cliffs, New Jersey, 1982.
The Word, by Rene Cappon, The Associated Press, New York, 1982.
Writing for Your Readers, by Donald Murray. The Globe Pequot Press, Boston, 1983.

EXERCISE 1

Identify the 5 W's and H from the following leads:

1. Students at Vallejo College will pay more for going to school. The Vallejo Board of Trustees, citing the surprising costs of an aggressive building plan, raised tuition by 10 percent Tuesday, the largest jump in the school's history.

2. Bellevue University won its first conference title in basketball Saturday, defeating Hammersmith, 71–70, on its own court when a desperation shot from just past the midcourt line went in as time expired.
3. Police arrested three men Friday for robbing five Franklin students last month at gunpoint.
4. Scott Washington became president of Halladay University's Student Association, promising to end student infighting after weeks of a bitter campaign.
5. Southport students told president Edwin Bartlett on Tuesday that they wanted the university to become a green campus by closing off access for cars and using alternative fuels.

EXERCISE 2

Write a lead from each set of facts:

6. Prescott College student, Jeff Lam, foreign exchange student from Leeds, England, freshman, 18, majored in finance, fell out of his dorm window, by himself, fell four floors to the parking lot of Huffington Dorm, pronounced dead at the scene, at 9:30 p.m. Saturday, about four hours after the Prescott football game, which the Pride won, breaking a 30-game losing streak, those in the dorm room said he had been celebrating the win all afternoon, he was drinking.
7. Interview with Chancellor Elizabeth Wirstein:
   "We believe that Edmonton College is the best institute of higher education in the land and has the finest student body of many colleges on the same level as we are. That's why we need to continue to move forward, to be at the cutting edge of universities, and so we're going to start this scholarship to attract minorities to our school that's almost completely white. The scholarship will be the richest one we've got, and it comes to us from the local newspaper, *The Edmonton Times*, and it will give us the leverage we need to attract a group that has previously decided to go elsewhere."
8. From the engineering school at Winkworth University:
   We are pleased to announce today that one of our very own students has won a most prestigious award. We are announcing that Tatiana Hermoz has been awarded the Penny Award. That goes to the best engineering student who is a junior in the country. Tatiana has a 3.9 grade point average and is one of the most pleasant students in our school. She is the first Winkworth student to ever win the award and the first Latina to win it nationally. "You can't get a higher award for engineering students in the country," said William Potter, the engineering school dean. Please join us in congratulating Tatiana. Who will be the first person to ask her what she'll do with her $10,000 prize money?
9. Fire in apartments just off campus. The Hilltop Apartments. Two units burst into flame on Thursday morning at about 9. Four students from Van Buren College were sent to the hospital suffering from smoke inhalation. Three more students can't move back into their apartments. The fire started from a cigarette. Another unit caught on fire before firefighter put out the blaze. In that unit lived the basketball player, Jamal Paulus, who was burned so badly that he's probably out for the season, the sports information department says. He was second team All-America last year and the Van Buren Broncos leading scorer.

CHAPTER 4

Writing Simply

IN THIS CHAPTER, YOU WILL LEARN:

- Writing simply lies at the core of effective popular writing.
- The better writers usually follow standard guidelines.
- Some writing advice is common sense.
- Reducing your stories to the barest form possible improves your writing.

You keep sentences simple and, if possible, short.

Marcus Hayes, reporter,
the *Philadelphia Daily News*

HENRY SCHULTE, THE LATE DEAN OF Syracuse University's communications school, once was answering typical parents' questions about tuition costs and jobs after graduation when one asked: What was Schulte's most difficult lesson to teach?

Schulte, a veteran wire service reporter and foreign correspondent in Spain, didn't flinch.

"To write a simple, declarative sentence in English," he said.

Accomplished writers might differ on style and approach. But they usually agree on this point: Writing is difficult, and writing simply even more difficult. Experienced writers know the craft requires both a sound idea of the story and an ability to tell it with grace. At the core rests Schulte's goal of the clear and simple sentence.

All journalists should strive for clarity. They never should give their readers a reason to leave the story because their writing was cloudy. How did they learn to write clearly? How do they construct the simplest sentences?

Discipline.

Much of writing the news clearly is resisting the temptation of indulgence. A journalist's style should never outdo the story. Disciplined writers know to weed their sentences of all that choke the reader's ability to comprehend. The unnecessary word, the overwritten phrase, the flowery language take a back seat to telling a story in the simplest way.

Disciplined writing takes a lifetime to learn. Donald Murray was teaching English in New Hampshire when editors at *The Boston Globe* asked him to help their reporters with their writing. Murray became a writing coach, one of the newspaper industry's first.

Murray later wrote about what he had learned at *The Globe* in his book *Writing for Your Readers*. He opens his book saying the best writers keep trying to master the simple sentence.

"Professional writers never learn to write; they continue to learn writing all their professional lives," Murray writes. "The good writer is forever a student of writing. . . ."

Murray suggests several guidelines that, if followed, will improve the writer's work. But he never says that strong writing is merely following rules.

Most seasoned writers understand that. Sometimes breaking the rules can mean a better, livelier sentence. Still, those same writers usually follow the guidelines carefully, picking their rebellious moments wisely.

Here are 10 suggested guidelines for writing that simple, declarative sentence Dean Schulte found so difficult a lesson to pass on:

1. KEEP ONE IDEA TO EACH SENTENCE

Beginning journalists must learn what writing style they should adopt, and what style they should avoid. To start, reject the long, twisted sentences that torture much of bureaucratic and academic writing. They can tempt the intimidated writer at first. Those sentences sound so learned that sometimes beginners believe that is quality writing.

The Art of Storytelling

Ever sit in a movie that had a lot of dialogue but not much action? You can almost hear yourself begging, "Will something please happen?"

Ever slide your car into gear, only to find you've accidentally selected neutral? Step on the gas and rev the engine: a big noise, but nothing moves.

In much the same way, writing with no action leaves readers waiting for something to happen, waiting for the story to go someplace.

Journalists who fail to remember this often-quoted mantra of nonfiction writing—use active verbs—are doomed to bore their readers: lots of words, lots of noise, not much going on. Let your language lapse into the inert, and you risk losing your readers.

The adage "use active verbs" never loses its truth. Journalists seeking vigorous sentences should attend to their verbs.

1. Put Action into Your Writing

Verbs are the engines that drive sentences. Active verbs give writing movement. Readers demand motion. They grow weary of sentences that sit idling, waiting for the light to turn green. They want the words to speed off ahead.

Verbs need to run, jump, hop, skip, leap, bound, soar, dash, streak, speed, race. They should take a sentence at rest and put it in play.

Turning dull verbs into exciting ones often means simply paying attention. Anytime you see "am," "are," "was" and "were," try to find a verb with more action.

Not:

Alcohol use among teenagers is much lower now than 10 years ago.

But:

Alcohol use among teenagers plummeted in the last 10 years.

Or:

Teenagers drink less alcohol than a decade ago.

Not:

Hillary Clinton is as popular today as she ever was.

But:

Hillary Clinton's popularity has soared to an all-time high.

Not:

There were no others who saw the shooting.

But:

No others saw the shooting.

Better:

No others saw Smith shoot his neighbor's dog.

2. Don't Confuse Action with Active Voice

Action verbs are not the same as active voice. Active voice means letting the subject control the action, such as "The boy mowed the grass." Passive construction would cast that sentence "The grass was mowed by the boy." The active voice is obviously preferred: It's more concise and moves quicker.

Writers should always try to use the active voice. But merely writing in the active voice won't give every sentence action.

Smith was voted off the board by the council.

In the active voice becomes:

The council voted Smith off the board.

Adding an action verb, this becomes:

The council kicked Smith off the board.

Or:

The council ousted Smith from the board.

3. Use Verbs That Carry Specific Action

Everything happens. Everything occurs. Everything results from something else. Use verbs specific to the action you describe.

Not:

An accident occurred Monday.

But:

Two cars crashed Monday.

Not:

Heavy rains resulted in widespread flooding.

(continues)

But:

Heavy rains flooded three counties.

Not:

The shooting, which happened in the home, left two dead

But:

The man shot and killed both his in-laws during an argument in the kitchen.

Writing in specific language lets your readers see the action. That makes the story easier to picture and to read.

4. Verbs with "Ion" and "Ive" Endings Raise Red Flags

Popular English enjoys attaching endings to verbs that turn them into nouns. The installation began as install, elimination as eliminate, creation as create. When writers see words that end in "ion" or "ive," they should see if the word can become a verb again and improve their sentence.

Not:

The school will pay for the installation of the computers.

But:

The school will pay to install the computers.

Not:

The administration is supportive of the idea.

But:

The administration supports the idea.

Better:

The administration believes smaller classes help students learn.

5. Make Action Put Pictures in Your Readers' Minds

Often, new writers will settle for language that could use more action. Action will put pictures in your readers' minds.

Not:

The company is aiming to boost profitability through a reduction in payroll.

But:

The company will try to make more money by cutting jobs.

Not:

At United, compensations and benefits accounted for 45 percent of operating expenses last year.

But:

Paying its workers' salaries and benefits cost United nearly half its budget last year.

Not:

The board voted against the public using the school's athletic facilities.

But:

The board banned joggers from the school's track and basketball players from its gym.

Not:

It is impossible for the panel . . . to conceive a mechanism through which the levee system can be rebuilt and operated effectively and efficiently with such organizational discontinuity and chaos.

But:

The infighting and petty politics will block rebuilding and operating the levees, the panel said.

Not:

The nickel defense was effective.

But:

The nickel defense stopped the Browns.

Better, more specific:

The nickel defense smothered the Browns' receivers, giving Smith no chance to throw.

Some Quick Advice from Marcus Hayes

Marcus Hayes, a sports writer from the *Philadelphia Daily News*, says he writes as if he were speaking to a large crowd. What would hold its attention? Imagining the audience spurs his writing to action.

"You move [the story] by telling a story," Hayes says. "You pretend you are orating, trying to keep an audience of 200 interested for 20 minutes."

But Hayes also says vigorous writing stems from using active language as well.

(continues)

"You use action verbs, but not exclusively and not for their own sake," he says. "You use words that punch you: 'Spat' instead of 'forcefully said,' and 'Cracked' instead of 'hit,' 'dead' instead of 'passed away,' etc.

"You infuse cadence or meter and you create images with aggressive verbs, and don't be afraid to break rules: i.e., 'Steve Sax crabbed down to first base on his little bowed legs.' Now, 'crabbed' isn't a verb and there should be a comma between 'little' and 'bowed,' but the created verb works and meter is better without the comma."

Hayes still works to make his writing clear and his prose as sparse as possible.

"You keep sentences simple, and, if possible, short. Periods usually work better than semicolons and they almost always work better than commas. And never try to write over your head. Write to your own level, not Poe's or Dickens'."

Marcus Hayes—sports writer for the *Philadelphia Daily News.*

On the contrary, journalists have found the simpler the better. The more writers add to their sentences, the denser their prose.

Keep one idea to each sentence. That lets readers grasp the meaning sooner. They don't have to reread to fully understand. Often, they won't bother to reread and instead go to something else.

Sometimes deleting the connectors—"and," "or"—fixes everything.

> Drivers trying to avoid Hurricane Rita snarled traffic for hours, and many were forced to sit in long lines for gas.

Eliminate "and," then break this into two sentences.

> Drivers fleeing Hurricane Rita snarled traffic for hours. Many sat in long lines for gas.

Attaching clauses to the main thought merely adds words, not simplicity. Shorter sentences can make the writing clearer.

> Cicero neighbors have lived with the odor for weeks, saying the smell from the lake's algae have made it impossible to hold barbeques in their backyards, wash their cars in their driveways or do any outdoor activity.

This sentence becomes several, and more specific.

> The lake's algae give off a stifling odor. Cicero neighbors complain the smell has driven them indoors. They can't barbeque in their backyards. They can't wash their cars in their driveways.

Long introductory clauses add too many thoughts to a sentence. They also make the reader work too hard. These clauses tell the reader to hold the thought until the writer gets to the main point.

> Seeing from the start that the university lacked enough money to support many of his initiatives, the chancellor announced a year-long campaign to add to the school's endowment.
>
> Broken down, this now becomes:
>
> The chancellor quickly saw the university couldn't pay for his ideas. He began a year-long campaign to increase the school's endowment.

Notice the second revised sentences read more direct. They also move the reader along at a faster pace.

2. USE FEWER ADJECTIVES AND ADVERBS

One important lesson to learn about writing is to take Mark Twain's advice: When you find an adjective, kill it.

Relying on modifiers to make your writing sparkle is futile. Overuse them, your writing bogs down. Often just eliminating most adjectives and their cousins, adverbs, frees your sentences.

> His balding, white hair and soft, wrinkled face tell you he's old. But his rail thin body speaks of probable athletic glory from years past.

What's wrong with these sentences? Using too many modifiers, and relying on them for color. Eliminating a few simplifies the prose.

> His white hair and wrinkled face tell you he's old. But his thin body speaks of past athletic glory.

One can't write without modifiers. But if writers trust them to add color, they should just rewrite.

The corollary to fewer adjectives and adverbs is to rely on nouns and verbs. Clear English depends on them. Subjects (nouns) act, and verbs prompt the acting. When your writing moves, readers stay engaged.

Notice how few modifiers are in these paragraphs from *The New York Times*:

> At 6 a.m. Thursday, as soon as curfew broke, she started out for ice and water. She went first to the mall, where the police told her to go to the parking lot at Hoods; she waited in line there for more than an hour, only to be told that the trucks would be another four hours. She was driving to her brother's house where she saw an

emergency supply truck under police escort doling out bags of ice and water along Pass Road.

"You see a white truck, follow it!" said Howard Waugh, her neighbor in the line where she now waited with a cooler and her two small children.

The action and specific language carry the reader through these paragraphs and send them into the rest of the story.

3. OMIT NEEDLESS WORDS

Will Strunk and E. B. White, collaborating nearly a half century apart, make a strong case for eliminating extra words.

"Vigorous writing is concise," they write in their book, *Elements of Style*. "A sentence should have no unnecessary words, a paragraph no unnecessary sentences, for the same reason a drawing should have no unnecessary lines and a machine no unnecessary parts."

Extra words clog writing. In speech, it's usually tolerable to hear duplication and verbosity. Inflections, gestures and volume mask the faults of saying too much.

Author and humorist E. B. White.

With writing, the game changes. Fewer are better. Less is best. Concise, fine-tuned paragraphs travel far. Some ways to eliminate extra words are merely mechanical.

- In order to—to
- The fact that—that
- At that point in time—at that time
- A small number of—a few
- In an attempt to—to
- All of the—all

Other ways to write in the sparsest prose possible is by eliminating unnecessary direction words. We don't need to say "sit down." That is the action of sitting, although it is different from sitting up. The careful writer avoids saying "Lift up" because "lift" implies up. Those who write "take away" usually can shorten to simply "take."

All these might strike beginners as picky. But the careful writer combs sentences for the unnecessary to emphasize the necessary. Readers win in the end.

4. AVOID OVERUSING PREPOSITIONS

Prepositions show the relationship between words. In the phrase "spokesperson for the group" shows that spokesperson and group belong together.

Prepositions are necessary for writers of modern English. But our language has grown cluttered with them. The more writers use them, the more wooden their prose.

Avoid prepositions—"about," "above," "along," "among," "at," "before," "between," "except," "for," "from," "in," "off," "on," "over," "since," "toward," "under," "until," "unto," "up with," "without"—or take extra care to use fewer.

The path of the storm started from the north and went to the east.

Rewrite this using fewer prepositions:

The storm blew from the north, then turned east.

Eliminating prepositions can help reach the goal of relying on nouns and verbs.

A small number of students traveled along with the boosters.

Remove the prepositions, and this becomes:

A few students accompanied the boosters.

The mayor has been supportive of the efforts of the group from the start.

This becomes:

The mayor has always supported the group.

Excess prepositions sometimes signal the passive voice. Deleting as many as possible transforms sentences from the passive to the active voice.

Recommendations by a committee studying truck traffic problems in and around Geneva will be the focus of a public meeting tonight.

Rewritten, this becomes:

A committee studying Geneva's truck traffic patterns tonight will recommend rebuilding a dangerous stretch of highway.

Perhaps the most overused prepositional phrase is "of the." Question yourself each time you use it. Try to recast the sentence to improve its clarity.

Members of the committee—committee members
The future of the city—the city's future
The leaders of the group—the group's leaders
Residents of the community—the community's residents

5. KEEP NUMBERS TO A MINIMUM

Numbers can be numbing. Use them carefully. Give readers time to grasp their size before springing another one on them. Using them one after another confuses even the sharpest reader.

Named after the Roseland Amusement Park, which closed in 1985, Roseland Waterpark began operations in the summer of 2001. Feasibility studies conducted in 1998 and early 2000 projected that the park would draw approximately 250,000 visitors each summer season. Instead, the $17 million, 58-acre park received 150,000 visitors in 2001 and between 130,000 and 140,000 this summer.

The information in this paragraph is necessary to fully understand the story. But cramming them into this paragraph slows down the reader. Present the numbers at a more comfortable pace.

> Roseland Waterpark opened in 2001, more than 15 years after its namesake, Roseland Amusement Park, shut down. Early studies promised 250,000 visitors each summer. Instead, about two-thirds of that number showed the first year, and even fewer—about 140,000—this summer.

Journalists shouldn't fear numbers. They are facts, and writers must use them to support their stories. But readers need help swallowing them. A few tricks help the medicine go down easier.

- Use the equivalent word when context allows. Instead of 10 years, use "decade." "Century" is better than 100 years, although "score" for 20 has become archaic. "Generation" might be better.
- Do the math for the reader. Instead of writing "she was born in 1985, when the drinking age was not standard," write "she was born 22 years ago, before the drinking age became standard in all states."
- Use counting numbers to explain percent. "The price of gasoline jumped 20 percent" becomes "gas increased 15 cents a gallon, a jump of 20 percent." "The city's population decreased by 2 percent" becomes "About 5,000 residents left Oswego, a 2 percent drop."

Numbers support your stories and show readers that your stories are true. Just pace them throughout so the reader has a chance to digest them. Show their relationship to other numbers and use the word equivalent when possible.

6. AVOID PROPER NAMES CLOSE TOGETHER

Beginning writers often make the mistake of using too many proper names at once, especially in leads. The long names of government committees and law firms are needed, but not before the writer has introduced them to the reader. The less familiar the name, the more difficult to grasp quickly. Therefore, the careful writers weigh when to introduce the name to the reader.

> The Travis County Board of Zoning Appeals denied the Smithfield and Loomis Inc. request to upgrade its zoning status on the Byrne Dairy tract.

The proper nouns get in the way of the reader understanding the news. The writer can gain clarity if she makes the board and business more generic.

> The county denied a developer's request to upgrade the zoning on the Byrne Dairy tract.

Once readers understand the news, you are free to introduce the key players one-by-one. Readers stand a better chance of understanding.

The better known a person or group, the freer the writer to use the proper name from the start. George W. Bush, Julia Roberts and Michael Jordan all carry recognition. Still, that doesn't give the writer a free pass to cloudiness.

President Bush flew to the hard-hit areas of Pass Christian, Biloxi and Gulfport in Mississippi, then traveled to Baton Rouge and New Orleans, stopping in the suburbs of Kenner, Metairie and Chalmette and then at the historic French Quarter.

A better way to write this eliminates some of the lesser-known proper nouns.

President Bush flew to the hard-hit areas along Mississippi's Gulf Coast, then traveled to Baton Rouge and several New Orleans suburbs before stopping at the historic French Quarter.

7. PUT VERBS AS CLOSE TO THE SUBJECT AS POSSIBLE

This sounds easy at first. But at times we have so much information to add to a sentence that the verb can get lost.

Careful writers keep track of where they place their verb. If it strays too far from its subject, pull it back to quicken the sentence's pace. Grammatically, the writer can place the verb nearly anywhere. The best writers are not so indifferent.

A new county budget, which includes pay raises for the sheriff and several top managers but avoids a tax increase, on Saturday was approved unanimously by the legislature.

Depending on the most important news, recast this way:

1. The county's sheriff and several top new managers will make more money, but residents won't pay more taxes in the new budget approved Saturday.
2. County residents won't see their tax bills increase despite the legislature Saturday approving pay raises for the sheriff and several managers.
3. The county legislature approved its new budget Saturday, giving the sheriff and several key managers pay increases without raising taxes.

By keeping the verb close to its subject, the writer also resists the temptation to add parenthetical clauses, that is, phrases that add to the sentence's meaning but hurt its readability. When the writer has more than one thought, it's usually better to break one sentence into two.

This is from *The New York Times*:

But for now, it seems that Chinese authorities have decided that the fashion magazines, which promote whiter skin—a popular theme—Western styles and an obsession with brands, and the men's magazines—which promote toned bodies and carry lifestyle and sex advice that would not be out of place on a newsstand in New York—are safe.

Placing the verb closer to its subject and using more sentences help this writing.

But for now, it seems that Chinese authorities have decided fashion and men's magazines are safe. Fashion magazines promote brands, Western style and white skin, a popular theme. Men's magazines promote toned bodies and carry lifestyle and sex advice that would be at home on a newsstand in New York.

8. AVOID USING NOT

Strunk and White advocate putting phrases in positive terms. This idea has withstood the test of time: Tell me what it is.

Avoiding the word "not" lets writers express themselves with more power than at first glance. Their sentences can grow shorter, more compact.

"Not on time" becomes "late." "Did not remember" becomes "forgot." "Was not happy" becomes "sad" or "upset." "Paid no attention to" becomes "ignored." "Did not know" becomes "was unaware."

Avoiding the negative also allows for other phrasing. About sources in the Valerie Plame case, where information from the White House outed a CIA spy:

> For two years, White House spokesman Scott McClellan said Rove and Libby weren't involved.

> This is improved by no negative and more specific words:

> For two years, White House spokesman Scott McClellan said neither Rove nor Libby were sources.

At times, avoiding the negative lets the writer give her prose an edge. *The Wall Street Journal* could have written this:

> . . . persuade affluent consumers, who don't have any problem making big-ticket purchases online, to embrace shopping through their TVs.

> Instead, *The Journal* wrote in the positive:

> . . . persuade affluent consumers, who have no problem making big-ticket purchases online, to embrace shopping through their TVs.

9. AVOID REPETITIVE PHRASES

Often, colorful phrases at first seem wonderful in their richness. But a closer look reveals that many of these phrases need editing. Some could be deleted.

If the goal is to be clear and concise, then avoid the following phrases. To use them only makes your reader work harder.

The "here and now," "front and center," "each and every," "pick and choose," "ready and willing," "able and willing" can all be shortened or eliminated.

10. WRITE WITH ANGLO-SAXON WORDS

Anyone who has spent an hour trying to write English soon discovers two ways to express most sentences. One uses the complex wording of bureaucrats: indirection, passive construction, euphemisms. *Proceeding down this path would threaten the integrity of this proposal.* The other way would say: *This is the wrong move.*

Government is a particularly bad offender of the complicated. When the United States sent troops to the tiny island of Grenada in 1983, politicians called it a pre-emptive defense strike. That is, we invaded. It was laughable at the time, but 20 years later when the United States was sending troops into Iraq, even journalists called the invasion a pre-emptive action.

The comic George Carlin, during his routines, tracks the origin of what soldiers suffer after their time in battle. In World War I, the military called it "shell shock." By World War II, it had changed to "battle fatigue." By the Vietnam War, it had become "post traumatic stress syndrome." The early versions are easy to understand. They have a ring to them. The Vietnam version sounds weak, impotent. It certainly lacks the punch of "shell shock."

Bedeviling the language is our preference to *commence* rather than *begin*, to *articulate* rather than *say*, to *utilize* rather than *use*. We live in *residences* or *abodes*, not *house* or *homes*. We render someone *aid*, not *help*.

English is full of these separate ways to describe the same. It has been so since the eighth century when Christianity was introduced to the warring tribes of Angles, Saxons, Jutes and probably Frisians on the island of Britain. The evangelists brought with them education and scholarship, but all in Latin, the church's official language. The new Christians introduced terms that had no equal in English. And the English either adopted the new words outright, or made up their own to describe the same thoughts. They rejected evangelium, that is, the message of a risen Christ. They chose instead "good news" or "glad tidings," which came out as God-spell. Eventually, we had gospel. But who wants to hear evangelium when you can hear some good news.

English has since survived several Latin onslaughts. The Norman conquest of 1066 changed the language in ways we still see. The Normans not only introduced French, a Latin derivative, but also ignored English, letting it linger unfettered in the lower classes until it changed beyond recognition of its earlier relative. It dropped its cumbersome word endings and assignments of gender. It began to use word order to produce meaning. And it borrowed foreign words with abandon.

The result? Middle English, which looked nothing like its earlier cousin named Old English, or Anglo-Saxon. Especially lost was the rich power of Anglo-Saxon words. About three-fourths of those have been replaced, chiefly by French and Latin. Yet the ones left behind are sturdy words that never seem to wear out. We use them constantly in informal speech. They have grown into the building blocks of our language, unadorned and unembellished. They power our sentences with punch and vigor. They are the words, a study at Brown University found, that we use the most. Researchers discovered that of the 300 most-used words in common documents, almost all are Anglo-Saxon origin.

We seem never to tire of them. They are, of course, the easy ones: all, a, the, and. Who could go a few sentences without using them? But they also are the power words, the words that take little effort to form an image in our minds. In their book, *The Story of English*, Robert McCrum, William Cran and Robert MacNeil tell the story of when Winston Churchill wanted to summon the courage of Great Britain as its people faced air raids from Germany in World War II, he called upon not Latin

Here are some Anglo-Saxon words, with their Latin equivalent. The Latin phrases seem impotent next to the plain, gritty Anglo-Saxon.

Anglo-Saxon	**Latin**
die	perish
chance	opportunity
live	reside
begin	commence
give up	surrender
put out	extinguish
house	domicile
eat	consume
run	operate
tough	onerous
make	manufacture
use	utilize
rise	elevate
speak	articulate
late	tardy

or French but Anglo-Saxon: "We will fight them on the beaches. We will fight them in the air. We will fight them on the landing grounds. We will never surrender."

All are Anglo-Saxon words, except for "surrender." A closer look (not examination) of Churchill's words reveals a visual element. A writer or speaker wants to create pictures in the minds of the listeners or readers.

Plain speaking and plain writing carry their own reward. Writers may be eloquent with larger words, but with Anglo-Saxon, they are understood. That's the goal of most writing.

Anglo-Saxon words pack a punch. They are guttural, sturdy. A writer who uses them writes solid English that is crystal clear and full of energy.

Because Latin-based words are euphemistic, they are in great demand from the bureaucrats who use them. Journalists who cover bureaucrats sometimes fall into the trap of imitating them. The bureaucrats' phrases sneak into the journalists' copy.

WIRED AND WIRELESS | TV

The lessons learned from writing simply translate particularly well to digital and visual journalism. The best writing on television and online is conversational. Journalists might be describing a profound event. But telling their viewers through conversational English is an art. It makes viewers feel as if they are speaking face-to-face with the reporter. The relaxed atmosphere journalists create relaxes viewers, and they learn more.

Clearly written stories and scripts also help viewers' comprehension. On television and radio, viewers and listeners don't have the luxury of rereading an unclear sentence. Reporters have to nail it on the first delivery, or they have lost their chance to communicate with their audience—a journalist's ultimate goal.

For digital journalism, the role of clear writing takes on greater importance. Many veteran journalists have likened writing on the web to wire service reporting of *The Associated Press*. On a breaking story, wire service reporters update stories constantly. The need to write clearly and concisely can't be overstated. Readers need to understand the stories immediately.

That clarity grows essential for the web, as one of its great strengths is on a breaking news story. Even though other platforms help tell the story, such as video from cell phones or a photo gallery from staff photographers at the site, the information conveyed in the words represent the story's heart. Readers and viewers must be able to digest the essential message. A simple, clear sentence fulfills that mission.

Talent Showcase

RON HUTCHESON ▶

Former White House Correspondent, McClatchy Newspapers

Former White House correspondent Ron Hutcheson writes as tightly as anyone in the business. But to hear him tell it, he used to use more words. What made him stop? An inspiring editor? Feedback from readers? Cutbacks on space?

"It was having kids," he says, with no trace of humor.

Kids?

"Because when you have other demands on your time, you realize how quickly reading the newspaper can fall by the wayside," he says. "So it was a big realization to me that when you are single and have all the time in the world to read the paper and savor it, you think 'Oh boy, I'm really going to get artistic here.'

"But when you've got tons of stuff to do and got to get the kids fed and to school, this better be good or I'm bailing out. So I'm very mindful of that. It's helped me to make the stories shorter."

Family is important to Hutcheson, even professionally. His children helped him to write tightly. His wife helped him think of his leads. He pictured himself walking through the door at night, fielding the question: "What happened today?"

"The first words out of your mouth are the things [that] are the most interesting or exciting or attention-getting. So I always think I can use my wife or my editor, like if I come back into the newsroom I'm thinking, 'OK, now how do I tell this guy what happened here?' The lead is usually somewhere in there, by definition.

"I'm a big believer in keep it short and keep it simple and get straight to the point. The days of throat-clearing leads are gone."

What is a throat-clearing lead?

"You know you kind of take a little bit to warm up and then you get to the story. Sadly, anecdotal leads can fall into that category, where you tell a meaningless anecdote lead and then you get to what the story is all about."

Hutcheson often wrote some of the more important breaking stories of the day on tight deadlines. He also filed for McClatchy's online service before writing his stories for the newspapers' news service.

When Supreme Court Chief Justice John Roberts was nominated, Hutcheson's editors wanted a story quickly.

"Truth is, I didn't know jack about Roberts," he said.

He put together a story quickly, using the background material available to him. He said he had to write so quickly for the web, he slightly misrepresented one of Roberts' positions.

"I was over at the White House at 7:45 and got the name there and had to have something off by 9:10. . . . The president's speech wasn't until 9.

"First of all, 7:45 is when the briefing started. I left the briefing by 8, had to make the 10-minute walk back [to his office], and then start writing cold. And in the meantime, [I] had to start writing for the web."

Hutcheson wrote that Roberts had previously written that *Roe v. Wade,* which establishes the legal right to an abortion, should be overturned.

"What I didn't know until like five minutes after I had sent the thing in for the web that at his more recent confirmation hearing, he said yeah but it's the set-

(continued)

Talent Showcase (continued)

tled law of the land and that I was just doing that as an advocate. I mean that's a key distinction."

He fixed the story in later versions.

Hutcheson hasn't missed the mark much during his career. He graduated from the University of Texas and began working immediately for the *Fort Worth Star-Telegram*. He covered municipal assignments, then state government, then Washington for the *Star-Telegram*. After the 2000 election, Knight Ridder asked him to move from the *Star-Telegram* to the news service Washington bureau. Knight Ridder later sold its newspaper empire to McClatchy.

Hutcheson learned to write more tightly than when he began. Sparser is better.

"I think the big thing is I've pretty much abandoned anecdotal leads. I've gotten more conscious of using quotes to propel the story as opposed to setting up the quote and having a quote that echoes what you've used in the setup, which is a mistake I see all the time.

"So in that sense, I think it's tighter, more concise. Again, it all goes back to the longer I'm in this business, and looking at what has happened to this business, I've become very conscious that we've got to do everything we can to make the stories more compelling to readers. The last thing you want to do is say well that paper was boring."

Hutcheson thought often about readers, both when he was deciding what was a story and when he wrote his stark leads.

"I've always thought that the lead by far is the most important part of the story because that's what makes me read or not read a story, other than the headline."

For Hutcheson, readers judge what's interesting.

"The big thing is to look at the story not through your eyes or your colleague's eyes and certainly not through the source's eyes, but through your neighbors who aren't invested in it. The twists and turns of a city council fight really aren't that interesting unless you're intimately involved.

"You just got to put yourself in the place of average readers."

Bureaucrats	**Anglo-Saxon**
negative cash flow	losing money
100 percent mortality rate	all died
heavy precipitation over higher elevations	snow on the hilltops
We need a reversal of this trend to stay fiscally viable.	If we don't make money, we'll go bankrupt.

There are many more. Journalists concerned about clarity keep a constant vigil on their writing to keep these phrases out. They do their copy little good.

IN CONCLUSION

The need for clear writing is a must for a journalist. It takes a lifetime of trial and error, experimentation and discipline, to learn the lesson. As Murray says, writers learn to write their entire professional career. The goal of simplicity carries the potential for escape each time they try their hand at a declarative sentence. Guidelines can keep clarity corralled. And the best journalists follow those guidelines, rebelling only when the odd moment inspires.

TOOL KIT

Some books to consider:

The Elements of Style, by William Strunk Jr. and E. B. White, 4th ed. Allyn & Bacon, Boston, 1999.
On Writing Well, by William Zinsser, Harper & Row Publishers, New York, 1985.

EXERCISE 1

Put these sentences into S-V-O form:

1. The attack was countered by the Iraqis.
2. The fire was put out by the sons.
3. Smith's rental properties were found to be in violation of the building codes.
4. There are 23 fraternities and sororities that hold charters at the school.
5. Of all those who face re-election, Smith's might be the toughest.
6. On that day, most of the garbage will be collected by the city.
7. With several counts of embezzling against him, the vice chancellor, Smith, was fired by Byrne University on Tuesday.
8. A quiet corner in the library is where the student found she could study.
9. With three seconds left, Smith's shot was blocked by O'Neal.
10. The winning goal was made by Smith.

EXERCISE 2

Omit extra words:

1. The girl went to Starbucks in order to buy coffee.
2. The student was failing at that point in time.
3. Some of the students enjoyed the class. Some of them didn't.
4. The SGA will conduct a poll to discover students' study habits and if they use Smith Library for it.
5. The administration announced the names of the fraternities who had been suspended.
6. All of the students have chosen to use buses to go from their dorms to their classes.
7. Smith College will continue offering Greek despite the fact that few students register for the course.
8. A small number of fans showed up for the game.
9. In an attempt to fill the stadium, Smith University officials gave away tickets for free.
10. Many of the students chose to stay home.

EXERCISE 3

Eliminate "there is, there are" construction:

1. There were those who thought the class a waste of their time.
2. There is an abundance of bars on Smith Street, the chancellor said.
3. There are times when students are overwhelmed with the work, the counselor said she had observed.
4. There were courses that were set up by professors to deliberately fail students, the study found.
5. There were lines of students waiting at the bookstore that went out the door, around the corner and up the stairs.
6. There were many who decided to skip class that day.
7. There was a cache of guns found by the police.
8. There were many former students who attended the ceremony.
9. There were a number of bills introduced by legislators that year.
10. There is a place that Smith knows he can escape the crowds.

EXERCISE 4

Turn nouns into verbs:

1. The school will pay for the installation of the computers.
2. Some of the residents said they would help in the restoration of the home.
3. Smith was supportive of his roommate's run for office.
4. Smith scored the crucial point that led to her rival's elimination from the tournament.
5. Smith joined her teammates in their victory celebration.
6. The mayor, who stands in opposition to the program, voted against the measure.
7. He said the exploitation of children has got to end.
8. Smith was critical of new building, saying it fell short of the school's architectural guidelines.
9. She believed the new class was beneficial to her work.
10. An inspection of the home by plumbers found the leak.

EXERCISE 5

Make these verbs more active:

1. Smith is a believer in counseling.
2. The Eagles have a poor record in punting.
3. The professor is funny when lecturing.
4. The university is in the red this year.
5. Employment is lower this month than last.
6. Student morale is higher, the study showed.
7. The car was in the wrong lane, resulting in a head-on crash.
8. Philadelphia is where the labor movement started.
9. The speaker was late when he strolled across the stage.
10. She was a standout on the newspaper staff, especially her biting essays.

EXERCISE 6

Simplify the sentences:

1. An inspection of the nursing home by state Health Department officials in February resulted in a 38-page list of violations. The problems must be corrected by May 13 or the facility could lose its Medicaid and Medicare funding, 90 percent of its budget.
2. The principal and teacher have been supportive of Smith's efforts from the start. Though they must measure their words carefully lest they inspire the anger of their bosses, they have expressed no regrets over the coverage and have had many complimentary things to say about the work Smith has done.
3. Beginning the next semester, and ending with the summer session, students will be forced to wait in lines to register for the fall semester. A faulty computer program is to be blamed, and until university officials buy and install a new system, students will feel the brunt of inconvenience.
4. Smith's first songs demonstrated why he has grown popular in the past year. "I'm Alive," "Painful Melodies," and "Go Feel It" were sung with such emotion that the crowd reacted with energy. They jumped up and down in their seats and began dancing in the aisles.

CHAPTER 5

How to Structure a News Story

IN THIS CHAPTER YOU WILL LEARN:

- Effective writers assemble a story in pieces: beginning, middle and end.
- When done well, the middle of a news story supports the lead and encourages readers to reach the end.
- The importance and function of nut graphs.
- Narrative writing techniques.
- How to self-edit to maintain a story's pace and keep readers focused.

There's nothing wrong with the inverted pyramid, just as there is nothing wrong with a hamburger as a meal. But if you have only hamburger on the plate, and you have it every day, then you are undernourished and meals become unappealing.

Roy Wenzl, advocating narrative writing as a cure for reader malaise

DIEDTRA HENDERSON, FORMER REPORTER FOR *THE BOSTON GLOBE* and other newspapers likens story structure to building a house.

"You know going into it the foundation—that's the nut graph. Paint—that's the color. The windows show people a world they haven't seen before.

"You put that together, but if there's no roof, everyone is going to know there's a big part of this house that's missing."

In other words, the successful news story has an indispensable lead. Beneath it, recognizable parts that reporters keep in mind while gathering information.

Traditional journalism relies on the inverted pyramid story structure, with the outcome first. Narrative writers, following the "new journalism" lead of author Tom Wolfe and two-time Pulitzer Prize winner Jon Franklin, prefer different shapes, such as hourglasses, where the story begins with people and settings, gets to the nut graph and then advances via suspenseful chronology to the outcome.

Although there is seldom just one way to pursue or to write an exceptional news story, each of these approaches has something in common: A successful story has structure, a definable beginning, middle and end—interwoven seamlessly with the thread of well-crafted transitions.

"It's not about pretty words, pretty sentences," says Roy Wenzl, who is admired for his graceful narrative writing at *The Wichita Eagle*. "It's about ideas and structure."

Just as a building needs structural integrity, each of the building blocks in a story must be well-constructed. A weak beginning, middle or end will undermine the other sections. The collapsing story chases readers away.

TECHNIQUES BEFORE, DURING AND AFTER WRITING

Anything beautifully written—news stories, essays, books, plays or music—evokes artistic notions about an author's gifts, inspiration and eloquence. Wenzl and other top-flight writers know that great results also require discipline.

News stories require discipline before, during and after they are written, because the process of reporting and writing them has a beginning, middle and end, too.

In the beginning, a reporter conceives the story and pursues it, gathering the raw materials—five Ws, quotes, illuminating detail, contextual background and more—for the construction job ahead.

Then, the story is constructed, section by section. "Constructed" lacks the artistic appeal of "created" or even "crafted," but superb writers invariably agree that they are well aware of each of the building blocks they must collect and combine. They are aware long before writing. The pieces missing from their inventory direct their reporting. They check their inventory again just before writing.

"I learned about writing while you're reporting," Leonora LaPeter told the American Society of Newspaper Editors (ASNE) upon winning the Society's Distinguished Writing Award. "In other words, thinking about how you write the story while you report it. Basically, the second I got to the courthouse every morning, I

HOW TO
Write a News Story

Before you write, think. Ask yourself several questions. The answers will tell you how to write your story.

1. **What is the central point to this story?** Perhaps the most difficult, and important, question, this tells writers whether they fully understand their story. It also tells them how they should write their lead.
2. **What is your lead?** Focus on the clearest, most compelling way to tell the essence of your story.
3. **What is my nut graph?** How can you tell the main parts of this story in a few sentences? How do you boil down the essentials to a nut graph?
4. **What is the supporting information?** Follow the suggestions in this chapter to support the lead: illuminating detail, supporting evidence, necessary background.
5. **What are my best quotes?** Do you have quotes from the various sides of this story? Do you have quotes that are both entertaining and informative? What quotes work best with what parts of your story? Is there one I can use as a kicker ending?

Let your story flow logically, making sure you support your lead. Write the most important information high in the story.

Many journalists outline their stories. This can be detailed, with each point joined to a supporting quote. Or it can be informal, with just a few words representing the story's progression. Organizing your thoughts this way helps you write more clearly.

At each moment, ask yourself if you are writing as clearly as possible. Never assume the reader fully comprehends.

was looking for my lead. I would be looking for details. I would be looking for quotes. I'd be thinking about transition. I would also be looking for the structure of my story."

She wasn't thinking about writing style as much as she was searching for the missing components of her story.

"It wasn't *how* I was going to write it. It was *what* I was going to write. It was what details I was going to use."

Diedtra Henderson agrees. "I'm already writing while I'm reporting. If I hear a great quote, I'll flag that in my notebook. I might be considering that for a kicker [to end the story]. I'll be thinking of a transition."

With this checklist in mind as they gather information, reporters develop an instinct about when they have everything they need. Then they start assembling their stories in their heads while returning to the office.

Thus prepared, these writers often are able to write rapidly as soon as they reach their keyboards. If they report the story by phone, they take time to organize the story in their minds before writing a word. A news reporter staring intently at a blank computer screen for several minutes may be a very capable writer organizing the first half-dozen paragraphs—even the entire story—before writing anything at all. Others prepare by typing a few sentences or some key words that help them put all the pieces in the right order.

Young writers can take encouragement from this blueprint. Although many aspire to artistic heights, the discipline of story structure can be duplicated even by journalists just getting grounded in their careers. As your experience grows, your confidence will soar. You will become instinctive about when you have all the raw materials for a fine story. Until then, the blueprint shows you the path to success.

Finally, the story is revised. Great writers edit themselves at least as rigorously as any subsequent editor will. The story that is perfect as first written is the rarest of all creations.

Often, the difference between a good writer and a great one is in the editing—not what someone else will do with your copy, but how you will edit yourself. Can you find the unnecessary words? The places where the pace drags? The digressions, however fascinating, that make your story's theme veer off course?

Famed writers Mark Twain and Henry David Thoreau have been quoted in variations of a statement on self-editing first attributed to author Blaise Pascal: "I have made this letter longer than usual, because I lack the time to make it short."

"In some ways, self-editing is the most important part of writing," Tina Griego of the *Rocky Mountain News* says. "Editing *is* writing. If I have the time, I will spend as much time on editing as writing. I'll print out my story. I can see things on the printout that I don't see on the single screen. Inevitably, I'll see more that way, things that I can change."

THE ESSENTIAL NUT GRAPH

We devote other chapters to news leads and to the various effective ways to end stories. This one dwells on the paragraphs in between. They are no less crucial. These are the paragraphs that deliver on the promises of the lead. These are the paragraphs that compel readers to the payoff at the end of a well-constructed story.

Unfortunately, all too often, this is where promising stories go to die. These are the paragraphs that determine whether a story is too long, too boring, or just right.

The beginning of any story is more than its lead paragraph. The beginning consists of several critical paragraphs. This is all the time you have to convince the reader to stick with your story.

The seminal study on reader behavior, *Eyes on the News*, by Mario Garcia and Pegie Stark Adam, used mechanical devices to track the eye movement of newspaper readers. Generally, readers have to be hooked in the first four paragraphs, the study found.

With that in mind, better newspapers insist that writers provide what have become known as a "nut graph"—the paragraph that provides context, significance and a convincing case why this story must be read now. The nut graph ought to appear by the fourth paragraph, or, if later, always before the story jumps to another page.

This cannot be overemphasized. Readers who jump from the first page of a story to the next often finish the story. But getting the reader to turn the page never should be taken for granted. The demands of reader impatience require swift progression from lead to nut graph.

The lead must express the theme of the story. This is done directly in the case of an inverted-pyramid lead. This may be done more indirectly with a compelling anecdote that showcases the person or situation that illustrates the heart of the story. For example, a story about American soldiers with extended stays in Iraq might focus first on a soldier who was scheduled to return home and the celebration planned for him, only to learn a week before then that he would need to stay in life-threatening conditions for another six months. A story on competitive Christmas shoppers might begin with the scene in the aisles of the store with the hottest new toy.

In narrative writing, writers concentrate on telling the story by hinting at the outcome without revealing it early. They establish the theme more subtly, but

Talent Showcase

ROY WENZL ▶

Senior Journalist, *The Wichita Eagle*

Devoted to the craft of narrative journalism, Roy Wenzl is as passionate in his advocacy as he is in his storytelling.

"The reason why circulation is slipping has very little to do with accusations of bias, accuracy and the Jayson Blair effect. That has been with newspapers from the beginning. We hurt because we're boring. You can read the headline, the lead and a few paragraphs and you can tell the ending, so why read the story? That's boring.

"There's nothing wrong with the inverted pyramid, just as there is nothing wrong with a hamburger as a meal. But if you have only hamburger on the plate, and you have it every day, then you are undernourished and meals become unappealing.

"We don't give readers engagement, surprise. There's no humor. Everything is a hamburger, poorly cooked."

Although he has been honing his craft for years, and has clusters of writing awards to show for it, Wenzl coaches young writers to employ narrative storytelling early in their careers. Although narrative is adopted most readily by feature writers, Wenzl has taken his missionary zeal to beat writers and to a national convention of investigative reporters. He has relied on narrative himself to offer insight into the BTK serial killer who preyed on Kansans.

Although narrative techniques such as indirect leads, foreshadowing and dialogue generally require more column inches than inverted pyramid leads and direct quotes, Wenzl is adamant that narratives can be used to tell a tale brightly in as few as six inches.

The example on the following page is not one of Wenzl's better-known narratives. It wasn't inspired by mega-news or societal shifts. It wasn't the product of weeks of eyewitness-reporting. Instead, this piece about a baby born in the front seat of a speeding car was an impromptu assignment from the City Desk that Wenzl handled by phone and completed in two hours. This example illustrates Wenzl's point that narrative writing doesn't require extraordinary investment of time and space, only the writer's determination to search for the most interesting way to tell a story.

And yet, this story earned raves from Jon Franklin, the guru of narrative journalism, a two-time Pulitzer winner (including the first Pulitzer for feature writing), and author of the narrative-writing bible, *Writing for Story*.

As you read, take note of how this story differs from other news-writing forms:

- Unlike the inverted pyramid, the tension in this story builds, rather than descends from top to bottom. "In the narrative, the end has a pop; it's a payoff," Wenzl instructs.
- The story emphasizes action. Sense the movement.
- Similarly, most of the quotes are presented as dialogue, not as someone being interviewed. "One of the worst things we do is turn people into talking heads," Wenzl scolds.
- The action and dialogue have the effect of making the reader an eyewitness. In this case, since Wenzl was not an eyewitness, he had to report more deeply to get the details that would permit telling the story this way.
- Narrative writers seize on the telling details that create the drama and/or conflict and give life to the principal characters. Notice the roles that the towels and the gender of the baby play in this drama.

By Roy Wenzl

The mystery child was born in a 2003 Chevy Tahoe speeding along Kellogg in front of the east-side Lowe's Home Improvement Store just before midnight Tuesday.

Baby's condition: good.

Speed at time of delivery: 90 mph.

Birthplace: front passenger seat.

The mother, Monica Lichlyter, coolly delivered the mystery child herself, reaching down, working the baby out of the birth canal.

Derek Lichlyter, sitting at the Tahoe's wheel, said two words upon his child's arrival. The first word was "Holy . . ." The second word was not.

For 10 minutes, until they reached the hospital, Monica didn't look to see whether the child was boy or girl.

She wanted to know. Boy or girl? Cash Quinten or Charlize Ann? They had the boy name and the girl name, and now they had the baby.

But it was cold in the air-conditioned Tahoe, and she'd wrapped the kid in a towel, and the kid looked cozy. Why make the kid cold?

So she hugged the bundle to her chest as Derek broke speed limits to St. Joe.

Boy or girl?

A mystery.

An adventure.

Monica's contractions had begun a short time earlier, at the Lichlyter home in Augusta. Derek, 34, works in program management for Raytheon. Monica is 37, a compliance coordinator for a pipeline company. She has a reputation in her family for doing sensible things, even under pressure.

On the way out the door, Monica picked up several towels, in case her water broke on the way to the hospital. Sensible Monica, Derek said later.

They headed from Augusta to Via Christi Regional Medical Center-St. Joseph Campus in Wichita. Derek drove at a reasonable speed.

This would last for hours, they thought. Their first child, Duke, born a year and a half earlier, had been so reluctant to appear that doctors had to induce him, after hours and hours of labor.

They rode west. When they reached Andover, Monica looked at the digital clock on the dashboard: 11:55 p.m.

A contraction. OW!

Her water broke.

"Turn on your emergency blinkers," Monica said through gritted teeth. "And drive."

Derek freaked out pretty good, Monica said. He cranked the Tahoe up to 90.

That put them in front of the Lowe's store two minutes later, 11:57 p.m.

Another contraction.

"This baby is coming now," Monica said.

Derek spoke the two holy words.

He watched Monica reach down and tug out 5 pounds and 13 ounces of wet, squirming baby.

She pulled the baby to her chest. The baby cried out.

Monica wrapped it in a towel. The whole thing took just fractions of seconds.

By this time Derek had braked the Tahoe from 90 mph to a screeching halt.

Monica looked at him.

"There's no point in stopping now," Monica said.

Derek hit the gas again.

He called 911 on his cell phone.

"Put the mother on the phone," the dispatcher said.

(continued)

Talent Showcase *(continued)*

"The baby is breathing," Monica told them.

"Is it a boy or a girl?" the dispatcher asked.

"I don't know," Monica said.

A hospital team, notified by 911 dispatchers, met them in the parking lot.

A woman took the baby from Monica, took the baby out of the towel, took the umbilical cord in hand.

She cut it, and spoke.

"It's a girl."

This story was instructive for Wenzl, too. After interviewing the mother, one of the grandfathers and someone at the hospital, Wenzl wrote a six-inch "bright." It was good enough to be published, but Wenzl hated it. He second-guessed himself.

"The mother said she wrapped the baby in a blanket. Why? There's got to be more than I got out of this."

Wenzl said he had made a typical reporting mistake. "When I talked to her I got the facts. I wasn't thinking like a parent. She was trying to be a good mother. She was shielding the baby from the air-conditioning. I called her back a second time. Only then did I realize that she hadn't bothered to notice whether this was a boy or girl.

"I realized that I could build a narrative with some suspense. What's the first thing you want to know about a new-born? It's alive, and has all 10 fingers. The next thing, is it a boy or girl? But this woman waited. So I asked about every detail."

Wenzl readily acknowledges that sometimes, the inverted pyramid is the best way to report.

"If my taxes are going up, I don't want the story to have a long wind-up. Just get to it. Tell me what the deal is, tell me why and tell me what I can do about it. That's all I need."

But he encourages beat reporters, even those with heavy story loads, to try to make half their stories narrative. The inverted pyramid might be the best way to handle mid-week breaking news. For the weekend, however, consider the narrative to follow-up on that story with untold insight.

Early commitment to narrative is essential, Wenzl insists.

"I'm thinking structure from the moment I conceive of the story idea. What kind of story is this? I will not make this story a cliché. How am I not going to make this a cliché? You map this out from the beginning. So your interview questions are much more on target—but you don't want to go in with any pre-conceived notion about the facts."

Then Wenzl invoked a quote from Truman Capote, author of the book-length narrative, *In Cold Blood*. "If you don't think hard about some type of outline or structure, 'that's not writing, it's typing.' "

seductively, through foreshadowing that entices the reader to find out what happens next. For instance, the story about competitive Christmas shoppers might begin with a father's desperation not to disappoint the daughter he has often disappointed and how, this time, it might all come down to being one of the first 25 customers at Toys 'R' Us the day after Thanksgiving. Readers learn the main characters and the plot early. But the outcome is delayed while complications develop in the competition for the hot new toy.

After the lead, the next paragraphs must advance the theme in the lead. They reveal more detail—perhaps more specificity to amplify the lead, perhaps additional

WIRED AND WIRELESS | NARRATIVE WRITING AND THE WEB

Narrative writing handles attribution sparingly. The attribution is necessary, but it sometimes appears briefer and later than in other news writing. Before it was a best-selling book and a popular movie, *Black Hawk Down* was a 29-part series in the *Philadelphia Inquirer*, each told in 25-inch to 30-inch narratives with special demands for attribution.

The *Inquirer* and its reporter, Mark Bowden, made creative and unique use of their newspaper website. The website not only helped tell the story in multimedia and in more depth, but to cement the attribution for curious and skeptical readers.

Bowden explained how that worked while recalling a particularly dramatic passage involving a U.S. Army Ranger unit descending 70 feet down a taut rope into the heart of Mogadishu, Somalia. The beginning of that fateful raid was told through the experience of Staff Sgt. Matt Eversmann.

"We had the series running on the Internet at the same time, so a lot of the sourcing was immediately available," Bowden told an audience at a convention of the American Society of Newspaper Editors. "For instance, readers on the Internet who might start off reading the story thinking, 'Well, how could Mark Bowden possibly know what was going through Matt Eversmann's mind at that point?' have a hyperlink on Eversmann's name where they can click and listen to him describing what was going on in his mind as he was going down the rope. So all of these details are gathered through careful reporting."

Mark Bowden, best-selling author of *Black Hawk Down* and former reporter for the *Philadelphia Inquirer*.

remarkable facts. Perhaps one of these paragraphs will be a quote that captures the human drama vividly, or sets the stage for the debate to follow.

Regardless, the progression from lead to nut graph will be concise. The sequence should indicate movement, either in action or in logic—preferably both.

Most news-writing advice focuses on leads—for good reason, given reader impatience in a world of time-stress, abundant information and countless providers. The nut graph is nearly as critical. This is the place where the story's urgency and broader implications become clear. This is the place where writers make the case for their stories. The power of this paragraph not only determines whether the story will maintain reader interest, but often determines the prominence of the story's play in that day's news report.

Here are some examples of this progression, and the role of nut graphs.

The New York Times
By Steve Lohr

Wal-Mart, the nation's largest retailer, often intimidates its competitors and suppliers. Makers of goods from diapers to DVD's must cater to its whims. But there is one company that even Wal-Mart eyes warily these days; Google, a seven-year-old business in a seemingly distant industry.

"We watch Google very closely at Wal-Mart," said Jim Breyer, a member of Wal-Mart's board.

In Google, Wal-Mart sees both a technology pioneer and the seed of a threat, said Mr. Breyer, who is also a partner in a venture capital firm. The worry is that by making information available everywhere, Google might soon be able to tell Wal-Mart shoppers if better bargains are available nearby.

Wal-Mart is scarcely alone in its concern. As Google increasingly becomes the starting point for finding information and buying products and services, companies that even a year ago did not see themselves as competing with Google are beginning to view the company with some angst—mixed with admiration.

The Wall Street Journal
By Peter Sanders

Last Wednesday, the furry red Muppet named Elmo learned the hard way that Hollywood Boulevard is a long way from Sesame Street.

In plain sight of children and tourists, Elmo—or, at least, a man named Don Harper in a knockoff Elmo costume—was arrested here by the Los Angeles Police Department. Elmo was taken down by a special task force created to combat a growing nuisance in the Hollywood tourist district: famous costumed characters who try to be photographed with tourists and sometimes badger them relentlessly for tips.

USA Today
By Jim Hopkins

Wal-Mart's critics, opening a new front in their war on the retail goliath, are borrowing from actor-director Mel Gibson's promotional playbook.

Producers of a new documentary, *Wal-Mart: The High Cost of Low Price*, will show it in about 1,000 churches, synagogues and religious sites nationwide on Nov. 13 in a bid to force changes in Wal-Mart's employment and other practices.

The film, by the director of *Outfoxed: Rupert Murdoch's War on Journalism*, comes as Wal-Mart mounts a new effort to polish its battered image. The movie is part of a broader campaign by a disparate group of critics who now include ministers asserting Wal-Mart's tactics are a moral as well as economic issue.

In each case above, the story starts with a timely fact. This news—"Elmo's" arrest, the documentary opening—could be the substance for a minor story. The reporters' ability to find the larger context for these events magnified the stories. *The New York Times* and *The Wall Street Journal* stories ran above the fold on Page One. The *USA Today* story was stripped across the top of the Money section.

WRITING EFFECTIVE NUT GRAPHS

Now let's take a hypothetical story, a type likely to occur early and often in your career wherever you report news.

> Mayor Don Dickens and Police Chief Sam Torcato announced Thursday a four-pronged attack calculated to eliminate two-thirds of illegal drug trafficking in Midland City.
>
> Thirty police officers will be redeployed to increase street beats in high-risk neighborhoods. Drug-sniffing dogs will be available to each beat cop for the first time. City Council will be asked to relax restrictions on "no-knock" raids. And the city will petition the state for legislation that will increase the certainty of convictions and double the length of sentences.

As important as this story sounds, efforts to combat illegal drugs are perpetual and often ineffective. As elections near, public pronouncements multiply. No politician ever lost votes by being too tough on crime. However, here are some plausible nut graphs that broaden the impact of "Thursday's" announcement.

The Trend Nut Graph

The pledges add Midland City to a rapidly growing number of communities that have embraced the recommendations made last month by Governor Simmons' drug task force.

The Counter-Trend Nut Graph

With their emphasis on no-knock raids, Dickens and Torcato place Midland City at odds with the law-making trends elsewhere in the state following last year's sweeping Supreme Court ruling that sharply reduced most local police powers.

The Timing Nut Graph (Two Variations)

The pronouncements by Midland City's traditionally laissez-faire government comes at a time when politically conservative challengers have been attacking Dickens and Torcato as being soft on crime.

The crackdown comes amid a new wave of drug-related violence that has put Midland City on every national television network and on the lips of a dozen nationally prominent officials.

The Counter-Intuitive Nut Graph

The announcements caught leaders of Midland City's minority community off-guard. They said they felt betrayed by a mayor they supported last year when he pledged to reform a police department criticized for abuse of no-knock raids and overly aggressive police dogs. The raids and dogs had been deployed disproportionately on the mostly black and Hispanic North Side.

The Analytical Nut Graph

Though certain to be popular with the electorate that votes next month, the proposals are fraught with controversy on all fronts. The dogs would tax a city budget already in the red by an additional $125,000 per year. The police union, already complaining of being understaffed and underpaid, promptly indicated it does not welcome simultaneously riskier assignments. Before the city's rules were relaxed, no-knock raids were contested regularly in court. And the state legislature rewrote sentencing guidelines just two years ago.

The facts in the above examples could *all* be true. Which nut graph would you favor?

Most news organizations are devoted to localizing regional, national and global news. Fewer capture the importance of local stories by "globalizing" them. The **trend** and **counter-trend** nut graphs above show how a story gains stature and urgency by placing it in a larger context. Is today's development catching up to a trend or bucking one? Is it setting a new standard as the first or the largest?

The **timing** nut graphs strengthen today's news by connecting it to other timely news. The phrase "at a time" (in the first example) is often used to signal this connection. In the second example, note the specificity of "every national television network" and "the lips of a dozen nationally prominent officials." That's reporting. This is superior to the lazy and hackneyed "made news" or "made headlines" phrases used so often. That's commentary. Individuals and organizations "make news" and "make headlines" when reporters and editors decide that they do.

Counter-intuitive stories are among the most appealing. Unexpected outcomes (favorable or detrimental) present the element of surprise. That's almost always newsworthy. News organizations gain extraordinary value when they consistently tell readers what they did not expect to learn.

The **analytical** nut graph propels today's news forward. Helping readers anticipate future developments has always been valuable, but never more so than in the current ultracompetitive news environment. The nut graph above suggests a variety of enterprising ways to distinguish this news story from anything else available. The multiple story angles this nut graph suggests present opportunities for this reporter to dominate coverage of this ongoing story for days to come.

NARRATIVE TECHNIQUES

Most of the examples above are "straight-news" formats, following inverted-pyramid leads. The others follow indirect (e.g., anecdotal) leads. All benefit from the explanatory nut graph.

At first glance, narrative writing appears even more indirect. The lead looks softer, the story less dependent on a nut graph that reveals significance early. Not so. Nor does narrative writing need be confined to feature writing.

Here is how Leonora LaPeter captured a day of murder-trial testimony for the *Savannah Morning News*:

> Tap. Tap. Tap. Tap. Pause. Tap. Tap. Tap. Ashley Lewis hit the counter of the oak witness box with his index finger, mimicking what he heard through a crack in the bathroom window the night of Dec. 4, 1997, as he got ready for bed.
>
> It sounded like a typewriter. But Lewis, testifying on the first day in the death penalty trial of Jerry Scott Heidler for the murder of a family in Santa Claus a year and a half ago, found it hard to believe his mother, a secretary, would break out her typewriter at almost 2 a.m. Just a half hour before, she had told him to turn the television off and go to bed.
>
> Lewis walked to his mother's room and turned on the light. She was asleep in bed. He walked through the house, turning on other lights. Nothing.
>
> "I got this real eerie feeling," Lewis said.
>
> Lewis did not know it yet, but a half-mile away, four of his neighbors lay dead.

With her opening paragraph, LaPeter takes readers into the courtroom and into Ashley Lewis' sense of foreboding. She has conveyed the "how" of Lewis' testimony by showing us rather than telling us. Her second paragraph gives us who-what-where-when of a trial that has just begun. Her final sentence is her nut graph, now making the significance of "tap, tap, tap, tap" clear.

Narrative works equally well in news features. The news feature adopts feature-style writing to highly topical news. These are often hard-news topics that have gained prominence through an escalating trend. Isabel Wilkerson of *The New York Times* is a master of the news-feature narrative, as this piece, an ASNE Distinguished Writing Award winner, demonstrates:

> It is a gray winter's morning, zero degrees outside, and school starts for everybody in less than half an hour. The children line up, all scarves and coats and legs. The boys bow their heads so their mother, late for class herself, can brush their hair one last time. There's a mad scramble for a lost mitten.
>
> Then she sprays them. She shakes an aerosol can and sprays their coats, their heads, their tiny outstretched hands. She sprays them back and front to protect them as they go off to school, facing bullets and gang recruiters and a crazy dangerous world. It is a special religious oil that smells like drugstore perfume, and the children shut their eyes tight as she sprays them long and serious so they will come back to her, alive and safe at day's end.
>
> These are the rules for Angela Whitiker's children, recounted at the Formica-top, dining room table.
>
> "Don't stop off playing," Willy said.
>
> "When you hear shootin', don't stand around—run," Nicholas said.
>
> "Because a bullet don't have no eyes," the two boys shouted.
>
> "She prays for us, every day," Willy said.

Note the powerful progression from the chaos in the first paragraph to the order in the second, from the commonplace to the extraordinary, from the actions

The **Art** of **Storytelling**

"Tell me a story," the TV news director played by Robert Redford challenged his staff in the film *Up Close and Personal.*

"Make me see," the blind city editor in rural North Carolina challenged his young reporter, Gene Roberts, who later became executive editor at the *Philadelphia Inquirer.*

"Bad writing is bad thinking," former Dow Jones Chairman Warren Phillips admonished.

These simple words create tougher challenges. But the thoughtful reporter tells a big story by condensing it into something visible to all, told from the vantage point of those who saw it.

Whether challenged to write something unique amid vast print and electronic competition, or to write about a unique topic, you can get the story worth telling by answering a few questions.

Where can you go to be an eyewitness? That's where to capture motion, dialogue and setting—the moving, living parts in a narrative.

Where might you find the unexpected story? No matter how obvious some people are affected, there are almost always others—in locales a bit below the radar, perhaps, but affected just as profoundly in their worlds.

Photo of Robert Redford and Michelle Pfeiffer from the film *Up Close and Personal*

of a caring mother to one who loves with desperation, from "sprays" to "prays." Very swiftly, we are taken from an experience every parent can appreciate to the perpetual fear—"*every day*"—that too many must endure. In just a few paragraphs, we know already this is a story about love and violence, of unsympathetic killers and truly innocent victims.

From whose perspective is this story best told? If the audience can see themselves in that person's place, they can experience the story much more personally.

Who can tell you a story? If you can't witness the action as it happens, find someone who did.

That's the concept. Now the practice: After a hurricane, where would you go to witness the damage? To flooded neighborhoods? Certainly. How will you find those who can tell you their stories? By going to a shelter? Perhaps. Perhaps also by shadowing insurance agents, who in a span of hours will learn of myriad afflictions, common and peculiar.

After Hurricane Ivan flooded Gulf Shores, Ala. in 2004, two reporters from *The Washington Post* went to the zoo. The story they found there resulted in this lead paragraph:

> Sometimes Chucky has three-chicken days, and sometimes Chucky has six-chicken days. But Chucky does not enjoy no-chicken days—and Thursday was his second in a row.

"And this was a problem," the story warned, because Chucky is a 12-foot alligator who had escaped his long-time home when the storm destroyed the walls that contained him.

The Washington Post story demonstrates how diverse victims are. In this case, they included the zoo and its animals. And in the specific case of Chucky, the potential victims included just about anyone who might suddenly be confronted by a starving gator, twice the size of a large man and on its own for food for the first time in 15 years, navigating the flood waters in a residential neighborhood.

To find the unexpected story, always consider the range of potential stakeholders—all of those who have a stake in the outcome. Stories and storytellers may flourish in each of those places.

When the stakeholder could have been any of us, there's a story with special power and potential.

The words are so elegantly simple and so descriptively clear that this is effortless to read. This is not effortless writing. We are the beneficiaries of the writer's superb discipline—the discipline of reporting dozens of details, and condensing her hours (or days) of reporting into a few time-saving paragraphs. By the second paragraph we know what this story is about. By the next, we care mightily about Angela Whitiker. We want to find out whether her obedient youngsters will live for one more day.

Because she has gathered her building blocks with such care, Wilkerson has constructed a passage complete with meaning, without straining to make her points.

SUPPORT THE LEAD

Whatever the writing style, the well-written nut graph works in concert with the lead as a task master for the rest of the story. The nut graph is the transition from the beginning of the story to the middle. It is a bridge to a section of the story that itself is a bridge between the beginning and the end. The construction works when the rest of the story delivers on the promises of the lead and nut graph.

Look at how this story follows a logical structure

Rep. George Atwater scolded a crowd of Mesa University students Wednesday, blaming them for his near-defeat and saying they had left him with "a hole in my heart."	**Lead (26 words. Note verbs: scolded, blaming)**
Atwater (R-Mesa) said Mesa students nearly ended his 16 years in Congress last fall when he won re-election by the narrowest margin of his political career. Mesa students voted overwhelmingly for his opponent, who campaigned against student loans cuts and for transforming the university into an environmentally friendly area, or green zone. Atwater said the issues would hurt the area's economy.	**Nut graph, explaining the conflict**
"I have never been so disappointed in voters in my life," said Atwater, who had been invited to speak at Mesa Young Republicans Club. "I have given my heart and soul to helping Mesa University succeed. I have brought home many federal projects to help the university. I will return to Washington with a hole in my heart."	**Quote that supports the lead**
Atwater defeated Maria DeGuerro by 500 votes, or 50.3 percent. He and Mesa political science professors blamed the narrow win on vocal student opposition.	**Background to bring context**
Shelby McAdams, Mesa student government president, said she felt no remorse for Atwater. "He's ignored students' wishes from the start," McAdams said after Atwater's speech. "If he's got a hole in his heart, maybe he should just fill it with the money from all those special-interest lobbyists he courts in Washington."	**Opposing viewpoint that shows conflict**
Atwater and Mesa students clashed over how a green university would hurt the economy. Forcing environmental regulations onto the school was a bad idea, he said. "It would hurt too many businesses, and then let's see where you kids will be when you graduate and go to look for jobs," the congressman told the crowd. But McAdams vowed to fight Atwater again during his next campaign.	**Setup graph that leads into the quote**
"He's returning to Washington. I say let him stay there," she said. "Look out in another two years when he's up for re-election."	**Kicker ending**

Support the lead. This is the key to writing a clear, concise, credible story that progresses logically from beginning to end: Support the lead. Can you back it up? What do you have to back it up?

Whether your building blocks are eyewitness accounts, quotes, documents, numbers, and/or paragraphs showing your command of recent history (the background of a story), you can make confident decisions about what to put in and what to leave out. If it doesn't support the lead, cut it.

Thus committed, you are far more likely to find the right lead in the first place and to express it clearly. Your lead will be the strongest expression that your building blocks can support.

Support the lead. These three words also help you solve such tricky puzzles as "How much do I quote?" and "How much background is enough?"

Answer: As much as necessary to support the lead, but no more. The support should be persuasive, as unequivocal as possible. Avoid redundancy or other long-windedness. As in conversation, these villains make writing less clear, less convincing.

Do this, and you are ready to move your story from one building block to the next. This document supports the assertion in the lead. This citation reveals the significance of that document. This number establishes the trend cited in the nut graph. These eyewitnesses validate the number. This description from eyewitnesses places readers at the scene. These quotes from eyewitnesses describe what no one else has seen.

As long as these building blocks support the lead, your story gains authority and the ability to compel readers to the next convincing fact, or to the next illuminating quote.

Support the lead. Relentless pursuit of the necessary leads to the ruthless execution of the dead spots in a story that will bore, distract or overwhelm readers.

SELF-EDITING

Newspapers are criticized for publishing stories that are too long. Television and radio are criticized for stories that are too short. Size rarely matters. Content does. Editing can produce better results in both cases.

No story that answers the urgent questions is too short. No story that compels readership to the end is too long. A story might be too long because the topic simply doesn't warrant the space—it lacks urgency, or it doesn't touch enough lives. More often, a story is too long because its pace is too sluggish, its information too redundant or extraneous. These things send readers away long before the end.

PACE

Many writing offenses slow story pace to a crawl. Here's how to avoid some of them:

- Vary sentence length and paragraph length. Use subheads and bullets to divide text into more digestible portions.

- Condense attribution. If you face continual attribution to one source, try a single attribution in advance.

  Police gave this account:
  Sullivan described his ordeal:
  The court's majority opinion provided this reasoning:

- Avoid bureaucratic jargon. Avoid both the unique terms of government and its infernal affection for turning nouns into verbs (e.g., "monetize"). The education bureaucracy is the worst.
- Beware of tortured syntax. Among many phrasing travesties, this is common: "the" followed by a verb ending in "ing" followed by "of."

  The school board approved the banning of the Harry Potter books.

  Make it: The school board banned the Harry Potter books.

  Another debilitating phrase: "the fact that"

  AIDS research has suffered due to the fact that foundations have been shifting donations to cancer and more recently discovered illnesses.

  Make it: AIDS research has suffered since foundations began shifting donations to cancer and more recently discovered illnesses.

  Also beware of phrases beginning with "is" (e.g., "is to," "is that," and "is because"). These signal the passive voice.

  One way to save money is to use frequent-flier miles.

  Make it: Save money by using frequent-flier miles.

  A common complaint is that too few seats are available to travelers using frequent-flier miles.

  Make it:

  A common complaint: Too few seats can be reserved with frequent-flier miles.

  A reason airlines make frequent-flier miles easier to earn is because they are more difficult to redeem for flights.

  Make it: Airlines make frequent-flier miles easier to earn, but more difficult to redeem for flights.

- If you encounter difficulty mid-sentence, start over. Expect much better results by rewriting than trying to salvage bad work.

REDUNDANCY

When readers reach familiar ground, they sense that it's time to move on to something new. End of story. Here are some tips to avoid the most common redundancies:

- If you find yourself trying to make the point stronger or clearer by adding a paragraph, try improving the first one instead.
- The most common redundancy occurs in transitions before quotes. If your transition says nearly the same thing as the quote, use one, not the other.
- If you have used an astonishing quote in the lead, be very sure before deciding to repeat it later.

EXTRANEOUS INFORMATION

Most good reporters collect more information than they need. Most good writers refuse to put it all in one story.

- Don't feel obliged to quote everyone. You interviewed a dozen people to learn the truth, not to quote a dozen people. Your obligation is to readers. Write the truth. Use the best quotes to make the truth clear.
- Use only the background that readers need to understand today's story. Too much old news can't be good.
- Can't resist using that fascinating anecdote, even though it has nothing to do with today's theme? Make it a sidebar or save it for another day.
- When you need to save space, cut whole passages first. Then tighten the others. Why bother to tighten something that is going to get cut entirely?

The *Los Angeles Times*' Steve Lopez, renowned for the freshness and humor in his well-reported columns, turns them over to newsroom colleagues for critique before he turns them over to his editor. Diedtra Henderson suggests finding the office curmudgeon if you want the unsympathetic judgment that your story will face from the typical reader.

Other admired writers have learned to be brutally honest with themselves.

"I found that when 1,000 (words) became 730, good almost always became better," Pulitzer-Prize winning *New York Times* columnist Anna Quindlen told the American Society of Newspaper Editors. "I had to make the distinction between what words and phrases were really necessary and what was merely me in love with the sound of my own voice."

How was she able to hear her own "voice" in her written words?

"I always read aloud to myself when I finish the piece, which makes me look a little crazy in the newsroom."

Griego of the *Rocky Mountain News* does the same. "Reading your stories out loud—though your colleagues might think you're a little nuts; you can murmur—it's amazing. When you put it down in writing, it feels so good. But when you actually speak it, it's not so pretty."

Griego is talking about the rhythmic flow of her stories and the strength of the words that need to carry the emphasis in a sentence. But she's also looking for gaps in logic. When she finds that, "either I'm not transitioning very well, or I've put this in the wrong order."

Logic, associated with numbers as often as words, is clear thinking. It's never too early in the life of a story for that.

"Part of that is in chatting with your editor early on, in the idea stage and then again before writing," Henderson said. That allowed her to organize, and then write her stories more confidently.

She could tell she was making progress by noticing "how [seldom] things got changed. Then, I moved on to bigger and bigger challenges. I used to read *National Geographic* and say, 'Wow! I'd like to be able to do that.'

"Now, I can do that. I have done that."

EXERCISE 1

Write a story from these facts:

A Worthington University cheerleader had a girlfriend. She was not a student. The cheerleader and his girlfriend had a baby. The cheerleader was a jealous person. The cheerleader, Robert Jones, and the girlfriend, Tori Elliott, often were seen arguing in the parking lot of the off-campus apartment building where they lived together. One Saturday night, at a basketball game in February, Jones failed to show. The other cheerleaders notified the athletic department. When Jones failed to show for practice the next day, the faculty sponsor for the cheerleaders and two other cheerleaders went to look for Jones. At his apartment, they found the door open. They knocked. No one answered. They went in and found the body of Jones' girlfriend, Tori Elliott. They called police. Police began to look for Jones. They found him at his mother's house with his baby, who was safe. Police arrested Jones, charging him with a homicide. They said he told them he and Elliott were arguing over the baby late Friday night, and he knocked her down and took the baby to his mother's house. He didn't think she had died. He thought she hadn't called because she was mad at him.

EXERCISE 2

Write a story from these facts:

Jerry Landers got a call on Wednesday. The professor of English at Payne College was in for a surprise. On the other line was a representative from the MacArthur Foundation. Landers had won a MacArthur Foundation award, commonly known as a genius award. Landers said, "I can't believe it was me. I pick up the phone and suddenly I'm a genius." He was laughing as he said it. Landers has written five books of fiction. Only two have made it on *The New York Times* bestseller list. One of them, *The Last of the Moonlighters*, won the Pulitzer Prize for fiction last year. The other book, *Messages from Ivan*, was on the bestseller list for more than a year. Landers is 70. He didn't even begin publishing his work until 10 years ago. He had retired from the Payne City Water Department where he worked as a purchaser. He said he had always wanted to be a professor, so he began teaching at age 55 in the English department. He finished his first novel 10 years ago and has been turning out one every two years. "I'm amazed at my success," he said. "This doesn't even feel like work." His dean, Mary Oswalt, says she's thrilled at the result. "This is a great day for Payne. Jerry has helped our college out so much with this award." What is *The Last of the Moonlighters* about? A water department worker who retires and becomes a professor late in life, then wins the Pulitzer Prize for fiction.

EXERCISE 3

Write a story from these facts:

Saba Aljeerz is vice president of the student association at Canfeld University. The elections for president are in two weeks. She is the only one running until someone enters with five minutes to the deadline, which was 5 p.m. yesterday. Now running is William

Mulvy, the student association's comptroller. Mulvy and Aljeerz have clashed all semester long over how the student association spends its money. The association hands out money to all student organizations on campus. the money comes from the student fees charged to all 12,000 students at Canfeld, which is a private university. It comes to about $50 per student. Yes, that $600,000. Aljeerz thinks the association should give it all away to the 78 student groups at Canfeld. "We could do a lot with that money," she says in an interview after Mulvy entered the race. "We need to support all students in whatever group they belong to. That's a lot of money, $600,000 is, and if you look at it objectively and with no blinders on and such you'll see that money could go to good use. I am bitterly opposed to leaving out any one group for no good reason." Mulvy thinks the student association should be building up a bank account for the future. "I think we could have a big impact on this campus. We could get the best music acts to play. We could bring in the biggest guest speakers. We could do something positive, rather than just let the money go to any group that brings a proposal to the board for approval and getting money." The two clashed also over funding to religious groups. "I am an atheist and I don't see any reason we should hand over our money to religious groups. We should support groups that are more representative of all Canfeld students," Mulvy says. "We should not be in the business of saying which students can form groups and which should not," Aljeerz says. "I am Muslim, but any group, Christian, Jewish, whatever, should be supported by us. The last time I looked, we all lived in America." The vote for president is next Tuesday.

CHAPTER 6

Interviewing Well

IN THIS CHAPTER YOU WILL LEARN:

- Ways to prepare for interviews.
- How to establish rapport with interview subjects.
- Interviewing techniques.
- Guidelines on anonymous sources.

Do your best to master the subject, so you are not at the mercy of the person you are interviewing.
Bill Marimow

In Jacqueline Winspear's novel, *Maisie Dobbs*, the young private detective benefits by remembering her mentor's wisdom at a crucial moment during an important interview:

> *"Never follow a story with a question, Maisie, not immediately. And remember to acknowledge the storyteller, for in some way even the messenger is affected by the story he brings."*
>
> *She waited a few more minutes, watching Billy sip his tea, lost in his memories as he looked out over the rooftops.*
>
> *"Billy, thank you for finding this out for me. You must have worked hard to track the details down."*

This passage from a work of fiction offers timeless lessons to those seeking the truth for today's chronicles of fact. It teaches the value of patience, observation and respect for your sources in order to become the consummate listener. Many interviews have been spoiled by reporters' impatient focus only on their own sequence of questions.

Interviewing is the most important skill a reporter must master. Armed with eyewitness information and vivid quotes from essential sources, the accomplished interviewer is a giant step closer to being an accomplished writer.

Less-gifted writers can dominate the top stories by gaining access to the best sources and asking the best questions. Powerful stories consist of powerful facts. Powerful facts come from many places, but most of all from successful interviews.

Here is some guidance on how to prepare for and conduct interviews that lead to powerful stories.

PREPARATION

Reporters have to be able to interview on a moment's notice. They can cover the basics by remembering Who, What, Where, When, Why and How. But reporters who prepare for interviews gain many advantages.

Especially for beginners, but even for accomplished veterans, preparation equals confidence. The prepared reporter is more knowledgeable and has key questions ready to keep the interview essential and on track.

The time spent preparing saves more time later. It will seldom be necessary to track down sources twice for questions you didn't know to ask the first time. The more prominent the sources, the less likely you will be able to reach them twice before your deadline.

Prepared reporters earn more respect. They don't force their sources to spend valuable interview time providing basic background information. They demonstrate sincere interest in the source, the topic and in getting the story right. These reporters gain trust. Their sources divulge more information.

Preparation is the ideal defense against reluctant, evasive and deceptive sources. A source is much less likely to risk deceit when speaking to someone who knows enough to detect the deception.

The Art of Storytelling

Fine storytelling requires deeper character development. Characters become more authentic when the audience can understand the life events that motivated the leading characters' passion and actions.

In each of the examples below, a person being interviewed divulged details that would have been difficult to obtain otherwise. By being sincerely interested in the interview subject as a person, you gain keen insight—and telling details for your story. These details about people in the public eye help your story paint pictures for readers—pictures that convey contrast, irony and motivation. Your characters gain depth far beyond cardboard stereotypes.

- The risk-taking entrepreneur whose leisure time is spent on extreme sports. Risk taking comes naturally to her. It's much of her life.
- The combative urban college basketball coach who first had to survive the toughest streets in the city where he still coaches. He is suspicious of outsiders and circles the wagons in defense of his players and his university, fiercely loyal to both.
- The open government advocate on City Council who is married to a journalist. He has an understanding of the issues that few on his council appreciate.
- The trial lawyer who also coaches award-winning debate teams. She loves an argument, and her team's success matches her own in the courtroom.
- The neighborhood dad who began coaching youth football after his only son was killed in a school-bus accident. He might never have coached otherwise. He spends more time with the boys than other coaches do. His undefeated team compensates for a small part of his loss.
- The high-living corporate executive who grew up in poverty. He didn't always have the good life, so he enjoys it while he's got it. Subordinates far below him aren't jealous because he understands their needs.
- The computer-game-company founder whose primary hobby is playing board games. Quite the irony—his inventions have made some of his other passions nearly obsolete.
- The death-penalty-activist state senator whose mother was murdered. He has pursued tougher laws with a vengeance.

The more detail you can obtain about these life-changing events, the more story you have to tell about the leading characters in current events.

HOW TO Tell If a Source Is Being Evasive

Here's an interview every reporter can benefit from: Ask a professional interviewer—a detective, for instance—how they can tell when someone being interviewed is being evasive.

You will hear about how the subject avoids eye contact, suddenly taking extraordinary interest in the lint on his clothes and the condition of his fingernails. You will hear about indirect answers—responses, not answers—and unnecessarily long, convoluted answers to direct questions. You will hear that inconsistent answers are most suspicious of all.

None of these things proves that the subject is lying. But these are red flags that make interviewers wonder if the subject has something to hide. They are signals that further, narrower questioning is in order—and that the subject's information should be checked with special care.

Effective stories built on successful interviews lead to more success. The potential sources on a beat or in an area of specialty expertise quickly learn the reputations of those who might interview them. They spend more time—and are more willing to be interviewed in the first place—by reporters known for their knowledge, thoroughness and fairness.

KNOW YOUR SUBJECTS—both the news topic and the person you will interview.

If the topic is complex and foreign, you won't become an expert soon, but a short amount of study can make you familiar with timely issues, controversies and their stakeholders. Above all, ask yourself: "What do my readers really need to know?" For instance, when interviewing an expert on stem-cell research, you don't have to know the finest details in the science to understand the conflict involving medical and religious ethics. Or to understand that many readers have deep interest in whether these considerations outweigh the potential, but unproven, remedies to previously incurable diseases that inflict millions.

Start by reading what has already been published. *But heed this caution: Never accept others' work as fact.* Just because it was published doesn't guarantee its accuracy. You don't know what steps the other publication took—or skipped. Treat other published works as tips to be verified. This is more important than ever, because it is easier to find other writers' work. There are vastly more media outlets today than a generation ago, and the Internet archives some work indefinitely. These twin benefits too often lure journalists to dangerous reporting shortcuts. The worst of these is plagiarism—many of the scandals that have cost journalists their jobs in recent years began with material copied from the Internet. A less-malicious problem is even more common: Verification standards are deficient in many places. Repeating someone else's error through your own lack of diligence cannot be justified.

Next, speak to colleagues and more familiar sources. You may learn something helpful about recent developments or the credibility of your interview subject.

OUTLINE KEY QUESTIONS. You want to be certain to ask them. The best interviews can stray into interesting new territory. As Bill Marimow suggests in this chapter, bring the most important half-dozen questions with you to the interview, written down in a place you won't overlook them. Something as simple as one-word reminders at the front of your notebook will help keep the interview focused on essential matters.

HAVE A BACKUP PLAN. Perhaps the source will prove reluctant, inarticulate or otherwise unhelpful. Your interview won't be a total loss if the source will share informative documents and/or refer you to other knowledgeable people to be interviewed.

Without presuming too much in advance of reporting, journalists may envision the potential for any given story. Think of this as a maximum story and a minimum story that is still essential to readers.

A simple example: In the face of a record-setting crime wave, you are trying to confirm rumors that a very popular police chief is going to resign, igniting a major new issue in an already-nasty mayoral election campaign. You are unable to confirm this. However, by remaining open to the minimum story—how the city will respond to the crime wave—you are the first to report that for the first time in three decades, your city will impose summer curfews beginning next week. This will trigger many potential stories about July 4 fireworks shows, the financial state of seasonal teen hang-outs and more.

Similarly, reporters must remain open-minded. Always guard against preconceived notions about a story. This is the true test of objectivity's triumph over bias. The story often changes shape as you collect information. If the original assumption—the reason for pursing the story in the first place—proves false, you must be prepared to discard the idea. But a new story may emerge from your reporting. Be open to that.

RAPPORT WITH SOURCES

People have different motivations for speaking to a reporter. The reporter who understands and appreciates which one(s) influence a particular interview will be more persuasive and will be able to get more revealing answers.

Some of the most common motivators:

Celebrity. Many are thrilled by the idea of having their names in the newspaper or their faces on television.

Ego. It's human nature to be eager to reveal that I know something you (and others) don't.

My Side of the Story. In a controversy, it's important to be heard.

Agenda. Many speakers want their "spin" to become part of the debate. Others initiate the debate through the press—for instance, floating a proposal as a trial balloon to find out what reaction it will generate. Stories built on anonymous sources from Washington, D.C., fit this category.

Conscience. Whistle-blowers and others more introverted want to do what's right to expose an injustice, even if it puts their jobs and families at risk.

Accuracy. Speakers who have no interest in seeing this story in print may still contribute because, once the decision to publish has been made, they are most concerned that the story be told accurately and responsibly.

Obligation. Public officials (who are paid with taxpayer money), company spokesmen and others may accept that it is their job to address public issues. Even media-wary company executives find times when they agree that no one else can speak for the company on vital matters.

WIRED AND WIRELESS | INTERVIEWING WITH E-MAIL

Interviewing via written questions robs reporters of many advantages they have when interviewing in person. So interviewing via e-mail is a poor way to interview sources. But it is an excellent way to find them.

If you have encountered the risks of conversing via e-mail, you know the risks of interviewing that way. Unable to hear chuckles or sarcasm, unable to see expressions of shock, anger or amusement, you can misconstrue the spirit and the content of the message, sometimes to severe embarrassment.

Reporters interviewing by e-mail also lose the opportunity to notice surroundings and mannerisms, as well as the subtle indications of sincerity or deceit. They lose the use of silence as an interviewing technique. The interview loses spontaneity. Someone interviewed in writing is more likely to answer formally, as if his lawyer is looking over his shoulder.

When an interview in writing is the only remaining option, the speed of e-mail compensates somewhat. The e-mail will arrive sooner. Recipients are more likely to reply promptly to an e-mail than to a letter. There may be enough time left to pose follow-up questions.

However, e-mail can bring miraculous results in locating sources. Ken Sands, former managing editor of Online and New Media at *The Spokesman-Review* in Spokane, Wash., and now executive editor for innovation at *Congressional Quarterly* attests to this on the Committee for Concerned Journalists website.

"At 9 a.m. on Sept. 11, I sent out e-mail to nearly 1,000 readers, asking for their personal connections to the terrorist attacks. Within minutes, the responses began pouring in: the husband of one reader's cousin had just exited the World Trade Center when the first building collapsed and his cell phone went dead; several other readers had friends or relatives in the air, in the Pentagon or in the World Trade Center. Some of their comments were included in that afternoon's special edition."

Another time, "a reporter was doing a feature story about the state Capitol dome closing for three years for repairs. That building is 300 miles away, but he wanted to find local people with fun, personal anecdotes about the building. So we sent out e-mail. . . ."

The reporter later wrote to Sands, "Here's a woman in remote Wilbur, who, 37 years ago, was stuck atop the dome during a honeymoon tour with her [still] husband. It's a great anecdote and she was a fun phone interview. I don't know how we ever would've found her any other way."

Sands again: "When the [racial profiling] issue surfaced in 2001, a reporter spent a great deal of time and energy—without success—trying to find someone to go on the record with complaints. Initial public meetings were sparsely attended. So the initial news stories didn't have the RH [real human] factor. I stumbled upon an e-mail list of about 200 members of the minority community and sent them a message asking for their personal experiences with racial profiling. The quantity of response was low, but the quality was outstanding. We published guest columns and a half-page of letters to the editor on the opinion pages, and provided the reporter with enough good RH sources to write a decent advance of a public meeting with the police chief. Partly as a result of our thorough coverage of this issue, the public meeting was packed, and testimony went on for hours."

Despite the success stories, Sands cautions, "The use of the e-mail tool is not a replacement for traditional reporting, and is not appropriate for many stories. It is simply a cool new tool and should be used judiciously."

Find Sands' "how-to" advice and more from his experience here: www.journalism.org/resources/tools/reporting/interviewing/email.asp?from=print

Television and radio reporters have additional obligations when recording telephone conversations.

Federal Communications Commission regulations specify that in order to use the taped conversation on air, the station's representative (in this case, a reporter) "shall inform any party to the call of its intention to broadcast the conversation, except where such party is aware, or may be presumed to be aware from the circumstances of the conversation, that it is being or likely will be broadcast."

With so many motivators driving interest in speaking to the press, reporters should seldom be persuaded to accept off-the-record interviews (more on use of anonymous sources later).

INTERVIEW INTEGRITY

No matter why a person agrees to talk, an interview is a test of your integrity. Recognizing this will help you complete successful interviews.

BE HONEST. You won't appreciate a source who tries to deceive you. That works both ways. Someone being interviewed isn't obliged to answer more than you ask, but you expect honest answers. Reporters aren't obliged to reveal all that they know, but the people being interviewed have a right to expect reporters to represent themselves honestly. That includes identifying yourself and your news organization and to explain, at minimum, that you are researching a story. While most people should understand that reporters ask questions to publish answers, this disclosure guards against misunderstandings, especially with people who are not media-savvy.

BE RESPECTFUL. The tigerish, overly aggressive reporter is the stereotype for newsmen in movies, but much less common in newsrooms. Undoubtedly, you will find times when you must be firm and stand your ground. But no one earns respect without giving it.

INTERVIEW FACE-TO-FACE WHEN POSSIBLE. Distance and deadlines often preclude this, so meet face-to-face whenever you can. You learn much more by adding your powers of observation to your listening skills. The source should gain greater comfort with you, and the result is a welcome, ongoing reporter-source relationship.

INTERVIEW ON THE SOURCE'S TURF WHEN PRACTICAL. This is especially important for profiles and other news features, where surroundings contribute valuable insight to a story. Then, it can be more helpful to follow these sources to each of their environments—office, home and the places where they spend a good bit of their leisure time. Sources are more likely to be at ease in such places.

WIRED AND WIRELESS | TV

This is an eyebrow-raiser. Television, which measures its value by the precious second, dreads dead time. And yet, in an interview with *Time* Magazine, Mike Wallace of CBS *60 Minutes* fame described the value of a TV interviewer's dramatic pauses:

"They get embarrassed by the silence," Wallace explained of his interview subjects, "and they begin to fill the silence. Suddenly they begin to really talk."

Throughout this book, reporters who describe interviewing on camera, on the phone or with pen and paper make two related points:

- Don't rush to your next question. Let the subject talk. Listen well.
- Silence can be a reporter's powerful ally. The reporters wish they had learned this sooner. The technique is often rewarded with more complete, and more revealing, answers.

At least five writers, several with Pulitzer Prizes in their portfolios, told the authors of their regard for silence as a reporting tool and an interviewing technique. Silence was one of the pieces of advice they were most eager to offer to young journalists.

Recent Jailed Reporters

- **1984, Richard Hargraves, Belleville, Ill.** Newspaper reporter jailed over a weekend in connection with libel case. Released when source came forward.
- **1985, Chris Van Ness, Calif.** Freelancer subpoenaed in connection with John Belushi murder. Jailed for several hours; revealed source; released.
- **1986, Brad Stone, Detroit.** TV reporter refused to reveal identities of gang members interviewed several weeks prior to cop killing. Jailed for one day; released pending appeal. Grand jury then dismissed.
- **1987, Roxana Kopetman, Los Angeles.** Newspaper reporter jailed for six hours for resisting prosecution subpoena seeking eyewitness testimony. Appealed; court ruled against her, but criminal case was long over.
- **1990, Brian Karem, San Antonio.** TV reporter subpoenaed by defense and prosecution; refused to reveal name of individuals who arranged jailhouse interview. Jailed for 13 days. Released when sources came forward.
- **1990, Libby Averyt, Corpus Christi, Texas.** Newspaper reporter subpoenaed for info about jailhouse interview. Jailed over a weekend; released when judge convinced she would never turn over the unpublished information sought.
- **1990, Tim Roche, Stuart, Fla.** Newspaper reporter subpoenaed to reveal source for leaked court order supposed to have been sealed. Jailed briefly, released pending appeal. Later sentenced to 30 days for criminal contempt. Served 18 days in 1993, and was released.
- **1991, Sid Gaulden, Schuyler Kropf, Cindi Scoppe, Andrew Shain; Columbia, S. C.** Jailed for eight hours; released for appeal, which they lost, but trial was over. Prosecutors sought unpublished conversations with state senator on trial for corruption.
- **1991, Felix Sanchez and James Campbell, Houston.** Newspaper reporters locked in judge's chambers for several hours; had refused to stand in the back of courtroom and identify possible eyewitnesses to crime. Appeal successful through habeas corpus petition.
- **1994, Lisa Abraham, Warren, Ohio.** Newspaper reporter jailed from Jan. 19 to February 10, for refusing to testify before a state grand jury about jailhouse interview.
- **1996, Bruce Anderson, Ukiah, Calif.** Editor of *Anderson Valley Independent* found in civil contempt, jailed for total of 13 days for refusing to turn over original letter to the editor received from prisoner. After a week, he tried to turn over the letter, but judge refused to believe it was the original because it was typed. After another week, judge finally accepted that the typewritten letter was the original.
- **1996, David Kidwell, Palm Beach County, Fla.** *Miami Herald* reporter found in criminal contempt, sentenced to 70 days for refusing to testify for prosecution about jailhouse interview. Served 14 days before being released on own recognizance after filing federal *habeas corpus* petition.
- **2000, Timothy Crews, Red Bluff, Calif.** *Sacramento Valley Mirror* editor and publisher served a five-day sentence for refusing to reveal his confidential sources in a story involving the sale of an allegedly stolen firearm by a state patrol officer.
- **2001, Vanessa Leggett, Houston.** Author researching "true crime" book jailed for 168 days by federal judge for refusing to disclose her research and the identities of her sources to a federal grand jury investigating a murder. Leggett was freed only after the term of the grand jury expired. A subsequent grand jury indicted the key suspect in the murder without any need for her testimony. Leggett may again face a subpoena during his murder trial.
- **2004, Jim Taricani, Providence, R.I.** A WJAR television reporter obtained and aired in February 2001 a portion of the videotape showing a Providence city official accepting a bribe from an undercover FBI informant. The tape was sealed evidence in an FBI investigation into corruption by Providence officials, including former Mayor Vincent "Buddy" Cianci Jr. Taricani was subpoenaed, but refused to reveal his source and was found in civil contempt of court. After a failed appeal to the U.S. Court of Appeals in Boston (1st Cir.), NBC, WJAR's network, paid $85,000 in fines. In November, Taricani was found in criminal contempt of court and a month later, was sentenced to six months home confinement. He was granted early release after being confined for four months.
- **2005, Judith Miller, Washington, D.C.** *New York Times* reporter jailed for refusing to testify about news sources in the investigation into leaks of a CIA operative's name by White House officials. She spent 85 days in jail, and was released when she agreed to provide limited testimony to the grand jury regarding conversations with vice presidential aide Lewis "Scooter" Libby without revealing her other sources.
- **2006, Joshua Wolf, San Francisco, Calif.** Freelance video blogger initially jailed for a month when he refused to turn over a videotape that federal officials said contained footage of protesters damaging a police car. Wolf was released on bail on Sept. 1, but an appeals court panel confirmed the contempt order against him, and Wolf returned to jail, where he remained as of late October. His lawyers are seeking an *en banc* hearing to appeal the contempt order again.

Source: Reporters Committee for Freedom of the Press; www.refp.org.

Talent Showcase

BILL MARIMOW ▸

Editor, *Philadelphia Inquirer*

Former vice president for news, National Public Radio. Former editor of *The Baltimore Sun*, Two-time Pulitzer Prize-winning investigative reporter for the *Philadelphia Inquirer.*

Preparation produces precise questions and precise questions make the difference in crucial interviews, Bill Marimow advises.

"It's the art of formulating questions with such specificity that when someone tries to evade or not answer that you would know instantly that the answer was not responsive," says the two-time Pulitzer Prize-winning investigative journalist. "There's an important corollary, too, and that is listening with great care and concentration."

Marimow offers an example that is a modern twist on the classic story of *The Emperor's New Clothes*. Call it *The Mayor's New Suits*.

While investigating allegations that a union official had misused union money, the FBI unearthed evidence that the union was making gifts of expensive men's suits to city officials. It turned out that Mayor Wilson Goode of Philadelphia received 24 suits valued at up to $300 each.

As Goode later explained, "What I wanted to imply was that I did not ask anyone for any free suits; that I did not receive any free suits; and I asked to be billed and, for those I was billed for, I, in fact, paid."

"Dissect his statement," Marimow instructs. "He never asked. The only person who can know what he expected is Wilson Goode. Maybe he expected he was going to get a bill. But, at the time I interviewed him, he had not yet received *any* bills."

To Marimow, Goode's statement represented "a lie of the technical truth in which every word was technically true, but the overall effect of the statement was to flagrantly mislead the listener."

Marimow's precise questioning forced Goode to answer differently: "I expected to pay for the suits and was, in fact, billed and, in fact, paid for the suits through that process." Goode's more precise answer could be—and later was—proved false.

SHOW SINCERE INTEREST IN YOUR SOURCE. When you show genuine curiosity about the person and genuine interest in what your source has to say, human nature dictates that the person is much more likely to open up and to divulge personal details.

You may demonstrate this interest several ways, but you must be sincere. Most people can tell when someone is being deceptive—too many subconscious signals betray that.

You demonstrate sincere interest by noticing and commenting on personal items in your source's office, home or car. Family photos, framed awards, evidence of hobbies. This conversation may turn out to be nothing more than an ice-breaker. More

Records showed that Goode did not pay for the suits until three weeks after his interview by Marimow.

Mastering an interview in this way takes preparation.

"Thoroughly research what you came to talk about," Marimow counsels. "Especially with key people, do your best to master the subject, so you are not at the mercy of the person you are interviewing."

Even when thoroughly prepared, resist the temptation to begin with "the thorniest, most difficult questions." Instead, the opening questions should be "designed to get the person to talk freely, uninhibitedly, expansively." This question can be procedural or generic.

"Let's say you're the labor writer and you're interviewing one of three members of an arbitration panel that will decide the contract for 8,000 police officers. Begin with something like, 'I'd like to hear your thoughts about [the labor law at issue], what's working, what's not.' Then ask what other cases the arbitrator is working on."

Once the person has warmed to being interviewed, get to the core questions, including your pre-prepared list of "six or seven questions that I didn't want to leave without asking."

A common interviewing flaw is to be so eager to ask the next question that you neglect to get a full answer to the last one.

"Listen with intense concentration," Marimow emphasizes, knowing that answers in tough interviews can include a word or phrase that tips off an attentive reporter to evasion or provides an impetus for strong follow-up questions.

"On the key questions, I will repeat what I've heard, prefacing that with, 'I want to make sure that I've captured the spirit and substance of your answers.' "

Experience has made Marimow so confident of the effectiveness of this discipline that he is sure the deposition of President Clinton under oath would have gone differently if he had been asking the questions.

"If I were the lawyer asking the president questions, I would never ask, 'Did you have sex with Monica Lewinsky?' because sex can be defined a number of ways.

"I would have started with a preface, telling the president that I was going to ask some specific, precise and uncomfortable questions but that 'as a lawyer yourself, you understand why this is necessary.' Then I would ask 20 or 30 questions, beginning with, 'Did you ever touch Monica Lewinsky's arm? Did you ever touch her hand?' And then I would proceed to each and every body part.

"At some point, the president's lawyers would ask for a recess, because they would conclude that I knew something they didn't know. Because Clinton obviously told them he didn't have sex with her. My questions would have required Clinton to either tell the truth, which would have been devastating because he hadn't told his own lawyers the truth, or he would lie, which would have been devastating when the truth came out, as it did."

often, it will disclose some personal relationship to the source's public personality that will make your story better.

You demonstrate sincere interest by asking follow-up questions. This shows your interest in the value of what was just said and your interest in getting the facts right. You are there not just to record answers, but to understand well enough to write clearly for readers.

Finally, you demonstrate sincere interest by giving the source the chance to expand the interview with a question such as, "Is there anything else you would like to talk about?" This is a courtesy that does not commit you to anything more than to listen. Meanwhile, it opens the door to disclosures you might not have learned otherwise.

INTERVIEWING TECHNIQUES

We have mentioned a few techniques. Probably the most fundamental of the others is when to ask open-ended questions and when to ask close-ended questions.

Open-ended questions cannot be answered with a simple "Yes" or No." These questions seek expansive answers—a philosophy, an explanation or a description, for instance. They are best used in preface to close-ended questions that seek more specific answers.

Let's say you had the rare opportunity to interview the Roman Catholic cardinal who oversees the Catholic bishops in your area. You have some sensitive questions to ask, including those about child-molesting priests, declining church membership, and increasing political activity among churches in local dioceses. It might be best to initiate the interview with some open-ended questions:

- "Why is this an important time for you to make an appearance in Florida?"
- "What is the best opportunity for growth of the Catholic Church in America?"
- "What are the most difficult obstacles you face in achieving these goals?"

Note the progression of these questions from least sensitive to most sensitive. Each of the earlier questions might elicit answers that provoke the tougher questions, and the even-tougher close-ended questions to follow:

- "How much damage has been done to the Church because of the priest-molestation issue?"
- "What has this cost the Church in dollars, membership and priest recruitment?"
- "In what ways can the increasing political activity by churches here compensate for these losses?"

Open-ended questions are valuable for building rapport and trust, and for exposing issues and story ideas that you had not yet considered. Close-ended questions seek specific answers. They demonstrate to your source that you are well-prepared and the answers enrich your stories with telling detail.

Close-ended questions can require a simple "Yes" or "No" response. This is not a problem with publicity-seeking sources, who are likely to expand their answers anyway. Generally, however, you do not want to give a tight-lipped source this option.

The "yes/no" question is most valuable when you seek confirmation of something said earlier in the interview or of something you learned elsewhere. In these cases, a simple "Yes" or "No" is exactly what you need, better than a wordy, "it-all-depends" reply.

"Do I have this right?" (followed by your assertion)

"Do you agree that . . . ?"

Take special care with the "Yes" or "No" answer. On camera, it is clear the speaker is agreeing with someone else's words, but not speaking them. In print, the writer must be careful not to put too many words in the source's mouth.

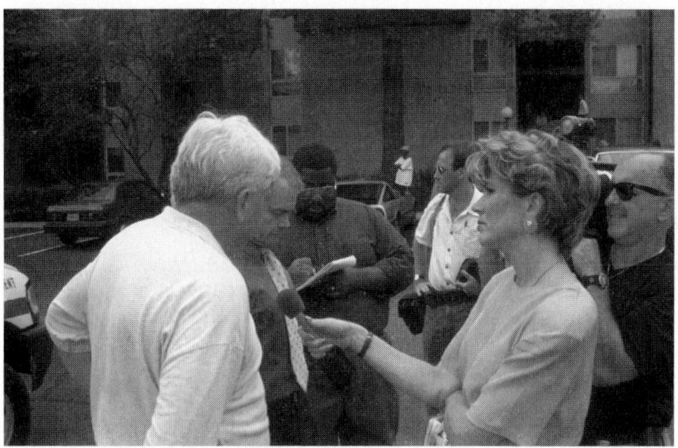

Whenever practical, interview in person, as here after a tornado has struck in Maryland.

A common mistake: "Commissioner Jones said taxpayers will be paying twice what they ought to for the toll bridge" (when all Jones really said was "Yes").

In such cases, *said* may not be your best verb. Replace it with the word in your question. "Commissioner Jones agreed with the view that taxpayers will be paying twice what they ought to for the toll bridge." Or, "Commissioner Jones said he agreed with the view that taxpayers will be paying twice what they ought to for the toll bridge."

Most often, reporters will learn more and get more to use by asking questions that cannot be answered with a simple "Yes" or "No." After all, your primary functions in interviews are listening, gaining information and obtaining useful quotes.

ASK QUESTIONS WHEN YOU ALREADY KNOW THE ANSWER

In a trial, lawyers ask witnesses questions that the lawyers already know the answers to. Their goal: Get the witness to say it.

That's an honorable goal for the reporter, too. Readers want to hear more from people like them or from people in authority, especially if it's a matter of opinion or other comment on a matter in dispute. The quote often carries more weight than the reporter's declarative sentence, which can be accused of bias. Quotes brighten stories, too, making them easier to read.

Obtaining a bright quote is reason enough to ask a question when you already know the answer, but there are others: A question tests the truthfulness of your source, and it can confirm what you *think* you already knew.

BUT LEAVE YOURSELF OPEN TO SURPRISE

The Committee of Concerned Journalists teaches that journalists should exercise humility about what they know. It's dangerous to assume you know or that you can deduce what is meant.

A reporter gains major advantages from long experience on a beat. However, after remaining on the same beat for years, reporters must guard against the complacency of having seen it all before, having written about it twice before. Keep things fresh by keeping an open mind and reviving the curiosity that is a reporter's greatest asset. If you don't leave yourself open to being surprised, you will miss things that fascinate newer reporters to the beat.

Here are a couple simple questions to keep things fresh for you and the sources you see day-in, day-out:

"What are you spending your time on today?"

"If you were a reporter, what would you be checking into today?"

These are simple, nonthreatening questions. But the answers to the first question have alerted reporters to the urgent activity of underlings during a hidden crisis involving the CEO or mayor. The second question sometimes discloses a pet peeve or outrage that has started reporters on investigative stories.

INSIST ON ANSWERS, NOT MERELY RESPONSES

Politicians, increasingly coached by their handlers to stay on message, have become ever-more adept at responding to questions without answering them. A self-proclaimed "education governor" (pick a state), asked about why test scores aren't improving more, may reply that public education gets the largest share of the state budget (true in almost every state) or that "since I've been in office, we've added $XX million to the education budget." This response evades the question and substitutes a self-serving campaign speech.

Athletic coaches, asked about reports that they are candidates for coaching jobs elsewhere, often reply, "I haven't been contacted by anyone at Team Other," when in fact such sensitive, high-level contacts usually are made by go-betweens.

THE POWER OF SILENCE

A popular television commercial was built around basketball star Tim Duncan's inscrutable game face. Across the table in negotiation with an auto salesman, Duncan says nothing and never changes his serious facial expression, causing the salesman to keep talking, repeatedly sweetening the deal he is offering.

On occasion, silence can be a potent interviewing tool, too. Given ambiguous or unresponsive answers, reporters often make the mistake of charging ahead to their next questions. Another common interviewing mistake: Talking too much. Silence is a reporter's ally. The reporter is there to listen and learn, after all. In the face of an inadequate answer to a good question, silence conveys that you are waiting for a more complete, more coherent, more plausible answer. Without a word, it's as if the interviewer is saying, "It's still your turn to talk."

ADVANCED TIP
The Ultrasensitive Source

In rare circumstances, a source who risks his job—even his life—by speaking to a reporter will be so reticent and so nervous that merely pulling out a notebook will scare him off.

In that case, try this: Concentrate intently on everything the source says, including verbatim quotes. Then, the moment you and the source part company, pull out your notebook and write everything you can remember. This is not recommended for any but extreme circumstances. But you may be pleasantly surprised how much you can remember this way.

If the interview subject is as patient with silence as the reporter is, the reporter can prompt a better answer with open-ended questions like these:

"Why do you say that?"
"Please give me an example of that."
"What else do you know about that?"
"Hmm. That's different from the way I heard it from XX. What accounts for this discrepancy?"

SEEK DESCRIPTIVE ANSWERS

Often, the difference between a competent story and a superb one is the level of detail. This is essential in storytelling methods such as narratives and reconstructions of spot news. Even in a first-day hard news story, the extra detail can elevate the story to more prominent display and wider readership.

Say, for example, that a source characterizes someone you are profiling as "combative" or "generous to a fault."

Take that opportunity to follow-up with questions such as these:

- What examples can you think of?
- What made you think of that?
- What brings that out in her?
- What do you think made him that way?

Then, when you have an excellent example, ask your interview subject to be an eyewitness:

"Describe that scene—tell me what you saw, what you heard, what the mood was. Put me there."

Delivering eyewitness accounts—taking readers to places they have never been—is among the most valuable services a reporter can provide.

ABOVE ALL, DON'T LEAVE THE INTERVIEW CONFUSED

Conscientious reporters have had nightmares about poorly written paragraphs constructed when, on deadline, they realized they did not understand something well enough at all. At that point, call-backs are time-consuming—and it's no sure thing you will find the person in time. Uncertainty produces vague and ineffective writing. It can get worse when you try to overcome vague writing with a declarative sentence, but without confidence in the supporting facts. Then, you've declared something to be so, without being absolutely sure that it is.

TAKING NOTES AND RECORDING INTERVIEWS

Few reporters can write as fast as their interview subjects talk. So develop your own note-taking shorthand. Crucial: review your notes as soon as possible after the interview. Notes written swiftly have a way of becoming confusing by the next day.

Shorthand techniques vary by the person. Some reporters use mathematical symbols in place of frequently uttered phrases.

> = more than
< = less than
~ = about
X = time or times

Abbreviations are popular—among countless examples, the two-letter postal codes for states; simply the capital letter Y for yes and N for no.

Trial reporters taking notes on testimony may eliminate quote marks altogether, by underlining the witness replies to separate it from the lawyer's question. Or simply by indenting the reply.

Recording devices have become more commonplace in interviews. They are standard fare at press conferences and in sports locker rooms. They protect both the interviewer and source if ever there is a question about what was said and in what context.

Still, some sources are skittish about being recorded. It's a matter of courtesy and fairness to ask permission to record or to inform your source that you are recording. Face-to-face, it's best to leave the recorder in plain view. Many interview subjects gradually forget they are being recorded as the interview progresses.

The advantages of recording are offset somewhat by the possibility that the recorder is not functioning properly and by the long and tedious process of transcribing a lengthy interview. Reporters using recording devices should also take written notes, both as a backup and as a reference sheet to help them find recorded passages more swiftly.

Take special care when recording telephone conversations. Some states require that both parties consent to the recording. Know the laws of your state—and the state you are calling. Some states require only "one-party consent." In that case, it is legal if only the caller knows the conversation is being recorded.

Wash., D.C. Rep. John McHugh (far left), Sen. Evan Bayh and Sen. Hillary Clinton speak to the media during a press conference on Capitol Hill to discuss their trip to Iraq and Afghanistan.

The most careful note-takers will miss a word or misunderstand one from time to time. If there is any doubt about what has been said, it's appropriate to read back quotes to the source to check on accuracy and intent. News organizations discourage reading other parts of the story to a source or turning over copies of stories prior to publication. That, in effect, inappropriately delegates editing the story to someone outside the news organization.

ANONYMOUS SOURCES

Anonymous sources almost always undermine the credibility of the news stories in which they appear. Readers wonder: Is the reporter making this up? If not, where is this news organization's allegiance? Who is it protecting, and why?

Consider anonymous sources a high-risk investment. If the reward is high enough—a *vital* story hinges on the information provided where anonymity is *required*—then the reward may be worth the risk. But anonymity should always be a last resort.

Generally, there are three levels of anonymity. Although definitions vary, these are widely accepted:

Not for Attribution. The news report may quote the source, but not by name or in any other way that identifies the source.

Off-the-Record. Neither the information nor the identity may be used for publication. However, the information may be used to assist further reporting.

Background. The information and identity must be kept so confidential that it may not even be used as the basis for further inquiries.

Some news organizations apply these terms differently. There is such confusion over the terms—among sources and journalists—that when a source and journalist discuss the *possibility* of anonymity they should define their expectations.

Although requests for any of these levels of anonymity are always negotiable, reporters should think long in advance about whether they *ever* want to grant such requests. The possible value of reporting an exclusive story because of anonymity is offset by the possible embarrassment of seeing the story of a harder-working competitor who confirmed the information on-the-record.

Accepting information on background is particularly dubious. You have information you cannot use and your further reporting is handcuffed, while competitors are free to report.

Consequently, reporters should throw up a stop sign before accepting information off-the-record or on background on an unknown topic. If off-the-record information is valuable at all, it is to confirm what the reporter already suspects is true, but is not yet in sound position to assert.

A co-author of this book, Glenn Guzzo, set this policy for the news staff when he was editor of *The Denver Post*:

> Anonymous sources will not appear in the newspaper without the approval of either the Editor or the Managing Editor. [This requirement alone reduced reliance upon anonymous sources because journalists did not want to have to overcome that hurdle.]
>
> News staff should expect these questions when they bring a request for anonymity, so they should consider this list a checklist of their own:
>
> - *Is the information essential to the story?*
> - *Is the information fact, not judgment? We will not allow anonymity for judgmental statements.*

- *Is our source truly in a position to know—are we talking about an eyewitness?*
- *What other indicators of reliability do we have (multiple sources, independent corroboration, experience with the source)?*
- *Is there a legitimate reason for anonymity?*
- *Finally, what descriptors can we use so that readers can decide what weight to assign to this source?*

Too many journalists are too ready to grant anonymity. Lacking time, discipline and/or confidence, some journalists—even experienced, talented journalists—make the serious mistake of *offering* anonymity to their sources. Rather than expecting to get the information on the record, they expect they will fail to do so and concede the point up front, ensuring their failure.

Those who adopt an attitude that they *expect* to get it all on the record often do. Remember, there are reasons why the source wants to speak to you in the first place.

Here's a corollary: The great investigative reporters Don Barlett and Jim Steele *expect* that for each fact they want to declare in a story, they will be able to find a document to support the declaration. Consequently, they find much more documentation than other reporters do, and in places most others would not think to look.

To give yourself the best chance to get it all on the record:

- Never offer anonymity.
- Don't be so quick to say yes to those who request it. It's negotiable. You will be surprised how often a source flip-flops on this request.

The reporter who succeeds at this not only gets the more credible story, but builds self-confidence and a valuable reputation among sources as well as colleagues. There are examples of reporters, having insisted on this measure of integrity with their sources, getting the exclusive calls on important stories because the sources have confidence that those reporters can (a) get the story and (b) get it right.

Guzzo's policy is more rigorous than most others. In the face of journalism scandals (including fabrications) and the general decline of public trust in the media, many news organizations have been restricting use of anonymous sources and setting the bar higher for determining when anonymous sources are permissible. The reporter who can master Guzzo's checklist should be able to thrive under the rules in any newsroom.

IN CONCLUSION

Excellent reporting requires successful interviewing. The details obtained in successful interviews often determine the strength of a reporter's story.

Some of the keys to success are preparation, recognizing the motivation of your sources, interviewing them in person when practical and using silence as a powerful listening tool.

Professional journalists reflect their integrity in the way they interview sources. Use of anonymous sources erodes credibility. Use them sparingly and as a last resort, only when their information is first-hand, essential and unable to be obtained elsewhere.

TOOL KIT

www.journalism.org/resources/tools/reporting/interviewing/print.asp
www.poynter.org/content/content_view.asp?id=1190

EXERCISE 1

1. Go interview four students and ask all of them one of these questions:
   a. When does the steady drumbeat from the mass media about celebrities and their private lives become too much and step over the line? What was a time when you found the coverage was out of bounds?
   b. The conflict in Iraq showed the U.S. military needs more troops. What should the government consider before re-instating the draft?
   c. Images of the perfect woman saturate our culture, in movies, magazines, ads and TV. Are the mass media to blame for women who fall prey to eating disorders and a desire to be too thin?
   d. Why shouldn't athletes in college be paid to play sports since many of them—football players, especially—bring in so much money for the university?
2. Now write a story based on what the students said. Write a lead that either summarizes what the four students said, or write a lead that goes with the student who gave you the most dramatic and compelling answers.

EXERCISE 2

Examine a story in the local newspaper, student newspaper or a magazine. Look at the quotes and information offered from the sources interviewed. Write a one-page discussion paper on what kinds of questions a journalist had to ask to elicit the responses. Write four questions that would get you the same information offered in the article.

EXERCISE 3

Write a story from the following:

From an interview with Jane Nguyen:

"I grew up in Ellington, Texas, and that was kind of wild for me since I was the only Asian kid in every school I went to except for high school when there was another but she was from Korea and my parents are from Vietnam. I was born here but my parents had to escape Vietnam when they were just married. I have an older brother and sister. I'm the youngest. My life's ambition is to help people like my mom and dad who came to this country with nothing and had to work themselves up. So I'm starting the club here at Fairmont University to do just that. We just started, and had our first meeting last week after the student association approved our membership. We have 15 people, and you don't have to be Asian, and it's called ASK, or Asian Student Kaleidoscope. We are going to help any person who needs help. Just ask ASK. We are offering study groups, help on writing papers, rides to the mall, anything. It's to give back. We have been blessed by the chance our parents never had. We need to pay it forward. So we've met and already we have had 20 students who have needed some assistance. Just yesterday, we took a student who is a freshman and arranged a ride for him to go home to see his family. They just live an hour away but they're kind of in the sticks and there's no way to get to there by bus or whatever so we just drove him home. I went, too. Once there, his mother greeted him and our club member at the door with tears. It was the most moving time of my life here at Fairmont. If I ever doubted that this was the right thing to do, seeing the mother made it all worth it. I'm a junior, majoring in pre-law. I wish I had started this sooner. It makes you a different person inside when you can help someone who really needs it."

CHAPTER 7

Using Quotations Well

IN THIS CHAPTER, YOU'LL LEARN:

- Whom to quote and how to quote them.
- Which quotes are the most effective.
- How to use quotes properly in sentence structure and story structure.
- Ways to keep quotes concise.
- Obvious and not-so-obvious forms of bias and deceit in quoting practices.

Our tendency is to use a lot of quotes. If we use them sparingly, they really have a punch, and more significance.
Tina Griego

AS A NEW PRESIDENTIAL CAMPAIGN WAS BEGINNING, *The Washington Post* built a story and a next-day political column out of a quote that, *The Post* emphasized, showed Democratic candidate Al Gore's tendency to exaggerate his accomplishments.

The Post quoted then-Vice President Gore as telling an audience of high school students that he had been responsible for bringing the environmental hazard at Love Canal in upstate New York to light. In 1978, homes in the area were evacuated after discovery that soil was contaminated by toxic waste containing the deadly chemical dioxin.

"I was the one that started it all," *The Post* quoted Gore in late 1999.

But *The Post* had one word wrong. And that wrong word so changed the meaning of Gore's statement that *The Post* had to correct two stories:

> A Dec. 1 article and Dec. 2 Politics column item about Vice President Gore's involvement in the Love Canal hazardous waste case quoted Gore as saying "I was the one that started it all," In fact, Gore said, "That was the one that started it all," referring to the congressional hearings on the subject that he called.

Compounding the error, the first story would have been quite different and the Politics-column item never would have been written had *The Post* quoted Gore correctly. One of the high school students was especially outraged. The vice president of the United States had answered students' questions about how they could become involved in making America a better place, the student lectured the journalists. Gore had used Love Canal (and another contaminated site in Toone, Tenn., which had been called to his attention by a high school student there) to show how citizen action could make a difference. What did *The Post* do with that? It presented a snarky political attack that had nothing to do with the issue that concerned the students. The student concluded that was a poor civics lesson for the students: The media will emphasize petty personal politics over serious policy issues.

This anecdote has been used by the Committee of Concerned Journalists in its workshops to show how bias creeps into news stories. The anecdote also illustrates how a news story can inflame public opinion against the press when something as common as quotations is handled poorly.

Accurate quotes from eyewitnesses and others in position to know add authority and credibility to your story. Colorful quotes brighten it. Quotes from multiple stakeholders add balance and fairness. Concise quotes make your story easier to read. Dialogue helps communicate motion, which draws readers deeper into your story.

Despite these advantages, experienced journalists disagree on much about quoting. Some use more quotes, others fewer. Some insist on quoting interview subjects grammatically. Others insist that all quotes be verbatim, flaws intact. Some prefer repetitive attribution, others sparer attribution. Some end most of their stories with quotes. Others try to find another conclusion as often as possible.

However, some practices are always sound, even if others find a different technique preferable. Some practices are rarely effective, but are regrettably common.

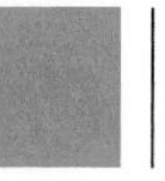

WHOM TO QUOTE

Quote momentous statements (often from speeches) from influential people. This is tomorrow's history.

Quote eyewitnesses. They add authenticity to your story and take readers to the scene.

Quote vivid conversations you have witnessed. Cross-examination, confrontations and other emotional exchanges make powerful dialogue.

Quote those in authority when they are candid and informative. Those in positions to know add credibility to your reporting, even when the truth of their comments is undetermined.

Quote other stakeholders—those with a stake in the outcome. Try to represent all points of view. Often there are more than two sides to a story.

Quote those who have been accused or criticized. In most cases, it's only fair that you seek them out for an opportunity to respond.

Quote those whose comments illustrate and emphasize key points.

Quote those who have the storytelling gift. They make your readers see. If they can make your readers laugh in good taste, that is precious.

Quote opinion and insight. Point of view requires attribution.

Use the fact, rather than the quote (or attribution) to state encyclopedic fact.

Use more precise and concise prose—or paraphrase—to avoid quoting bureaucrats about policy or governmental process. Choose your own words in favor of quoting anyone whose comments are dull, vague, inarticulate or unnecessarily long.

WHAT QUOTES TO USE

After writing just a few stories, you will begin to develop an ear for which quotes improve your stories and which interfere by slowing the story down or confusing readers.

So be selective. Use quotes that move the story forward. These quotes supplement the writer's prose. They answer, confirm or illustrate other content in the story. Quotes also enliven stories by adding voices that get readers' attention and keep them interested. These quotes can be commanding voices of authority, colloquial voices of natural storytellers or provocative voices of controversy. They can be full sentences or only a word or two.

Here are virtues of effective quotes:

- **Clear:** Good quotes follow the principles of good writing. They should be clear, concise and pointed. A muddled quote hurts a story. Readers have just as much

> **ADVANCED TIP**
> **Use Quotes Wisely**
>
> - Quotes should read as clearly as other sentences.
> - Quotes should propel the reader through the story.
> - Quotes should be authoritative, show someone's personality or surprise the reader.
> - Quotes should offer the reader a voice that differs from the writer.
> - Quotes should illuminate, not confuse. If they are difficult to read, paraphrase.
> - Quotes that are a part of a dialogue breathe life into stories.

The Art of Storytelling

Narrative storytellers prefer dialogue to other quotations.

Dialogue—the conversation between characters in your story—is spontaneous and more authentic-sounding than many speeches and carefully worded answers to reporters' questions.

Dialogue helps put readers at the scene.

Dialogue is part of the action—the motion that propels a narrative forward.

The unique ways characters speak and interact also assist character development in storytelling.

Despite all these advantages, dialogue is perhaps the most underused effective writing technique in American journalism.

Why? More reporting is required to witness or reconstruct dialogue than to interview someone in an office or by phone. Dialogue also is likely to take more column inches at a time when there are fewer inches to spare.

But this also is an era when journalists' credibility is challenged daily. Dialogue has the credibility of an eyewitness account.

In Chapter 5, reporter Roy Wenzel asserts that "one of the worst things we do is turn people into talking heads" by merely publishing their responses. He advocates dialogue as a way to show the action, rather than recite what happened.

Here are some of the countless ways you can incorporate riveting dialogue into your stories instead of more common quotes:

- **Trial Testimony:** Especially in cross-examination, when the lawyer-witness exchanges can get testy, the natural question-answer format often is best presented as dialogue. That might even take less space than using prose to explain the testimony context, followed by the witness's quote.
- **Top-of-Mind Stories:** When a news topic generates buzz in a community, discard the idea of droll, uninformed comments in "man-on-the-street" interviews. Instead, go to places where people gather publicly and listen. War talk at the neighborhood bar, barbershop or hair salon. Politics chatter in the square where federal workers gather for lunch. Sports talk at the mall. Health care concerns in the hospital cafeteria.
- **For Profiles and Other Celebrity Stories:** Follow them in the community. Capture the interaction with citizens, and the bystander chatter among the onlookers.
- **During Controversy at Public Meetings:** Try positioning yourself nearest the standing-room-only audience that is reacting to official comment, or arguing among themselves away from the podium.

- **On the Sidelines at Sporting Events:** Comments between teammates or players and coaches can capture emotion. They may reveal strategy valuable for postgame insight.
- **Among the Fans at Sporting Events:** Try sitting among them and listening to what's important to them. This could reveal sentiment about coaches and players, or it could show how these fans have weightier matters on their mind—the local economy, national foreign policy, health care.
- **In Classrooms:** Rather than thoughtful quotes from adults about education, the eager remarks from children might show what they are really learning. How refreshing.
- **In Strategy/Decision Sessions:** Access may be difficult, but if you can gain it, be a fly on the wall capturing the back-and-forth between decision makers. These can be elected officials, business executives, football coaches in a draft "war room," or citizens wrestling with a neighborhood concern.
- **On the Phone:** Any time you see the potential for narrative storytelling, find out if the people you interview can reconstruct pivotal conversations.

An Example

The following example is from the profile of a 60-year-old bounty hunter from California that ran in *The New Yorker* magazine. Notice how even the most insignificant dialogue adds to story's authenticity. Mackenzie Green, the bounty hunter, and her two assistants, Sergio Rosales and Bob Shandrew, come alive as they search an apartment complex looking for a man who has jumped bail.

> Green put her ear to the door and then kicked it, hard: "Open up!"
>
> A frightened female voice said, "Quien es?"
>
> "Policia!" Rosales shouted.
>
> The door was nudged open and a gray-haired woman peeked out, holding an infant. "We need to talk to Fernando!" Green said.
>
> "Quien?"
>
> "Rodrigo," clarified Rosales, who is accustomed to rectifying Green's misnomers. He showed the woman a Polaroid: "Rodrigo Hernandez." She looked mystified. As Rosales explained who they were, two toddlers appeared and stared at Shandrew's handcuffs. "She says we can look around inside, but she's never heard of him," Rosales said. "I think she's telling the truth."
>
> Green sighed, and Shandrew gave her an amused look. He favors patience, stakeouts, and visiting witnesses when you know they're at home, whereas Green sees stakeouts as a waste of time and relishes a blitzkrieg. She was still mad at

(continued)

Shandrew because when he visited Zabala's last known address he didn't rummage through the trash bags for leads.

"Let's talk to the manager," Green said. The crew trooped downstairs and rang the bell to apartment 103, which had "MANAGER" stenciled in red letters above the lintel. A sleepy woman with the impassive face of a Mayan sculpture eventually came to the door. Green showed her Hernandez's photograph and she shook her head. Green showed her Juan Zabala's photograph.

"He used to live here, oh yeah," the manager said. "With his wife." In concocting his fake address, Rodrigo Hernandez had unwisely borrowed from memory. "But they had so many relatives in the apartment I had to ask them to leave. Juan's wife's brother and his wife still live here"—she pointed across the hall. "The brother won't tell you anything, but his wife, Elizabeth, would. She doesn't like Juan because her husband had to put up some of his bail money."

Green's eyes flashed. The most common mistake fugitives make, aside from going home to their mother's house for Thanksgiving, is alienating a relative or a close friend. Bounty hunters sometimes call prospecting for this person "seeking out Judas." "What's your name?" Green asked, lowering her voice.

"Monica Perez," the woman said.

"Monica, there's a chunk of change in it if you can get a solid address out of Elizabeth," Shandrew said.

Perez nodded. "I'll talk to her tomorrow."

"But," Shandrew continued heavily, "if you were friends with Juan and had Elizabeth warn him, that would be aiding and abetting, and you'd go to jail."

"He was no friend of mine," Perez said.

Outside, Green gave Shandrew a high five. "It's so much fun to finally find that thread!" she exclaimed. "Yes!"

The dialogue, at times, was normal conversation one hears every day: what's your name, I'll talk to her tomorrow, yes. But even adding those—in small doses—to the scene gives the writing the ring of truth.

difficulty getting through a quote with bad syntax and grammar as they do other prose that has the same problems. *"I have no affinity for—and this of course is when it's served in butter—the vegetable broccoli, even though I know that a good number of people can and do think highly of the many dishes served with it."* This speaker meant: *"I hate broccoli, especially in butter, although others don't."* But she didn't say that, and there is no way to salvage any part of this quote without losing readers. Better to paraphrase this speaker.

- **Nonbureaucratic:** You aren't obligated to quote bureaucrats who use vague language. Ask yourself if their statements really add enough to justify the length of the quote. *"We're investigating the original allocation to see if we have the budget to alter the project regulating our municipal waste."* Often, a paraphrase in clearer, common language is the better option. *He said the council will see if the city has enough money to fix the sewers.*

- **Authoritative:** Sometimes reporters should quote a source just to back up the story's main point. Some stories make assertions that readers might question. The quote verifying the assertion settles this doubt, even if the quote is not vivid. *Mayor Bill Boyd broke his silence Tuesday, saying he was not running for governor. "I'm Herald's mayor today, and I'll be Herald's mayor after November," he said.*
- **Character:** Some speakers' colorful language makes great reading. *"I can't tell the difference between these Democrats or Republicans. They're like brown roosters and red roosters. Once you pluck the feathers off, they look just alike."*
- **Emotion:** Quotes that reveal a source's emotion appeal to readers. These quotes are especially powerful in narrative stories. *"I held out hope that he was still alive. But when I saw the officers standing at the front door, I just ran upstairs and pretended they weren't there. They never came. That way, I can still hope. Someday I'm going to see Trent again."*
- **Variety of Voice:** To pick the best quote, listen. Listen not only for clarity, but for rhythm that differs from your writing. These provide an effective change of pace that breaks monotony and keeps readers involved.

Look at the following example. In an interview, a person can give the reporter both facts that should be paraphrased or pithy statements that are best quoted directly.

> It doesn't work that way. If one member of the team has committed a crime of this nature, and at a party and where others have seen him, and he's possibly hurt, you know psychologically a woman maybe for the rest of her life, if she was raped, then it's important for the police to know. Someone needs to say something. They need to step forward, face the lights and the microphones and do the right thing.

Notice the first sentence is short and concise but it doesn't say much. It would be difficult for readers to understand the meaning unless the reporter put it in context. That probably would take too many words with too little payoff for the reader.

The second sentence has a lot of information but it is too wordy and awkward to follow easily. Therefore, it is a prime candidate for paraphrasing.

The last two sentences are quotable. They are clear, they show emotion and they get to the heart of the source's message.

The written story might read like this:

> Smith called on his players to quit protecting their teammate and say what happened during the party. If a player has raped someone, then his teammates should tell the police.

ADVANCED TIP

When to Paraphrase

Journalists often must decide if they should use a full quote or paraphrase their source. Quotes usually make stories livelier, but not if:

- The quote is confusing.
- The speaker uses academic or bureaucratic language.
- The speaker quotes encyclopedic facts.
- The quote is merely "Yes" or "No."

"Someone needs to say something," Smith said. "They need to step forward, face the lights and the microphones and do the right thing."

HOW TO QUOTE THEM

Quote speakers by name. Anonymous sources erode credibility.

Quote speakers by title. Better, add the credentials that give them standing to be quoted. These allow readers to decide what weight to assign to the speaker's words.

Examples:

Robert Smithson, a criminologist who has spent much of the last decade studying the effects of mass hysteria.

Jill McCracken, who discovered the body.

Shandra Collins, whose House district stands to gain the most federal aid if the bill becomes law.

If a title is long, it may be best to introduce the speaker by name and title in the paragraph before the quote. This will leave the content and rhythm of the quote undisturbed and give the quote more impact.

Christine McCaffey is the state Environmental Protection Agency's assistant director for regulation and enforcement. She has handled most of these cases for the EPA for the last nine years.

"Pollution of this sort is rare this far from a lake or river," she said. "This level of toxicity is unprecedented."

Usually, quote people in the past tense. Present tense indicates that the person is *still* saying this. Reporters seldom can be sure that a quote or the facts supporting it will remain unchanged by the time the quote is published.

For further clarity on the temporary nature of past-tense quotes, say when (*Riccardi said Tuesday*). Once is enough unless your story contains multiple time elements.

Quoting people in the past tense is always safer, but the risk of using present tense is small if quoting a long-held philosophy or opinion that is highly unlikely to change soon.

Examples:

"Pro-life advocacy compels opposition to abortion and the death penalty," the priest preaches.

"We will not soon see Winston Churchill's equal for public oratory," Wright says.

"For sheer power in America? J. Edgar Hoover and the 1927 Yankees," Farrell quips in the speech he makes twice a month.

Present tense is safest in the first two examples, because it is used to express a general point of view. Examine the statements by the priest and Wright without the quote marks. The point of view is likelier to persist than the precise quote.

Present-tense quotes also prevail when constructing a scene in present tense.

Usually, quote printed documents in the present tense. Their content remains in print. However, electronic documents can change more readily. Use past tense to quote a blog or other website entry, for instance.

Use neutral, verifiable words in attributing the quote: *said*, *asked*, *quipped*, *shouted*. "Noted" asserts that the statement is true. "Contended" or "claimed" introduces skepticism. "Believes" reveals a thought process—reporters know only what people *do*, or *say* they believe.

Avoid "refuted," a commonly misused attribution. Refuted indicates proof. The writer usually means "rebutted" which means to counter or argue against.

Quotes are spoken. Choose quote attributions that can be heard. Words such as "smiled," "grinned," "winced" and "grimaced" are physical expressions, not oral ones.

QUALITY TRUMPS QUANTITY

Most print journalists overquote. They quote too many speakers, and the quotes used are too long. This happens for sincere reasons.

We quote too many people to demonstrate the earnestness of our research and to include those whose time we have taken in interviews. We rely on others' words, even when longwinded and vague, rather than our own out of our desire to remain objective. We let imprecise speakers take paragraphs to conclude their point because there are worthwhile remarks among the chaff.

Conversely, broadcast journalists overrely on sound bites that capture the most vivid remarks at the expense of context. Politicians and others have learned that detailed explanations and complex issues are nonstarters on TV news stories. They have learned that a short, colorful response is more likely to earn them air time than a thoughtful answer.

Overreporting can be a virtue. Overwriting is not. When it is necessary to interview many people to learn the truth, focus your writing on the truth, not on the voices. Include only those speakers whose comments enlighten and illustrate the truth.

"Sometimes when we interview, we feel we have an obligation to them for taking their time, and including them even when what they said doesn't add anything," *Rocky Mountain News* writer Tina Griego said. "But our obligation is to readers, it's not about making our news sources feel good about seeing their names in the newspapers.

"It can be helpful to explain to the source: 'I'm not sure how this is going to come together. I'm still gathering information. A lot of this might be just for my information.' "

Quote or paraphrase? Griego has a simple test.

"If they speak in bureaucratic language, it's better to paraphrase. Any time they use jargon. When they sound human—surprise, anger—it's better to quote them."

When the scope of the story demands that many different stakeholders be heard, assist the many readers who are less familiar with the topic than you are. Try to organize the quotes by speaker. If you can complete the quotes of one speaker before moving onto the next, that is best. Failing to do so often forces readers to stop and then search earlier paragraphs to re-identify the speaker. If segregating speakers is not feasible, organize the quotes by subject, completing that thought before advancing the story.

Quoting a single speaker for several paragraphs at a time may be inevitable—and effective—in a one-source story (such as some of the shorter pieces in this book showcasing prominent journalists). Otherwise, be wary. Subconsciously, the reader demands change of pace to maintain interest. Quotes provide that change of pace to your prose, and vice versa.

"Our tendency is to use a lot of quotes," Griego said of writers in general. "If we use them sparingly, they really have a punch, and more significance."

Even so, Griego has an instinct about when to quote more.

"I will quote at length when it is important for a person to explain a philosophy in their own words—if it illuminates their way of thinking, a unique way of speaking, reveals their personality."

STRUCTURING QUOTES

The first words of your story should communicate significant meaning. They are best reserved to identify subject and actors. Therefore, it is rarely effective to begin a news story with a time element, static nouns and verbs like "It was" or quotations. Quotes work best after providing context.

Reader preference for the active voice applies to quotations, too. Make your quote attribution *Gonzalez said* rather than *said Gonzalez*. In conversation, how often do you hear "said I," "said she" or "said the grocer"? Deviating from familiar syntax causes readers to hesitate, when you want them to proceed smoothly to the next sentence.

The exception: When introducing a speaker who has a long title. A lengthy title puts too much distance between speaker and verb ("said") and too much of the sentence's load on a dependent clause. In such case, the passive attribution is the lesser of evils.

> Weaker: *"We'll give it two days, then time's up," John D'Angelo, interim captain of the New Constantine County Organized Crime Strike Force, said.*
>
> Better: *"We'll give it two days, then time's up," said John D'Angelo, interim captain of the New Constantine County Organized Crime Strike Force.*
>
> In this case, the quote might be more potent if it is set up by introducing the speaker first.
>
> *The interim captain of the New Constantine County Organized Crime Strike Force is losing patience with the negotiations.*
>
> *"We'll give it two days, then time's up," John D'Angelo said.*

Punctuation goes inside the closing quotation mark.

> *"Timothy had everything to live for," Robinson said.*
>
> *"Get him!" the police dog-handler commanded.*
>
> *"When will we stand up to this threat?" neighborhood block captain Ernst Bauer asked.*

This is true even with a series of quotes within a sentence—as when we wrote above: *Words like "smiled," "grinned," "winced" and "grimaced" are physical expressions, not oral ones.*

The exception occurs when the sentence is a question, but the quote is not—as when we wrote above: . . . *how often do you hear "said I," "said she" or "said the grocer"?*

Quotes within quotes are set off with single quotes.

"What part of 'no' don't you understand?" Szymanski challenged.

When it works best to quote a speaker for two or more consecutive paragraphs, begin each new paragraph with a quotation mark. However, leave the end quotation mark off all but the final paragraph of quote.

In prose, ellipses (. . .) suggest a dramatic pause, or a shift to a different time or place. But in quotations, ellipses indicate that something has been left out. Much too often, writers do not grasp the distinction and misuse ellipses to indicate a speaker's hesitation.

Ellipses can help a writer condense a long-winded quote with too much wind between nuggets of solid content. However, use this device sparingly and beware of the risk.

"As a reader, I always wonder what isn't there," the *Rocky Mountain News*' Griego said. "So I try not to use them because I know how I react to them as a reader."

To deliver the dramatic pause in a quote, divide it into two parts.

"Give me liberty," the patriot Patrick Henry proclaimed, "or give me death."

In a long quote, this technique also helps identify the speaker more swiftly.

When a lengthy quote has only a kernel of value, a concise quote fragment may work better than ellipses.

WIRED AND WIRELESS | QUOTES CAN BE DECEITFUL

More extreme forms of deceit have grown disturbingly common in recent years.

News reporters, feature writers and columnists have been fired for inventing quotes and the supposed speakers. Others have been fired for failing to attribute the source of the material in their stories, thus presenting the work of other journalists as their own.

In early 2006, Thomas Warhover, executive editor of the *Columbia Missourian* and an associate professor of journalism at the University of Missouri, said he fails a student or two each term for lifting published material, including quotes, from the Internet and inserting it, unattributed, into their own stories.

That's plagiarism. In most places, that offense warrants firing, expulsion or a failing grade on its first commission. Even the freshest rookie journalist is expected to know better. Even the most decorated veteran can be fired when one act of plagiarism outweighs decades of award-winning accomplishment.

Aside from plagiarism as an act of theft, it undermines accuracy. In numerous cases, the material plagiarized was inaccurate—even defamatory—to begin with. Lifting the material without verification, then spreading its falsity, compounds the felony.

Do your own work.

In a story contrasting views about how much of New Orleans should be rebuilt following Hurricane Katrina, the *Los Angeles Times*' Peter H. King wrote this paragraph:

> *They warned against what some of them termed "the bulldozer approach," challenging any notion that health and environmental concerns, not to mention the sheer logistics involved, demand a more rapid reconstruction.*

"When most of us speak we meander," Griego observed. "This is a good way to keep it tight. This is a way to keep the heart of the quote and its meaning clear."

When introducing a quote with prose, take special care that your words and the speaker's complement each other. Readers and good writers have a pet peeve: The transition and subsequent quote that are redundant. This is always unnecessary. Delete one.

ETHICAL QUOTING

Accurate, insightful, eyewitness quotations are allies of the news story's delivery of credible fact and pursuit of truth. Used improperly, quotes are agents of deceit and inappropriate bias.

Always take care to preserve the speaker's meaning. When writers are careless with context, quote fragments or paraphrasing, they falsify the message, even if the phrases are quoted accurately.

Similarly, keep your words out of other speakers' mouths. If you ask a source whether he agrees with a statement, you do not have license to say the source made that statement. Sound obvious? This is a common error. Instead, report, for instance, *the university chancellor* <u>*said he agreed*</u> *that tuition increases had helped lower enrollment by out-of-state students.*

Increasingly, print publications are insisting on verbatim quoting, even if the quote makes the speaker look uneducated.

Editors disagree on this.

One philosophy maintains that printing ungrammatical quotes embarrasses the speaker unnecessarily and does nothing to help readers with *their* command of proper English. If the slip, especially in spontaneous remarks, is minor—say, subject-verb agreement—some organizations permit the writer to "clean up" that quote and present it grammatically.

Others complain that this standard is applied inconsistently. The college president, city council member or business executive may get this benefit of the doubt, while the factory worker, crime-scene bystander or hip-hop teenager's grammar, slang, dialect and street vernacular are quoted verbatim.

More fundamentally, *Denver Post* Editor Greg Moore said, it's a matter of authenticity. *The Post* has adopted this written policy:

> The words of our sources and the people we cover must never be altered. Quote marks are intended to bracket the true voices and exact words of people. If a reporter or editor is concerned that ungrammatical or clumsily worded remarks may

expose the source to embarrassment or ridicule, then they may agree to use another quote from that person conveying the same or a similar point, or they may agree to paraphrase the source.

If it was ever appropriate, the practice of "cleaning up" quotes is out of date, Moore said.

"We live in a world where people are using tape recorders, digital devices and cameras," he said. Not only does this make it easier for the reporter to get the quote verbatim, readers who watch television news and Internet video feeds know the difference.

Moore offered the example of a former professional football player who is an analyst on network TV pregame shows.

"Shannon Sharpe stomps all over the English language and you're watching him do it. So to have him speak the King's English in *The Post* is not an accurate reflection of who Shannon Sharpe is. To clean up his language and have him speak as if he's a Nobel Prize winner is just not right."

Quotations are involved in more subtle forms of deceit.

Fair-minded journalists prefer to let all interested parties have their say. But do not be party to a lie. Do not quote what you know is untrue, unless it is important to show that the person is lying or uninformed—and you are prepared to prove it, immediately.

Balance, generally a virtue in a news story, is not always accurate if balance means giving equal weight to all sides. In some controversies—for instance, scientists debating intelligent design or global warming—opinion is not evenly divided. In an attempt to be fair, a reporter might give each side the same number of quotes. But without other prose describing the preponderance of opinion, the story may inaccurately describe the state of the controversy and the truth as it is currently understood.

Finally, there is the matter of The Last Word.

Although quality journalists apply an objective process—principally through thoroughness and fairness—subjective judgments are made at every stage of a story. Among those judgments is who will be quoted, for how long, and at what point in the story.

Quotations are overused as ways to end news stories. Often, this will provoke no controversy. However, when the story itself showcases divided opinion, giving the final word to one side may reflect an inappropriate bias in favor of that view, or that person. Beware. (And read more on ways to end news stories in Chapter 17 of this book.)

IN CONCLUSION

Although preferences vary, there are some always-acceptable methods for quoting and some methods that are never effective.

Effective quotes mirror effective writing: They are clear, interesting and add information.

Good intentions can produce bad results. Quoting everyone can overburden a story. Quoting all sides equally can put a story out of balance.

Quoting accurately is vital. Quoting inaccurately undermines journalistic credibility. Quoting fraudulently is a firing offense.

Deciding whom to quote, how often, how soon and who gets the last word are subjective judgments. Take care that they do not betray inappropriate bias.

Dialogue is an underused writing technique. Ending stories with quotes is an overused technique.

EXERCISE 1

Pick out the best quotes from the following:

Interview with Freeman Lyons, vice president for student affairs, Tully University:

"This is a new program we've just decided to start this year. Because the Onondaga Nation is just 10 miles away, we've decided to pick 40 Native American students this year and offer them a full scholarship. There's nothing else like this. This program shows that Tully believes Native Americans have suffered too long and universities have an obligation to help improve their lives. Education is a key part. This will give them the chance to better themselves. One of the ways this program will work is through the clan mothers. They will work with counselors at the high school and help us choose the students. They can major in whatever they want and they can live wherever they want. Most students so far have chosen to live in the dorms with others. We are astounded at the response, overwhelmed, pleased, surprised, warmed. It is truly heart touching to see the students accept the offer and arrive with energy of youth and wisdom of an ancient people. So get back with us soon to see how the program is developing.

EXERCISE 2

Pick out the best quotes from the following:

Interview with Carolyn Ann Brown, director of public safety, Tillman-Weeks College:

"We are asking the entire university community to be on the lookout for a person who is sneaking into professors' offices and stealing their belongings during work hours. This student is a male, about 25 years old but looks younger. In fact, he looks just like a student. He acts just like a student. When classes change, he blends in just like a student. We simply can't catch him. So far he's stolen, and let me get this clear, he's stolen several cell phones and purses but no laptops. They seem too bulky. It's odd. Professors leave their doors open to go down the hall to check their mail. When they return, their stuff is gone. How do we know it's a male? Well, we have a surveillance tape and we have a picture of him. He's been slippery though. We know what he looks like but we just can't seem to set the right trap. Well, he's hit several buildings but he really seems to like the A. M. Rothchild School of Human Services. Most professors there are women, and he seems to target women for their purses. He's preying on those who are trusting. We can't let him continue.

EXERCISE 3

Write a story from the following:

Interview with William Everest speaking to a class at Elmwood University.

"As publisher of the *Lake Mountain Times*, I'm sure you know that these are not great times for newspapers. But don't let that fool you. For one, no mass medium has ever gone out of business. It simply changed its focus or found a new audience. Take radio, for instance. When television came into being and took away its programming and advertisers, radio just became something you listened to in your car commuting to work. And so you had drive time and Top-40 and suddenly, radio was vital again. Same thing with newspapers. The world will always need journalists. We'll always need someone to go out and cover events we can't get to or see for ourselves. Now most people get hung up on if we'll keep printing on paper. Well, if you're honest, paper is portable and useful, but it is inefficient and in some ways, environmentally unsound, you know, the way it's made and all that. So what if we move to the Internet and go online? Did you know that the most-visited web sites of any community are the newspaper's. No contest. People still want news, and they want news given to them by professionals, and they want the news in an impartial way. They might like blogs, and people who give them the news with a political opinion in mind, especially if that opinion agrees with their own view of the world. But you can't rely on them to be accurate or impartial. If something doesn't agree with their viewpoint, they won't put it on their blog. They'll conveniently forget to tell you about it. But a professional newspaper reporter will give it to you straight, no matter if they like the information or hate the information. That's their job. Tell it like it is, and then let you make up your mind. That's a commodity that will still be needed 100 years from now."

CHAPTER 8

Writing News about Crime

IN THIS CHAPTER YOU WILL LEARN:

- Why crime stories are so popular.
- Crime story essentials.
- Accident story essentials.
- Fire story essentials.
- How to handle sensitive identification of victims and suspects.

The sources who paid off when I needed it—I didn't have a phone relationship with those sources.
Michael Connelly

WHY CRIME STORIES ARE SO POPULAR

When surveyed, readers and viewers consistently say there is too much bad news, citing crime as the leading example. Then they admit they read and watch the crime news more than most other content.

The evidence suggests they cannot get enough of crime stories.

The maxim, "If it bleeds, it leads," still is widely practiced on local television news. Ratings for the televised O. J. Simpson murder trial encouraged some national cable stations to push aside other programming for weeks. Its influence is still seen today on television courtroom dramas and police shows featuring crime-scene detectives. Online, where breaking news rules, crime stories regularly are among the best read on the websites of print and broadcast news organizations.

Network and cable television offer more than 60 hours a day of crime stories. Shows such as *CSI*, *The Closer* and *Law & Order* fetch top ratings. Reruns of *NYPD Blue* and many other crime series are on at almost every hour of every day. Cerebral British mysteries featuring Sherlock Holmes, Agatha Christie's sleuths and others are among the Public Broadcasting System's most popular shows in the United States.

Typically, crime novels dominate the best-sellers lists.

Some disdainful analysts see this as lowest-common-denominator behavior by media and citizens. However, crime stories reveal fundamental truths about news and news consumers. Sudden and dramatic, crime stories are news in the extreme. These are matters of life and death. Like disasters and war, crime stories compel readers with urgency too often absent in daily stories about such coverage staples as government and religion.

Montgomery County police chief Charles Moose briefs the media at police headquarters in Rockville, MD, confirming that the sniper shooting of a bus driver the day before in Aspen Hill is linked to the sniper shootings in greater Washington over the past three weeks.

CRIME IS A PERSONAL STORY

Many readers have been crime victims. Almost everyone knows a relative, neighbor, coworker or close friend who has been burglarized, robbed, raped or otherwise victimized. Readers can see themselves in the misfortunes of strangers, can feel the terror of some crime victims and admire the courage of others.

When a serial criminal continues to rape, murder or rob banks, readers worry: It could happen to me next. Seldom has this been more vivid than during the sniper shootings that killed 10 and wounded three others in Washington, D.C., and nearby areas of Maryland and Virginia. The October 2002 shootings induced widespread fear

ADVANCED TIP

Criminal Justice Timeline (State Felonies)

Arrest

Jail (bail possible)

Charge—by grand jury or district attorney

Arraignment before judge or magistrate—defendant's plea (bail possible)

Pretrial hearing(s)

Trial in state court—defendant chooses jury or judge for guilt phase

If conviction, defendant chooses jury or judge for penalty phase

Formal sentencing by judge (if first conviction, probation possible)

Probation or prison

Convict may elect one or more appeals

- First to state court of appeals
- Then to state Supreme Court
- Then to U.S. Supreme Court

Parole from prison possible for some crimes

as victims with nothing in common were shot down during their normal lives—a 72-year-old man walking on a street in Washington, a 47-year-old woman outside a Home Depot in Virginia, a 13-year-old arriving at his middle school in Maryland, a commuter bus driver on the job in a second Maryland county. The snipers killed five on Oct. 3 alone. The Oct. 24 arrests of 41-year-old John Allen Muhammad and 17-year old Lee Boyd Malvo finally eased three weeks of terror.

Ultimately, crime stories can arouse citizens to action. Readers sharing their community's outrage can participate in efforts to assist victims and make their communities safer.

CRIME IS A PEOPLE STORY

Crime creates authentic theater with a cast of dramatic characters. Victims, perpetrators, witnesses, investigators, lawyers, judges and juries hold power over human life—imprisonment or liberty, life or death. These are heroes and villains, often scarred and tragic figures. Their stories are among the most riveting any journalist will tell.

"Listen to the pain and let it teach you," *Los Angeles Times* reporter Jill Leovy says of her interviews with the families of murder victims in South Central Los Angeles. "Only when I stopped trying to orchestrate my reporting did I get the best material. I stopped asking questions; I let people talk . . .

"Grief proved to be a gateway to broader topics, from the mechanics of the urban gang culture to the institutional problems with police and emergency services. I learned to be quiet, to listen, and to see the power of trauma to enlighten."

Leovy's comments come from *Best Newspaper Writing 2004*, which showcased her uncommonly perceptive "Mortal Wounds" series on the families and communities devastated by epidemic homicide.

CRIME IS A COMMUNITY STORY

Almost everywhere in America, citizens consistently rate crime and public safety as the number one or number two problems facing their communities. Poor neighborhoods despair of the crime that surrounds them. Rich neighborhoods fear the invasion of their safer spaces.

This is reason enough to report thoroughly and thoughtfully on crime.

Another: Citizens take greater responsibility for their neighborhoods' safety. When coauthor Glenn Guzzo oversaw the Neighbors sections at *The Philadelphia Inquirer* in the early 1980s, the comprehensive coverage of crime in those community-news sections—all felonies, fires, and unusually interesting misdemeanors—prompted a typical citizen response: new Neighborhood Watch programs supported by police.

Alert reporters understand that while the crimes themselves make fascinating stories, other coverage should be focused on crime prevention. In this way, news coverage offsets the bad news with coverage that helps citizens overcome their fear and despair.

CRIME IS A TREND STORY

The most powerful crime stories are those told through people, but numbers help tell these tales.

Annual FBI statistics, compiled from the reports of individual police agencies, show which crimes are increasing and decreasing, locally and nationally. These numbers put individual crimes into context. They are springboards to stories about the cause of recent crime trends and what local law enforcement is doing to combat specific crimes.

Be alert to trends in criminal prosecution. Are prosecutors accepting more or fewer plea bargains for certain crimes? Are they seeking longer sentences for some crimes? Are the sentences delivered by juries and judges becoming harsher? Why?

CRIME IS A POLITICAL STORY

Many judges and prosecutors are elected to office.

Political analysts have an axiom: "No politician ever lost an election by being too tough on crime." That's only a slight exaggeration. Once elected, mayors and city councils are accountable for the actions of the police departments they oversee. But they also derive some of their more forceful power from that oversight.

CRIME NEVER CEASES TO AMAZE

As the Washington Beltway snipers story shows, the extreme nature of crime often demonstrates that truth is stranger than fiction.

Crime reporter-turned-best-selling novelist Michael Connelly emphasized that in an interview with the Mystery Guild book club:

"There were lots of weird little crimes that I wrote about that seemed like the stuff of fiction but really weren't because if presented as fiction they would have smacked of being unbelievable.

"My first novel was based on an intricate heist that actually occurred in Los Angeles. As a reporter I had the details of how the crime was committed and used them

The Art of Storytelling

How obvious can it be that crime stories lend themselves naturally to the suspense of great narrative writing? Undoubtedly, more mayhem rampages in novels and screenplays each year than in America's streets.

And yet, because truth is stranger than fiction, the most compelling stories may be in your local county courthouse.

> The 21-year-old Air Force employee in Texas reported his live-in, go-go dancer girlfriend missing. But when her body was found, hack-sawed in half at the waist and dumped in separate crates at a local landfill, the airman was swiftly arrested. The crates were lined with newspapers from the airman's Indiana hometown. The girlfriend had been killed on a Friday. Friends say they attended a party at the airman's apartment that night—unbeknownst to them, apparently the body was in a closet at the time. While awaiting trial, the airman was confined at an Air Force base with a psychiatric unit. At the base, the airman and another psychiatric patient attended a movie together—*The Texas Chainsaw Massacre.*
>
> * * *
>
> The wife on trial for killing her husband testified that she had been terrorized by his extreme sexual desires. In graphic detail, she described how it took increasingly bizarre, and violent, behavior to gratify him. Finally she shot him in what she said was self-defense. The defense attorney called the case "The .44-caliber divorce."
>
> * * *
>
> The mother of a young man facing an armed-robbery charge pleaded with his accomplice-friend not to testify against her son next week. Then she changed tactics. She gave him a Coke. It was poisoned. When that did not kill him, she attacked him with an axe multiple times. He was still breathing, and struggling to get away. So she fired a bullet from a powerful handgun into his head. That finished the job.
>
> * * *
>
> While in jail for armed robbery, the teenager vowed that, next time, there would be no eyewitnesses. Soon after his release, he held up a convenience store and ordered the lone clerk into a corner. When she was shot dead, the clerk was pregnant. From the position of the body, prosecutors said, it was clear that she also had been facing her killer and praying, perhaps pleading, for two lives. The killer was caught anyway. At age 18, he was the youngest ever in his state to be sentenced to death.
>
> * * *
>
> The multi-millionaire oil man faced the death penalty in the death of his 12-year-old step-daughter, the first to die in a night of shootings that left two dead and two others near death at a $6-million mansion. Claiming innocence despite three

surviving eyewitnesses, the millionaire hired the best lawyers to attack the credibility of the accusers. The lawyers presented dozens of witnesses, including drug dealers, a professional motorcycle racer and a self-proclaimed witch. The medical examiner arrived for testimony with blood stains on the pant legs of his gray suit. One defense witness was an eyewitness to a controversial scene. This was somewhat undermined by the fact that he had only one eye. He testified while dressed in an iridescent suit and, when asked the color of his pickup, said it was "every color" because of all the vehicles he had hit.

* * *

Most of these plots and characters would be rejected as implausible if they didn't happen to be authentic. All of these stories, and many others nearly as sensational, unraveled within a few years while the coauthors of this textbook were reporters in Fort Worth, Texas.

The characters and plots for narrative crime stories dwell in many places.

Los Angeles Times writer Jill Leovy walks the neighborhoods where criminals win more than they lose. She interviews those with the internal wounds.

"Listen to the pain and let it teach you," she counsels other reporters.

Crime novelist Michael Connelly finds material in cold-case files and the long memories of investigators who refuse to forgive and forget.

"It's like time travel," he suggests.

By all means, get your fingernails dirty in the streets and rummage in the dusty file cabinets. But reporters seldom find a tidier package of narrative elements than in a criminal trial.

Here we find evil and innocence, tragic victims and scarred survivors. Sometimes, we even find heroes.

Some of them even tell their stories under oath. The needs of the law and the jury are the needs of the reporter. Tell us what you saw, the lawyers ask the witnesses. Tell us what you heard. Where were you? How can you be sure? What happened next? And after that?

In short order, we have eyewitness testimony, dialogue and chronology in an evolving drama with authentic characters at the defining moments in their lives and deaths. Witnesses gesture and grimace, whisper and shout, plead and cry.

"It's human nature with all its pretenses stripped away," Chicago Judge Michael Bolan says in a story by *Chicago Tribune* reporter Linnet Myers. "Headquarters for tales from the dark side."

Some reporters watch and listen. The storyteller sees and hears. Then lets readers use their senses:

(continued)

Millionaire Thomas Cullen Davis flashed five fingers three times and calmly ordered the deaths of 15 people, the key prosecution witness at Davis' murder-for-hire trial testified Friday.

—*The Associated Press* writer Mike Cochran

Tap. Tap. Tap. Tap. Pause. Tap. Tap. Tap. Ashley Lewis hit the counter of the oak witness box with his index finger, mimicking what he heard through a crack in the bathroom window.

—*Savannah Morning News* writer Leonora LaPeter, on the gun shots that killed four people in Georgia

in the novel. When the book was reviewed by *The Washington Post* it received a very positive critique. But the one rub for the reviewer was that the heist seemed too farfetched to be real. The fact that it was the only thing in the book that *was* real was a good lesson to learn at that early stage in my career."

When there are no tragic victims, a reporter's lighter touch can turn crime stories into humor.

Everyone got a laugh at the would-be bank robber who was caught because he signed the note demanding money from the teller.

Years ago in Lincoln Park, Mich., a man set out to rob a chain restaurant and demonstrated his seriousness by firing two shots into the air. A patron who realized the robber had just emptied his shotgun rallied the other customers to jump the man, beat him silly and hold him for police.

A man arrested for drunk driving in Fort Worth, Texas, won in court despite the arresting officer's testimony that the driver could not walk a straight line, had soiled his pants and had bloodshot eyes—both of them. In court, the accused proved he had a wooden leg, a colostomy bag, and a glass eye, which he removed and set on the judge's bench. Case dismissed.

CRIME IS AN ENTERPRISE STORY

A trend story about a crime wave, effective crime-fighting or sentencing is one form of enterprise reporting.

Another is revisiting unsolved cold cases. For victims' families, these stories renew hope that new interest in the case will help catch a killer. For investigators, the public attention may produce new leads. For readers, the unsolved mystery is a fascinating puzzle. For reporters, these stories are rich in possibilities.

Connelly selected several unsolved-murder stories for his book *Crime Beat*, a compilation from his 14 years as a newspaper reporter. In an interview for this textbook, Connelly first referred to the practice of revisiting old cases as "a journalism gimmick—when things are slow, pick a date 10 years old, or 20 years old, whatever."

But he quickly cited the merits of these stories:

"A—you find good stories. And B—cops and prosecutors, even the family, are able to open up and talk so much more after the heat is off.

"You also end up revisiting the cop, the neighborhood, the city. The passage of time offers hindsight about the sociology of the city. You add the technological advancement to crime-solving. And now there are new levels of the story. It's like time travel. Los Angeles in '94. Compare it to 2006.

"As a writer of fiction, it's a tremendously cool tool to use. You can apply that to non-fiction. Those were some of the best stories—the best experiences—I had."

The consequences of crime and the power of police present numerous opportunities for investigative reporting. In the past four decades, more than a dozen Pulitzer Prizes have been awarded for stories unveiling police corruption and abuse of power, exposing the flaws in unjust convictions and more.

CRIME STORY ESSENTIALS

The crime beat consists of covering violent crime and more:

- **Felonies:** the crimes for which someone can be sent to state or federal prison.
- **Misdemeanors:** lower-level crimes usually punishable by 90-day or shorter terms in local jails and/or fines.
- **Traffic accidents:** and sometimes other accidents, that result in death or serious injury.
- **Fires:** both arsons and accidental fires.

These stories are incidents. Crime-beat reporters also follow the investigations leading to arrests. Typically, especially at larger newspapers, other reporters cover the prosecution of those suspects—the work of the local district attorney and the results in the courtroom.

The crime-beat reporter may also have responsibility for covering the police administration. This could involve crime-fighting policies and internal-affairs investigations into possible discipline of officers. More often, it would involve budgets, labor issues, and politics.

ADVANCE TIP

Knowing Your Way around Court

Rules vary by state, but here are some typical differences between criminal and civil trials and other things to remember in court.

Court	*Criminal*	*Civil*
Jury size	12 for felonies, 12 or 6 for misdemeanors	12 or 6
Verdicts	must be unanimous	may be 10-2 or 9-3
Finding	"beyond a reasonable doubt"	by "preponderance of the evidence"

Language

Motions are Granted or Denied
Objections are Sustained or Overruled
Verdicts (when appealed) are Upheld or Overturned

WRITING THE INCIDENT STORY

Incident stories may be reported from interviews, written police reports, or both. Written incident reports are required for each police action and they are public records. Reporters and all others are entitled to read these reports at the police station on demand during the normal business hours of the building where the records are kept. Subsequent investigative reports may not be public records unless they are made part of a court record.

As breaking news, incident stories may be written with an inverted-pyramid lead, an alternative lead or as a narrative. In each case, some general principles apply:

- With rare exceptions, give more weight to loss of human life than to loss of animal life or property damage. Report those killed first, those injured second. *Example: Four people were killed and three more seriously injured in a fire that destroyed the popular Oblivion night club on the city's South Side Friday.*
- Because most incidents involve people not widely known in the community, their identities likely will be secondary to the incident itself and more revealing identifiers (such as the suspect or victim's age).
- Because suspect and victim names can be similar or identical to others uninvolved in the crime, identities must be as thorough as necessary to leave no doubt. Complete names, ages and residence addresses usually suffice. Other identifiers may be appropriate description, though under some conditions they are not (see page 139 for those guidelines).
- Because the criminal or suicidal mind confounds most of us, when motive is known it deserves prominent position in the story.
- Remember that often much is unclear on the first day of a crime story and may not be determined until a trial. Words such as "murder" are legal findings. In the first-day crime story, it's a "shooting death," "stabbing death" or "strangulation death," not murder.
- Suspects are first arrested, then jailed, then formally charged with the crime—at which time they may be freed on bond, a payment that will be forfeited if the suspect does not show up at court proceedings. In many locales, charges are leveled by a grand jury—a group of citizens appointed temporarily to decide whether enough evidence exists to warrant a trial.
- Remember that in the American justice system, someone arrested or charged with a crime is presumed innocent until found guilty by a judge or jury. News accounts do not assign guilt until such a verdict. Instead, make sure to report that the person is a suspect or defendant. The person is "accused of . . . ," "charged with . . . ," "held on charges of . . ." or has been "arrested in the shooting. . . ."
- Careful attribution is essential, but overly repetitive attributions such as "police said" can overburden a story. Look for opportunities to attribute long passages of detail with a single introductory phrase, such as "Police gave this account":

Crime and motive appear more prominently than the suspect's name in the following news stories. Note how the writers handled identifications.

By Nicole Fuller
The Baltimore Sun

A Prince George's County man who authorities say was planning to attack an abortion clinic was arrested on charges of manufacturing an explosive device, a pipe bomb that police detonated in a friend's house after trying to disable it.

Robert F. Weiler Jr., 25, who had a loaded gun at the time of his arrest, surrendered to police early yesterday at a Garrett County highway rest stop, authorities said.

Weiler was charged with possessing an illegal explosive device, making an illegal explosive device, illegally possessing a firearm with a previous felony conviction and possessing a stolen firearm.

Police said that the target was a College Park abortion clinic and doctors who perform the procedures.

The bomb—made with black powder, galvanized pipe, nails, seven feet of fuse and one-inch-diameter end caps—was discovered in the closet of a friend's home in Riverdale and detonated about 3:30 a.m., after Prince George's police bomb technicians were unable to disable it using a robot, said Mike Campbell, a spokesman for the federal Bureau of Alcohol, Tobacco, Firearms and Explosives.

The house was damaged and caught fire, but no one was injured, police said.

Weiler, of the 3200 block of Maygreen Ave. in Forestville, was ordered held without bail at the Garrett County Detention Center pending a hearing in U.S. District Court in Greenbelt on the four charges.

Note that Fuller's story about a man not widely known first identifies him by his better-known hometown and the newsworthy event. Identification by name waits until the second paragraph, but it is usually necessary by then after this type of lead. Ultimately, the arrested man is identified by name, age and address.

The story carries careful attribution. All but two paragraphs are specifically attributed to police or even more specifically to a law-enforcement officer. The remaining two paragraphs are separately verifiable fact from the judicial process—charges and whether the suspect is jailed or free on bond.

Similarly, although the accusations against the arrested man are detailed, the presumption of innocence is intact. He's a "man who authorities say" was involved in illegal activity. He "was charged with" the crimes listed. He will have a future court date.

Nonetheless, the story spares no description. It contains precise times and locations. Identities are clear. It communicates possible motive through reported detail, not speculation—"police said the target was a College Park abortion clinic and doctors who perform the procedures."

In sum, this story covers Who, What, When, Where, Why and How in the span of four paragraphs. Each adds detail and context. The story concludes with three more paragraphs that offer additional detail for those interested in more.

This story is told in inverted-pyramid form, but the story shows as well as tells—the rest-stop arrest, the loaded gun, the bomb ingredients, its detonation and the damaged home. These are elements a writer of narrative journalism would investigate further, adding dialogue and chronology to keep the action and the story moving.

Identifying a little-known victim early can be an essential part of telling a story in narrative form. Doing so in the following story signals the reader that the victim is an important character helping to tell the story.

By Kathy Jefcoats
The Atlanta Journal-Constitution

Alexis Norals was sitting in traffic in Stockbridge Thursday afternoon when a bleeding man opened the passenger door and jumped inside her car.

"He was screaming at me to drive, just go," Norals said. "I was screaming, 'What are you doing? Get out of my car!'

Norals didn't know a crime spree was about to end inside her 1997 Oldsmobile Cutlass.

Authorities said two men snatched an item from a clerk at Fancy That Fine Jewelry store on Hudson Bridge Road in Henry County about 4:30 p.m., then drove north on I-75. Henry sheriff's deputy Jeff Poole spotted the car and gave chase.

The men got off the interstate after five miles at Ga. 138 in Clayton County, but the car hit an embankment. The men jumped from the still-running vehicle. One ran into the woods behind Lowe's. The other man, bleeding and unarmed, jumped into Norals' car and started screaming.

That didn't last long. A hand holding a pistol thrust inside the open car window.

"I said, 'Please don't shoot me!' " Norals said.

Lucky for her, the handgun belonged to Poole, the deputy, who pulled the man out of the Cutlass and subdued him with pepper spray, said Henry County Sheriff Maj. Keith McBrayer.

Said Norals, "I just freaked out from there."

Police identified the man as Alfred William Hardy, 22, of College Park. The state corrections department website said he was released a month ago after serving almost four years of a five-year Gwinnett County sentence for robbery by intimidation. He now faces a host of new charges, including armed robbery.

The man who ran into the woods has not been identified. Norals, who recently moved to Georgia, said she'd just left a job interview.

"I just moved here," she said, "but I think I'm gonna go back to Mississippi."

Note the point of view in the narrative: Norals' eyewitness experience rather than the distant third-person voice of a formal police report. Readers can imagine themselves in Norals' place and the story's attention to detail propels the story forward. The writer is telling a story, not merely reciting from a document.

IDENTITY ISSUES

Identifying suspects and victims presents some of the most sensitive issues for journalists. Most widely practiced guidelines seek to protect innocent victims. The guidelines are much more likely to be the customs of news organizations rather than laws dictating journalistic behavior.

VICTIMS. News accounts generally withhold the names of victims of sexual assault. Sexual assault is an act of violence, not sex, but the misperception is still a stigma

HOW TO
Avoid Rookie Mistakes

Reporting experience matters in criminal justice more than most beats. It takes time to learn the important provisions in your state's penal code (penal codes differ significantly from state to state) and the local customs of police, prosecutors and judges. Until you do, you can be misled easily.

* * *

Beware of "echo" sources in law enforcement. Before attributing information to "several police sources" make sure to test their knowledge. Is each of these officers investigating the case, or are some of them merely repeating what they have heard in the hall?

* * *

Not all grand jury testimony is secret. The lawyers and grand jurors are bound to secrecy, but witnesses can discuss their own testimony, including what questions they were asked. The latter can be extraordinarily useful to reporters seeking to know more about high-profile cases.

* * *

Before announcing their verdicts, many juries decide among themselves not to discuss their deliberations with reporters. This agreement seldom holds up. Typically one or more jurors speak when asked. Then, others will join the discussion.

* * *

Following convictions, "motions for a new trial" seldom are newsworthy. These motions are procedural. By law, convicts must be denied a new trial before they can appeal to a higher court. They earn a new trial only if new evidence not available at trial has come to light. New evidence important enough to suggest a different verdict almost never occurs in the short time the lawyers have to make their motion.

* * *

Juries never find a defendant "innocent." The term is "not guilty"—literally that the prosecution did not prove its case up to the legal standard. Many news reports will use "innocent" nonetheless—not in ignorance, but in an abundance of caution over fear that the word "not" in "not guilty" will drop out of copy (it has been known to do so). When possible, try to use "acquit" as your verb and "acquittal" as your noun.

that many victims prefer to avoid. Unless the victim consents to be identified—some do to underscore that victims ought to be angry, not ashamed—almost all news organizations withhold names.

Journalists also won't publish names when identifying victims would jeopardize their safety. This can be as extreme as a life at risk. It can be as routine as not using the name or address of a victim whose car was stolen away from home—the thief may have the victim's house key, too.

SUSPECTS. Many news accounts withhold identities of juvenile suspects unless the justice system chooses to charge them as adults. Some news organizations make other exceptions, such as violent incidents causing death or incidents involving deliberate shootings.

Other suspect identifiers can create third-party victims. Journalists generally avoid these practices:

- **Specific Residence Addresses:** Suspects may not live alone. They may live in rental units with the same address as uninvolved citizens. It's best to cite addresses this way: "The 2700 block of Station Avenue" rather than "2713 Station Ave." Victim residential addresses should be similarly general. Business addresses should be precise.
- **Specific Employers:** If arrested burglar John Doe is a car mechanic, his occupation and company name may be irrelevant. If he used his mechanic's tools to enter houses, then his occupation is relevant, but his employer may not be. If all the victims had their cars in for repair at John Doe's shop, then the employer company would be relevant.
- **Race/Ethnicity:** Unless race is central to the crime (e.g., race riots, hate crimes), a suspect or victim's race is irrelevant. However, in detailed descriptions of criminals on the loose, race can be an important identifier. The key is that race is helpful only when

Talent Showcase

MICHAEL CONNELLY ▸

Best-selling Crime Novelist

Former crime reporter: *Los Angeles Times*, *South Florida Sun-Sentinel* and *Daytona Beach News-Journal*

In the digital world, Michael Connelly urges crime reporters to rely instead on "shoe leather." Even now that Connelly is writing crime fiction after 14 years as a newspaper reporter. Even now that shoe-leather reporting requires Connelly to travel from his Florida home to California each month to research his crime novels set in Los Angeles.

"Shoe leather is the catch-all for being there in person," the author of such best-selling books as *The Lincoln Lawyer, The Closers*, and *The Narrows* explains. Being at crime scenes and elsewhere when police are on the job builds source relationships and trust. "So much of that beat comes down to trust."

Cell phones may have revolutionized communication since Connelly left daily reporting more than a decade ago, but they have done little to help crime-beat reporters, he suggests.

"A lot of this [reporting today] is done over the phone, on the run. But there's a lot of value face to face. When there is no crime scene, go to the police department to become familiar with the people and how they do their jobs. When I had to call, I didn't say 'Give me the details.' I said, 'I will be there in 15 minutes.'

"The sources who paid off when I needed it—I didn't have a phone relationship with those sources."

That payoff is on display in Connelly's book *Crime Beat*, a compilation of his best journalism from the *Los Angeles Times* and the *South Florida Sun-Sentinel*.

Crime Beat begins with "The Call"—the detailed eyewitness story Connelly crafted after earning a week of thorough access to Fort Lauderdale's homicide squad just as the city's murder rate was soaring.

"Full access," Connelly writes in the introduction to *Crime Beat*. "I was given a pager and if the homicide squad got called out, then so would I."

In an interview for this textbook, Connelly said another chapter of *Crime Beat*, "Death of an Heiress," contains "one of the best scoops I ever had. You could say that scoop was years in the making."

Connelly had written in 1990 of an unsolved Los Angeles murder five years earlier. Then eight months later he had the exclusive story that police finally had a suspect in the shooting death—the heiress's nephew. He cited a public document—the return of a search warrant police had executed. Connelly now says the true source was a police lieutenant.

"Lieutenants often are the keepers of the information, but they are more likely to be into the politics of the department, too," Connelly said. "This one concluded the best way to deal with the media was not to deal with it."

Yet, after watching Connelly work for years, this lieutenant gave Connelly a "backdoor tip" to check the paperwork on the just-returned warrant. This was crucial: Search warrants, obtained with judicial approval, are not public records until investigators file the paperwork to inform the judge what the search produced. A big-city police department conducts thousands of searches each year. Reporters are unlikely to know whether an old case has become current again unless they are developing sources.

Connelly's first rule for reporters on the crime beat: Understand that the police distrust you. You are a threat because you are around to notice—and to tell the world—when the cops foul up.

"I was always a threat" in the eyes of those he covered even after years reporting on the same police department, Connelly acknowledges. "If they did something wrong, as in the Rodney King case [the

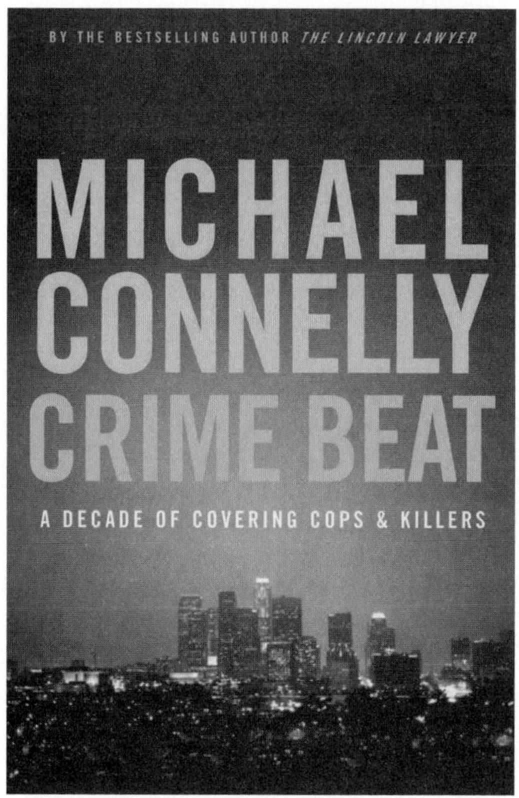

police brutality incident that triggered riots in Los Angeles], I was going to write about it.

BY THE BESTSELLING AUTHOR THE LINCOLN LAWYER
MICHAEL CONNELLY
CRIME BEAT
A DECADE OF COVERING COPS & KILLERS

"As a rookie reporter, it's 'Hi, I'm Michael Connelly and I'm on the police beat'—you're an 80 percent threat. Even when I was only a 10 percent threat years later, the distrust never went away.

"The minute I turned in my press pass, my access [to the police and their work] dramatically increased."

Connelly's experience suggests these tips to overcome some of that distrust:

- Report in person. See and be seen. "You see stuff, maybe stuff you shouldn't see—and how you handle that determines a lot."
- Rely most on your actions, not words, to develop source relationships. "I was very professional. I never once went to a cop bar on my own after hours to fraternize, or out to dinner. I never had a social life with the cops I covered. No matter how professional, it was how accurate, how fair my work was."
- Build your reputation with each story. "It's like an inverted pyramid. It starts with a small story, then larger stories, then wider coverage."
- Be sincere. Detectives who wouldn't even return his calls at first eventually became his best sources, Connelly said, when they became convinced by his work that he was trying to faithfully describe their world—"that I was trying to get it right."
- Be thorough. Connelly's novels and his news stories in *Crime Beat* are written efficiently, but are rich in the detail, context and apt quotes that only thorough reporting can produce. "The fuller story is the truer story," he says.

Most of all, Connelly emphasizes the shoe leather. A decade of returning to the Los Angeles police headquarters each month has made a big impression.

"I'm in LA three or four days a month. There's probably not a day I spend in the Parker Center that I don't say, 'Man, I wish I was a police reporter.' Invariably I'm hearing about the internal workings of the police department that are newsworthy. And I'm thinking, 'The community should know this.'

"In those 10 years, I have never seen a reporter there. Maybe there's not enough people on these beats. Maybe they can't get in there—maybe it's indicative of access."

But he can't help thinking that this accounts for the shift he sees in crime reporting since he left the *Los Angeles Times* to write his novels.

"I always felt that when I was a police reporter at the LA *Times*, we always dictated the order of the day when it came to crime," Connelly says. "Today it seems to me it's dictated by TV. Obviously, I think [crime] is an important part of our society. It's very prevalent on people's minds. The newspaper should be the ones presenting that to the public, because we go beneath the surface."

Note the "we" in that last sentence. The successful novelist is still a reporter.

"I hope and believe that my books are reportorial."

the description is sufficiently detailed to help narrow the potential suspects significantly. "A black male of medium height" doesn't do that. "A dark-complexioned female in her early 20's, with short dark hair and a rose tattoo on the palm of her left hand" does.

The next story withholds an identity.

Jaxon Van Derbeken
San Francisco Chronicle

A San Francisco man kidnapped a Roman Catholic nun while she was driving in the Mission District, held her for eight hours and sexually assaulted her before letting her go at 5 a.m., police said Thursday.

Leroy Racklin, 31, turned up at the Mission District police station Wednesday afternoon, hours after the alleged attack. Police say he was driving the 50-year-old nun's car and told officers he was simply trying to return it to its owner.

Racklin, who police said frequents the Mission District, was charged Thursday with several crimes, including two counts of rape, one count of assault with great bodily injury as well as charges of kidnapping, carjacking and crack cocaine possession.

In a jailhouse interview, Racklin denied the allegations and said he had simply borrowed the woman's car. He said he hadn't known she was a nun.

WRITING ACCIDENT STORIES

Drivers who cause traffic accidents can face felony criminal charges in case of death or injury (if the charge is driving while intoxicated).

Even without criminal charges, accidents that cause death or massive traffic problems are newsworthy.

These stories often are written similarly to crime stories, leading with the dead and injured, then providing the details.

Some fundamental details in traffic-accident reporting:

- Identify the drivers and significant passengers.
- Describe the action: The direction of the vehicles (e.g., southbound), the collision (head-on?), and anything in between. Did one driver swerve, and another brake hard? Did one car turn over three times and land in a ditch or on the other side of the median?
- Determine other factors that may have influenced the collision and its severity: Was a driver speeding? Were the victims wearing seat belts? Was a driver under the influence of alcohol or other drugs? If so, report how much higher than the state's legal limit (generally a blood-alcohol level of .08 or .10).
- Emphasize the human angle, especially any circumstances that make the collision ironic or especially heart-wrenching.
- Again, respect the presumption of innocence. Resist the reflex to assign blame for the collision based solely on an incident report. Take care to attribute witness statements and police reports.

The Associated Press

WAGON MOUND, N.M. (July 1)—A former Colorado State University runner and her fiance died in a crash on Interstate 25, days before their wedding, school officials said.

State police said 21-year-old Valerie McGregor and 23-year-old Samuel Zawada were in a 2003 Tacoma pickup that rolled off Interstate 25 near Wagon Mound in northeastern New Mexico early Thursday.

The two were on their way to McGregor's home in Tucson, Ariz., where they planned to wed July 8, according to the school.

McGregor, who was driving, died at the scene, State Police Lt. Jimmy Glascock said. Zawada was flown to St. Vincent's Hospital in Santa Fe, where he died.

Both were wearing seat belts, and alcohol was not involved, Glascock said.

WRITING FIRE STORIES

Fires, whether caused by arson, neglect or chance, kill thousands of Americans and cause billions of dollars in damage. Like crime-incident stories, fire stories focus on the casualties, then the property damage, then the explanatory details.

Like crime stories, fire stories can be written several ways. Here are leads for a typical fire story. Each might appear as written, but each successive lead benefits from more detailed reporting to produce more vivid writing.

BASIC. Three people were killed in a fire that destroyed a home Tuesday night on the city's Northwest side.

BASIC, WITH CONTEXT. Three people were killed in a fire that destroyed a home Tuesday night on the city's fire-plagued Northwest side. In the past five weeks, eight fires have claimed fifteen victims and more than a dozen buildings in this densely populated, low-income sector of the city.

SHARPER FOCUS ON VICTIMS AND CAUSE. A teenager and the two toddlers she was babysitting were killed last night when a cigarette ignited blankets and a fast-spreading fire through a home on the city's Northwest side.

Two survivors, teenage friends of the babysitter, said she had fallen asleep while holding the lit cigarette, the first she had ever tried to smoke.

THE CAUSE AS A TELLING DETAIL. Fifteen-year-old Dawn Ashmore had been "dying to smoke her first cigarette," say her two friends who survived the fire that killed Ashmore and the two toddlers she was babysitting Tuesday night.

Fire officials and the two survivors, Josh Phillips and Tina Brandon, said they believed that Ashmore's lit cigarette ignited the blaze while she and 2-year-olds Paul and Carla Swanson slept in the Northwest Springfield home that was destroyed in the fire.

Case Study

A CRIME REPORTER ON HER BEAT ▶

The text below is heavily excerpted from a five-day journal Jill Leovy wrote in 2003 for *Slate*, the online magazine.

Covering the high-crime 77th police precinct of South Central Los Angeles for the *Los Angeles Times*, Leovy demonstrated uncommon perceptivity. Being a keenly attentive eyewitness and a sincerely interested listener helped Leovy reconstruct vivid scenes.

Monday: *Leovy goes to two murder scenes one night; the next night, she's on a ride-along that ends at the scene of a domestic-violence case.*

The specifics of the dispute are byzantine, and there is much "loud-talking" and profanity. However, one protagonist stands out: the couple's 11-year-old son, his face a sullen, tear-streaked mask of anger. The boy quietly tells the police that his father is the better caretaker, the mother has a drug problem; he says he wants to stay out of gangs and begs to be placed with his grandmother.

The mother rails; her clothes and hair are in disarray, and she is behaving somewhat erratically. The boy stomps away from her, his thin shoulders tense as iron. The situation is made more complex by the cops' suspicion that the woman has lied, and that the father has committed no crime. But under domestic violence laws, they must arrest him and let her take the kids. So, the distraught boy is packed into the back seat, and the mother drives off to a shelter.

A minute later, the grandmother pulls to the curb—gracious, neat, well-dressed, anxiously looking for her grandson.

The sergeant leaves unhappy. The image of this boy is eating at her.

She refers back to it all evening. She transferred recently from one of the city's safest divisions, in the San Fernando Valley. Over Chinese fast food later, she speculates about what will happen to this boy, then says, "Before I came here, I never believed that people's choices were dictated by their environment. South Los Angeles has changed me," she says. "I no longer think everyone has choices."

Tuesday: *Leovy's movements recall "a feature I wrote last week."*

The story was about how the bereaved scream and sometimes become quarrelsome or dangerous at homicide scenes—how this creates practical difficulties for police trying to protect evidence and adds to the suffering of survivors.

People typically find out about homicides on the street, called there by friends, or upon arriving home. They will show up at the tape, frantic, breathless, still hoping for a miracle, demanding information. When they learn of the murder, they scream or wail, or run away, or lose their balance. Twice I have seen mothers taken away in ambulances shortly after learning of their children's deaths. Many people talk about the screams. A paramedic from Compton told me it is the only part of his job he finds unbearable—that distinctive homicide scream. Emergency workers sometimes tell of being attacked by hysterical family members. Last week, a 77th detective told me how the grief-stricken brother of a murder victim once brandished a gun at him.

Wednesday: *More murder scenes in South Central LA.*

The community I write about is not uniformly poor and stagnant but restless and varied. It's hard to convey the tranquility and normalcy of these neighborhoods—the skateboarding kids, the Pizza Huts, the garage sales—while still presenting a truthful picture of their crime problems.

In fact, what many people in Los Angeles think of as this city's "bad neighborhoods" are in many ways indistinguishable from those with milder reputations. They brim with aspiration and middle-class comfort, even as they distill every kind of despair. I pass blocks of graffiti on Slauson Avenue in the morning before stopping in at the bright new Western Avenue Starbucks, inevitably full of well-dressed commuters listening to cutting-edge blues. This is just northwest of where the 1992 riots broke out, and the area is now booming, construction everywhere: a new Gigante grocery store, a new Subway sandwich shop. But just across the street is the permanent swap meet where a shootout broke out recently amid a crowd in daylight.

Thursday: *Leovy finds that talking with murder victims' families is harder months and years later than it is right after the crime.*

I sometimes stay in touch with victims' family members, and there are a few I know who are slipping: They are drinking all the time, talking about suicide. I think the most painful interview I ever did was with a mother who had lost her 16-year-old son a full six years before. She couldn't get any words out, sat choked and rigid, staring at the floor, fidgeting, unable even to cry. One call I made to the relative of a recent Southeast murder victim this week went awry yesterday: The family tells me this relative died, suddenly, of an asthma attack, about two weeks after the homicide. This happens, too: I have dealt with at least three cases in which mothers died unexpectedly of health problems within a few months of their children's murders.

The pain of sudden death often comes with an incalculable burden of anger and helplessness. This is especially true when—as with many gang shootings in South Los Angeles—the murder is never solved. And victims' families often endure astounding indignities. I know of a mother who learned of her son's murder from a pair of tennis shoes. She had been given a claim check at the hospital and told to take it to the property room, where she was wordlessly handed his shoes.

Friday: *Images.*

(1) His name is Gregory, and he is 18 and black, in baggy pants and a baseball cap. He has just spent about 20 minutes, in handcuffs and against a wall, being questioned by police.

He told them he had been a gang member, but he's named in no warrants. They have let him go. And now, describing the experience, he gives a shiver, wraps his arms around himself as if he's cold and glances sideways at the police.

We talk a little bit—about crimes he committed, how he likes poetry, how he wants to go to Trade-Tech and about the time that someone shot at him. He was 13; he heard the bullet whiz by his ear, like a blast of hot wind, he says. He exhales sharply for me, to imitate the sound. He relaxes and smiles once, when he mentions his mother. He does not seem bad, he does not seem good. He seems "just a kid," as the officer I'm riding with says later, and now, a fretful, indignant kid.

(2) I am often assured by officers that there are very few "real" or "true" victims among the victims—by this, they mean that most assault and homicide victims are gang members—and then, in the next breath, they will assert with equal sincerity that death is death and rail against wider society for not caring. Those I've talked to in depth often express more frustration and bafflement than anything else. "Tell me what to do and I will do it," a black sergeant I know once burst out a couple hours into a discussion about black men and homicide. He was pounding on the steering wheel, appealing to thin air. "Just tell me what to do."

(3) Gregory slips off into the night, pushing his bicycle, heading alone down dark streets on which—as a gang member in the area once told me—young black men at night are bull's-eyes.

Leovy's entire online journal is at:
www.slate.com/id/2090015/entry/2090081/

* * *

(continued)

(continued)

Things to Consider

- What did you learn by reading these journal excerpts that contradicted your preconceptions about people and places in an area known for its violent crime?
- Think about the range of people Leovy spoke to in these five days. Thanks to her assertiveness, with one week's work, she knows more about the community she covered than most reporters know about their beat in a year of talking only to officials.
- Which of these passages are most memorable? What makes them so memorable? How many of them involve a picture in your mind—*he was pounding on the steering wheel, appealing to thin air*—because of Leovy's precise description of what she sees?
- There are only a few direct quotes in these passages. Yet Leovy's statements carry the voice of authority. How does she back up those statements? Look at how being an eyewitnesses substitutes for quotes.

NARRATIVE. Josh Phillips awoke to the crackling noises. Tina Brandon smelled the smoke. Closest to the door of a ramshackle bungalow on the city's impoverished Northwest side, they saved themselves, but were too scared and too far to rescue their best friend and the sleeping twin toddlers she was baby-sitting.

Some fundamental details in fire stories:

- Identify the victims and the reasons they were present.
- As soon as possible, cite the cause of the fire. This may not be immediately known, but interview the fire department investigator, who will appear at the scene soon after the rescue squads do. Readers want to know whether the fire was deliberately set (arson), was caused by carelessness (such as the lit cigarette), or was caused by something the victims could not avoid (e.g., lightning or a furnace explosion).
- Cite the structural damage estimate (in dollars), also obtained by interviewing fire officials.
- Cite the duration of the fire—the time it started and the time that the fire department declares the fire "under control."
- Find the vivid stories from survivors. What allowed—or prevented—escape?
- Find other witnesses. Fires attract crowds. They may provide details that fire officials do not yet know.
- As always, describe the action. A devastating fire can happen to anyone. Readers easily can see themselves in the place of victims, survivors and fire fighters reacting to an emergency.

REPORT MORE, WRITE LESS

Some of these examples of crime, accident and fire stories come entirely from law enforcement. Others involve independent interviewing. With the need for precision in crime reporting, Michael Connelly discussed the importance of reporting broadly and writing narrowly.

"No doubt that I come from the school that less is more," he said. "In the newspaper, you have limited space so you hone things down, you get to the point—the explosive quote that sums things up. Nothing is wasted, less is more. That's how I was as a reporter and it carried over into my novels."

Although Connelly's news reporting abetted his long-term plan to write detailed novels, he said his newspaper work benefited from "always looking for details—I had no problem throwing a big net and then for the purposes of a newspaper story hone it down.

"That philosophy works best in creating momentum. I try to keep things short and sweet. Keep it moving, with velocity. You have to be aware of the reading process.

"Whether you're writing a 12-inch story or a long novel, what kind of writer are you if you don't want your readers to get to the end?"

IN CONCLUSION

Sudden and dramatic, crime stories are news in the extreme, urgent matters of life and death. That compels readers, even those who complain of too much bad news.

Crime stories are personal. They are people stories and community stories. They are most often written as breaking news, but also feed trend stories and other enterprise, including investigative journalism.

Remember that the human toll of crime, accidents and fires is the most dramatic fact.

With so much at stake—life and death, liberty or imprisonment—journalists must seek precision, although essential facts may not be immediately known. This requires reporting in detail, but writing concisely. Often stranger than fiction, crime, accident and fire stories do not need to be embellished to be riveting.

Take special care in identifying victims and suspects. Mistakes here can be especially painful to story subjects and innocent victims.

TOOL KIT

Covering Crime and Justice, written and edited by Criminal Justice journalists, © 2003, funded by the Ford Foundation.
www.justicejournalism.org/crimeguide/

Inside the Police Beat

www.poynter.org/content/content_view.asp?id=92447
For TV: Bringing Court Stories to Life:
www.newslab.org/strategies/courtstories.htm
For TV: From CBS News on covering trials:
www.journalism.org/resources/tools/writing/fairness/trials.asp?from=print

EXERCISE 1

Write a story from the following:

You are an ace reporter for the school newspaper and website at Balford State University. As part of your routine duties, you visit the police station once a week at Elfington City Hall, the town where your college is. Usually nothing new happens. But today, you are going through the police reports with one of the officers on duty and you find something you didn't know about. Apparently there was a two-car accident involving students from Balford State. You read the report. The students were driving by the lake on the Balford campus. Somehow both cars wound up partially submerged after they made contact. No student was hurt. But you get the four students' names. Ashley Weymont was driving a Ford Explorer SUV. Her passengers were Jessica Rubin and Adriane Messing. The other car was driven by Gary Dodson. The Elfington police were charging Dodson with driving while intoxicated. They said his blood alcohol level was .10, which is legally drunk in Elfington. "This was an odd accident," Sgt. Larry Princeton said. "Apparently the passengers and drivers of both cars were yelling at each other as they were driving by the lake. No one quite knows what happened next, but the two cars hit each other and they wound up in the water. They're mighty lucky no one drowned." Princeton said Dodson posted bail and is out of jail. You thank him, and then look up the addresses for those involved. You find one of the passengers, Jessica Rubin. "We were driving and this guy in the other car has on the Buffalo head suit. We couldn't believe he was the guy who is the student mascot, and we had just come from the basketball game. So we started doing cheers and singing the school fight song. And Ashley is steering the car back and forth to the beat of the song, you know. And then she just rams into him and we all go to the lake." You also find out all three women are seniors. You then contact Dodson, who won't talk to you. But he does confirm he is the school's mascot: the mighty Buffalo. You are getting close to deadline but finally track down Ashley Weymont. "It was the stupidest thing I've ever done. We had just beaten St. Thomas and we were so happy. And then we see the guy who's the mighty Buffalo and we're singing and everything. I don't know what happened. One minute we're driving. The next our cars are in Lake Balford right by the school shrine. We all got soaking wet. But we had to pull the mascot guy out of his car or he would have drowned. The Buffalo suit was so heavy and the water wasn't that deep, but we all just pulled him back onto the shore." You head back to your dorm room to write something for the web, but have to make a quick call first to Princeton. He confirms that the three women saved Dodson from drowning, and the cars were at the Buffalo shrine, which greets visitors to the campus. Oh, and it happened at 10:30 p.m. You now sit down and write.

EXERCISE 2

Analyze the following story. What are its strengths? Where could it improve?

A University of South Running student, apparently imitating a stunt from the television show *Jackass*, died Thursday while running through streets in a hospital gown brandishing a chain saw.

The student, Brandon Taylor, 19, was struck by a truck that couldn't stop in time. He was hit on Fourth Street, a block from his dorm. He was pronounced dead at Crane Hospital.

"He wasn't on drugs or anything," said university spokesman, Henry Welderman. "He was a bright student. He just saw this crazy stunt on television and thought it would be funny."

Taylor, a television, radio and film major, was watching the show with his roommates early Thursday evening when the stunt was aired on the television show, police said. According to police, he jumped from the room, put on the hospital gown, grabbed a chainsaw and ran out into the streets.

"We didn't even know he owned a chainsaw," said his roommate, Gary Johnson. " He wasn't on drugs or drunk or anything. He just thought it would be funny."

Taylor was struck at about 7 p.m. by a truck driven by Emery Hileman. Hileman, who was not ticketed, said he never saw Taylor until it was too late.

"I just was driving and I saw this student right in front of me," Hileman said. "I tried to stop but I couldn't in time."

Taylor, a sophomore, was from DeKalb.

1. Does the lead capture the essence of the story?
2. How important is it to give the reason the student was running through the street?
3. Where does the quote from the driver of the truck belong?
4. Notice the number of quotes. How do they add to the story?

CHAPTER 9

Writing about Victims of Crimes

IN THIS CHAPTER, YOU'LL LEARN:

- The best crime reporters talk to victims and their families.
- Victims often are willing to talk about their experiences.
- Journalists should treat victims with the utmost respect and honor their wishes if they decline an interview request.
- Victims fill in the blanks of missing detail often left out of official reports.
- Told correctly, victims' stories can be dramatically powerful and emotionally moving.

To not include people who may, for example, have lost a family member in a crime . . . is to leave the puzzle undone.
Louise Kiernan,
Chicago Tribune

ED PALATTELLA'S EDITOR FROM THE *ERIE TIMES-NEWS* in Pennsylvania called him at home one Friday night. An area middle school student had shot and killed a teacher outside a school dance. Apparently the teacher was just the first person the student met at the door.

The shooting was one of several at middle and high schools across the country at the time. The next day, Palattella began canvassing the small community of Edinboro, where both teacher and student lived. Palattella spent the next week retracing the teacher's and student's steps that Friday, piecing together the two random paths that ended the moment they crossed outside the dance.

Palattella talked to neighbors, classmates, school administrators, police. After a few days, he had a timeline of the night's events. Then Palattella performed one of the more necessary and uncomfortable parts of his job as a journalist.

He contacted the family of the slain teacher.

"I knew I wasn't going to get much from the family," Palattella said. "They weren't talking, and understandably so. They were in shock."

Palattella had gathered so much information from his interviews that he had a streamlined list of questions for the family "just to confirm some details leading up to the shooting. So they were more open to providing that than, you know, talking about what happened. So it was more like what was he wearing that day and things like that."

Palattella kept the interview short. But the family shared with him the detail needed to make his story compelling. The interview yielded a cruelly ironic and telling anecdote: the final words the teacher, John Gillette, would say to his wife concerned the dance where he would die.

> John Gillette called his wife at work that afternoon. He wanted to know where he could buy a registry book, like the kind a bride and groom use at their wedding and treasure for years.
>
> I want to know all the kids who were at the dance, John said on the phone.
>
> Debbie Gillette gave him some ideas. She said goodbye.
>
> The conversation was the last she would have with her husband.

Palattella's story helped him earn writer-of-the-year honors from the Pennsylvania Newspaper Association, competing against journalists from the larger markets of Philadelphia and Pittsburgh.

Each day, in markets of all sizes, journalists such as Palattella make the uncomfortable visit or phone call to victims and families of tragic events. The journalists do so not to be sensational but to verify facts, give victims and their families a chance to comment and to paint a more human picture of the tragedy.

Surprising to nonjournalists, reporters find these victims and survivors often remarkably open to telling the public their ordeal. The information fills out the details of what actually happened. Those interviewed can either verify or refute official versions. In the case of deaths, they can reveal victims' personalities, their passions, their last small moments that death magnifies.

But nearly always when victims and families choose to share their experiences, the emotional drama of how humans live through tragedy plays out. Journalists who capture those moments also capture their readers.

WHY TALK TO VICTIMS

Leonora LaPeter, a national-award-winning reporter for the *St. Petersburg Times* in Florida, once was sent to a troubled neighborhood after a young man had been shot and killed with an assault rifle. Her assignment was to capture the neighborhood's mood and show readers where the teenager grew up.

LaPeter went to the sidewalk where the man had died and a memorial stood. But the shrine, she discovered, was for another young man killed a few months earlier. A crowd gathered. She spent about four hours watching as, one-by-one, community leaders showed up to speak to television cameras and those milling about. She interviewed several neighbors, friends, family and the victim's former girlfriend and mother to his two children.

She found a neighborhood in decline, and the neighbors both angry and sad. During the afternoon, police officers arrived, encountering young men similar to the victim, 24-year-old Jacobie Spradley.

> A police cruiser pulls up and three officers get out. Several men hanging out on front porches disappear.
>
> "What," asks Officer Patrick McGovern, "you don't want to talk to me?"
>
> He says this area of Melrose has had 15 to 20 shootings in the eight years he has been an officer. He points to the ground. "There's enough crack baggies to make a plastic recycling plant out here."
>
> A young man with dreadlocks, wearing black jeans and a tank top, is sitting on stairs in front of a turquoise duplex, just feet from where Spradley was shot.
>
> "What happened to the killer?" he yells at the officers. "Those reefer bags y'all digging up, that's petty. You just want to talk about dope. This is about murder, man. This has got nothing to do with dope."

LaPeter could have stayed with the official version of the shooting, looking at it from law enforcement's and politicians' viewpoints. Had LaPeter ignored the friends and neighbors who gathered that day, her story would have missed how residents felt about their neighborhood.

"It [not only] brought the victim to life, but also the victim's circumstances and his neighborhood to life and the people in his community and what they thought about what happened," LaPeter says.

LaPeter was rewarded with a story that breathed life because she practiced the type of journalism that seeks stories beyond the official versions. Those reporters who, especially on crime and disaster stories, look for the victims or those who knew the victim often discover the same pot of gold LaPeter found.

Filling in the Puzzle

Journalists who want fuller, livelier stories should make it a matter of routine that they talk to the victims.

- **Journalists should use police and other official reports as a place to start:** "For one, official reports aren't always right," says Louise Kiernan, a Pulitzer Prize winner from the *Chicago Tribune*. "But more importantly they represent just one piece of the puzzle that you're trying to fill in. And to not include the people who may, for example, have lost a family member in a crime, or people who are otherwise affected by the crime, is to leave the puzzle undone."

- **Seasoned journalists know official reports leave out human interest:** "Police don't get the types of details we get as reporters," LaPeter says. "And so it's kind of like their versions are very lackluster, very straight down the middle. They only get the information they need for their purposes but they don't get what we need, which is: Who are these people? What was going on at the time that it happened? You know, just what was going on through their minds?"
- **Journalists often use the phrase "the story comes to life" when they include comments, insights and information from victims:** "A story can go from one dimension to three dimensions if you can explain what it did to people, why they were victims, how did they feel, who they are, all of those things," says Mary Flood, a veteran reporter at the *Houston Chronicle*. ". . . There are all sort of pieces of everything, every story you cover."
- **In the sense of fairness, journalists should allow a victim or survivors to comment on stories where they're mentioned:** "But more than anything else," LaPeter says, "this person's life is going to be in the paper, and they have a right to contribute to whatever you do on it because they were part of it, it happened to them and they are going to be the person who knows the most about it, is able to tell you what happened the most accurately, the best way, the most vividly."
- **Journalists should give a voice to the victims and those who know them:** "I think that when the case gets in the justice system, everything is centered on the defendant, protecting the defendant's rights, the Fifth Amendment, or whatever," Palattella says. "The victim is just a bit part after a while, so it seems to the victim. . . . The victims just feel left out."

HOW TO APPROACH VICTIMS

When the news broke that one of the world's largest energy corporations was failing, editors at the *Houston Chronicle* assigned the story to veteran reporter Mary Flood. She quickly became one of the leading reporters in the country on the Enron scandal.

Part of her task was to interview those who lost their pensions and life savings. She called their homes and new jobs. When she reached them, she asked for other names. She left postings on websites run by ex-employees.

The response surprised her. She found many who wanted to speak. Hardly any she contacted didn't want to say something about Enron.

"These people felt victimized, angry, put out, and they knew that a lot of people cared about them because it had become sort of this iconic story for the problems with our economy and the fall of the stock market, the fall of trust in corporate America," she says, adding that "most of these people were extremely approachable."

The Art of Storytelling

Louise Kiernan's remarkable year of 2000 saw her write the lead story for the *Chicago Tribune*'s Pulitzer Prize-winning entry in explanatory journalism. The story studied the bottleneck that is Chicago's O'Hare Airport on a bad weather day.

Incredibly, Kiernan wrote another story that year that finished second in the same category. Rarely does a reporter win a Pulitzer, much less finish one-two in the same category.

Her second story was a haunting, emotional account of when glass from a broken Chicago skyscraper window fell to the street, killing a young mother, Ana Flores, as she and her 3-year-old daughter walked hand-in-hand on the sidewalk.

Kiernan's reporting demonstrates why reporters seek out the victims of crimes and tragic events. Her story described the random cruelty of how a piece of glass could kill someone in one spot and spare another inches away. She documented how the building's owner ignored fixing the broken window promptly.

Her journalism also shows outstanding techniques for approaching families with sensitivity.

"It's better not to call first," Kiernan says. "I just got their address and I went down one evening and knocked on their door. And because I knew I would have some time with that story, I didn't say coming in 'I'd like to interview you.'

"I said 'I'm a reporter and I would be interested in writing about Ana and I just want to tell you a little bit about who I am and what I'm doing.' "

Reporters facing deadlines sometimes work too fast. They fail to give families unaccustomed to interviews the time to absorb the request and what it will mean to have their story shown to the community. For Kiernan, she tries to explain her job and how journalism works. She seldom sets up an interview during the first meeting.

"It helps particularly with people who are reluctant or don't have much trust in reporters. Sometimes I'll bring stories that I've done or agree to meet them somewhere out of their home if they're not comfortable with that," she says.

Kiernan spent several months on the story. She obtained documents under the Freedom of Information Act. She interviewed family and friends. She even tried to interview those who had been walking on the same sidewalk where Flores died.

This is how Kiernan led her story describing the glass falling from the sky.

> The glass falls like a shadow, swift and silent, a dark blur swooping through the wet sky.
>
> For weeks, the cracked window on the 29th floor of the CNA building strained against the adhesive film that held it in place 340 feet above the ground, expanding almost imperceptibly in the heat of the afternoon sun, contracting with the nighttime chill. Cracks slowly crept across its surface, pieces pushing and pulling with each gust of wind.
>
> Now, a fragment breaks free. It is a jagged triangle, no larger than a cafeteria tray, dark with dirt on one side, covered with white film on the other.
>
> Below, the west side of South Wabash Avenue bustles with Friday lunchtime traffic. People walk quickly, heads ducked against the drizzle.
>
> A college student is headed to the camera supply store. Three construction workers decide to make the best of a workday cut short by rain and go out for lunch. A parking lot attendant stands in the booth and wonders if he should run next door to pick up some food.
>
> A 3-year-old girl walks a step or two ahead of her mother. The mother is on her way to a job interview. They hold hands.

"If you look at that opening sequence, it talks about how the glass fell like a shadow. That information came from a document that I obtained under the Freedom of Information Act. I got all the police reports and the city building department reports on the accident, and used those to go back and re-interview all the people who were witnesses to the accident.

"So if you look at that whole opening sequence, that's not something that I imagined or extrapolated. It's all documents based, and documents that were supported by interviews."

Kiernan rechecked even the smallest facts. She examined the official photographs of the accident. She also verified that it had rained that day.

"I looked at all the weather reports for that day to make sure that how people remembered the weather was actually what the weather was. So many people don't remember that accurately," she says.

For much of her story, which ran in two parts, Kiernan wrote in scenes. To get the detail needed to write vividly, she asked her subjects more than once to describe their experiences.

(continues)

"Over and over again, I'll interview people again about things that to them may seem minor or irrelevant but I am really trying to understand how things looked and felt and to paint a scene that involves all five senses," she says.

The result is writing that puts readers into the story and lets them experience the emotional drama that plays out during traumatic moments. These two scenes show how Ana Flores' friend, Carmen Taborda, and Flores' husband, Tony, were told of Ana's death.

> At her bungalow down the block from Centro Cristiano, Ana's best friend, Carmen Taborda, waited too. Her family and a few friends had gathered for her birthday, but she refused to cut the cake until Ana arrived. Just a few hours before, when she hugged Carmen goodbye at the front door, Ana had promised she would come.
>
> Four o'clock passed. Then 5.
>
> Carmen's children grew impatient. No, she told them. We have to wait for Ana.
>
> The telephone rang. As soon as Carmen asked "What happened?" everyone knew something was wrong.
>
> She sank onto the couch.
>
> All afternoon, Tony sat in a classroom near O'Hare International Airport, in a training session for his job loading and unloading bags for United. He didn't know that Anita—as he called his wife—had gone downtown.
>
> Around 6, there was a knock at the classroom door, a stranger whispering a few words to the instructor.
>
> Then, the long, quiet ride to the terminal where his two brothers-in-law waited to break the news. On the way home, Tony insisted they drive to the morgue.
>
> "I wasn't thinking real straight. I was hoping they had made a mistake," he says. "It took a long time to get to the morgue. I don't even know where we went.
>
> "And it was Anita."

"What you are doing is putting the reader inside that scene, inside the story, that they feel they're a part," Kiernan says. "So that they come to care about the people who are a part of the story so they feel something when they're reading it, that they're engaged.

"And at the most basic level, so that they get to the end."

Though journalists, imagining a negative response, might feel reluctant to call victims of crimes, many victims don't mind talking to reporters. Newer journalists especially need to resist the fear that families will respond in anger. That does happen. But if the reporter is polite and respectful, the response might be positive.

HOW TO
Approach Victims

Mary Flood, the lead reporter at the *Houston Chronicle* for the Enron scandal, says reporters should approach victims with empathy and respect. The result will be a story that shows the human side of crimes and disasters.

One of her earliest assignments—covering a destructive tornado in Texas in 1979—taught her that lesson.

"I came from the Northeast and from Michigan, and I had never seen what a tornado could do. I remember walking up to a house and a woman (was) there crying, holding her baby and crying, and asking her what happened.

". . . What she told me about was having that same baby in her arms, hearing the cliché sound like a train's coming at them, getting into the bathtub, putting a mattress over her, holding the mattress and the baby simultaneously and screaming the Lord's Prayer at the top of her lungs.

"Telling people that the shopping mall near her the roof fell in and some people were hurt, that some cars were tossed around, that the twister took mirrors and etched into the glass of a door a swirling pattern—none of that says quite the same thing as 'I was screaming the Lord's Prayer while holding this baby and holding a mattress.'

"It just brings a story to life. It lets you understand what you really want to understand, which is, what does it mean to be a human being.

"It makes the story a real story instead of statistics."

To approach victims and their families, the first rule is respect: respect the tragedy, respect the victims, respect their time, respect their wishes. They are not obliged to talk to a reporter. But if reporters show professionalism and compassion and explain what they seek, people surprisingly will agree to an interview.

"I think different people react differently," Flood says. ". . . My experience has been that most bereaved families would prefer to speak to you if you are kind and respectful than not—because they think that something incredibly important has happened that they have lost a loved one.

"And if you call and are respectful, that is reinforcing something they know is . . . important, and if you verify that in a respectful and polite way, they often are willing to share things with you."

The second rule is to go slowly. Victims and their families have suffered a tragedy. Journalists sensitive to that will succeed.

One of the authors of this book, Bob Lloyd, discovered just that. Lloyd was covering the police in Arlington, Texas, for the *Fort Worth Star-Telegram*. A man in his early 20s had chased an intruder out of his apartment where his wife and infant daughter were sleeping. The intruder, wielding a knife, turned on the man. After a struggle, the man stabbed the intruder. The man brought the intruder into his home, but he watched the intruder die on his living room floor.

Police interviewed the man, then let him go as the district attorney sent his case to a grand jury to see if the man should be indicted for the killing. The grand jury took several days before saying no.

During that time, Lloyd tried unsuccessfully to contact the man. Finally, on the day of the grand jury's decision, Lloyd found the man sitting in his truck outside his apartment, a few feet from the spot where he had struggled with the intruder. Lloyd thought the man would be relieved, but he was agitated. The man had just argued with his wife.

Lloyd, kneeling on the pavement next to the truck, didn't ask about the killing. After a few moments—which included a bit of commiserating about the opposite sex—the man agreed to meet at a pizza place. There he talked for more than two hours, telling full details about that night, his subsequent nightmares, his still vivid

Tips from the DART Center for Journalism and Trauma for interviewing victims and families

- Journalists can help victims and survivors tell their stories in ways that are constructive and in ways that make for great journalism.
- Sometimes you can't avoid intruding upon someone in grief. If you can't postpone your contact, remember to be sensitive and respectful in your approach.
- "I'm sorry for your loss," is a good way to start the conversation.
- Don't assume a victim or family member won't want to talk; often they are eager to share their story and memories with a journalist.
- If someone doesn't want to talk to you, be respectful and polite. And don't forget to leave your business card; at some point, the person may decide to talk to a reporter, and they will likely call the one that made the best impression.
- Make sure the person understands the terms of the interview. Tell them: "This is an interview for a story I'm writing. Your quotes will appear in the newspaper along with your name." Remind them of the terms periodically.
- Pay attention to your own emotions during the interview and let your reactions inform your reporting (while remaining professional). If you find something emotionally stirring, chances are readers will, too.

For more about reporting on victims of tragedy, visit the Dart Center for Journalism & Trauma website at www.dartcenter.com. Also read the Dart Center's free publication, *Tragedies & Journalists: A Guide for More Effective Coverage.*

Source: DART Center for Journalism and Trauma

fear waiting for the grand jury's decision, wondering if he would be charged with manslaughter.

Some journalists believe reluctance to contact victims or their families is misguided. Kiernan of the *Chicago Tribune* blames popular culture's false images in movies and on television for perpetuating the notion that journalists grow callous to victims' sufferings.

"I think the hardest part of doing those kind of stories can be picking up the phone or making that first knock on the door," she says. "I think in part because of how reporters are often portrayed in popular culture and, perhaps, because unfortunately, a few reporters do actually act like vultures, that younger reporters or more inexperienced reporters can feel that what they are doing is in some way intrinsically wrong. And it's not.

"All you're doing is giving people an opportunity to lend their voice to your story. If you treat them with respect and integrity, what you're doing is really only helping them and not hurting them."

THE WHIPPY DIP

Sometimes victims' responses can surprise even veteran journalists. Palattella of the *Erie Times-News* covered an odd robbery at an area ice cream stand with the even odder name of "The Whippy Dip."

ADVANCED TIP
Why Journalists Talk to the Victims

- **Voice:** Journalists give a voice to both the victims and those who know them.
- **Fairness:** Just out of fairness, journalists should try to let victims or survivors comment on stories where they're mentioned.
- **Experience:** Including the victims' or survivors' accounts puts the readers inside the story and helps them see what the victims or survivors experienced.
- **Human Interest:** Police reports often leave out the human interest inherent in any crime or disaster.

The robbers, using a false gun, tried to hold a worker hostage. Palattella covered the story, later discovering the worker held hostage was the son of owners of a popular Italian restaurant in Erie.

A few years later, the Italian restaurant also was robbed at gunpoint. Palattella covered that trial "where the owner spoke about how it pained her so much" because she had gone through the same experience as her son.

When Palattella heard the owner's testimony, he knew he wanted to ask the owner more about her experience. He understood the story would hold wide appeal because of the human interest and the restaurant's popularity.

"You never know what you're going to get until you ask," Palattella says. "I mean I thought she'd be angry at me because of the story I did on her son when he was jammed up in the Whippy Dip case."

After the trial, Palattella approached her. To his surprise, she was delighted to talk.

"I thought she resented the paper. It turns out she didn't at all because of the way we had covered those stories," he says.

Many journalists say the victims' reactions can catch them off guard. At most newspapers and television stations, talking to the victims is merely part of the job. How they handle that initial contact can harm or help their chances of talking to the person.

"The worst someone's going to do is say no," Palattella says. ". . . You'd just be surprised if you treat people with respect and your odds of getting a story are much greater."

ELEMENTS OF A VICTIM'S STORY

Journalists follow no formula when writing stories about victims. Common to most though are four elements: the victim's experience, a sense of what put the victim in the path of the crime, what followed after the crime and revealing the victim's personality.

- **Let readers live the victims' experiences:** Seasoned journalists concentrate on vivid language that shows the experience in a storytelling form. Nearly always, a traumatic event has occurred. It began and ended. Journalists can capture the power of storytelling by giving a chronological recount interspersed with the victim's or family's own thoughts as they were going through the event.
- **Explain how the victim got into the situation:** The pressing question that needs answering in these stories starts with "Why." Why did this occur? Why were

Talent Showcase

TINA GRIEGO ▶

Reporter/Columnist, *Rocky Mountain News*

Formerly, columnist for *The Denver Post*, reporter for *The Los Angeles Herald Examiner*

Tina Griego's writing is uncommonly effective at connecting with readers because she is uncommonly effective at connecting with the people she interviews.

It shows in her columns and in her year-long reporting projects. She earned those lofty roles only after a journalistic baptism that forced her to overcome her own shyness. Introverted and insecure, rookie reporter Griego had to get victims of tragedy to open up to her when their first instincts were to slam the door in her face.

As a first-year reporter at *The Los Angeles Herald Examiner*, she had a role that many veterans dread and shun: Interviewing victims of violent crime. Right away, she was dispatched to Compton, the Los Angeles suburb notorious for its wars between competing gangs. A 3-year-old had been killed in a drive-by shooting.

Her assignment had all the elements predicting rejection and failure. The family, already outraged over the crime and their loss, was hostile towards the newspaper. The racial implications were obvious. Characteristically, poor, minority neighborhoods feel that they are not covered at all until there is bad news. The family was black. Griego wasn't. Indeed, it was her maiden voyage to Compton and this type of situation.

"I told the grandmother I really wanted to get to know the family," Griego recalls. That just set the grandmother off.

"I had to let her be angry. It was difficult because I wanted to take it personally. That's the first instinct. I could feel my face flush. Hot. She's laying into me. Who was I and how could we come down there at this time? I wanted to say, 'But I'm a *good person*!'

"I just had to shut up and to let her get it all out. I let her have her say. And when she was done, I gave her my card. I said it was, of course, her prerogative, but I'd really like to talk to her and her daughter. A day passed and I heard from her daughter (the mother of the murdered child)."

Next, a stalker went to the door of sitcom actress Rebecca Schaefer and gunned her down. With the family walling itself off from the LA media horde, Griego wrote a letter to the family and put it into a doorjamb. She got the interview.

In these cases, Griego relied on her instincts and fundamental human emotion.

"So many people want their son, their daughter and their auntie to be remembered as people, and not just as a headline buried in the local section. These people are almost seized by this desire to speak and to say, 'You didn't know my daughter, but you would have liked her. And this is what she was like.' "

Understanding why victims might talk about tragedy is one thing. Being the person they choose to tell takes skill and some other virtues.

"Interviewing is an art," says Griego, who sees her stories not as mere news accounts, but as a continuing conversation that begins with sources and progresses to readers.

"I tell a lot of stories. I tell other people's stories. I always remember that they are other people's stories. It's a matter of respect. Like looking at people when they talk to you. And listening. Really listening. People know when they have captured you. When they sense that you are there with them, you will always get more from them, even if it's an antagonistic interview."

When there is time to prepare for an interview, Griego will find what else has been written about the person that she may need to know.

"That will guide my questions, inform my questions, create new questions. I want a good idea of what I'm going to ask, but not a script. I'm never so focused on the questions that I stop listening. That was an early mistake. I'd have my questions and I was ready to go. I was concentrating on my questions. Now, the answers will guide my questions. The best interviews are not interviews. Not question, answer, question, answer. They are truly conversations."

Easier said than done, this starts with Griego's empathy. It's her nature. Less-gifted, less-sensitive reporters can at least emulate comparable attentiveness, curiosity and patience.

"If I get into a personal area, I'll talk about my own experience. I'll admit some vulnerability or some confusion over an issue. People want to help, to find some common ground. It's human nature for most people to do that. So it turns out that they talk about their own experience."

When that rapport hasn't been established yet, silence has its virtue, especially on the phone, Griego advises.

"Some folks are reticent, but you can sense that there's more that they want to say. You can keep silent while you're writing notes [she would seldom want to break eye contact in person]. They want to fill it. They keep talking because they're made uncomfortable by the silence.

"For example, someone who has suffered a loss is grieving and angry. They feel pain. In that situation, you have to be very respectful and you have to listen. They have emotions that they have a hard time articulating. They have to put into words what they feel they *can't* put into words. If you give it time to percolate, maybe they can."

Dealing with victims of tragedy has taught Griego to do a "continual gut check with your own humanity." There's a fine, but visible line between the sensitivity that heightens awareness and allows a writer to match words with emotion, and the sensitivity that renders the writer too emotional to function.

Griego learned lessons about detachment in an elementary school playground in Stockton, Calif., after a deranged Vietnam veteran opened fire there. Five children died. Twenty-nine others and a teacher were wounded. The gunman then killed himself.

"That was my first experience with the media circus. There were reporters from all over the country at this school. Parents were crying. The principal came out to make a statement. People were jockeying for position. I remember a radio reporter interviewing the principal. As he did, he was looking around to see if there was somebody better to interview. I remember thinking that it would only take two or three minutes to give the principal the respect of looking at him. I said to myself I would never do that, and if I did do that, I couldn't be a reporter anymore."

Griego says that day in the schoolyard has helped her deal with her own losses.

"Then, I had never experienced death in my life. But since then I have lost my dad and my mom. Now, I draw insight from that day. And I draw insight from my own losses when I interview others."

Tina Griego came to journalism almost accidentally. In college, she was an engineering student who switched to English and who began working for her school newspaper because "I had to do something practical."

It changed her world.

"In some ways, journalism was for me like slipping into an alter-ego. In my real life at the time, I was very, very shy and uncertain and much more of an introverted person, not a socially comfortable person. But by being a journalist, I could slip on this magic cloak and I could

(continued)

Talent Showcase *(continued)*

go places that I didn't have reason to go and I could ask people impertinent questions, and, best of all, I could then tell other people. I can learn every day, and then I get to teach other people."

More than 20 years later, "I can still say, 'I love my job.' But I would not tell people who are not curious that they should be reporters. What speaks to you—change the world, challenge the establishment—those loftier goals will sustain you. But you need something in a day-to-day way. You have to engage. If you're not curious and you don't like people, this is not the job for you."

victims where they were when it happened? Why did the events unfold as they did? Journalists answer these questions through interviewing the victim or those surrounding the victim and filling in the blanks left by official reports.

- **Show readers the victim's personality:** The story should reveal not only what happened but also who the person is. A journalist attracts readers by telling them of a person's life and personality.
- **Tell what has happened since:** The aftermath of a traumatic event is part of the story. The event usually influences a host of feelings and actions. Public policies might change. People's personalities usually undergo an assault of emotions.

"Ultimately . . . these are people," Palattella says. "No matter what you think about a defendant or victim, they are people.

"I once had a private detective tell me, and I'll never forget it, the victim is entitled to justice just as much as anyone else. No matter what their life might have been like, no matter what they did, no matter what you agree or disagree with, they're entitled to justice just for being a person."

WRITING THE VICTIM'S SIDE

When LaPeter worked for the *Savannah Morning News*, she covered a trial of a man accused of killing a family of four. Each day, she wrote a story, trying to capture not only the trial's testimony but also its drama.

One day she sat behind the mother's sister. The prosecution played a video police taped, just after the shootings, that went from room to room, showing how police found each victim dead. The mother's sister bowed her head and didn't watch. A friend next to her watched and told her when she could look.

> Connie Smith bowed her head and kept it there.
>
> Sitting in the front row of a Monroe courtroom Tuesday—surrounded by family and friends—she couldn't bear to look at the television screen.
>
> It showed the inside of her sister, Kim Daniels', home in Santa Claus the morning of Dec. 4, 1997, about seven hours after Kim, 33, her husband, Danny, 47, and their two children, Jessica, 16, and Bryant, 8, died from shotgun blasts as they slept in their beds.

"They're in Bryant's room now," whispered Amy Tomberlin, a best friend from church, into Smith's ear.

The video camera panned through young Bryant's room, showing the bunk beds where he and brother, Corey, 4, slept. A toy truck on the floor near a shotgun shell and a boy's jacket. A closet with boys' clothes and a bowling pin on the floor.

And blood. Splattered on the walls next to the bed, near a framed photo of Bryant in a red baseball cap holding a bat. The boy's arm poked out from beneath a sheet on the top bunk bed.

Smith, 33, grasped a tissue and wiped her eyes, still keeping her head down.

Across the courtroom, the man accused of killing the Daniels' family also kept his head down, staring at a spot on the gray-blue rug in front of him for hours on end.

Jerry Scott Heidler, 22, sat solitary at the defense table as his lawyers, the prosecutors and observers moved over to the other side of the room and gathered around a single television that showed the carnage he is accused of causing.

"What a scene that is because . . . you have them going through the house with a video and showing you and here's the reaction of the family member. So that for sure the light bulb went on," says LaPeter, who won a deadline writing award from the American Society of Newspaper Editors and saw three of her stories reprinted in the book, *Best Newspaper Writing*, published by the Poynter Institute.

LaPeter tries to write these stories with scenes. She has discovered that writing with pictures lets her readers experience her subjects' actions and emotions.

"Scenes bring it to life," LaPeter says, adding that they put readers in the place where her subjects act. That's better, she says, than many news stories that quote officials using bureaucratic jargon.

"You just have to have a pretty good scene," she says. "And that involves being there. It involves watching all the details, and looking at how people react, and what they're wearing, how they interact with people."

WHAT TO ASK

When Kiernan began working for the *Chicago Tribune*, her editors decided to write about every homicide victim in the Chicago area. So for a year, Kiernan interviewed family after family about loved ones lost.

The important lesson learned during that year: Find out who the victim was as a person, not a statistic. Ask much later about the event.

"When you sit down with people to talk to them about someone in their family who's been a crime victim, you don't start by asking about the crime," she says. "Start at the beginning, about who this person was, what they were like as a baby. If it's somebody's wife, how they met.

"Your goal and the goal that you want to communicate to the family [is] you're interested in who this was, not in what happened to them, that you're really there to understand the person and to take your time. Even if you know that you don't

WIRED AND WIRELESS | WEB

Almost the moment after a gunman at Virginia Tech University killed 32 students and professors, journalists reached victims' friends and family in a way that until a few years ago had been difficult or impossible.

Those who knew the victims at Virginia Tech created digital memorials and tributes using Facebook, MySpace and personal web pages. Students immediately began blogging, posting video and still photos shot with cell phones. E-mail portals were clogged with messages. Communication that came naturally to students flew quickly through cyberspace as they learned about their friends from other friends.

These postings—all but obscure or unavailable just a few years ago—let reporters find a new list of sources and witnesses. Journalists from all media went online to query students. They went to the memorial pages, requesting interviews and looking for witnesses. Some found the inquires intrusive, yet others said yes. It was akin to what journalists did before the Internet: knock on doors and either be invited in or shooed off the porch.

The Wall Street Journal told the story of journalists at the student newspaper at Virginia Tech who were able to gather nearly half the names of those who had died just from memorials on Facebook. The university had yet to officially announce the victims' names. The student journalists began to cull the list from the many visitors to websites.

In the end, the student journalists had to call friends of the victims to confirm the deaths, but it was clear that the digital postings had overcome the silence from the university, which was waiting until it notified victims' families.

Though less intrusive than a reporter knocking at the door, cyber-journalists did attract the same criticism for disturbing those still trying to gather their thoughts and emotions.

"Completing the circle, subscribers to Internet sites railed against journalists creeping inside their social networks seeking quotes," wrote Joanne Ostrow, the television critic for *The Denver Post*. "Call it Journalism 2.0: the search for sources now leads to cyber-sites. Instead of perusing phone directories or distributing business cards, reporters now post online requests for eyewitness footage."

Some mainstream media websites simply linked to a student blogger at Virginia Tech, who was telling his story as it unfolded during the day.

But with new methods come new sensitivities about the relationship between journalists and their sources.

Officials at Facebook criticized some media for using the social networking pages to lift quotes and ask for interviews.

"We absolutely do not support how the media has been using Facebook in many cases," Brandee Barker, a Facebook spokeswoman told the *Boston Herald* the day after the shootings. "We see this as a violation of user privacy."

The Facebook official argued that the information on the pages should not be used without permission. Many journalists countered that the pages are designed for public discussion and therefore in the public domain.

The debate demonstrates that as journalism and technology evolve, professional newsgathering standards will be under constant scrutiny and review.

have much time with them . . . act as though you have all the time in the world to sit down with them."

Once she gains a family's trust, she also asks for anything that might be a written record. These can be the ordinary ones, such as birth certificates, baptism records, report cards. They might also be letters or private journals. They even could be notes on scraps of paper or dates highlighted on a calendar.

These prove invaluable. Journalists can quote from them, for one. They also may jar a memory that had lain dormant. But also these may show a side to the person that the friends and families have yet to reveal or may not have known.

"Always think about the kinds of documents that people have in their lives," she says.

Flood of the *Houston Chronicle* says to avoid asking the trite "How does this feel?" in those words. However, she says that is precisely the question that needs answering. Get inside the minds of the victim or those close to them. That gives stories a human quality and lets readers see what they saw.

"You need to ask how did it feel in about 10 different ways without being too cliché," Flood says. "You need to get details. The more detail you have the richer it is. Detail about what they're wearing. Ask them where they were when things happened. What they remember. If you can get sights, smells, anything like that. Detail makes things much richer."

The danger, Flood says, is letting those interviewed stop when they have described how they feel. To show readers the emotions, journalists need action, or stories that reveal the emotions through how the characters acted. Instead of saying that a mother is sad, show the mother softly touching the photograph of her lost child, her eyes focused in the distance.

"Everybody's going to say I am horribly sad, I am really mad. The words that describe their emotion or their reaction is not as sufficient as the actions and the specifics of what they did," Flood says.

What happens when a victim or family declines to talk? Be polite, back away, let them know where they can reach you later, and leave.

"There are people who find it intrusive and you have to know that when you're talking to someone who is a victim, who has lost somebody, who has lost their home, who is in some sort of mental distress, that if you say I'm a reporter may I speak to you and they say no, then you walk away immediately and you do not push that person," Flood says.

She has found that showing respect and not pushing the victims can pay off.

"If they push everybody away and you're the one who backed off and said you're sorry and left, then when they are ready to speak you are the first one to call as well. It's respect. It's about respect. It's about respect with everybody."

For Kiernan, the knock on the door and request for access can be different for each person.

"For some people they might just be in shock, and you're getting them at that time and they're just unloading on you. Other people I think they do understand that it's important in some way to document who this person was and for the people who ultimately read this story to understand that this was an individual who mattered at least to somebody in the world and not just another statistic."

A LAST EXAMPLE

At times, reporters catch victims at just the right moment when they are eager to share their thoughts. Palattella covered a story where a Russian immigrant had been arrested for manslaughter.

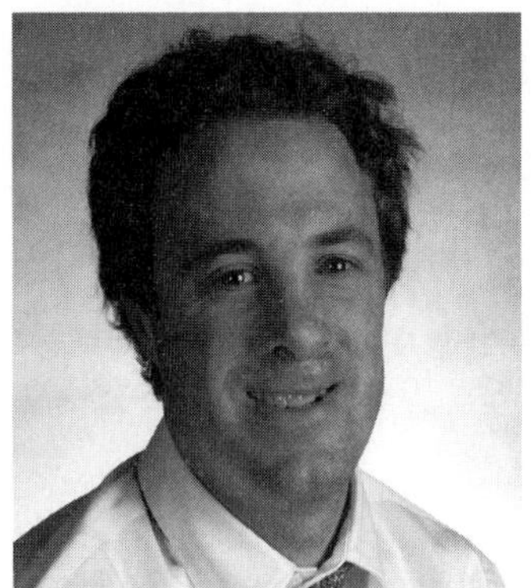
Ed Palattella

The Russian and his girlfriend had been asleep at a motel when a man broke through the door. Through a bizarre case of mistaken identity, the intruder thought the Russian, Denis Borisov, was someone else. He attacked Borisov, who killed the man, claiming self-defense.

Police arrested Borisov, holding him until they believed his innocence. Borisov's lawyer alerted Palattella, who caught Borisov at his lawyer's office a few minutes after his release.

"It was one of those things where everything just turned out. But it happens so rarely," Palattella says.

Palattella's story, written that night on deadline, captured the thoughts of an immigrant who was innocent but faced the American criminal system for the first time.

Someday, maybe soon, Denis Borisov hopes to pick up the telephone and call the family of the man he stabbed in the heart in self-defense.

Borisov still wonders what he will say.

He didn't know the man, 19-year-old Sergey A. Hodakovsky, and he doesn't know his family. He has no idea what their phone number is.

But someday, Denis Borisov said after his release from prison Friday night, he will call.

"I wish I could talk to his family, because I am so sorry," Borisov said. "I'm kind of scared. What would you do? Your son is killed and this guy wants to talk to you?

"I will talk to them," he said. "There is a big cut in my heart right now. And I wish I could change that this happened."

Denis Borisov, 20, started to cry.

IN CONCLUSION

Though uncomfortable, talking to victims lets journalists tell their readers a more complete story. They can captivate their readers if they show what a victim thought or felt and let the experience unfold through the victim's eyes. Journalists should respect the wishes of victims and their families should they not feel up to an interview. But more often than not, victims and those close to them are willing to share their traumatic event. Those reporters who rely chiefly on official reports run the risk of missing the best stories.

EXERCISE

Write a story from the following:

Elizabeth Johnson, president of Remnick College:

We are gathered today because of the one-year anniversary of one of the saddest moments at Remnick. A year ago today the airliner bearing 30 Remnick students studying abroad in London was blown up by terrorists. I wish that I never had to live through this tragedy and it is my awful duty to be president during this time. We remember the students with much pain. One of my favorites, class president Wayne Cassidy, was on that flight. But I knew Wayne, and he would want us to carry on, to go forward, to remember him with dignity and grace. He would not want us to be mired in bad thoughts. He would want us to conquer new horizons. That is my wish for this college and the students left to fulfill the destiny and desires of those 30.

Felicity Danbridge, student president of Remnick College:

All of us can remember where we were when we heard the news. I remember where I was. I was sitting in my dorm missing my best friend Ellen O'Donnell. I knew that later that day I would be picking her up from the airport. We were going to spend much of the holidays together. That's because Ellen and I had been best friends since the first day of kindergarten. In high school, I hadn't wanted to come to Remnick. But Ellen convinced me to go by promising that we would room together except for the semester she wanted to go abroad to London. We had planned to be the maids of honor at each other's weddings. We were going to go visit London after graduation and she was going to show me all the sights. I don't think I'll ever go to London now. I won't be able to see Big Ben or the Tower of London. I will only see Ellen O'Donnell, my best friend, now gone for but a year, even though I know it will be for a lifetime.

Kevin Barber, president of the Remembrance Committee:

We all have a story, and mine was Heidi Martin. I met Heidi during my freshman year at Remnick, and I have to say that I didn't like her much for most of that year. I think it's safe to say that Heidi didn't like me, either. As most of you know, Heidi was openly gay. She didn't flaunt it or put it in your face. But she didn't hide it. I didn't like it much, and told her so. And since we lived in the same dorm, we frequently had a lot of what some would call vigorous discussions. What was cool about Heidi is after even the most heated argument, she would still talk to me. One time, she even defended me to one of her friends, who also was gay. I can't honestly say I became a convert to the cause, but I did become a convert to Heidi. We worked on the school newspaper together last year before she went to London. There in the heat of deadline, she and I became friends. I respected her for her ability to edit a story on deadline. No one could make it as clean as Heidi. When we heard the news about the plane, and I was standing in the middle of the newsroom wishing I had someone like Heidi to help edit the story, I knew then that I had to do something to keep her memory alive. So we started this day of remembrance, one year later, and I hope we keep the memory of Heidi and the other 29 students alive forever.

CHAPTER 10

Writing about Disasters

IN THIS CHAPTER, YOU WILL LEARN ABOUT KEY ELEMENTS OF COVERING NATURAL AND MAN-MADE DISASTERS:

- First, the essential breaking news.
- Next, the invaluable daily enterprise.
- Eventually, the opportunity for public-service journalism.
- Inevitably, the opportunities that each of these offer to report and write at the top of your skills.

What happened spoke so vibrantly and profoundly and horribly for itself that you didn't need words like vibrant and profound and horrible.
Bryan Gruley, about his lead story on 9/11 for *The Wall Street Journal*

AFTER HURRICANE KATRINA OBLITERATED THE MISSISSIPPI GULF COAST, Biloxi *Sun Herald* Executive Editor Stan Tiner told his readers how his staff of 50 journalists had set aside their personal misfortunes. They understood their urgent role—the lifeline for survivors of a storm that damaged or destroyed 75 percent of all structures in three counties:

> Many, perhaps even most, journalists chose the profession because of their belief that they could do good—and provide a public service for the communities they serve.
>
> In these days those dreams have been realized by many who are toiling out of the newsroom of this little newspaper. The stories of courage, and destruction, of life and death, have taken them to the pinnacle of their careers.
>
> There will be much more to tell in the weeks and months ahead. We will probe how this could have happened, even asking the tough question—should it have happened?
>
> And we will tell of the rebuilding of the Coast, and of the spirit of the people who will do that.

In those few paragraphs, Tiner outlined the essential role of journalists and their journalism when communities need them most.

First, when the unimaginable hits home and chaos replaces order, journalists delivering breaking news become nearly as valuable as rescue squads delivering fresh water. Survivors need to know the extent of the disaster, the fate of loved ones and how to cope until order can be restored. Information literally is their lifeline. When a disaster kills power and phone lines, a newspaper is precious, supplying answers when desperate questions abound, and helping to conquer fear of the unknown. When those elsewhere are cut off from people and businesses in the disaster zone, they rely on news organizations' websites for vital information about whom and what has survived, whom they can contact and how they can help.

Then, as it sinks in that lives have changed suddenly and permanently, communities count on enterprising journalists to help them understand their options.

BREAKING NEWS

When momentous news breaks, the inverted pyramid lead does its best work.

Even when alternative leads work well, their writers quickly return to the basics: The 5 Ws and chronology, told through eyewitness accounts.

Many writers learn this painfully. Faced with writing the story of their lives, they may strain too hard to create art, when life (and death) has already provided unforgettable images.

These writers search for profound, hidden meaning when the facts in plain sight already are more powerful than imagination.

For generations, journalists have passed down a tale about a wire service reporter assigned to cover the devastating Johnstown flood of 1889.

When the New York office learned that the reporter on the scene was one infamous for writing purple prose, it cautioned him: Tell the story straight. Stick to the facts.

Yet, when the initial dispatch arrived, it began:

"God looked down on this forsaken land and saw death and destruction . . ."

Upon which New York interrupted the transmission with new instructions:

"Forget the flood. Interview God. Get art if possible."

This story has been told in so many variations that it is almost certainly apocryphal. But its lesson is real, and timeless: Report, don't interpret. Focus on the urgent.

The Johnstown flood was considered the worst flood in America for more than a century. The flooding that surpassed it earned spot-news leads as Hurricane Katrina first threatened, then battered the Gulf Coast in August 2005.

Note the progression of breaking news as reporters covered the approach of Hurricane Katrina, its assault on the Gulf Coast and the desperate conditions that impeded rescue efforts.

As a storm approaches, essential information includes the seriousness of the threat, the speed of the hurricane and evacuation information:

August 28—The Associated Press

Louisiana coastal residents jammed freeways and gas stations Saturday as they rushed to get out of the way of Hurricane Katrina, a vicious storm that is threatening to gain even more strength and make a direct hit on the New Orleans area.

August 29—The New York Times

Hurricane Katrina, one of the most powerful storms ever to threaten the United States, bore down on the Gulf Coast on Sunday, sending hundreds of thousands of people fleeing the approach of its 160-mile-an-hour winds and prompting a mandatory evacuation of New Orleans, a city perilously below sea level.

When a hurricane hits, the essential information answers the question: How hard? Both the AP and *The Times* note the force of the hurricane and the death and flooding it inflicted. Also note that while human life is most precious, in hurricanes property damage is typically more extensive because most people had warning enough to evacuate or seek shelter.

August 30—The Associated Press

Announcing itself with shrieking 145-mph winds, Hurricane Katrina slammed into the Gulf

HOW TO
Organize a Story on Disasters

1. **Lead:** Usually the inverted pyramid works the best for stories on disasters. The destruction is so monumental that simply using the 5W's and H formula is enough.
2. **Impact:** Tell your readers the scope of the disaster, how many people have been hurt or are in harm's way. Use numbers and best estimates from public officials.
3. **Update:** Tell your readers the latest information you have before deadline of what is occurring or what rescue and public safety workers hope to do in the next few hours or days.
4. **Quotes:** An official quote of the magnitude of the disaster adds to overall storytelling.
5. **Personal Stories:** Anyone who has been a victim or has a story to tell puts a human face on the disaster.
6. **Chronological Recount:** At some point in your story, you should start from when the disaster began and then lead your readers through the timeline of events.

Coast just outside New Orleans on Monday, submerging entire neighborhoods up to their roofs, swamping Mississippi's beachfront casinos and killing at least 55 people.

August 30—The New York Times

Hurricane Katrina pounded the Gulf Coast with devastating force at daybreak on Monday, sparing New Orleans the catastrophic hit that had been feared but inundating parts of the city and heaping damage on neighboring Mississippi, where it tossed boats, ripped away scores of roofs and left many of the major coastal roadways impassable.

Packing 145-mile-and-hour winds as it made landfall, the storm left more than a million people in three states without power and submerged highways even hundreds of miles from its center.

Officials reported at least 55 deaths, with 50 alone in Harrison County, Miss., which includes Gulfport and Biloxi. Emergency workers feared that they would find more dead among people believed to be trapped underwater and in collapsed buildings.

Once a hurricane has passed, reporters focus on rescue and recovery. Katrina was unique in America—its flood waters didn't overwhelm lakes and levees in New Orleans until after Katrina had passed by. That caused a second day of disaster that needed to be covered while reporters also focused on rescues.

August 31—The Associated Press

Rescuers along the hurricane-ravaged Gulf Coast pushed aside the dead to reach the living Tuesday in a race against time and rising waters, while New Orleans sank deeper into crisis and Louisiana's governor ordered storm refugees out of this drowning city.

Two levees broke and sent water coursing into the streets of the Big Easy a full day after New Orleans appeared to have escaped widespread destruction from Hurricane Katrina. An estimated 80 percent of the below-sea-level city was under water, up to 20 feet deep in places, with miles and miles of homes swamped.

"The situation is untenable," Gov. Kathleen Blanco said. "It's just heartbreaking."

One Mississippi county alone said its number of dead was at least 100, and officials are "very, very worried that this is going to go a lot higher," said Joe Spraggins, civil defense director for Harrison County, home to Biloxi and Gulfport.

With the weather having done its worst, reporting moved on to recovery—a process made immeasurably worse by government procrastination and blame-shifting. Reporters focused on the vivid details of tragedy to alert the nation to the expanding emergency and awaken rescue efforts stalled by bureaucrats.

September 2—The (New Orleans) *Times-Picayune*

New Orleans on Thursday pulled back from an almost complete collapse of public order, a near anarchy that had supplanted receding floodwaters as the gravest threat to the city's still tenuous recovery.

WIRED AND WIRELESS | WEB

When Hurricane Katrina blew away *The* (New Orleans) *Times-Picayune* disaster plan, the newspaper's website saved the day and, some say, their lives.

The newspaper had built a hurricane bunker at the innermost part of the fortress-like *Times-Picayune* building. It had emergency power and off-site printing arrangements. Elaborate plans to outfit reporters and photographers with cell phones, satellite phones, radios and other emergency equipment gave the news staff confidence, especially after all went well during Hurricane George in 1998.

It was, after all, *The Times-Picayune* that had warned New Orleans in a 2002 series that a Category 3 hurricane could overwhelm the levees holding back the lake waters above this below-sea-level city. The newspaper had taken its own advice and prepared for the worst.

Then Katrina blew out *The Times-Picayune*'s bulletproof windows. Water filled the streets around the building. Thirty hours after the news staff had huddled in the hurricane bunker, they faced a now-or-never decision: Get out on the last circulation trucks or stay in an unsafe building unsure whether they could work or when they could leave.

Katrina attacked early Monday morning. *The Times-Picayune* could not print a newspaper that day, Tuesday, Wednesday, or Thursday. Katrina's storm surge had swelled Lake Pontchartrain, which spilled its flood waters over and through New Orleans' levees, filling the city with water as high as 14 feet. Eighty percent of New Orleans was flooded, 200,000 homes destroyed, a million people evacuated. Suddenly, the paper's website, nola.com, became *The Times-Picayune*—the only resort for a desperate news staff and its suffering community.

"There's nothing like sitting on the biggest story of your career and not having any way to do it," said Jon Donley, who was the founding editor of nola.com in 1997, after 20 years as a newspaperman.

Nola.com allowed *Times-Picayune* journalists to reach their community, supply trusted information during a time of panic and send out the SOS to bureaucrats who had been clueless for days.

Jon Donley, founding and current editor of nola.com, website of *The* (New Orleans) *Times-Picayune*.

They used a quick-publishing tool for breaking news. "Movable type" permitted writers to file directly to nola.com without a web staffer to post for them. Some had already been trained on blogging and other Internet tools. The rest got crash courses.

"When all was said and done, everybody had a training session," Donley said.

The staff already knew that online forums would be lifelines for locals, evacuees and distant family, friends and coworkers.

"In 1998, we had a big evacuation for Hurricane George," Donley explained. "When people got to wherever they evacuated, a good number of them posted to nola's forums on their evacuation routes and were asking when they could come home."

This time, forums simultaneously told of desperation and signs of life. A Missing Persons forum was established Wednesday. More than 4,000 posts went there that day. A Found Persons forum and a "Tell Them You're Okay" forum followed. Nola.com had sites for relief aid, volunteers and pet rescues. Frantic people got helpful information from strangers about missing loved ones.

Rescuers got clues about where to find stranded homeowners. People in need sent out an SOS.

Online traffic spiked from a norm of 800,000 page views a day to nearly 40 times that—30 million page views. Nola.com, host of high-demand Mardi Gras content online, was ready for that, too.

The Times-Picayune staff won two Pulitzer Prizes for its storm coverage. The community shares those honors. It contributed to the content.

"The clearest, truest pictures of what was happening to our city did not come from professional journalists, but from the people," Donley said.

Three days after the storm Donley received photos from a girl who was evacuated on a bus to the Astrodome in Houston.

"She had taken pictures of the work by an artist who had sketched a woman with tears running down her face. She sent a photo of the feet of boy who used two MRE (Meals Ready to Eat) packages with string for sandals because he didn't have any shoes.

"Here we have a core black person who got those photos to us on the Internet. It turns out there's a lot of street kids who have their own website."

Nola.com received 82 photos from a man in Chalmette, the largest city in St. Bernard Parish, where only five homes were not flooded.

"In the first photos, he sat in his living room with a digital camera. The water was outside, halfway up to his window like an aquarium," Donley described. "Then he got up into the attic and got photos of the water rising. Then onto the roof with photos of his neighbors' houses floating by.

"I have those 82 photos and no professional photographer can recapture that moment."

It turned out that nola.com was a lifeline for *The Times-Picayune* staff, too, in more ways than one.

"Everybody in town was traumatized," Donley said. "Everyone at *The Times-Picayune* had a hardship.

"I'd see them write their stories with their teeth clenched, then walk into the hall and you'd see them, just heaving the tears. That was pure gut journalism at its finest."

The staff had posted full newspaper-like pages online from temporary offices in Baton Rouge. They blogged, filed notes, photos and full stories as if they had a whole newspaper to fill with the only story that mattered.

Donley understood the significance: "Just the ability to get the story and photos out was life-saving for everyone. If you have the ability to work, you have a job and hope. If you're huddled in a shelter, all you have is despair."

That included Donley, who could not find his daughter Sarah, then 20. She had been in the area of a 12-foot storm surge. Nearly every tree was down, cutting off access, in or out.

"I was almost suicidal part of the time," Donley admitted. "If I hadn't been able to work . . ."

He had plenty of work, and savvy. "I was using all my own tools" in his search for his daughter.

He spent 72 hours under the police scanners, reporting what he heard on his blog, but keeping an ear for signs of hope about Sarah. He joined the posters on forums. Four days later, a friend who had finally gotten his electricity back saw Donley's post that his daughter's area had not been completely evacuated. It was still almost impassable, with trees every two feet. The friend, an ex-policeman, found Sarah and her boyfriend, cooking a sausage over a candle.

Donley was in the midst of a TV interview with NBC when his daughter walked into *The Times-Picayune*'s temporary newsroom in Baton Rouge. He started crying on the air, explaining to a national audience, "My daughter just walked in."

And on Friday, when the newspaper was finally able to resume limited print publishing, grateful citizens had a similar sensation.

"Seeing *The Times-Picayune* was a sign that the city wasn't completely dead," Donley said.

Evidence that authorities were beginning to get a grip on gargantuan problems varied from the successful and orderly evacuation of Baptist Mercy Hospital to a sharp reduction in the menacing bands of idle refugees, many of them intent on looting that had haunted Uptown neighborhoods in the immediate aftermath of Hurricane Katrina.

September 4—The Washington Post

Tens of thousands of people spent a fifth day awaiting evacuation from this ruined city, as Bush administration officials blamed state and local authorities for what leaders at all levels have called a failure of the country's emergency management.

The White House dispatched 7,200 more troops to the area, bringing the total in the region to more than 40,000 National Guard and active-duty soldiers. Authorities reported progress in restoring order and electricity and repairing levees, as a hospital ship arrived and cruise ships were sent to provide temporary housing for victims.

Note that the inverted pyramid served journalists and their readers well for a week or more. Many other formats were used to tell stories of horror, heroics and outrage during this week. But some of the stories above would rival any for power. The facts were that potent.

Also note that the inverted-pyramid leads did not rob writers of their ability to provide meaningful context.

HOW EYEWITNESSES CAN HELP TELL THE STORY

A hurricane scatters potential victims and denies reporters access to them during the storm. Despite the thousands killed in the Sept. 11, 2001 terrorist attacks on New York and Washington, reporters had legions of eyewitnesses. Disaster reporters sought them for tales so vivid that no official accounts can match.

Bryan Gruley customarily took weeks to craft his Page One stories for *The Wall Street Journal*. After New York and Washington were attacked, he had one hour to turn 300 inches of notes into his paper's lead story.

Gruley wrote about a dozen inches of copy in that first hour. After filing "little three and four paragraph snippets" for the next two hours, he had a 3,000-word story worthy of the American Society of Newspaper Editors' Distinguished Writing Award.

Here is one of those snippets:

The streets of downtown Manhattan were strewn with body parts, clothing, shoes and mangled flesh, including a severed head with long, dark hair and a severed arm resting along a highway about 300 yards from the crash site. People fleeing the attacks stampeded through downtown and streamed across the Brooklyn Bridge while looking over their shoulders at the astonishing sight of the World Trade Center collapsing in a pile of smoke and ash.

> Andrew Lenney, 37 years old, a financial analyst for the New York City Council, was walking to work a few blocks from the trade center when, he said, "I saw the plane out of the corner of my eye. You're accustomed to a plane taking up a certain amount of space in the sky. This plane was huge. I just froze and watched the plane.
>
> "It was coming down the Hudson. It was banking toward me. I saw the tops of both wings," he said. "It was turning to make sure it hit the intended target. It plowed in about 20 stories down dead center into the north face of the building. I thought it was a movie," Mr. Lenney said. "I couldn't believe it. It was such a perfect pyrotechnic display. It was symmetrical."

Gruley worked from dispatches e-mailed by *The Journal*'s reporters at Ground Zero and throughout New York City. Accustomed to writing from the notes his colleagues filed, Gruley found these dispatches superior because his colleagues "didn't have time to interpret."

"It was names. It was action. It was description. It was real things."

Gruley applied the same lesson to his own writing.

"What happened spoke so vibrantly and profoundly and horribly for itself that you didn't need words like *vibrant* and *profound* and *horrible*," he said at an ASNE meeting seven months later. "I read it again today. I was marking out things that I would, had I had more time, taken out—people listening in horror. What else would they be listening in? And there were some adverbs that snuck in there. I don't like adverbs. You could see this stuff. It was cinematic. It was just a matter of putting it in order."

"Putting it in order" is the function of chronology. Superior stories often begin with a vivid, dramatic scene—a revealing moment. Then the stories rely on chronology to show how events got to that point. The stories conclude with a memorable fact or quote that ties back into the lead. This is what is sometimes referred to as "hourglass" story structure.

DAILY ENTERPRISE

The next order of business is enterprise. When the scarcely imaginable happens, people turn to their news organizations for understanding. They are anchored in front of televisions for long hours. Then they turn to newspapers and websites for more.

It's remarkable: even as people had 24-hour access to electronic news, millions of additional newspapers were sold on Sept. 12, 2001, then again in the days after Hurricane Katrina.

Nothing sells newspapers quite like news. When readers well-versed in the headlines turn to print, that is an ideal time to treat them to enterprise unavailable elsewhere.

Enterprise journalism is exclusive. If you didn't find it here, you wouldn't know about it. It is gathered on the initiative of reporters and photographers, rather than the news that *comes to us* in the form of breaking news.

The Art of Storytelling

When a work of nonfiction is praised because it "reads like a novel," invariably the piece is a narrative story, reconstructed in exquisite detail from eyewitness accounts. News story or book, it has character and plot, dialogue and action.

Although such reconstructions can spring from other careful reporting, they most often appear in news accounts following spectacular acts of breaking news—terrorist attacks, school shootings or natural disasters, for instance.

They may appear days, weeks or months after the breaking news, but reconstructions have several key elements in common:

- They answer "How?": *How Sept. 11 Hijackers Beat Airport Security, How Katrina Overwhelmed New Orleans' Levees.*
- They rely on fine detail for insight and character development.
- They use narrative story structure.
- They tell the story in chronological sequence.
- The writing constantly moves the plot forward, creating the sensation of motion.

Character development, plot development and dialogue can consume columns of space. Or they can be accomplished in one column, like this story by James Dwyer of *The New York Times*. We have excerpted a portion of the story about a man who escaped from an elevator in the World Trade Center with six others because he had his squeegee with him on Sept. 11, 2001.

> After 10 minutes, a live voice delivered a blunt message over the intercom. There had been an explosion. Then the intercom went silent. Smoke seeped into the elevator cabin. One man cursed skyscrapers. Mr. Phoenix, the tallest, a Port Authority engineer, poked for a ceiling hatch. Others pried apart the car doors, propping them open with the long wooden handle of Mr. Demczur's squeegee.
>
> There was no exit.
>
> They faced a wall, stenciled with the number "50." That particular elevator bank did not serve the 50th floor, so there was no need for an opening. To escape, they would have to make one themselves.
>
> Mr. Demczur felt the wall. Sheetrock. Having worked in construction in his early days as a Polish immigrant, he knew that it could be cut with a sharp knife.
>
> No one had a knife.
>
> From his bucket, Mr. Demczur drew his squeegee. He slid its metal edge against the wall, back and forth, over and over. He was spelled by the other men. Against the smoke, they breathed through handkerchiefs dampened in a container of milk Mr. Phoenix had just bought.
>
> Sheetrock comes in panels about one inch thick, Mr. Demczur recalled. They cut an inch, then two inches. Mr. Demczuk's hand ached. As he carved into the third panel, his hand shook, he fumbled the squeegee and it dropped down the shaft.

Asked what makes a good short story work, Dwyer spoke about structure.

"There's a beginning, a middle and an end in this story," he told the American Society of Newspaper Editors. "They're trapped. They struggle to escape. They get out. There's even a postscript. The three acts are a key element. . . .

"If you can find the three acts that are part of the story, then walk it down that way. The other piece is you have to be very savage about cutting. For instance, in the case of the squeegee story, I watched the men on the 'Today' show a couple of days after my piece ran. I swear I couldn't follow them, not because they were telling different stories. You have to be brutal about trimming your narrative down to absolute vital, hot core. If you don't you're going to end up having people babbling like they sometimes do on the 'Today' show. In this particular case, they just didn't order it. You have to talk to each one of these guys, and you finally figure which version is pretty true. There's a lot of stuff that you have to throw out."

Buzz Bissinger does not wait for breaking news to write reconstructions. Each of his nonfiction books are built that way.

"Chronology is essential," he says, invoking the core of his signature story of a plunging airplane and his books *Friday Night Lights*, *3 Nights in August* and *Prayer for the City*: "44 seconds, a football season, a three-game series, four years of a mayor's term. Each has some finite beginning, middle and end. When I don't have that, I find the stories tend to drift and it makes writing much, much harder."

He quoted Bill Eddins, then an editor at *The Philadelphia Inquirer*'s Sunday magazine: "Keep it simple, stupid. Keep it chronological. Very few people in arts and letters can pull off a complex narrative—and you're not one of them, Buzz."

The chronology also helps Bissinger edit himself before an editor sees his writing.

"As a young writer, I wrote way too long. I had a pretty good gift for storytelling. But we become enamored of our notes and all that we've gathered.

"I remember another editor in Saint Paul, Deborah Howell, telling me, 'You're not writing for yourself. You're writing for readers. How can we get that balance—give them information, give them drama and keep the pace going?'

"Indignant, I walked away. I know now that she was right.

"Now I'm always paying attention to pace (to propel readers to each new paragraph). I'm looking at any extra words—is this interesting information really germane to the piece or is it just being in love with the music of your own voice?"

Bissinger said he learned a lot about self-editing by reading Steve Lopez, then in Philadelphia and now a local columnist for the *Los Angeles Times*.

"He had exactly 17.2 inches. He could not waste a word. A marvelous columnist. You could learn a lot from the way he wrote. Constant self-editing. He had no choice."

Nothing demands—and rewards—a reporter's curiosity more than enterprise does. Driven by a reporter's ability to wonder Why? and How? the possibilities are otherwise limitless.

The obvious enterprise following a disaster like a terrorist strike or a deadly hurricane is in the gripping tales of survival. As the events following Sept. 11, 2001, and Hurricane Katrina demonstrated, extreme circumstances bring out the best and worst in people. Heroism, compassion and selflessness contrast with acts of cowardice, hate and greed. All make jaw-dropping stories.

The following few examples demonstrate, however, that the range of possibilities is much greater. All appeared in the Business section of *The New York Times* in the second week following Hurricane Katrina. These examples from one reporting team in a less-obvious area of hurricane news coverage illustrate that enterprise results primarily from determination to produce it.

Sept. 7: Next to a story announcing that hurricane-influenced gasoline prices were receding at last, a story headlined "The Perils of Casinos That Float" described the destruction of offshore casinos near Biloxi, Miss. The story explained that Mississippi law requires casinos to be on water, separate from nearby communities, then offered this insight:

> The wreckage could even hold a silver lining. The extensive damage has set off a debate over whether casino owners should be allowed to rebuild on land. Even one of the industry's most vocal opponents is resigned to seeing dry-land casinos in the near future, but wants to extract a hefty price in return.

Sept. 8: Devastated homeowners in southern Louisiana might have trouble collecting insurance based on this question: Was the damage caused by hurricane winds or subsequent flooding?

> A majority of businesses and homeowners in the storm-ravaged area have insurance that covers wind damage. While many businesses bought flood insurance as well, relatively few homeowners did. In Orleans Parish, for example, the federal government treated flood insurance as largely optional because of the protection offered by levees. Only two in five households bought the relatively expensive coverage.

Sept. 9: Two unique stories ran on the section front. One addresses the plight of displaced workers.

> With some one million people from New Orleans and the Mississippi Gulf Coast suddenly tossed out of their jobs by Hurricane Katrina, the newly unemployed are now fanning out across the South and the rest of the country, getting help from friends, family, employers or government agencies. In many ways, the potpourri of relief efforts is serving as a testament to the economy's flexibility.
>
> But the makeup of the Gulf Coast work force—heavy on warehouse employees and blackjack dealers, light on bankers and factory workers—has already complicated relief efforts and appears likely to add to Hurricane Katrina's economic damage.
>
> With a population less educated than the nation as a whole, New Orleans and coastal Mississippi employed many people without the kind of skills that would help

WE'RE WHITER.

WHITE		BLACK	
PRE KATRINA	POST KATRINA	PRE KATRINA	POST KATRINA
59%	73%	37%	22%

Many African-Americans have not returned to their homes, such as those in eastern New Orleans, while more white residents resettled close to home.
STAFF FILE PHOTO BY CHUCK COOK

WE'RE OLDER.

MEDIAN AGE		CHILDREN 3 & OLDER ENROLLED IN SCHOOL	
PRE KATRINA	POST KATRINA	PRE KATRINA	POST KATRINA
37.7	41.6	312,899	170,269

Because many schools like Jean Gordon Elementary could not reopen, families with school-age children stayed away. That trend has been partly reversed since January as some schools reopened.
STAFF PHOTO BY TED JACKSON

WE'RE MORE AFFLUENT.

MEAN HOUSEHOLD INCOME	
PRE KATRINA	POST KATRINA
$55,326	$64,122

Fewer poor people who lived in public housing could return because much of it was too damaged to reopen, such as the St. Bernard housing development. So, mean household income figures increased.
STAFF FILE PHOTO BY ELLIS LUCIA

Source: U.S. Census Bureau survey of the New Orleans area January-August 2005 and September-December 2005

The Times-Picayune and nola.com employed a series of interactive graphics to help citizens understand the effects of Hurricane Katrina and its aftermath. In this one, database reporting and modern Internet technology combine to show how New Orleans is repopulating after the massive evacuations. In earlier graphics, users could see the sequence of flooding by pressing a button, or could check the progress of reconstruction in their neighborhoods by clicking on a map.

> **ADVANCED TIP**
> **Covering 9/11**
>
> "What happened spoke so vibrantly and profoundly and horribly for itself that you didn't need words like *vibrant* and *profound* and *horrible*. I read it again today. I was marking out things that I would, had I had more time, taken out—people listening in horror. What else would they be listening in? And there were some adverbs that snuck in there. I don't like adverbs. You could see this stuff. It was cinematic. It was just a matter of putting it in order."—*The Wall Street Journal* reporter Bryan Gruley, telling the American Society of Newspaper Editors about covering the Sept. 11, 2001, terrorists attacks.

them quickly find new jobs. The Gulf Coast economy also had more than its fair share of workers who made their living waiting tables, fixing houses or otherwise serving a local economy that, for now, does not exist.

The second story focuses on the tough decision by executives of Ruth's Chris Steak House, an 88-restaurant chain headquartered outside New Orleans. Meeting in Orlando, Fla., the executives decided unanimously not to return. The headquarters would move, permanently.

Many other businesses in New Orleans, particularly those with public shareholders, face a similar quandary. And as others struggle to get back on their feet, the quick, practical decision by Ruth's Chris may foreshadow a painful exodus of a number of other companies from the city and surrounding region.

Sept. 11: The headline, "Disasters Waiting to Happen / Has a Zeal for Budget Cuts Undermined Public Safety?" suggests a story from New Orleans. It is not.

More than a thousand miles of levees stretch from San Francisco Bay. They protect the cities and the farmland in the Sacramento–San Joaquin delta of California and keep salt from the bay out of the drinking water of millions of people. But those levees are deteriorating, experts say, raising the odds of a Katrina-like disaster for the nation's most populous state.

The delta and its maze of levees are high on the list of public infrastructure considered to be subpar. That list—which also includes highways, dams, ports and bridges—is growing as government outlays for repair lose out to budget cutting. . . .

. . . Infrastructure deteriorates in more than one way. There is lack of maintenance: roughly 13,000 highway fatalities each year, for example, are a result of inadequate maintenance on aging highways, the civil engineers say. And there is overuse: the levees in California, many of them built by farmers to convert marshes to farmland, now must be strengthened to prevent the destruction of newly built communities.

Sept. 14: Two more unique stories. One is headlined, "When Good Will is Also Good Business"

As companies reach into their corporate coffers in a time-honored gesture of corporate good will, they have grown increasingly creative, even strategic, about the way they approach their philanthropy. Many are tapping their particular expertise, and in contrast to the government's initial response, they have applied hallmark speed and efficiency to the process of sending in goods and services.

Corporations are rising to the challenge out of a spirit of charity but also to burnish their image. The money spent not only redounds in good will but also serves to publicize a company's products or business.

The second story is blunt:

> The New Orleans medical system has been devastated by Hurricane Katrina, and no one can say how many hospitals will ever re-open.
>
> Although some local officials are calling for a central plan, decisions are likely to be based mainly on economic forces—not necessarily on the city's health care needs. Deregulation at the state and local level over the last few decades has meant that the main force in the hospital industry now is the invisible hand of the marketplace.

ENTERPRISE: START WITH STAKEHOLDERS

Each of these examples teaches us things that may not have occurred to us. *The Times* found these stories by considering all stakeholders—many people with a stake in the outcome are far from the center of the action.

Consider the stakeholders in these stories: people whose homes have been flooded, displaced workers, business owners, those who would rebuild the Gulf Coast, policy makers and even those elsewhere who have new warnings about disasters waiting to happen.

Identifying stakeholders is one discipline to generate enterprise story ideas. Here's another: Each of the above stories fits into the category of whether and how New Orleans will be rebuilt.

When a disaster creates chaos, reporters and their editors can help their community focus by organizing news coverage into areas of inquiry.

After Sept. 11, 2001, for instance, those categories included:

- The investigation into the terrorist attacks
- The victims (including survivors)
- The relief effort
- How to help and how to cope (including issues involving religion and travel)
- Al Qaeda and its place in the Muslim world
- America's preparation for war (including military activity, political action, protests and civil liberties)

This focuses the journalism, too, and applies to local disasters as well as those of national significance. A disastrous fire that causes many deaths and much property destruction would direct enterprising coverage to the investigation (arson or accident?), the victims, safety issues (was this catastrophe preventable?) and rebuilding plans, among other possible areas of inquiry.

RESISTING DISTRACTION

Note the inclusion of official investigations as a major area of inquiry. When blockbuster news breaks, some journalists get distracted by the enormity of the implications. These—global concerns and political ramifications among them—are important to pursue. But remember the fundamentals, too. On one important level, these require the same focus as crime stories—incidents, victims and evidence.

In 1978, the Peoples Temple religious cult led by the Rev. Jim Jones ended in an apparent mass suicide of more than 900 followers. This happened within hours of the murders of a congressman and three journalists who traveled to South America to investigate on behalf of anxious California parents.

Immediately after discovery of a poisoned drink that followers were believed to have consumed together in a suicide ceremony, news stories morphed into studies of cult religions and their implications. Reporters for the *Chicago Tribune* followed a different path.

Checking the coroner's reports, they discovered that hundreds of the followers did not swallow the cyanide-laced drink. They had been injected with poison—and the position of the needle marks argued against self-injection. Some of the victims had been shot. Suddenly, the story of brainwashed followers and their mad leader became a story of mass murder.

After his exclusive story, *Tribune* reporter Tim McNulty said he always kept one thing in mind: "This was a police story." He had reacted to the body count with a reporter's discipline. The coroner's office, which determines cause of death, is one of the checkpoints.

The reporting and writing fundamentals described in this chapter apply to all disasters, large and smaller. Call them into action when your town is victim to tornados, flash floods, toxic poisoning, factory explosions, school shootings and other tragic disasters.

PUBLIC SERVICE JOURNALISM

An explosion on Jan. 4, 2006, trapped 13 workers in the Sago Mine in West Virginia. With little oxygen and surrounded by toxic gases, all but one soon died. Less than 48 hours after the explosion, *Washington Post* reporter Joby Warrick produced this news lead:

> Time and again over the past four years, federal mining inspectors documented the same litany of problems at central West Virginia's Sago Mine: mine roofs that tended to collapse without warning. Faulty or inadequate tunnel supports. A dangerous buildup of flammable coal dust.
>
> Yesterday, the mine's safety record came into sharp focus as officials searched for explanations to Monday's underground explosion. That record, as reflected in dozens of federal inspection reports, shows a succession of operators struggling to overcome serious, long-standing safety problems, some of which could be part of the investigation into the cause of the explosion that trapped 13 miners.

This and similar stories almost immediately forced public officials to focus on how to prevent future mine disasters. Documenting dangers, sounding the alarms and influencing changes that help make communities safer are ingredients of public service journalism.

The term is intentionally imprecise, envisioning a wide range of good that journalism can accomplish. Disasters present journalists with extraordinary opportunity to fulfill the highest calling of the profession.

That can be accomplished by sounding the alarm in advance, as *The Times-Picayune* did when it warned, in a 2002 series of stories, about the circumstances that could overwhelm the levee system that protects New Orleans from catastrophic flooding.

When the worst happens, journalists have a vital role in helping their communities cope, then recover. After hurricanes, terrorist strikes and more, journalists have given victims hope—linking separated families, connecting those in need of help with those who can give it, and making it possible for officials to pass vital information to its scared and scattered citizens.

Subsequent journalistic diligence—investigating causes and educating about solutions—can increase the likelihood of a safer future.

PULITZER PRIZE EXAMPLES

The Pulitzer Board presented its highest honor—the Pulitzer Gold Medal for Meritorious Public Service—to *The Miami Herald* in 1993 "for coverage that not only helped readers cope with Hurricane Andrew's devastation but also showed how lax zoning, inspection and building codes had contributed to the destruction."

In 1998, the Pulitzer Board presented its gold medal to a much smaller newspaper, the *Grand Forks Herald* in North Dakota, "for its sustained and informative coverage, vividly illustrated with photographs, that helped hold its community together in the wake of flooding, a blizzard and a fire that devastated much of the city, including the newspaper plant itself."

And in 2002, the gold medal was presented to *The New York Times* "for 'A Nation Challenged,' a special section published regularly after the September 11th terrorist attacks on America, which coherently and comprehensively covered the tragic events, profiled the victims, and tracked the developing story, locally and globally."

Whether the disaster is natural or man-made, local or global in scope, covered by small, medium or large organizations, in any region of the country, the profession often confers its highest praise on those journalists who rise above adversity when their communities need them the most.

IN CONCLUSION

Natural and man-made disasters demand urgent coverage of breaking news, thoughtful enterprise and courageous public service journalism.

This can require journalistic effort that is demanding physically and emotionally, but serves the best traditions of our profession.

When covering breaking news, stay focused on the urgent, the important. Resist the temptation to overwrite.

Follow leads to unique enterprise by recognizing all who have a stake in the outcome of recent events. Chronicle the impact of sudden events by helping others understand how their lives will change.

Fulfill journalism's public service promise by helping communities cope and regain hope. Investigate dangers and help find solutions that will make a safer future.

TOOL KIT

The Wall Street Journal's award-winning stories from Sept. 12, 2001: www.asne.org/index.cfm?ID=3426#Stands

Tragedies and Journalists: A Guide for More Effective Coverage, by Joe Hight and Frank Smyth. A publication of the Dart Center for Journalism & Trauma, Seattle, Wash.

EXERCISE 1

Write a story from the following:

You are a reporter for your university's newspaper and website. You are with your roommates in your dorm at about 6 p.m. on a stormy Wednesday when you hear something that sounds like a train go overhead. You don't think much of it until somebody from down the hall comes rushing in and says the storm has blown off the roof of Archeletta Hall. That's a small dorm on the other side of campus. You know just what to do. You grab your notebook, camera and tape recorder and head for Archeletta. When you arrive, this is what you see.

Fire trucks, firefighters and police officers are swarming across the yard leading to the old dorm. You find the police department's spokesperson, Bob Wainright, who tells you this:

"We have 22 students in the dorm and all but three are accounted for. From what we can tell, the storm took the roof off the place, then collapsed the back of the building. We hope the students who in there are gone."

You find a couple of students sitting under a blanket by themselves looking somewhat disheveled. One of them is sophomore Wendy Harnell.

"We were just getting ready to go eat when we heard this noise like a train. It was the scariest noise I have ever heard. The building began shaking. I thought I was going to die. I have never been so scared. I just jumped to the floor and crawled under my bed and asked God to save us. Then it was over. We walked outside and saw the roof was gone."

You locate the university's spokesperson, Preston Wayne. He tells you that this has only happened to the university once before, the storm of 1962. No one was injured then.

"This is the worst storm ever to hit our school," he tells you.

You have just finished talking to him when you hear shouting. Apparently the firefighters are pulling students out of the rubble. From what you can see, the three students are walking. Ambulance workers are looking at them. Wayne walks over and then comes back to you.

"All three students are OK. They apparently were trapped but it appears that they have some cuts and bruises but that's all. We are very fortunate, and those students are very fortunate."

You ask if you can talk to them. He leads you to Kiki Masden.

"I had just come back from physics class, and I was wet from walking in the rain. I turned to ask my roommate a question and suddenly he was gone and I was falling and then I realized I had stopped. But I couldn't move my leg. It didn't hurt but part of the building was on it. I just waited and then I heard the firefighters yelling. I said, "Over here," and they came and pushed the debris aside and pulled me out. I'm really lucky. I'm just thankful that's all that happened."

You thank him and then find Wayne again, who tells you the university will begin rebuilding as soon as possible. It hopes to preserve the building, which he says is the oldest on campus. Oh, that's also where the first storm struck in 1962.

You go back to your dorm, but on the way home call the weather service from your cell. A spokesperson blames the storm on a severe down draft that hit the area at 5:52 p.m. It uprooted some trees nearby but they know of no other damage.

You now sit down at your computer, and write an award-winning story.

EXERCISE 2

Write a story from the following:

What: Sleet overnight. Interstate 81 overpasses are frozen over. Tractor-trailer loses control, smashes into a passenger car. Eighteen-car pileup. Twenty-five people injured. One man killed. 18-year-old Harold Mead of New York City. Riding in a Santa Fe SUV with his 7-year-old brother, Nathan. Nathan is unhurt. Most of the 25 injured are treated at Serafim Hospital and released. Four remain in the hospital and are in serious condition.

When: The accident occurred at 7:35 a.m. on Monday. Traffic was tied up for three hours.

Where: At mile marker 83 near the village of Tully.

Why: Rain through much of the night turned to sleet, icing up the roads. State police said the overpasses iced up the heaviest.

How: The tractor-trailer was traveling north when it hit a patch of ice on an overpass. The tractor-trailer jackknifed, then rolled over, hitting the passenger car that was traveling in the next lane.

Who: Harold Mead. Freshman at Carelton State University. Majoring in speech communications. Lived at Hendricks dorm.

Quotes: State trooper Jerry Mariano: "It was like a sheet of ice on that overpass. Once the tractor-trailer went down, I don't think the rest of these cars had a chance. This is the worst pileup I've seen in the last two years."

Driver Hector Salsito, 32, in a Taurus: "I saw the big tractor flip up ahead and on a normal road, I would have had plenty of time to stop. But my brakes just wouldn't work on that ice. I feel lucky to walk away from this."

Amy Rainwright, dean of student affairs at Carelton State: "We're saddened by the death of Harold. He was on his way back to Carelton after visiting his family in New York City. He was hoping one day to follow his father's footsteps and go into politics. His father is Patrick Mead, who served one term as governor about 20 years ago."

CHAPTER 11

How to Write News from Speeches, Press Conferences and Press Releases

IN THIS CHAPTER YOU WILL LEARN:

- Speeches, press conferences and press releases can lead to vital stories.
- How to prepare for and write stories from speeches.
- How to prepare for, participate in and write stories from press conferences.
- How to make the most of press releases and the traps to avoid.

If there's nothing in the first three to four sentences, it gets deleted.
Diedtra Henderson, on the need for urgency in press releases

ASPIRING NEWS REPORTERS might see themselves reporting from overseas battlegrounds and from the scenes of devastating disasters. They anticipate being the citizenry's watchdogs over government, as the United States Constitution envisions. They might crave the chance to chronicle the quests of medicine, space exploration or social agencies. They might hear a calling to be the voice of riveting personal stories from heroes and villains and victims.

All appeal to what attracts writers to journalism: serving community and country in the cause of democracy, witnessing history in the making, telling the uplifting and heart-breaking stories of deep human interest.

Reporters present and future are *not* likely to hear a siren's song calling them to speeches, press conferences and press releases. These public-relations functions of government, industry and other newsmakers often lack spontaneity, colorful scenes and human drama. Yet they are such a staple of news that journalists young and older can expect to be called to this duty. If they perform well, reporters will find a rich supply of sources and proximity to vital stories—stories that do serve democracy, chronicle the historic moments of our world and touch millions of lives.

Sometimes, these staged events carry dramatic news.

Former President Richard Nixon resigned during a speech. Celebrities (public officials, athletes, entertainers) have called press conferences to face public shame. Families of victims have summoned the media in desperate pleas for help, to call for justice or to protest wars. When dangerous prescription drugs, automobiles or toys were withdrawn from the market, press releases have carried the first word.

More often, these news vehicles initiate or supplement other reporting. Speeches and press conferences provide rare access to prominent and sometimes-reclusive sources. Impersonal press releases sometimes are paper trails as rich as a treasure map, directing reporters to priceless sources with amazing stories to tell.

SPEECHES

Unlike press conferences, speeches are one-way communication. Excellent journalism usually involves adding other voices.

Reporters will almost always find that speeches begin as public-relations functions. The president, accepting nomination for re-election, pauses often for applause at the well-scripted pageant. The tycoon returns to his hometown to accept a lifetime achievement award. The popular author makes a guest appearance while on tour promoting a new book. The political candidate, in town to collect money and votes, tells supporters what they want to hear.

Although the prominence of the newsmakers all but guarantees their involvement in issues of public concern, these events are staged to be controversy-free. They are celebrations before admiring audiences. Questions are prohibited or limited. Sensitive issues can be ignored.

Reporters translate public relations into news through additional reporting. But mind the speech. Some of the most famous quotes have come from well-orchestrated events.

Franklin Delano Roosevelt used his first inaugural address in 1933 to proclaim, "The only thing we have to fear is fear itself."

John Fitzgerald Kennedy used his inaugural in 1961 to challenge, "Ask not what your country can do for you; ask what you can do for your country."

Martin Luther King Jr. used the platform before fellow civil-rights marchers in Washington, D.C., in 1963 to deliver his immortal "I have a dream . . ." speech.

The reporter covering a speech has an obligation to quote the key speaker(s), often extensively. But even when equipped with legendary words, reporters are no mere stenographers. Their obligation extends to providing the context that permits readers to assign value and weight to the public comments.

Here are some ways to do that:

PREPARE: Research the speaker's previous comments on topical issues. If the speaker changes course, *that* may be the story. The more prominent the speech, the more likely an advance copy will be available. Search it for quotable lines, but especially for story angles. *Remember*: Make sure the speaker's remarks track the speech. Many speakers edit their speeches until the last moment, or deviate. Quoting something that wasn't said is a deep journalistic misstep.

INTERVIEW THE SPEAKER: Before and/or after the speech, you can make sure that the important questions are asked on topical issues. This could become the lead of your story, context for quotes lower in the story or a sidebar. If mixing speech and interview quotes in the same story, make sure to tell readers which are which, lest you lose credibility with those who heard the speech.

BE AN EYEWITNESS: Vivid descriptions trump general characterizations in the quest for detail and color, accuracy and context. Take note of the surroundings, the sounds, and the physical appearance of the speaker, including emotions and mannerisms. Is the location symbolic or ironic? Does the music convey a subtle message? Was that remark delivered with a snicker or sarcasm?

If you can choose your reporting location, you might be best at the side, where you have a full view of the speaker, the audience and the room.

REMEMBER THE AUDIENCE: President George W. Bush tended to speak publicly in front of invited supporters only. A speaker on a college campus might encounter hecklers. Whatever, the enthusiasm and involvement of the audience are part of the story.

REPORT THE PROTESTS: Political and other controversial figures often attract protesters. Their involvement usually is newsworthy. But make sure to place the protest in the proper context. Tell readers how many and how active. A frequently committed journalistic misdeed is to capture the best quotes without saying that, for instance, there were only 20 silent pickets, half sipping coffee while slouching against their placards indifferently, until the TV cameras showed up. The size of the opposition, the subject of their protest and the extent of their actions will determine whether this is a major or minor part of your story.

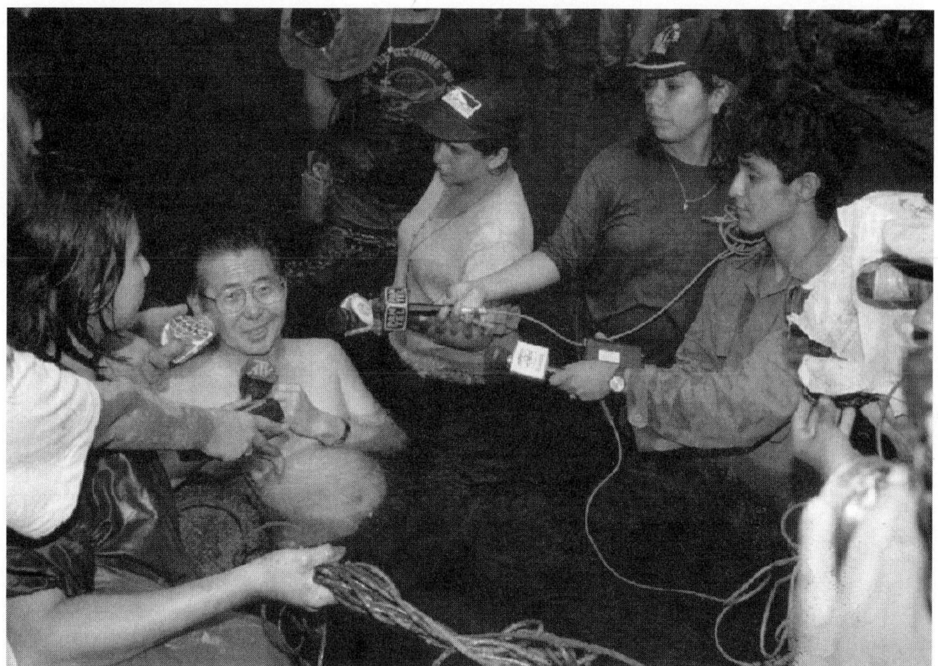

Reporters must be prepared to conduct press conferences on short notice and in unusual places. Here, a shirtless Peruvian President Alberto Fujimori conducts a press conference for members of the media standing in waist-deep water in the Cueva De Los Tayos outpost on February 24, 2007. Reporters covering press conferences should pay close attention to the spoken words and the surroundings for a story richer in context.

SEEK REACTION: If the speech is topical, opposing forces need not be present to be included in your story. If the story requires balance, reporters are expected to pursue it. Remember that balance is not necessarily equal time. If the main speaker's point of view is the dominant view in your community, you do not need to give equal space or find the same number of people with opposing views.

DON'T ASSUME: In *The Elements of Journalism*, Bill Kovach and Tom Rosenstiel quote former Tribune Co. Chairman Jack Fuller that reporters should be " 'modest in their judgments' about what they know and how they know it."

The book cites an incident involving a Pentecostal prayer revival on the steps of the United States Capitol. After "faith healings, calls for school prayer, condemnations of abortion and homosexuality—a fairly typical evangelical revival meeting," a Christian radio broadcaster concluded, "Let's pray that God will slay everyone in the Capitol." A reporter assumed that the speaker was calling on God to kill all the members of Congress. Her story resulted in a front-page correction after it was explained that in the Pentecostal tradition, this usage of "slay" means "slay in the

The **Art** of **Storytelling**

Though the challenge will be steeper, the determined storyteller can find narrative opportunities even in speeches, press conferences and press releases.

To do so, recognize a vital narrative component: The complication that the key character must resolve.

The character who initiates the speech, press conference or press release often is prominent. So far, so good: The character's name may attract readers.

Next, examine that character's motivation. Is he or she appearing before the public to confront a crisis? To promote thinking or behavior that might not happen without this public appearance? To encourage an audience that needs reassurance? This is the complication.

The key character might be a U.S. president promoting his position on a controversial issue, a business leader whose company needs a turn-around or a public-health official with a warning. It could be a desperate parent of a missing child, a scientist with research findings that challenge us to see the world differently or a new coach hired to make a team better.

All these story lines suggest the elements of drama—high stakes, conflict, urgency, emotion.

All these subjects imply an audience that must be persuaded. Perhaps the audience is there, where the speech is being delivered. Perhaps it is elsewhere—nationwide—and the key character needs to use the highly visible speech or press conference to spread the word far and fast.

In the right circumstances, the audience—the public in attendance or the inquiring press—might also exchange questions and comments with the key character, providing dialogue for your story.

Some speeches and press releases are far blander staples of community news that most journalists will cover. Let's put them to the narrative test.

The Award Banquet

Consider a speech at an awards ceremony, one of dozens staged every few months in your community. The honoree is not a unique news subject. This time, her principal achievement was writing a check with a lot of zeroes. Thanks to her generosity, the president of a local charitable group tells us, many more local children will have good books in their elementary-school libraries. Her brief speech is half thank-you, half remarks about how she hopes others will take up the cause, because it's important that young children read more. The audience is mostly admiring adults. However, the first row includes a few fidgety children, who appear to be present chiefly as props.

Even this unremarkable scene holds clues for the storyteller.

What's the problem? / What's at stake?
Presumably, your community has a child-literacy problem. Perhaps an adult-literacy problem, too, that may be remedied if educators can break the cycle of failure. This should be easy to document and could have been done in advance of tonight's banquet.

Why is there motivation?
Why is tonight's honoree involved? Is there something at stake in her personal or professional life? Was there a turning point that motivated her? She's there tonight—ask.

Where are the complications?
Is there really much prospect that others will follow her lead? Is she doing more than writing a check and showing up at this one public event? What will it take besides money to turn this thing around? Or has this problem become so persistent precisely because it generates so little energy? There are plenty of other supposedly concerned adults in the audience tonight. Question some.

How can you show (rather than tell) this story? Who can be the face of this story?
Far from least, the children present at the awards ceremony can tell you about their school libraries. Are they make-shift rooms with scant supplies of tattered covers on tired volumes? Would the kids find current, popular titles there? Is it a place the kids hang out in, or avoid? How much are they expected to read—as class work, as homework, and as leisure reading with or without parents? Maybe one of the kids you speak to tonight is a clear example of the problem. Perhaps another is the promise for a brighter future.

As storyteller, your reporting beyond the speech gives you options.

This could be a story that ends with a solution. Or it could be one whose tension builds to describe the height of the mountain that the community has just begun to climb.

The leading character might be the check-writing honoree. But a child would be a more compelling star in the leading role. An especially creative approach might cast illiteracy as the villain and principal character amid unwitting accomplices (adults) and innocent victims (children).

The Self-Congratulatory Press Release

Local University is flourishing and wants the world to know—so that its reputation will bring even more success. Today's press release informs us that when the new term's classes begin next week, new professors and hundreds more students

(continued)

will enjoy the sparkling new Engineering Building on campus. This is evidence that Local U. is on the leading edge to satisfy America's unmet demand for engineering talent.

The press release recites the numbers: How American companies have had to employ many thousands of immigrant engineers and to outsource high-paying jobs to India and elsewhere overseas. But with the latest computers and most scholarly engineering teachers, Local U. is preparing a new generation of American talent just when it is needed most. The press release describes the impressive new building and quotes a highly credentialed engineering professor.

An e-mail or piece of paper is even less personal than the staged ceremonial speech. Most self-congratulatory press releases end up as trash—they are ads, not news stories. But the determined storyteller, who remembers that a press release is a tip, could find a trail to follow here.

What's the problem? / What's at stake?

As the press release documents, America is critically short of engineers. Some of America's best-paying jobs are being exported. The jobs engineers do involve commerce, science and national defense.

Why is there motivation?

Presumably, it's important that Americans do some of the most sensitive jobs. Some of the professors ought to be asked why they are teaching instead of taking

spirit"—that the members of Congress be overcome with love for Jesus. If only she had asked before writing.

Assumptions are the enemy of fair, accurate and objective reporting. The humble reporter who asks questions in a postspeech interview achieves clarity and perhaps additional story angles, as well.

KEEP TOMORROW IN MIND: Diedtra Henderson, formerly of *The Boston Globe,* says that when she attends a speech at something like an awards dinner, she is "listening for something that sounds like a spark"—a spark of a story idea, or even a clue about future sources. Like the speaker from Johns Hopkins University who was so impressive speaking about stem cells. "I'm listening to the cadence of how people talk," Henderson says. "If the speaker is alert, on topic, and speaks in a way that is likely to get in the paper, that can be someone to call for another story."

PRESS CONFERENCES

When former Secretary of Defense Donald Rumsfeld conducted televised daily press conferences after the United States invaded Iraq, press critics laughed loudly some of those higher-paying jobs. Is Local University ahead of the pack or part of a nationwide movement?

Where are the complications?
Many years of American underachievement in K–12 math is coming home to roost. American universities have produced so few talented engineers that those who can teach usually are hired by companies instead. Still, a degree may not be a guarantee—companies also save money by hiring cheaper labor overseas. Immigration issues also may surface. The professors and some of the leading employers in your community ought to be ripe for interviews on these topics.

How can you show (rather than tell) this story? Who can be the face of this story?
Who are the students in the new Engineering Building? Are all of them American? Are all of them math-heads or has the employment crisis resulted in some creative outreach to students with different potential? Remember those state-of-the-art computers in the press release? Instead of telling readers about "engineering," show them what those computers can do, and what the students who use them will be accomplishing on the job.

Storytellers starting only with a press release must report more deeply for narrative elements. But the reporter with adequate curiosity will be grateful for the head start the press release provides.

and sarcastically at how Rumsfeld repeatedly seemed to outsmart his questioners. Rumsfeld confidently, patiently pointed out how naive the reporters were in matters of war. In fact, the journalists were much sharper than they appeared. In time, they were able to show that the Bush administration had been ill-prepared, then deceptive on many scores—naive, if you will, about the challenge of fighting terrorism this way and about the ability of others to recognize what was going wrong.

But that's the nature of press conferences. They make the press look bad at the time, but can prove helpful later.

Press conferences differ from speeches in that journalists are invited to ask questions. As it turns out, that's not nearly as much of a two-way conversation as a one-on-one interview, and the difference leaves the person conducting the press conference in control.

If the topic is urgent, journalists of every stripe—print, broadcast, online—will crowd into the room and then compete to ask questions. The "host," Rumsfeld for instance, can choose his questioners. He can move onto the next one, even after a partial answer, without giving the previous questioner a chance to follow up. He can end the conference at any time, leaving many of the journalists unable to ask any question at all. Shrewd "hosts" play favorites. They call on reporters from the pub-

WIRED AND WIRELESS | WEB

Many speeches are significant, but not entertaining. If they are as important as the president's State of the Union address, the entire speech demands wall-to-wall television coverage and a complete transcript in print. A governor's State of the State address may have equal importance to a smaller audience, but might not rate all that TV time and newsprint. This is when a news website can shine.

If the TV cameras are rolling for a key sound bite, the station's website can offer the complete coverage via streaming video, live and with later playback ability.

A newspaper website can publish the entire transcript, with links to that day's stories and to previous stories on the key topics. Podcasts can offer audio, as well.

Also consider collecting instant feedback from viewers and readers via online polls and chat rooms.

A strong TV-newspaper partnership, like those in many major cities, can accomplish all of this.

Think about other speeches where the Web can be an ally. Remembering a reporter's role to be the eyes and ears of citizens who can't be two places at once, the Web is an ideal archive for those who want to tune in later. That goes for a State of the State speech (the governor's blueprint for the coming year), which political junkies might want to refer back to months later for a progress check. That goes for speeches on other niche subjects with devoted followings. And it goes for speeches on high-demand topics, like a mother's plea for help locating a missing child.

lications they want to favor and ignore reporters who are likeliest to ask the toughest questions.

Journalists are taught, correctly, that there is no such thing as a dumb question. Better not to assume you know the answer. But in a televised press conference, the uninitiated viewer hears dumb questions all the time. They don't understand that, like a prosecutor conducting a cross-examination, the journalist often already knows the answer to the question. Readers want to hear the answer from the official, not from a reporter's assertion. Reporters also can seem adversarial at press conferences with questions seeking clarity in the face of conflicting answers. That's part of the press's role as the Fourth Estate, the citizenry's check on government's potential abuse of power.

PRESS CONFERENCE TIPS FROM VETERANS

For enterprising reporters seeking unique stories, being part of the journalist herd at a press conference is, at best, awkward. But veterans of press conferences develop ways to succeed.

Ron Hutcheson, former White House correspondent for the McClatchy newspaper group, offers these tips for asking effective questions at a press conference:

> "Most important: Listen to what the person is saying. It's tempting, if you're eager to ask a particular question, to tune out and focus on trying to get recognized. By doing so, you might miss a chance to ask a better question.

Ron Hutcheson, former White House correspondent for McClatchy Newspapers, questions President Bush during a presidential press conference.

"A real-life example: At one White House press conference, President Bush announced that he could accept some type of means testing for Social Security benefits—a big change from the current program. Most reporters ignored the president's announcement and asked their predetermined questions. I got the last question of the night, and I followed up on the Social Security issue. Several colleagues thanked me for fleshing out Bush's announcement, which was the news of the night. Bush later told me that he was surprised no one else asked about it.

"Second, frame your question in a way that is most likely to get a thoughtful response. Overtly hostile questions often put the subject in a defensive crouch. While that is sometimes the best approach, think it through before you speak.

"Third, don't turn it into a multiple choice test by stringing together a bunch of questions. If you have something you want to know, ask about it directly. Tossing in extra questions gives the subject a chance to dodge the key issue."

The herd of journalists hearing the same answers forces the question: Other than a turn of phrase, what does a reporter do to offer a better account than his readers could get from the wire service report available on dozens of websites?

"Do some reporting that goes beyond the press conference," Hutcheson advises. "Truth test and give context to the pronouncements from the podium. Seek out opposing views. Try to avoid steno journalism. We're not there to be a transcript service."

At *The Globe,* Henderson sometimes went to press conferences where she had little interest in the topic, just to gain access to tough-to-reach sources she needed

HOW TO **Use Websites**

Diedtra Henderson's story on maggots and leeches (see page 201) began with a press release from the Federal Drug and Administration, but quickly advanced to the website of the American Association for the Advancement of Science (publishers of *Science* magazine and the largest organization of scientists in the nation.

The search function there allowed her to type in "maggots" and "medicine" and she soon found expert researchers and doctors who have used the creatures for cures. That led Henderson to Barbara Enser and her doctor, plus others quoted in the story. All were located and interviewed in a few hours.

This is an ideal use of the Internet—finding sources that otherwise would take days or weeks to locate.

for another story. "It's tough to get to the leadership of the FDA (Federal Drug Administration). If you talk to the press office, they want to talk on background. But drug safety is not a background story. It's a real story that needs real sources."

She went to a press conference featuring U.S. Sen. Mike Enzi, R-Wyoming. As then-chairman of the Senate Health, Labor and Pensions Committee, Enzi "was at the center of the scrum" over legislation concerning prescription-drug advertising at the time of drug-safety concerns involving the popular arthritis drug Vioxx and other medications.

"I was staking out the stage, trying to get him on the way in or the way out," Henderson explained. "I had a tape recorder. As he came off the stage, down the stairs and out toward a taxi, I figured I had the chance for four questions. By time he reached the front row, I had introduced myself."

Henderson and Hutcheson agree that preparation is essential.

"If I get to ask the first question, that sometimes determines the topic" in a press conference where there may be no more than six or seven questions overall," Henderson says. "If others pick up my line of questions, it's as if I got in five questions instead of one."

"Try to have a question in mind anytime you go to a news conference," Hutcheson advises. "It helps you prepare and it guarantees that you won't be caught flat-footed if called on. A White House colleague who was once surprised by the chance to question Bush learned from that lesson and came up with an evergreen question: 'Where's Osama?' "

But press conferences often occur on short notice. And you might be the newest reporter to that story. In that case, Henderson counsels, listen: first to the speaker's prepared statement, then to the line of questions that the most knowledgeable reporters pursue. Those questions can inform you about the key details on the most urgent topics.

When your chance comes, "Ask short questions—clear, concise and to an open meadow, so you get expansive answers." The common mistake, she says, is asking long questions where the answer could only be yes or no.

WRITING THE STORY: PRESS CONFERENCES AND SPEECHES

A newsmaker has made a statement. Half a dozen reporters have asked questions, most of them on different topics. Three of the subjects will be of interest to your audience. Where do you start?

Keep it simple, Henderson advises. That usually means the focus is on a single issue. She starts thinking of her news lead *during* the press conference.

"The Center for Disease Control says it will make changes governing supply of the flu vaccine. What do people really want to know: 'Can I get the flu vaccine this year?'

"In Colorado, health officials made an announcement when they saw their first case of the West Nile virus. And this occurred earlier than last year. Hmm. That might mean it will be worse this year than last year."

By thinking of her lead while the press conference is progressing, Henderson avoids "getting trapped in a bunch of different questions." And she creates the opportunity to get more answers, either during the press conference or immediately after.

Then, it's make good use of the down time between the press conference and the writing time at the office.

In *Writing Tools*, Roy Peter Clark writes, "Transform procrastination into rehearsal, a way of writing a story in your head."

Henderson remembers the advice from Bill Rose, then her editor at *The Miami Herald* (now managing editor of *The Palm Beach Post*). "You ought to be writing in your head when you are coming back from the press conference. You're listening to it not just when you're writing it, but when you're in the car. You already have it in your head so that you can sit down at the keyboard, without even opening your notebook."

Here's an example from *The Tampa Tribune*'s Keith Epstein. Note how he led with one topic but quickly disclosed that the story would be covering more ground:

> WASHINGTON—U.S. Sen. Mel Martinez on Wednesday defended a taxpayer-financed retreat for his staff at an Orlando theme park hotel, saying it was a necessary gathering worth shutting down his offices for several days.
>
> Martinez described the price for the event as "modest," but he refused to disclose the cost.
>
> Martinez, who discussed a range of topics during an hour-long session with Florida reporters, also urged accepting Fidel Castro's offer of 1,586 Cuban doctors to treat victims of Hurricane Katrina.
>
> The Orlando Republican is the Senate's first Cuban-American and a fierce opponent of Fidel Castro's regime.
>
> "Times like these are not about politics," he said. If the United States needs skilled doctors in New Orleans and Cuba offers them, "then of course we should accept."
>
> Bush administration officials have given Castro the cold shoulder.
>
> Meanwhile, Hurricane Katrina's effect on energy supplies has sparked a drive to open once-sacrosanct areas of the Gulf of Mexico to oil and gas drilling, leaving outnumbered opponents, including Martinez, feeling like "the Lone Ranger."

Martinez did not choose to spend an hour with reporters so that he could give more attention to his taxpayer-funded retreat, or to rehash the political embarrassment that caused him to schedule the retreat in the first place. But Epstein capitalized on the access to Martinez to address a taxpayer concern.

Note how Epstein also provided meaningful context for the quote about Castro's offer, citing Martinez' historical opposition to the Cuban dictator and the Bush administration's current attitude.

Writing a speech story is not far different. The options for the opening paragraph: Focus on a single topic or several. Focus on the speaker's priorities or on higher priorities for readers. They might be the same thing.

The example below from the *Rocky Mountain News* sticks to the speech, adding audience involvement:

> Colorado has turned the corner on tough economic times but still faces battles on key fiscal, water and education issues, Gov. Bill Owens told state lawmakers Thursday.
>
> With a steady dose of optimism in his State of the State message to legislators, Owens outlined past accomplishments and set goals the state still must reach.
>
> "Today, I'm proud to say Colorado is back," Owens told a legislative audience that broke into applause. "After years of tough times and tight budgets, we're back. And we are getting stronger."
>
> The House was packed with lawmakers, Cabinet chiefs, military guests and others, including Denver Mayor John Hickenlooper, whom the governor singled out for helping him bring jobs to the state.

PRESS RELEASES

Press releases arrive from everywhere. Everywhere. The difference between lazy and successful reporters is whether the press release becomes the heart of your story or the inspiration for a better one.

At its best, a press release alerts you to news, directs you to sources you did not know existed and prompts questions you would not have known to ask. Often written by former journalists, they sometimes appear in story form.

At credible news organizations, even the most expertly crafted press releases from the most trusted organizations are *not* ready-to-publish stories. Nor is it acceptable to simply rewrite the press release.

Regard press releases as tips. Verify independently the parts that might appeal most to readers. Reporting should go beyond the sources named in the release. Anything used directly from the release should be attributed to the organization that issued it.

News organizations can be lax about this:

- Each holiday, the American Automobile Association (AAA) issues a press release estimating how many drivers will be on the roads. News organizations across the country dutifully echo the numbers without asking or explaining how AAA comes up with the numbers and whether they have proved reliable in the past.
- Various magazines develop "Top Ten" and "Top 100" stories rating communities, colleges, restaurants, you name it. The press releases arrive ahead of time to create extra interest in that magazine issue. News outlets eagerly publish the rankings that mention their communities. Only the most diligent investigate the

ADVANCED TIP
Online Exchanges

The Washington Post regularly connects readers and reporters via Internet exchanges. It's an excellent device for demystifying the news process. The answers help readers understand why reporters act the way they do, which can clear up suspicion and misunderstanding.

This exchange from Aug. 17, 2005, with *Post* White House reporter Jim VandeHei allowed readers to understand more about a White House press briefing's role in stories.

San Francisco, Calif.: *Why doesn't the press refuse to take briefings from Scott McClellan, who either lied to them about the (Valeri) Plame incident, or was lied to by the administration? Isn't his credibility shot?*

Jim VandeHei: Scott took a good beating when it was learned that the White House knew much more about the Plame leak than he and others let on last year. It's not entirely clear how much he knew about the involvement of other officials. But Scott has a lot of credibility with reporters. He is seen as someone who might not tell you a lot, but is not going to tell you a lie. More broadly, we go to the briefings if for no other reason to hear the White House spin on world events. They rarely figure into our daily reports because we will talk to Scott and others one on one and not in front of a crowd.

legitimacy of the rankings or seek alternate points of view.

Reporters should be especially inquisitive about press releases announcing the results of fresh research or opinion polls.

WHO FUNDED THE RESEARCH? This is more important than the name of the polling firm. No matter how professional and highly recognizable the polling company, the research belongs to those who paid for it. Invariably, commercially and politically funded research only comes to light when the results are favorable to the people paying for it.

WHAT DOES THE RESEARCH REALLY MEASURE? If a study of newspaper credibility questions only regular readers of the newspaper, then the results may skew more favorably towards the newspapers. Those who have so little regard for them that they don't read newspapers have been excluded.

WHAT CAN BE SAID LEGITIMATELY ABOUT THE RESULTS? Perhaps a study will announce triumphantly that "20 million Americans prefer herbal teas." Upon deeper analysis, it turns out that only 20 percent of those questioned—200 of 1,000 people—said they would "much rather" or "sometimes rather" have herbal tea. In fact, 80 percent of those questioned *don't* prefer herbal tea. Projecting the percentages to a much larger population is suspect. In this case, expressing the outcome in those terms is deceptive. The percentages tell a truer picture.

WHAT ABOUT THE MARGIN OF ERROR? Every study has one. Careful studies that conduct many thousands of interviews may have a margin of error +/– 1–2 percent. More are 3–4 percent. At a higher percentage than that, the study was probably done on the cheap.

Remember that the margin of error applies to every number in the study. If the margin of error is +/– 4 percent and the poll shows the Republican ahead of the Democrat by 52–48, the truth could be just the opposite. Or, the Republican could be ahead, 56–44. This is why "horse-race" polls tell us so little about a forthcoming election.

Reporters should remain skeptical, but not cynical. Don't assume that self-interested research or laudatory press releases are inaccurate or deceptive. Also, those who produce press releases can be reporters' allies.

Talent Showcase

DIEDTRA HENDERSON ▶

Former Reporter, *The Boston Globe*

With 200 new e-mailed press releases arriving every day, Diedtra Henderson had to be decisive to the point of being ruthless about when to hit the delete key. After more than a decade of covering health, technology and science, she had her system down to, well, a science.

Her techniques are instructive to reporters concerned about news judgment and time management and to public-relations agents trying to get a reporter's attention.

The e-mails are not spam. Covering the Federal Drug Administration for *The Boston Globe,* Henderson welcomed the press releases because they often contained sources or alerted her to something out of the ordinary.

But those gems are rare. Press releases, which push a single point of view, are not meant to be published, but to trigger further reporting for well-balanced stories. On Henderson's computer, few press releases had a life expectancy of more than a few seconds.

"If there's nothing in the first three to four sentences, it gets deleted. If the topic is something I think I might come back to, it goes into the file for a future story," she says.

Bottom line: Of 200, only five survive for a potential story that day. Twenty achieve dubious, "maybe someday" status and 175 get the computer-version of the guillotine.

Lesson one to press-release writers: Get to the point quickly. "The least helpful are those written in story form and bury the news below the lead," Henderson advises.

She preferred the science press releases from Washington University in St. Louis, which summarizes its items on the first page with a no-nonsense approach. "It's, here's the news. Here's the source. Then they devote no more than one more page to each of those items."

Henderson also found helpful the approach by the *New England Journal of Medicine*, which sorts its releases in order of newsworthiness, and divides them among those that are of public and political interest and those that are cutting-edge science.

When the reporter-source rapport has been well established, phone calls can be even more efficient.

"I don't need to see a whole press release," Henderson says. "Call me, say there's something going on and here's what's interesting about it. Instead of taking the time to polish a press release, and get your execs to sign off on it, run it by me."

That conversation might go like this:

PR person: "I've got this."

Henderson: "Nope."

"I've got this."

"Nope."

"Well, I've also got this."

"Okay, tell me more."

This efficiency is likelier when everyone understands what is newsworthy. While news judgment is just that—

Henderson says that when she was looking for human experience to explain medical issues, "some of the best sources for that are the drug companies. They know who would be a good person to speak from experience with passion and emotion."

In surprising contrast, "Patients groups and disease groups—such as those concerned with heart failure, diabetes, etc.—are getting multi-million dollar grants from the drug companies, so that even people on their advisory boards are conflicted."

judgment, not science—and subject to disagreement, some principles are nearly universal.

Even with its much larger news space than most newspapers, *The Boston Globe* is not trying to be the paper of record on the FDA, Henderson points out. That is going to be true almost everywhere on specialty beats such as science, health, the environment, labor, the military and many more. Increasingly, in this era of shrinking news staffs, that is also true on such bread-and-butter local news beats as crime and education.

In the competition for precious news space and precious reporting time, the winners are topics that are urgent and novel and touch the most lives.

"We're trying to focus on the stories that linger in people's minds," Henderson says.

This story started with a press release. Notice how Henderson blends information supplied by the FDA with her own enterprise reporting in this story for *The Boston Globe*.

> GAITHERSBURG, Md.—What do pacemakers, stents, and artificial hips have in common with leeches and maggots?
>
> According to the Food and Drug Administration, they are all medical devices. FDA advisers considering how much scrutiny to give to leeches and maggots used for medicinal purposes yesterday decided they should require a prescription.
>
> Leeches have been used by doctors for centuries to control bleeding. Maggot therapy was used hundreds of years ago by indigenous Australians and has been credited with disinfecting the wounds of World War I soldiers who lay untreated for days in battlefields.
>
> With FDA approval, doctors now use maggots to trim dead flesh with more precision than scalpels, and leeches to draw excess blood that can collect when severed fingers are reattached.
>
> For Barbara Enser, the old-fashioned technique succeeded when modern medicine failed.
>
> The 57-year-old diabetic said she is grossed out by creepy, crawly things. But she got over her revulsion within minutes after her doctor said maggots were the last option for saving her right foot.

There's much more to the story, but this small example is enough to demonstrate Henderson's relentless efforts to make her story accessible to all readers.

The story is free of medical jargon. The lead broadens the universe of potential readers by including many medical patients.

Henderson quickly moves to the day's news about FDA action and prescription status, and then to easily understood examples of how both maggots and leeches have been used historically and recently.

By the fifth paragraph, we're done with theory. We have a real person talking about real results. When we learn that this woman "is grossed out by creepy, crawly things," we know this is a story about people just like us, not some exception with all the sensitivity of a robot.

Ready to read more? Who wouldn't be?

Here's where to find the full story: www.boston.com/business/healthcare/articles/2005/08/26/for_fda_maggots_are_a_kind_of_device/

Similarly, effective public relations people are those who steer reporters in the right direction of legitimate news. Savvy organizations know that if they make reporters' work simpler, the reporters remain concentrated on that company's issues. Conversely, organizations that opt to obstruct and deceive reporters soon become distrusted. Suspicious reporters then work—sometimes all the harder—to avoid the PR staff when pursuing stories about those organizations.

IN CONCLUSION

Speeches, press conferences and press releases are only starting points for effective stories. Reporters should supply context and additional sources.

The well-prepared reporter will use the access to prominent speakers to seek topical answers not volunteered in the speech or press conference. But don't be so consumed with your own questions that you miss the value of other remarks.

Keep your questions clear and concise. Multiple questions and complicated ones give sources an easy route to evasion.

Begin thinking about the lead of your story while at the event. This may lead you to a new question. Continue to think of the lead on the way back to the office. Be ready to write as soon as you arrive.

Be especially inquisitive when research and polls are cited.

EXERCISE 1

Write a story from the following speech:

Bryce Ellis, professor of English, Whitman University:

> Thank you for your time this afternoon. I'll make this brief. I believe we are at a critical crossroads in our society. I fear for the future. I'm frightened at how those yet to come will look back at us who are here now. The question I ask of you is this: Will they in the future be able to understand a word that's being written now? I mean, look at this mess that's passing for the English language. How can anyone in the future know that "BTW" means "by the way?" Who will decipher "LOL" means "laugh out loud?" Because it could also mean "lots of laughs." I think it stands for "losing our literacy." I mean "U" for "you" and R for "are" and who knows what else. This is a train wreck waiting to happen and I can see the lead locomotive coming around the bend.
>
> Now I'm all for the English language changing. That's the nature of a living language. English has spread throughout the world. It is one of the more important languages of our age. But that headlong rush to speak English is mostly due to the Internet and the strength of American commerce. I'm afraid English as we know it today will disappear into this cyber-uber language that no current English speaker will recognize. Can you imagine: "We the peeps of the USA" or "4score&7yrsago" becoming part of a rewrite of history?
>
> Yes I know English changes. In no time did it change faster than when William the Conqueror made French the language of choice and sent English off to the fields to speak their language unencumbered. Yes, I know that Old English is unrecognizable to modern English. But it strikes me that this was a natural change, an organic change. It happened on its own. This stuff today is of our own volition. English mutates without fanfare. We are purposely using one of our language's greatest strengths to weaken what made it so strong in the first place.
>
> Expression is important. At one time in my life, "turn me on" made my parents cringe. I still have visions of Sister Marie standing over me with a ruler driving out any desire to say "ain't." But even now with no grammar police standing over my shoulder, and I myself having no desire to become one, still I feel compelled to pick up the

ruler and beg you to stop. The definition of loneliness is the inability to communicate. Use the English we all understand to communicate your message, whatever message that might be. Turn me on with great language. Thank you.

EXERCISE 2

Write a story from the following two press releases:

For immediate release

Greek Life Council

Keller College

Contact: David Leiberman

The Greek Life Council will hold a "Bust the Beer Bust" celebration this Friday, from 7–9 p.m. at the Kappa Beta Epsilon fraternity.

The "Bust the Beer Bust" is an alcohol-free party sponsored by the 10 fraternities and 13 sororities at Keller College. Price to attend is $5 at the door. Money raised at the party will support the Greek Life's project of the Sun Room, a center for underprivileged children to spend their time after school.

"This is a great way for sororities and fraternities on campus to show the rest of the student body that there's more to Greek life than drinking and parties," said David Lieberman. "We want all the community to come see that we are able to have fun and do it alcohol free."

The idea for "Bust the Beer Bust" originated with the Office of Student Life at Keller College. It was suggested that the fraternities and sororities at Keller demonstrate their commitment to the after-school program and to parties where alcohol was not served.

Sororities and fraternities have existed at Keller since 1905, with the founding of the Kappa Beta Epsilon fraternity. The Greek Life Council decided to hold the "Bust the Beer Bust" party at the same house where Greek Life began more than 100 years ago.

For immediate release

Keller City Police

Contact: Sgt. Anne Elway

Keller City Police have arrested four fraternity brothers Friday from Kappa Beta Epsilon fraternity at Keller College on a variety of charges in connection with a hazing incident last weekend.

Arrested are Ellis Wadsworth, 19; Perry McComb, 19; Wendell Stackmore, 21; and David Leiberman, 21, all of Keller. All are charged with disorderly conduct and resisting arrest. Stackmore and Leiberman are charged with serving alcohol to minors and assault with a weapon.

The arrests stem from a hazing incident last weekend where all four members of Kappa Beta Epsilon fraternity forced a freshman fraternity pledge to drink six beers in one hour. The freshman grew ill and was taken to St. Joseph's Hospital where he was treated for alcohol poisoning and several severe bruises throughout his body.

The freshman, a 17-year-old minor, told Keller police that he was forced to drink the beer and then crawl on the floor of the fraternity while other members beat him with canes.

All four fraternity members are still in the Keller City jail awaiting arraignment on Monday.

CHAPTER 12

Writing the Meeting Story

IN THIS CHAPTER YOU WILL LEARN:

- How news stories from governmental meetings serve the press' role in democracy.
- How to generate new sources and enterprise stories from meeting-agenda items.
- How to turn dull topics into essential reading.
- How to write meeting stories on deadline.

If you have any emotional reaction—you laughed, or it strikes you as sad—look at that as a source of a future story. This is a clue that there's a story to be told.
Jane Von Bergen

IN THE LATE 1980s, as voter turnout, public awareness of current events and newspaper readership were, uncoincidentally, at their lowest levels in modern times, nervous news organizations financed public-opinion research that offered this awakening:

Citizens sensed a "double-disconnect"—they felt as remote as ever from the elected officials in power, but also felt distant from their traditional ally, the news media covering government and politics. In the past, news reports had originated from the public's point of view, making sense of the often-confusing inner workings of politics. But as political campaigns grew increasingly media-savvy and manipulative, the press grew increasingly fascinated with the political process. The result: Fewer stories focused on the public, the consumers of government, and more focused on those who manufactured the political process. As the public saw more "news" reports focused on "inside politics," it sensed that news organizations had drifted from their traditional middle ground, growing closer to the politicians and further from those who vote for them.

This sense of alienation still contributes to the public's perception of media political bias. As a consequence, journalists at every level must fight the forces of human nature—the tendency to report from the perspective of those we see daily in government bureaucracy. Journalists must resist the tendency to do the stenographic reporting—this vote, that agenda—that is easiest to do because it is always in plentiful supply.

As we will soon see, reporting on the public's business need not—should not—be confined to the buildings that house our governments. You may be assigned to the city hall beat or the county courthouse beat or the school board beat or the police beat. Some reporters then trap themselves within those walls. Instead, consider that you are covering not the buildings and their workers, but the work they do for the public. You aren't covering the school board, but the way children are educated. Not the police, but public safety. Not the courthouse, but criminal justice. Not city hall, but the ways that city government is changing our lives, for better or worse.

Still, no matter how innovative and courageous their coverage, most reporters will write stories from meetings early in their careers and throughout their careers. How these stories are reported and written says much about the reporter's skill and whether readers find them to be essential.

Typically, these meetings will be matters of government, whether the local zoning board, school board or city council, the state turnpike commission or the U.S. House of Representatives. While these meetings are open to the public by law, few citizens can skip work or family responsibilities to attend regularly. They count on the press to be the public's eyes and ears and then to put the jargon of government into clear words. Indeed, that is what this nation's Founding Fathers envisioned by empowering the Fourth Estate of the press—a leg of democracy so vital that its scrutiny of government should be unhindered, and even adversarial if necessary to help citizens govern themselves. Thus, it is critically important that the press write for those they represent, not those in the bureaucracy with whom they might be more familiar.

ADVANCED TIP
What's Missing?

Like other people, elected officials will put off dealing with unpleasant matters as long as possible. They might need to raise property taxes. A new landfill might be needed, but its placement would anger nearby residents who fear their housing values will decline. Costly repairs to roads and equipment might be inevitable, but can't be paid for without new taxes. Declining enrollment might dictate closing some neighborhood schools. If the matter is unpopular and a governing body thinks it can avoid the problem until after the next election, it often will. That usually makes the problem worse.

Rather than follow the official agenda, enterprising reporters will follow the issues. Good reporters expose and quantify neglected problems of wide community concern. On those occasions, the appropriate question is *why* these problems *haven't* made it to public meetings and official votes.

Enterprising reporters might also be present at meetings of decision-making bodies of nongovernmental groups, such as labor unions, neighborhood associations, faculty organizations and more. While this chapter emphasizes governmental meetings, keep in mind that its lessons apply elsewhere, too.

AVOIDING A JOURNALISTIC DEAD END

A metropolitan area has hundreds of government taxing authorities, plus the many more at the state and federal levels. Most of these bureaucracies churn out tons of written reports each year. Collectively, they compile countless databases. Scarcely a day goes by without a public meeting or press conference, often several of each.

Politicians and government bureaucrats like to keep reporters busy this way, following the officials' agenda, rather than allowing you enough time to ask awkward questions elsewhere.

The volume is such that an entire local news staff can stay endlessly busy, and any government reporter can write the most stories of anyone at the news organization through mere dutiful coverage of government's staged events. This level of coverage requires no curiosity, enterprise or affection for readers. Fortunately, there are ways to avoid this journalistic dead end.

REPORTING THE MEETING STORY: GET AHEAD OF THE CURVE

Every meeting has an agenda, available to all in advance, as required by law. Nonetheless, coverage often is superficial, in part because many public meetings happen at night, when newspaper deadlines are near. Until an issue grows red-hot, newspapers usually are the only media tracking the public's business through the halls of government. This is true at all levels of government. Unless the topic is high profile, electronic media won't go to these meetings.

If the newspaper reporter is seeing the meeting agenda for the first time, coverage from the meeting might not go beyond the basics: the roll call vote, a quote and a bit of background on the issue. To take the lead with more meaningful, useful coverage, newspaper reporters ought to prepare well.

First, understand that nothing gets on a meeting agenda that hasn't been discussed several times elsewhere. Diligent reporters get to those earlier discussions.

Community problems usually surface in the community, not in government buildings. To learn of those problems in their infancy, connect often with the unelected leaders in the community—neighborhood leaders, business leaders, clergy and former elected officials, for instance. All have broad community connections and constituencies of their own. These folks have their ears to the ground. They can be your ears, too.

This early intervention offers many advantages:

- There's the enterprise story—you read it here first.
- Your sources will be more diverse, spread throughout the community, instead of relying so often on the same voices in high places.
- By explaining the problems through the experiences of citizens, you show readers their stake in the outcome, increasing their level of understanding and the likelihood that they will participate in self-governance.
- Telling readers early gives them time to get involved before the issue passes the point of no return in the governmental bureaucracy.

When community problems do find their way to city hall or school board offices, officials discuss the issues privately, days or weeks before they make it to a meeting agenda. Often, the next step is a written report and then a committee hearing. Finally, the public is invited to the meeting where open discussion and formal votes take place. If you are surprised by what appears on a meeting agenda, you have missed many chances to inform your readers sooner.

WRITING CLEARLY: KNOW THE LANGUAGE OF GOVERNMENT, THEN TRANSLATE IT

Although writers must fight for clarity to win the contest with the cloudy, contrived jargon of government, they must also *know* that foreign language. Only then can you understand the political maneuvers well enough to write confidently in clearer terms.

Meetings typically are governed by *Robert's Rules of Order*. While these venerable rules help prevent a meeting from devolving into chaos, master politicians know how to use them to force legislative gridlock and to present issues in deceptive ways. To stay alert, make sure you know the consequences when simple votes are replaced by amendments, filibusters and motions to table, reconsider or return to committee. For instance, a motion to reconsider is not about giving legislators more time to think through an issue for a future vote. Its passage reverses the outcome of an earlier official vote. It can only be offered by a voting member who voted with the original majority. That lawmaker is changing sides. If his motion to reconsider passes, his change of heart was decisive.

Having a copy of *Robert's Rules of Order* will help you in such times. Your command of a governing body's customs will help, too. For instance, at a certain stage in a several-month session of the state legislature, a successful motion to return an issue to committee effectively kills the issue for that session. There's not enough time left to restart and complete the political process for that legislation.

The Art of Storytelling

To the incurious reporter, government meetings can be the most boring hours. Local-news sections typically reflect this tedium, with story after story about the lawmaking process, bureaucracy and petty politics. These stories make readers yawn and stray.

But to the storyteller, whose senses are alert to conflict and consequence, a 4–3 vote that changes thousands of lives, or saves just one, is a wake-up call.

Workload, deadlines and the dense language of government can stifle journalistic creativity. But think for just a few minutes about the drama inherent when a small group of elected leaders decide matters affecting hundreds, thousands or millions of citizens:

- Though the elected board may be unanimous when it votes on a problem, the community seldom is.
- A divided community pits neighbor against neighbor. It's the recurring conflict between individual rights and the common good in a system of majority rule.
- Often, this is a conflict between competing values, both deeply felt and deeply rooted in constitutional rights.
- Eventually, officials will confront a similar classic choice: follow the will of the narrower interests who elected them, or lead with their best judgment for the greater good.
- Having taken oaths to uphold the law, when may officials follow their community's conscience in a matter of principle in conflict with the law?
- Short-term interests and long-term interests often collide.

This list easily could be a great deal longer. This is true whether the governing body presides over a city or a school district, a labor union or a business coalition, a neighborhood group or a professional association, a social-activist organization or a student body. The decision-makers could be an appeals court, a parole board or a turnpike commission.

In every case, journalists choose how best to tell the story of a people governing themselves through representative government. Journalists may choose to record history in the form of votes and quotes, or tell the narrative story of conflict and resolution. Like the competing interests described above, the journalistic choices are both legitimate. Neither approach is wrong. Both may be necessary—to give readers the essential facts rapidly, and to do so in a way that delivers the facts as essential reading.

New Town—Old Town

Many stories do not break. They evolve.

Consider a tale of two cities. They face issues most journalists will cover early and throughout their careers.

The first city is growing. Trees and farms have disappeared, replaced first by housing developments and then strip shopping centers. New schools and office buildings sprout every year. Jobs and new money flow freely. News—usually optimistic news about progress—focuses on the future. The city's present is not nearly as interesting as its potential, and the past is nearly forgotten.

Nearly. Residents who arrived first long for the past. They wanted large spaces, small government and peace. Now they have encroachment, new taxes for infrastructure—roads, sewers, full-time police departments and more—and noise. "You can't stop progress," they have been told again and again. And the next family has just as much right to live where it pleases as the first residents did when they moved out here 20 years ago. Still, there seems to be little sense and no end to the uncontrolled growth in the name of jobs and property values, which are both escalating rapidly. Some suspect improper alliances between city officials and developers. Economic progress always seems to prevail in debates about the land, the air and the water. Which is best for the bright future?

The second city is in decline—jobs and population have disappeared, replaced by vacant stores and for-sale signs. Crime, more frequent and more violent, raises the fear factor. City services, too little and too late, drive despair. News—usually pessimistic news about the downward spiral—is riveted in the present, while the city and its citizens cling to as much of the past as they can hold on to. The future is almost beside the point.

Almost. A relatively small group of neighborhood activists and entrepreneur developers press a persistent vision of hope. They would replace decay with modern apartments, shops and offices. But upscale prices and government-approved bulldozers threaten to displace generations of families with neither the desire nor the dollars to move. "You can't obstruct progress," they have been told again and again. The younger professionals have just as much right to occupy the pricier new downtown housing and the whole city will benefit. Still, some suspect the developers will benefit most of all, profiting extraordinarily from precious tax dollars. Other compromises in the name of economic progress mean allowing a prison and a toxic-waste dump to replace the jobs where once-bustling manufacturing plants are now vacant eyesores. Is this a brighter future?

(continued)

These problems face communities across America. As citizens and their elected decision-makers wrestle with tough choices, many votes will alter lives and neighborhoods dramatically.

Journalists will record that history.

But shun the convenience of describing these changes as colorless turns of the government bureaucracy.

Journalists also have the opportunity to tell that life-changing tale through the private and public tensions in a tug-of-war between competing values. It's a dynamic story with moving parts—characters, scenes, conflicts, plot twists, emotions and uncertain outcomes.

That's why we call them stories.

DULL, BUT IMPORTANT

Uninspired journalists who are content to do the minimum will excuse dry and dense meeting coverage as "DBI" stories—dull, but important. Supposedly, this is the medicine that readers might not *want*, but they *need*. This is a false dichotomy. A reader's wants and needs are not mutually exclusive. It's the writer's job to present important information in compelling fashion; to demonstrate the relevancy and urgency of the issue at hand; to make it clear why readers should care.

Here is the difference between writing from the bureaucracy's point of view and the public's point of view:

- Are you writing about which departments are the economic winners and losers in the debate over a new city budget, or whether there is going to be enough money this year for badly needed road repairs?
- Are you writing about how enrollment declines will affect the amount of state aid coming to your local school district, or how parents will get their kids to school on time?
- Are you writing about which legislators will gain power in the latest Republican-Democrat power shift at the statehouse, or how a new majority party will affect citizens when it changes tax, environment, and education laws?

Your answers will influence the structure of your stories, where you go for information and which sources you question.

When covering government and politics, it helps to think first in terms of issues. Better yet, use the language of the people, not the politicians—it's a *problem*, not an issue. The *Wichita Eagle* decided to concentrate its coverage of the 1990 Kansas governor's race on problems facing the state, not on the political personalities and vague campaign rhetoric. After voter turnout in Wichita was higher than expected, research showed that what most influenced citizens to vote was their clarity on these problems. The citizens clearest on the issues were those who read *The Eagle* most often. The research also showed that readers are clearer on the scope of problems when they can see their stake in the outcome. So think of your readers as the diverse stakeholders in a community problem. Each has something unique to gain or lose as the problem is addressed. If there weren't conflicting values and interests, there wouldn't *be* a problem.

We use the phrase "diverse stakeholders" rather than "both sides" because there may well be more than two sides to the story. "Stakeholders" is a broader term that includes both those at the core of a controversy and others who are affected. Even on such a seemingly straightforward matter as a labor-contract dispute between the school district and its teachers union, there are many more than two sides. If you think about the impact of starting the school year late while contract negotiations continue, you will quickly determine that stakeholders include the negotiators, the temporarily unemployed teachers, other school workers who can't do their jobs, students, parents and their employers, day care centers, vendors who provide supplies to schools, other school districts facing new contracts next year and on and on.

Once you have identified the ways that a problem becomes vital to various community stakeholders, you broaden the range of stories and sources. Your ongoing coverage remains ever fresh and urgent to readers.

WRITING THE MEETING STORY

The One-Issue Story

Although most meeting agendas contain many items, typically one issue will dominate coverage. It's the most controversial issue, the one that fills the meeting room with interested citizens. Or it's the issue with the highest price tag and the greatest impact.

Let's compare the benefits of several different writing approaches by examining a meeting with one dominant issue.

THE VOTE LEAD The Northtown School Board voted 4–3 Tuesday to close six elementary schools and two middle schools next fall to contend with declining enrollments, teacher shortages and a multi-million-dollar budget drain.

THE ISSUE LEAD Citing what one board member called the "triple threat" of declining enrollments, teacher shortages and a multi-million-dollar budget drain, the Northtown School Board decided Tuesday to close six elementary schools and two middle schools next fall.

THE IMPACT LEAD More than 3,000 of the area's youngest school children will be required to attend more distant schools next fall, following Tuesday night's vote by the Northtown School Board to close six elementary schools and two middle schools.

THE CONFLICT LEAD Choosing $6 million in annual savings for 20,000 taxpayers over the emotional pleas of more than 300 parents, a bitterly divided Northtown School Board voted 4–3 Tuesday to close six elementary schools and two middle schools next fall.

THE POLITICAL LEAD Republicans elected to the Northtown School Board last year as a slate of candidates promising fiscal reform used their slim majority Tuesday night in a controversial vote that will save the school district $6 million a year, at the expense of closing six neighborhood schools to thousands of the district's children.

THE HUMAN-INTEREST LEAD Janice Ashley made a quick calculation: $300 saved in school taxes against the prospect of quitting her $21,000-a-year job so that her twin 6-year-olds would not have to walk nearly a mile to school each day. An instant later, she was on her feet, joining hundreds of other parents who pled in vain Tuesday that their neighborhood schools should be saved from Northtown School District budget cuts.

ADVANCED TIP
A Matter of Time

Although the time element in a story is an essential W (When) in a news lead, to use the time element most effectively, the writer must develop an ear for the rhythm of sentences. Few mistakes do more violence to effective writing than putting the time element in the wrong place.

Here's a typically clumsy use of the time element:

The Northtown School Board Tuesday voted 4–3 to . . .

"Tuesday voted?" No one talks that way. When we read that syntax, we halt. The last thing a writer wants the reader to do is to stop. The last thing the reader wants to do is reread and struggle through awkward prose.

Another common flaw: placing the time element next to the wrong antecedent.

The Northtown School Board voted to close six schools Tuesday . . .

The schools did not close Tuesday, as this sentence says. The vote was Tuesday.

Try this: Most often, place the time element *after* the verb, but as near to it as possible. Then read the sentence aloud. If it doesn't sound right, find another spot where the time element works both in terms of content and maintaining the flow of words.

The Pros and Cons of Each Lead

Most daily news organizations would publish any of these leads, especially if the sharp deadlines following lengthy night meetings argued against reworking the story. Each offers different advantages and each sacrifices points of interest.

THE VOTE LEAD: This gives us the essential information—the governing body, its official vote, the time element and the reason (Who, What, When, Why)—quickest of all. Readers in a hurry (most of us) appreciate that. However, on an issue of this magnitude, presumably the news organization has informed its readers in advance that a vote was imminent on the fate of six schools, for the reasons stated in the meeting-story lead. In that case, this lead offers us the least new information of any lead we could choose.

THE ISSUE LEAD: This emphasizes the *issues, or problems*, facing the Northtown School Board, rather than the law-making body itself. In this lead, the vote tally is not as important as the decision. Presenting the issue first is more dramatic and more likely to seize the reader's attention. And this lead promises that we will hear from the decision-makers (the "triple threat" quote) if we keep reading. However, this lead offers little new information, scant hint of the conflict and focuses primarily on the government's role rather than the law's affect on the community.

THE IMPACT LEAD: The reporter writes from the perspective of the citizenry, the consumers of government. This addresses the consumer concern, "How does this affect me?" This story goes beyond the stenographic recording of the vote and repeating the issue. It calculates some of its impact and advances the story, perhaps beyond what any of the media competitors will do from this meeting. However, as we can see from the subsequent approaches, this lead focuses on but one stakeholder, the children who have further to travel to school.

THE CONFLICT LEAD: This blends numbers and emotion, drawing the battle lines and promising readers that they will read more about emotional parents and bitterly divided school board members. We see various stakeholders in this issue. However helpful it is to have the new numbers that explain the voting majority's rationale, we can see that they offer an incomplete picture. The $6 million spread among 20,000 taxpayers is $300 each—less than what a typical household might pay for its telephone, its cable-TV, its Internet service, its pet food or its newspaper. The 300 emotional parents at the meeting are a small slice of the 5,000 or so parents of the 3,000 affected school children.

THE POLITICAL LEAD: This offers unique context, a subplot or "back story" that suggests the will of the citizenry (the thousands who voted for the Republicans) may be much broader than the will of the parents. Again, there can be many different stakeholders. However, the focus of this story is on politics (party affiliation, campaign promises) and seems secondary to the more immediate concerns facing the large school community. This story might best be offered as a sidebar to the main story, or as an analytical second-day story.

THE HUMAN-INTEREST LEAD: This offers many of the advantages of the earlier leads—contextual numbers, emotion, impact, conflict. Focused on Janice Ashley, we see the face of this issue, which is no longer just a matter of government budgets and political philosophy. And we get a sense of movement—the writing makes us an eyewitness to the meeting. This is enterprise reporting that is unlikely to be found elsewhere, rewarding readers who come to this news report. This is the one lead that requires the reporter to do more than attend the meeting after preparing for it. Getting to Janice Ashley involves extra reporting, of course. That takes more time. And because many readers will not recognize Janice Ashley personally, they must identify with her predicament. Therefore, the reporter must find a person who is a representative example—"someone like me" or at least someone who is not in a unique, extreme situation with whom few others can empathize. Also note that this lead gets to the essential information—the decision to close schools—more slowly.

ADVANCED TIP
Jargon Is Your Enemy

It's human nature to adopt the language of the groups we associate with—the slang of social groups, the shorthand for familiar topics at work, the abbreviations in e-mail and the unique terms in sports.

But journalists must guard against adopting the jargon of government, which is difficult to read and understand.

Here are a few examples on the long list of words used daily in government buildings but in few other places:

Funds and *"monies"* are money or tax dollars.

Revenue enhancements are increases in taxes and government fees.

Legislation and *ordinances* are laws.

Facilities are buildings or offices.

When there is a *negative cash flow* someone is losing money.

Mortality rates are death rates.

The *public sector* is government; the *private sector* is business.

Impact is not a verb.

It is the longest of the leads shown here. Thus, the writer has the urgent burden of including the other elements very soon, while also telling us more about Janice Ashley's safety and economic concerns (and what numbers tell us that her dilemma is characteristic of many others).

Numbers as Context

Whichever approach is best for your story, the various examples above show the elements that should be present in *all* well-written, well-reported meeting stories. The reader wants the essential information about the vote and the issue, but also wants context—the rationale and the consequences (the cause and effect), expressed through human experience and/or meaningful numbers.

A word about numbers in news stories: Knowing the numbers helps you write more powerful words. When you know how the math works, your writing doesn't have to be conditional or vague. Your verbs can be stronger, clearer. Your sentences can be declarations of fact. This is not simple for most journalists, who prefer words and often are baffled by numbers.

To keep it simpler for you, keep it simpler for readers. The $6 million tax savings is just a number. Context—$6 million compared to what?—makes the number meaningful. Perhaps the $6 million is $1 out of every $6 in the school district budget. Perhaps it is enough to fund school books for every child in grades one through four. As tax dollars, it is $300 per taxpaying household. And $300 per year is equivalent to what else in a family's life?

A politician pushing his agenda will use the numbers that favor his position. The politician might like to use $6 million, which sounds like a lot more than what the average family pays for pet food. That $6 million per year spread among 20,000 taxpayers is $300 per year, or $25 per month. The politician might like to talk about 20,000 taxpayers, rather than 3,000 children and 5,000 parents. Go ahead, use the politician's numbers, especially when quoting him, but do your best to put those numbers in context so that everyone can understand the scope of the issue.

THE ROUNDUP STORY

When more than one newsworthy item must be reported from a single meeting or other event, the writer is at risk of burying newsworthy information by presenting everything in order of importance. Instead, the roundup story is an effective way to signal readers early that there is more than one topic of interest in this longer story.

Talent Showcase

JANE VON BERGEN ▶

Reporter, *Philadelphia Inquirer*

At some point, everyone is a rookie covering meetings, Jane Von Bergen notes with empathy. Whether it's your first meeting ever or it's your first in an unfamiliar community, the first time can be intimidating.

"Fear is a great motivator," says Von Bergen, who started a long reporting career at *The Philadelphia Inquirer* by covering communities for the suburban Neighbors sections. She overcame her own trepidations—"I was terrified"—with preparation and discipline. Nothing complicated—anyone can do it, really.

"Call ahead of time. Call the township manager and others, and ask, 'What is likely to happen? What's the most important thing on the agenda?' Get an explanation of anything technical. When you're writing you may hardly mention these things. But if you don't understand them, you'll have trouble writing.

"Try to learn the principles of municipal government. Basic civics, but in more detail: The taxation system, the process of bills and ordinances, zoning, planning, the sewer authority, mills, per capita tax, competitive bids. Review your state's open-meeting and open-document law and have a very good understanding of that."

Thus prepared, get to the meeting early. "You have to draw a picture of where each official is sitting and get the spelling of their names. Confirm that the right people are sitting behind the name placards in front of them.

"The other reason to arrive early: When each person arrives, introduce yourself, hand out business cards and ask why they are there. What's the significance of their being there? Get phone numbers for home, work and cell phones. Then you'll have the complainers and others—a list of sources you can use for months on many issues. These are the people involved in their community. If you are working for an editor who is paying attention to your story production, and the number of your sources, meetings are great for production. That night, you get the most important story. But government generates lots of other reports that can give you additional stories over the following days without that much more work—a couple of phone calls."

Once the meeting begins, things can happen fast, so the preparation pays off. "Today, you would use a Blackberry, or Microsoft phone book to store the numbers and notes. I like a leather portfolio with pockets to put pieces of paper, and a big tablet for notes from the meeting. A reporters' notebook is good for taking notes while standing up, but the big tablet works better when you're seated. On the big page, I draw a vertical line. On one side I put the facts, on the other emotion, color and description.

"If you have any emotional reaction—you laughed (something strikes you as funny or absurd) or it strikes you as sad—look at that as a source of a future story. This is a clue that there's a story to be told. You want to pay attention to your emotions, but you don't want to get caught up in them. Don't want to say you have no emotions at all, because that makes you a bad reporter."

The smaller the town, the less likely things will be done by the book. "Vigorously protest any closed meetings. You don't want to be unpleasant about it, but you want to be relentless, even if you think the officials might have a good reason to do so. You want to be on record about this and to discourage it from becoming routine."

(continued)

Talent Showcase *(continued)*

Encourage your editors to send you back to familiar towns, Von Bergen advises. Maintaining the beat is easier and more productive than starting all over each time.

"You must make your physical presence obvious. Show up at the municipal building and show up at community events. Just like an animal lifts its leg and marks its spot, you're marking your spot.

"Once in a while, it won't hurt to go out drinking when they all go out. But you must be very careful. Insist on a separate check. Be careful about how much you drink. Drink something like a vodka tonic—but instruct the bartender that you only want a tablespoon of vodka. Don't just go out with one faction. And don't be too quick to share with one faction what you learn from the other. Tell them, 'You wouldn't want me to tell the others what I hear from you.' "

Reporters who know their turf and prepare well will be far ahead on issues and stories. Then, "you should be able to write it all before the meeting begins. But you have to be prepared to throw it all out if things happen differently."

The roundup story is used often by reporters covering the periodic cluster of decisions from the U.S. Supreme Court. It is used when writing about government budgets. It can be used to write about a multi-issue meeting.

There are two popular techniques. The first gets as much information into the first paragraph as possible:

> *In moves that will affect almost every local citizen one way or another, the Southwerk City Council passed new laws Tuesday that set summer curfews, change trash pickup days, and raise fees on building permits, garage-sale licenses and pet licenses.*

The other technique leads with the most significant item, and then quickly tips off readers that there is more to come.

> *Anticipating the annual summer surge in crime and delinquency, the Southwerk City Council voted Tuesday to prohibit teens and pre-teens from being outside after 11 p.m. in July and August—a move that some predicted will create binge drinking and other problems in late June and early September.*
>
> *"This is going to cause more problems than it cures," Councilman Wilson Harding predicted before voting on the losing end of a 5–2 vote.*
>
> *In other votes Tuesday, the council:*
>
> - *Changed trash pickup days to save money by scheduling work crews more efficiently.*
> - *Doubled the cost of building permits to discourage shoddy repair work.*
> - *Raised fees for garage-sale licenses and pet licenses for the first time in five years.*
>
> *Hundreds of parents who signed petitions against the curfew considered it the most extreme approach to dealing with the crime sprees that have antagonized summer tourists.*

There are other ways to identify the secondary issues in the story, but the bullet points used above do the job efficiently. The short amount of text following each bullet helps the reader move swiftly through the story. The bullets also make it easy for readers to refer back to the issues if they need to find them.

Keep in mind that the content of bulleted material works like a single paragraph. Each item in this list is part of a series, so the grammar must be parallel. In the example above, each phrase following a bullet begins with a verb in the past tense.

IN CONCLUSION

A news report's proper vantage point is the view of the citizenry, the consumers of government. That is a free press' role in democracy.

Reporters achieve this by connecting with citizens in their neighborhoods rather than spending so much time with bureaucrats in government buildings. Alert reporters make seemingly dull topics interesting and essential by showing citizens their stake in the outcome.

Thus prepared, reporters have several ways to write meeting stories with context and urgency.

EXERCISE 1

Write a story from the following:

You are a student at Mainefield State, browsing your student newspaper's website, when you see the following item:

> Old pipes burst in the Billings Library sometime this weekend, flooding the basement and ruining a valuable collection of books stored there.
>
> Workers pumped out the water on Sunday, but Alice Beckworth, library director, called the leak "a disaster."
>
> Beckworth said the entire Chadwick collection was destroyed, thought to be the only surviving copies of magazines from the turn of the century. She estimated the collection's worth at $25 million.
>
> The Billings Library closed Monday but will reopen Tuesday.

As an enterprising reporter covering the university senate, you vaguely recall a request from the library staff to fix the plumbing. You sift through your notes, and there it is, four weeks ago, Beckworth spoke to the senators and school administrators. "I'm predicting a disaster that will set the Billings collection back 20 years. If these pipes break over a weekend, there's no way to prevent losing the entire Chadwick collection." Your notes say the senators and administrators tabled action on the proposal.

You call Beckworth's office, but she is declining interviews. You then contact the president's office. He was at the university senate meeting, but you are referred to the university spokeswoman, Hilary Rodriguez.

"Mainefield State has lost a valuable collection, and Billings Library has suffered an obviously terrible loss. But we'll let the insurance adjusters look at the situation and give us their best estimate of the damage that has occurred. Mainefield will continue to offer students the finest education in the state."

You feel stymied, when you remember a report that was offered at the meeting. You find it under the pile. In the executive summary is all you need. It says the pipes have been a problem for 10 years. A leak two years ago nearly turned into a flood but a student discovered and reported it, and maintenance stopped it in time. Here's a quote from Beckworth: "The pipes will cost $10,000 to fix. That's a small price to protect a $25 million collection that's one of its kind. If we don't do this soon, we run the risk of losing the irreplaceable."

You call back the spokeswoman.

"Yes, well, obviously we were aware of the problem. We were trying to take steps to fix it within two years," she says.

You go over to the library to look for yourself. There you find the assistant library director, Robert Fineman. "We warned them," he says, shaking his head. "We told them this would happen. Now look at it. All for just $10,000."

You go back to your room and write.

EXERCISE 2

Write a story from the following:

At the Appleton State board of trustees meeting, board members decide to raise tuition. They vote, 6–3, to raise tuition by $3,000. It will now be $15,000 a year to attend Appleton. That's a 25 percent increase.

"We have no other choice," says board president Victoria Hill during the meeting. "We are faced with a budget shortfall of $4 million. There's no other way to make up that amount of money without taking these drastic means. I know that some students might not be able to attend, but maybe we could help."

The board decides to set up a special scholarship fund for current students to help offset the increases and help them stay in school. That vote is 6–3.

The board also voted, 6–3, to fire the school president, David L. Brown. Brown had been president for five years.

"It's time for a change," Hill said. "We need a leader who understands budgeting better. Mr. Brown needed to provide stronger leadership during this time of budget crisis, a crisis he started."

Others at the meeting felt that way.

"This guy needed to go three years ago," said Harold Irving. "I believe his ambitious building plan was too much. I can remember sitting right here at this board meeting four years ago telling him we didn't have the money to launch that kind of building campaign. He just wouldn't listen."

One of the three negatives votes was cast by Beverly Pasiano.

"The building plan is our fault. We voted for it, told him to do it, and now we're going to punish our mistake by firing him? That may be legal but that's not right."

C H A P T E R 13

Writing Nontraditional Leads

IN THIS CHAPTER, YOU WILL LEARN:

- Nontraditional ways to begin stories can attract readers.
- These leads can be a few words or several paragraphs.
- Journalists use storytelling as an effective writing tool.
- Nontraditional leads help readers see the story.

You can recover from a good-not-great lead, but it's really hard to recover from . . . a really terrible lead.

Gayle Reaves, editor,
Fort Worth Weekly

AS A COMPETITIVE AND DETERMINED POLICE REPORTER FOR *THE MIAMI HERALD*, Edna Buchanan mastered the art of nontraditional lead writing. Buchanan wrote legendary stories about murders in Florida's Dade County. She earned a reputation for doggedly working a story until it became interesting enough to run on the *Herald*'s front page.

Buchanan's hallmark was her leads. Influenced by two-time Pulitzer Prize-winning *Herald* writer and editor Gene Miller, Buchanan learned to open her stories with ironic twists. She usually started with a few sentences that, left alone, would seem routine. She quickly followed with a short, punchy burst that surprised readers and woke them to the story's irony.

In his *New Yorker* profile of Buchanan called "Covering The Cops," writer Calvin Trillin said one *Miami Herald* staffer called Buchanan's leads the "Miller Chop" after her sometime editor. This one was Trillin's favorite and "the classic Edna lead:"

> The man she loved slapped her face. Furious, she says she told him never, ever to do that again. "What are your going to do, kill me?" he asked and handed her a gun. "Here, kill me," he challenged. She did.

Buchanan might have easily written: *A young woman shot and killed her boyfriend Wednesday after he slapped her and threatened her with his gun.*

There's nothing wrong with that lead. But Buchanan's writing is more creative, more evocative, more entertaining. It lets readers picture the action.

Buchanan's lead doesn't follow the formula of a traditional news lead. It promises readers that a story will follow—not just a straight reporting of facts, but a story with characters, conflict, intrigue.

Writing those types of stories begins with leads that push beyond the traditional 5 Ws and H. These stories beg for imaginative writers, journalists who can tell the day's news with flair and style.

REPORTING ENTERTAINING LEADS

Consider this lead to a story from the *Houston Chronicle* about a woman wrestling with the aftermath of Hurricane Rita, one of two powerful storms that damaged the Gulf Coast in the summer of 2005.

> Sandra Hall thinks she will eat a ham sandwich for Christmas dinner.
>
> From her recliner. By herself. Surrounded by pill bottles, books and boxes of microwave dinners good for hurricane victims and shut-ins.
>
> Temporarily, Hall is both.
>
> "I'm just not in the holiday spirit," she says. "How could I be?"
>
> Last September, the fearsome Rita barreled up her street in Bon Wier in deep East Texas, turning her 200-year-old home into a soggy cardboard box.
>
> Federal Emergency Management Agency representatives offered her $500 for what she estimates to be $10,000 in damage. Her kitchen floor is cracked in two,

her water heater, though still working, leans like the Tower of Pisa and her sieve of a roof is covered by a blue tarp.

A reporter could have written: *An East Texas woman says Hurricane Rita caused $10,000 in damage to her 200-year-old home, a figure 20 times higher than federal agents are willing to pay.*

There's little wrong with that lead. But the writers, Claudia Feldman and Jeannie Kever, let their readers see Sandra Hall's house and feel her despair during the holidays. They take the reader inside her kitchen. Who can't picture the water heater tilting as the Tower of Pisa?

Some nontraditional leads set scenes to show the story's main theme. This lead, from the *Los Angeles Times*, starts a story about the conflicted nature of those who oppose the war in Iraq but understand that soldiers must do the jobs assigned them.

> There's a diner called Peggy Sue's about eight miles outside of Barstow, Calif., and as hard as Lt. Col. Kenneth Parks tries, he can never seem to pay his bill.
>
> He orders a burger and chocolate shake. But before he is finished, the waitress informs him the tab has been taken care of by yet another stranger who prefers to remain anonymous, but who wants to do something for a soldier in uniform.
>
> Many Americans have conflicted feelings about the Iraq war, but not about the warriors. The gestures of gratitude and generosity that occur with regularity at Peggy Sue's—across Interstate 15 from Fort Irwin, a military desert-training site—have become commonplace across the United States.

These leads promise readers a different type of story. The information might be similar to a traditional news story. But the lead says the writing will be more entertaining.

STORYTELLING

Tales attract readers. Many of us learned to read through storybooks. Stories with characters and action usually capture more interest than straight recitations of facts. Nontraditional leads that take advantage of these storytelling techniques can improve an otherwise routine piece.

This lead from *The Associated Press* tells a quick story about a one-of-a-kind operation. Notice how the writer helps the reader to know early that this operation is unusual. The writer also gives readers a picture of what will happen. The chief conflict, and therefore the major change, is saved for last, though.

> CLEVELAND—In the next few weeks, five men and seven women will secretly visit the Cleveland Clinic to interview for the chance to undergo a radical operation that has never been tried anywhere in the world.
>
> They will smile, raise their eyebrows, close their eyes, open their mouths. Dr. Maria Siemionow will study their cheekbones, lips and noses. She will ask what they hope to gain and what they most fear.

ADVANCED TIP
Think Storytelling

To write effective nontraditional leads, reporters must ask themselves several questions.

- First, thinking visually, what scenes could they show readers? What could make the reader picture the story?
- What parts of their story would make a good tale? How would a storyteller relate the information?
- What conflicts are in their stories? Knowing where there are problems to overcome or changes that might occur tells writers what they should choose to begin their stories.

Then she will ask, "Are you afraid that you will look like another person?"

She will pose that question because whoever she chooses will endure the ultimate identity crisis.

Siemionow wants to attempt a face transplant.

Leads that tell stories don't have to be as serious as a face transplant. Some are whimsical looks at the day's trends. This beginning from *The Washington Post* lets the reader go through the thoughts of an upwardly mobile woman whose every purchase, including just the right Christmas tree, reveals the need for status. It also sets the stage for this recent trend: buying the largest Christmas tree on the block.

> WASHINGTON—With a living room ceiling that soars 22 feet above the carpeted floor, no ordinary Christmas tree would do. A standard 7-footer, Daphne Kessler decided, would look "kind of weird," dwarfed by the second-floor balcony and the towering Palladian window.
>
> She needed a tree as grand as the five-bedroom, 6,000-square-foot Great Falls, Va., home that Kessler moved into almost four years ago with her husband and two children. So Kessler bought a 12-foot behemoth that her interior designer decorated by climbing so high up a ladder that, he said, "I feel like a monkey up here."
>
> As estate-like homes have popped up across the suburbs, they've spawned a must-have seasonal accessory: the super-size Christmas tree. McMansions with their two-story foyers, cathedral ceilings and great rooms are fueling a demand for trees fit for Paul Bunyan with price tags fit for Daddy Warbucks—from $100 to more than $1,000.

The writer introduces the problem—not just any tree will do—and the reader follows along. The main character decides how to solve the problem and then enlists her interior designer for help. As soon as the example plays out, the writer introduces the story's theme.

Sometimes, using storytelling techniques simply means telling a story. This lead from *The Associated Press* tackles the issue of urban legends. What better way to begin a story on urban legends than by telling one?

> ATLANTA—The urgent e-mails usually come with a warning: Beware, this is a true story.
>
> Then the story unfolds: A woman gets into her car in a parking lot, starts the engine and shifts into reverse. As she backs up, she notices a piece of paper, some sort of advertisement, stuck on her rear window and blocking her view. She shifts into park, and gets out to remove the leaflet, leaving the engine running. As she walks to

the rear of the car, carjackers appear. They jump into the car and speed away with her purse, keys and identification.

At the end of the message, Detective Bledsoe of the Florissant, Mo., sheriff's office and Lt. Tony Bartholome of the Missouri Highway Patrol confirm that the incident happened in St. Louis County and urge motorists to take precaution, particularly around the holidays. It also gives an address and a telephone number for more information. But as it turns out, it is entirely made up.

Urban legends—those weird stories that seem to take on lives of their own as they travel from person to person—have likely been around for centuries. But in the last decade, the Internet has added a new, more encompassing dimension to the spread of false rumors.

Notice at the end of the lead, the writer makes it clear why the new story on an old subject: adding the Internet to the equation gives this dusty tale renewed energy. Readers now know enough to decide if they should keep reading.

ANECDOTES

To tell the news as a story, reporters must use anecdotes—not the amusing jokes told at the beginning of after-dinner speeches, but nuggets of action that reveal a character's personality or symbolize a larger issue.

An anecdote ordinarily is a scene—usually not funny—that holds up on its own. It has a defined beginning and a clear ending. Journalists use them for a reason: Anecdotes must have a point. They show the reader an example of the story's theme.

Leads that use anecdotes have grown common in both print and broadcast journalism. Some writers try to avoid them, fearing the leads use too many words or are overdone. But done correctly, anecdotes carry tremendous power. They show action, which engages the reader. They force the writer to focus on people, whom readers find more interesting. And they have a point to them.

This lead from *The Atlanta Journal-Constitution* tells the story of when a lobbyist encountered, through back channels, a national political figure who then was running for lieutenant governor of Georgia.

Notice how the anecdote follows a storyline, then ends with a punch that shows the reader why the writer put it in her story and why it is necessary to set up the story's point.

AUSTIN, Texas—Suzi Paynter, a lobbyist for Southern Baptists in Texas, says she's never met Ralph Reed. But she thinks she recognizes his work.

In the spring of 2001, while strolling the grounds of the state Capitol, her cell phone rang.

A local senator screamed in her ear. "Stop it. Stop the phone calls," he shouted. His office had been swamped with calls demanding the defeat of a bill to allow an Indian tribe to open a casino.

Paynter was puzzled. First, it was widely known the bill was doomed to fail. Also, Paynter maintains close contact with other anti-gambling groups and couldn't

The Art of Storytelling

Tasneem Grace Tewogbola began writing for *The* (Syracuse) *Post-Standard* just weeks after graduating from high school in Syracuse, N.Y. She worked at the paper every summer during college, and later joined the staff as a full-time reporter. She won a full scholarship to Syracuse University, graduating as a university scholar—one of the top 12 students in her class. She was chosen to deliver the valedictory address at the university's graduation. She later wrote for *The* (Nashville) *Tennessean* before moving back to Syracuse and *The Post-Standard*. Her advice on writing leads? Think storytelling: "What would you go home and tell somebody about your day? That's your lead."

QUESTION: If someone asked "How was your day?" and you told them what you were working on, how is it that you boil it down to the most important? What makes it important?

GRACE TEWOGBOLA: For me it has to be the most interesting component, and it's a personal decision. But sometimes when I'm doing the interview or sitting and observing something, it will occur to me that whatever I'm observing is the lead. I think, "OK, so this is it." At some moments, it's almost a feeling when I'm interviewing someone and they start getting dramatic, or something out of the ordinary happens. I go for those because I'm more drawn to those as a reader, those experiences, rather than the straight inverted pyramid style. That's what pulls me into a news story. So I look for those dramatic details that someone might find more in a feature story.

QUESTION: How do you define the drama? How do you say, "OK this is the dramatic moment?"

GRACE TEWOGBOLA: I decide it by any observation of emotion that goes beyond just the basic facts. So if I'm covering, say, a town meeting or something, and I'm noticing that one of the people at the table is scrunching up their face or sucking on the end of their pencil, then that gets me beyond the basic quote when I ask them, "Oh, what was your reaction to by-law blink, blink, blink?" I'll be able to allow people to see some of the humanity, some of the reaction that's not so boring. I know some people are really drawn to the basic fact lead—who, what, when, where, why. But I'm not as a reader.

QUESTION: How did you learn to write those [nontraditional leads]?

GRACE TEWOGBOLA: I learned to write them by paying attention to the news stories that actually got my attention. And wanting to enjoy the job of news writing better. I wanted to employ something that would invigorate me more. So just in the daily reading of the paper, if I find myself reading a story, "Hmm, I don't really care about [a local Syracuse project called] Destiny, so why am I caring now?" I'll look over the story and think "I'm caring because there's a voice in it. There's some emotion." There's something beyond what somebody read off a press release or dry quote. Again, it's all my own personal judgment and personal reading style. But then I started to play around. How could I adopt that into some of my own writing, make it more storytelling than fact-telling.

QUESTION: What are the points of storytelling that translate into news writing?

GRACE TEWOGBOLA: The points of storytelling that translates for me is element of voice beyond just the facts. It's like the reaction element. And it's also the little detail that sometimes you'll find in different kinds of writing but for some reason can be completely absent in news writing. So you might comment on a person's posture. You might talk about the sound their voice makes, their mannerisms. I would look for certain things that would give me a clue about who this person is beyond just their job titles.

QUESTION: How did you make that turn? When did you say, "Wait a minute. I can't keep writing like this. I've got to make this turn."

GRACE TEWOGBOLA: In my internship experience, I had some summers when I had to do straight news writing, and some summers where I was able to do more long-term assignments, which were news features. And when I saw that I could vary the style, that's when I stopped writing strictly from the inverted pyramid. That's when I started taking risks. "I don't know what the editors are going to think, but I like it." And hope that they kind of got it. They didn't always get it. But after three summers of interning, I was able to develop the confidence and say, "OK, I'll take the basic story, you're going to give me this assignment but what you get back may be a little different."

> imagine that any of them could afford automated phone banks. "I didn't know who it was," Paynter said. "Now I think I do."
>
> That year, and the next, Reed secretively worked Texas officials and the Legislature to kill pro-gambling initiatives on behalf of Washington lobbyist Jack Abramoff—and a Louisiana Indian tribe out to protect its casino. Documents show one of Reed's weapons of choice that spring was automated phone banks.
>
> This month, three government watchdog groups called on an Austin prosecutor to investigate Reed, arguing that he violated a strict Texas law requiring lobbyists to register with the state.

The anecdote's main point is also the story's main point: Reed wasn't always upfront with the public, and Georgia voters needed to know about the man running for the second-highest office in the state.

The lead also uses techniques normally found in fiction books, such as dialogue and scenes. Using these are fine, as long as the story is true and each fact—even walking across the Capitol grounds—is true. Using them helps readers see the story and hooks them into continuing to read.

SITUATIONERS

People's circumstances interest readers. Journalists have discovered that using a person's situation to explain their stories' main points draws readers into their stories. Finding the right people and their circumstances often can show readers the story more effectively.

This lead from *The Associated Press* introduces the remarkable story of the only known unvaccinated human survivor of rabies. The writer sets up the victim's contrasting circumstances from one year ago, letting the situation speak for itself.

> MILWAUKEE—Last December, Jeanna Giese spent Christmas in the hospital, unable to speak or walk as she suffered from the effects of rabies. This year, the 16-year-old is celebrating her survival at home with her family.
>
> The teenager, who is the world's only known unvaccinated human rabies survivor, is regaining her ability to walk and talk. She has returned to school and plans to return to the volleyball team next year and eventually, attend college.

When Hurricane Katrina hit New Orleans, journalists told the stories of victim after victim. Usually the most penetrating stories began with examples of what problems the evacuees faced. This lead in the *Atlanta Journal-Constitution* uses the situation of one victim to demonstrate the problems many fellow evacuees faced.

> Phyllis Agee thought she'd done everything she was supposed to do.
>
> The New Orleans realtor had flood insurance as well as homeowner's insurance on her house a few blocks from Lake Pontchartrain. When officials told people to evacuate before Katrina hit, she left her native city.
>
> Now, the 39-year-old single mom is living in an apartment in Douglasville and trying to figure how to rebuild her life.

Her insurance company hasn't paid out anything, and she can't find out when it is likely to cut a check. Her mortgage lenders told her last week that she will get another 90-day deferment on payments—unless she starts working before that, and then they want her to resume payments on her ruined house.

With car payments and other bills coming due, she wants to start working as soon as she can transfer her real estate license to Georgia. But she doesn't think she can juggle mortgage and rent if she doesn't get an insurance check soon. Even if she had that money, she isn't sure it makes sense to start rebuilding her house until the levees are repaired. Officials say the flood barriers should be repaired to pre-Katrina standards by June 1, the official start of the next hurricane season.

The Washington Post ran the following lead on a story about an inventor trying to use soybeans as fuel. The writer begins with a quick account of the subject's past inventions. Going through his background gives the lead an extra boost. The reader learns this man's idea for soybeans is not his first brainstorm, just one in a long line of a different way of thinking.

Larry Jarboe's quest for energy independence began years ago in the mangrove swamps of the Florida Keys, with a 15-foot canoe he bought for $75 at Sears. He installed an electric trolling motor to chase lobsters and realized "it was a really great way to live, and very clean."

After that came the homemade electric riding lawnmower, the solar-powered electric Toyota MR2 with a lightning bolt on the side, the electric bicycle and the wood-and-gas-powered sawmill. Now Jarboe has laid his hopes on a hard vegetable the size of a pencil eraser, one grown throughout southern Maryland: the soybean.

Already used in soaps, foams and salad dressing, the soybean is also the key ingredient for the burgeoning biodiesel fuel industry. Thanks to high petroleum prices, a tax incentive that began this year and a desire for cleaner-burning alternative fuels, biodiesel plants are popping up nationwide.

After the Tampa Bay Buccaneers lost in the National Football League playoffs, the *St. Petersburg Times* ran the following lead on its front page. The writer simply observed what he saw after the game to create a mood of grim acceptance.

The game ended. The sky was black. The night cold. And Buccaneer fans filed out of Raymond James Stadium glum-faced, toting their homemade signs and dashed playoff dreams.

As they trooped back to their cars, some stalwarts gathered in the chill, huddling around charcoal grills that glowed faintly in the parking lot.

North of the stadium in Al Lopez Park, somebody lit off fireworks anyway.

ADVANCED TIP
Nontraditional Leads

Here are some unconventional ways you can start your stories:

- **Anecdotes:** Leads with unusual power, these stories within the main story have a point and a beginning, middle and end.
- **Situationer:** This lead uses a person's unusual circumstances to draw readers into a story.
- **Roundup:** Put several related facts one after another and you clearly show readers an issue or trend.
- **Intriguing Statement:** A one-line sentence that captures a story's irony also captures readers.
- **Change in Direction:** This lead suddenly shifts direction to add surprise or conflict.
- **Humor:** The most difficult of writing, but this lead can capture a reader's attention.

The lead is particularly poignant when it describes the fans carrying something concrete—the homemade signs—and something emotional—dashed playoff dreams. The writer could have said the fans were disappointed. But by showing the reader the fans' actions, readers understand and discover the fans' mood by themselves—a better way to begin the story.

Situationer leads work because they show subjects as examples of a larger story or issue. These leads also are especially effective when the subjects' circumstances are what make the story worth reading. Simply showing these situations can lure readers into the story.

ROUNDUP

Some stories have several facts that, by themselves, seem impotent. But string them together and they suddenly have great strength. Putting routine facts side by side sometimes can infuse energy.

In his book *Magazine Editing*, J. T. W. (Jake) Hubbard called this lead a "roundup" or bullet. He was especially fond of calling it "bam-bam-bam" because of "the nuggets of information it spits, machine-gun-like, at the reader," he wrote. Usually three examples carry just the right cadence to get the writer's point across. Hubbard says this lead is an excellent way to begin stories that show trends or stretch across geographical lines.

The following lead from *The Associated Press* was written a few weeks after Hurricane Katrina devastated New Orleans. Lafayette is the first major city due west of the New Orleans area. Many refugees from the hurricane stayed there.

> LAFAYETTE, La.—Their homes are bursting with guests. Their schools are overwhelmed. Traffic has been at a standstill for three weeks since thousands of New Orleans hurricane evacuees arrived in search of shelter.
>
> But Lafayette, the capital of Cajun country, still knows how to party.
>
> Throngs turned out Saturday for the first full day of the Festivals Acadiens, billed as the largest Cajun festival in the world, in a show of just what "*joie de vivre*" means.

The writer could have written this in a more traditional way: *Throngs in Lafayette turned out for the first day of the Festivals Acadiens, three weeks after Hurricane Katrina forced thousands of New Orleans evacuees to seek shelter in the capital of Cajun country.*

The first version reads better. It lets readers understand that despite the problems caused by the swelling numbers, Louisianans kept a longstanding tradition. Notice the first paragraph uses three examples to make its point.

This technique works again in another story by *The Washington Post*. This lead began a piece that showed readers that many states had budget surpluses. Having each sentence seems matter of fact. Placed back-to-back, they show the scope of the story's points. The writer uses more than three examples, but stays in the same family by doubling three to use six examples.

> WASHINGTON—A tax refund in Hawaii of $300 million. A full day of kindergarten for every 5-year-old in Delaware. A light-rail line from Denver's airport to

downtown. Cheap health insurance for middle-class families in Illinois. Property-tax cuts in New Jersey and Pennsylvania. A tram for Wyoming's biggest ski resort.

The story's point is that state governments had finally crawled out of their financial black holes and had money to spend on special projects. Without placing the projects one after the other, the lead would have lost energy. This version is much stronger, and does what a lead should: carry the reader to the story's heart.

Sometimes in-depth stories generate several excellent examples whose information is more complex than a sentence can capture. A journalist still can string these examples together to show the expanse of the story's exposé.

This lead, on a story from *The Buffalo News*, grows stronger when these examples run one after another.

> Susan M. Lindgren wasn't expecting luxury accommodations when she was arrested and taken to the Erie County Holding Center on a domestic charge in July.
>
> But she also didn't expect to be denied her medication, or find out some inmates couldn't get toilet paper.
>
> Ellen M. Rodo also was shocked by the way she was treated at the jail. There wasn't enough water pressure, she said, to clean her colostomy bag.
>
> And 16-year-old Michelle D'Amico refused to sit on the floor or even lean against the walls of a holding cell where she was initially detained. The room, she said, was filthy and had a putrid smell.
>
> "They treated us like animals in that holding pen," said another prisoner, Madelyn V. Cheatham. "There were about 16 of us in this tiny room, and I had to sleep on the floor and it stunk of urine. It was hell."
>
> These stories and others inmates recounted to *The Buffalo News* paint a picture of an Erie County Holding Center where basic humanity has been lost to overcrowded conditions, overworked guards in an understaffed facility, and lack of basic supplies due to budget cuts.

The story could have begun with the information in the last paragraph. Showing readers the examples of the women in jail breathes life into the lead. The examples carry more power than the summary sentence of basic humanity lost to overcrowded conditions.

INTRIGUING STATEMENT

Reporters often can make their stories less typical by beginning with an unusual sentence or sentences. These statements sum up the story's essence in a few words. Leads such as these work especially well on news stories less somber than most.

Intriguing-statement leads are short and take up less space. They are fresh. They often mimic conversations, another reason for writing them.

The Associated Press wrote a lead about the success of a man who had a string of problems so difficult that any one of them alone would be devastating. The writer

Talent Showcase

GAYLE REAVES ▸

Editor, the *Fort Worth Weekly*

Gayle Reaves has spent 30 years writing stories that challenged authorities, exposed corruption and won awards.

Consider:

- She broke the story that led to accounting scandals at MCI Worldcom.
- She exposed a corrupt sheriff who ran the law near the Texas-Mexico border.
- She teamed with other reporters at *The Dallas Morning News* to tell about epidemic violence against women. Their efforts won the Pulitzer Prize for international reporting in 1994.

So, after hundreds of stories and all the accolades, writing leads should be a snap.

Or not.

"For me, finding what the lead is that I need to put on the story is a trial-and-error process," Reaves says. "Obviously, you want to draw people into the story. You don't want it to be clunked up details that can wait until some other point in the story."

Her leads must tell readers accurately what's going to be in that story and draw them into it.

Reaves, who now leads the editorial staff at the *Fort Worth Weekly*, an independent newspaper in Fort Worth, Texas, still writes as often as possible. She also edits her reporters. She has developed guideposts to judge her writers' leads, and to find her own.

- The lead has to reflect the story. "When I'm editing copy, and reading other people's stuff, the lead so often either stops people cold in their tracks, or it doesn't quite fit the rest of the story. Either it leads you to believe the story is going to be something [other] than it is, or it doesn't give you a clue that the story is going to be about all these different elements."
- An effective lead attracts readers. "It draws people in. It's clearly written. It's got the major elements in it. And it's the first part of telling people what you're going to tell them."
- Writers can't be lazy. Settling for second-best means fewer readers. "If it's bad, you've lost. It's really im-

listed them rapid-fire for effect, then twisted the lead to the positive by using a conversational phrase.

> NEW YORK—Dale Keyser: bipolar, alcoholic, homeless, jobless, estranged from his wife and children.
>
> But that's history.
>
> Days before Christmas, Keyser is playing Santa Claus on Fifth Avenue—now a man with a roof over his head and a job, who volunteers to entertain the side-

portant. I think you can have a decent lead that's not a great, great lead and . . . people are still going to follow along with you. They're going to give you another chance. They're going to keep going for another couple of more paragraphs. You can recover from a good-not-great lead, but it's really hard to recover from . . . a really terrible lead."

These guidelines work for both breaking news and less timely pieces. Reaves says she follows no formulas for starting her stories. Her leads can be long or short, just so they tell the story clearly and attract the reader.

Once Reaves was working election night covering a local election for *The Dallas Morning News*. Her story would run among a host of others. How could she distinguish hers from among the many?

"It was a very close race, and one guy got out ahead but he was just barely ahead. But he stayed ahead all night and he still won. So the lead said, 'So-and-so had a paper-thin lead that refused to tear.' That's a hard-news lead," she says.

Reaves is more concerned about quality and the reader than counting words. A three-paragraph lead is fine for her if "it covers what it needs to cover." She believes in streamlining the writing. Leave extraneous facts for later.

"It doesn't have to be a certain number of words. It can be fairly long. But it just has to be simple and clear. And . . . all the elements that are in the story have to be hinted at, have to be foreshadowed," she says.

Much of writing is rewriting. Reaves knows that well. When she finishes a story, she always rewrites.

"I used to write a whole lot of really long, complex sentences. I still do that. But I go back and I read them and then I kind of puke and then I redo them."

One of Reaves' former colleagues refers "to first drafts as upchucking on the page." The first draft covers what is needed to tell the story. Then the important job of rewriting begins.

"And then you go back through and you pick through that, and when you go back and reread, usually I find structures that are way too wordy that I can make more spare and clean," Reaves says. "There are some structures that are convoluted because of some fact I am writing around or some nuance that I'm trying to get across. And there's a reason why I did it the way I did it, but you can come up with a better way of doing it. You just have to work harder at it.

"So that's what I do. I go back and I winnow."

Why does she spend so much effort rewriting?

"Even if it's a long story, you want it to read short. . . . My stories and everybody else's here that I edit, I want them to read short, I want the writing to be fair and very accurate. A lot times that's what I go back and do."

walk crowds. And who will spend time with his own family during the holiday season.

The writer for the following lead from *The Associated Press* could have begun the story several ways. Yet the sentence's simplicity and plain words are attractive.

America's teens are smoking less and popping pain pills more.

The lure of the family medicine cabinet helped nearly one in 10 high school seniors to try prescription pain killers last year, even as their generation continued turning away, at least slightly, from smoking and many other drugs.

This next lead from *The Wall Street Journal* uses the second person "you" to affect a conversational tone. The reporter writes in the second person in the first two paragraphs before switching to the more conventional third person but still keeps a light touch.

> Before you drag out old family stories at holiday gatherings this season, researchers have some news for you.
>
> The tales you choose to tell, and the way you tell them, may play a bigger role than you think in shaping your children's self-esteem and their academic skills.
>
> A growing number of researchers are putting family stories under the microscope, recording and dissecting the plots and adults' storytelling techniques to uncover links to children's development. What they're finding is that a sense of family history is linked to self-esteem and resiliency in kids. And contrary to what adults may assume, happily-ever-after tales aren't always best. Instead, stories of relatives grappling with sad or difficult events may give children the wisdom and perspective they need to thrive.

The Associated Press story about an unusual flight from a bird looking for food for her chick began this way:

> BANGKOK—Talk about a working mother.
>
> A Christmas Island, Australia, Frigate bird named Lydia recently made a nonstop journey of just over 26 days, covering nearly 2,500 miles—across Indonesian volcanoes and some of Asia's busiest shipping lanes—in search of food for her baby.

This next lead from *The Arizona Republic* is longer than the others but still manages to engage the reader. A prisoner still is able to commit crimes—especially against the agent that put him in jail in the first place.

> Daniel G. Johnson was serving time at the Marana Community Correctional Treatment Facility near Tucson when he found a new way to make money from behind bars: He started ripping off Uncle Sam.
>
> The 28-year-old forger, who worked in the private prison's library, sent fraudulent tax forms to the Internal Revenue Service, seeking refunds of more than $200,000. Although tax schemes are rampant in Arizona's correctional systems, Johnson's case was exceptional because he was caught and prosecuted by the federal government.

These leads show you don't have to write long to be effective. Even one or two sentences can do the trick.

CHANGE IN DIRECTION

Describing the same person or event with opposites or a change in direction creates a tension. That tension lures readers into stories.

This lead from *USA Today* plots the fortunes of Jeanine Pirro, a district attorney near New York City, who had announced she would run for the New York state's senate seat. The opposite action makes the lead work.

> New York Republicans once begged Jeanine Pirro to take on Sen. Hillary Rodham Clinton when she runs for re-election in 2006. Now, many are begging her to get out of the Senate race and run instead for state attorney general—ASAP.

The Associated Press wrote about another Clinton, using the technique of stating a fact, but then asking a question.

> NEW YORK—Former president Bill Clinton managed to persuade a group of world and business leaders to commit to more than $1.25 billion worth of initiatives to solve major global problems.
>
> Now the question is, will they follow through?

Cox News Service and *The Associated Press* repeat that technique with a slight variation on the theme. These next leads state facts, but follow up with obvious and warranted skepticism. In both leads, putting the factual statement next to the skeptical one gives the writing tension. The urge to see how the tension is resolved will pull readers into both pieces.

> WASHINGTON—NASA Administrator Michael Griffin is set on grounding the space shuttles for good by 2010, no matter what.
>
> Whether that actually happens is still anyone's guess.

> WASHINGTON—Federal employees helping Katrina victims charged more than $39 million on government credit cards for disaster relief items. Congressional investigators want to make sure the taxpayers got a good deal.

Sometimes writers use direct opposites to add intrigue to their leads. This lead from *The Associated Press* begins a story about Puerto Rico using inmates to work on a cash crop.

> YAUCO, Puerto Rico—Cocaine sent Juan Rivera Cabrera to prison. Coffee got him out—at least for a few hours each day.
>
> Rivera, serving five to seven years for selling cocaine, is among 100 inmates who travel each morning to Puerto Rico's lush highlands to pick coffee beans.

ADVANCED TIP

Impact of a Weak Lead

Leads are the first words that greet readers. Journalists usually have just the one chance to convince those readers to stay with their stories. The beginning must catch the reader's eye. Sharp, focused leads give a good first impression. They signal to readers that the journalist knows the story's point, and why it is important. Anemic writing says the story is optional, and the reader can pass.

HUMOR

Amusing leads can be terribly effective. But writing humorous leads (or columns or essays or stories) might be the most difficult of assignments. Still, when the writing has an urbane feel, it adds spice to the bland.

This lead from *USA Today* began a story that was stale by the time it ran. Would the 2005 Indianapolis Colts go undefeated that season? We now know they didn't, but at the time the speculation had taken a life of its own. Only the 1972 Miami Dolphins had ever finished the season without losing a game.

To make the story fresh, a reporter found a new angle. The conversational tone adds just the right touch of mirth.

> When the 1972 Miami Dolphins etched their way into the history books as the NFL's only undefeated champions, just two players from the current Indianapolis Colts team flirting with a perfect season were even alive.
>
> So it is not shocking that some Colts might be sketchy on a few details.
>
> "The only player I know from that team is the running back: Butkus," said Colts rookie cornerback Marlin Jackson, born in 1983.
>
> Uh, Dick Butkus was a Chicago Bears linebacker from that era. The Dolphins' bruiser of a fullback who played like a linebacker was Larry Csonka.
>
> "Oh, Csonka," Jackson said. "Well, that's the guy. And what they did is very impressive. No other team has been able to do it."

IN CONCLUSION

The New Yorker profile on Edna Buchanan touched on her work habits and ability to gather information in a hurry. The piece's author, Calvin Trillin, kept returning to her leads, though.

Buchanan, who won the Pulitzer Prize in 1986 and now writes detective novels, once covered a story about a man who ran a television repair shop and was killed in a robbery attempt at the store. Her lead demonstrates the power of a nontraditional approach:

> On New Year's Eve Charles Curzio stayed later than planned at his small TV repair shop to make sure customers would have their sets in time to watch the King Orange Jamboree Parade. His kindness cost his life.

You can start your stories more than one way. When faced with a blank screen, think storytelling.

EXERCISE 1

Examine stories from your local newspaper, a website or a magazine. Choose three stories that have nontraditional leads. Discuss the following questions:

1. A lead should interest readers in a story. Do these leads grab the readers' attention?
2. What type of leads are these, that is, anecdotal, startling statement, among others?
3. Should the writer have used a different approach to grab the reader?
4. How far do you have to read before the writer tries to hook you into the story? What devices does the writer use to accomplish this?
5. Try rewriting these leads with a traditional 5W's and H. Which ones work better?

EXERCISE 2

Read the following and write four nontraditional leads using separate techniques:

Holbrook University has just lost the last football game of the season to its archrival, Hastings. The score was 21–20. Hastings won on a touchdown and extra point with five seconds left. This also was the last game Holbrook would play in its old stadium, LaGrove Field. The stadium, one of the first in college football, was built in 1914, but will be torn down. A new stadium will be built on the same spot. The crowds file out of the stadium following the game in a muffled silence. Few speak. "I'm shocked," one student says. She would not give her name. "I'm sad. I'm speechless. We should have won." Several male students are gathered in a grassy area just outside the gate. They are looking up at the stadium. One raises his fist. "We're going to miss you LaGrove," he yells. His name is Todd Miller, a junior. An elderly man files past, then pauses. "I played football in this stadium when I was in high school just after World War II. Then I played for Holbrook. When they tear this down, they're going to tear down a lot of memories."

1. Write a situationer lead.
2. Write an anecdotal lead.
3. Write a roundup lead.
4. Write an intriguing statement lead.

EXERCISE 3

Read the following and write a nontraditional lead of your choice:

You've noticed this man playing guitar outside the Starbucks just off campus for as long as you've gone to school. He plays nearly every day, driven indoors only when it rains or it's bitterly cold. You have seen him play once, though, in a snowfall. His guitar case is always open for passersby to drop money in. As people walk past him, he makes up words to his songs to fit them. "There goes a sweet-looking kid with books in her arms and a smile to light up the world" or "Here comes my favorite friend who's giving me a dollar before and I've sung to him until he hits the corner." Not great, but entertaining and charming. His case usually is full of dollar bills. One day you notice that his guitar is different. You stop and ask. He sings back: "Got me a good friend at the OD's Shoe Store right there. Comes out one day, says, 'Ray, I got a gift for you.' Gives me an ax that's as beautiful as the sky. Now I'm playing for the OD." You go into OD's Shoe Store and discover the manager, Pedro Ramirez, bought the guitar man—he only goes by Singin' Ray—a guitar last week. "He's made me smile for the last five years. Hey, he even made me laugh out loud a few times with his made-up lyrics. It's the least I could do."

CHAPTER 14

Obituaries: What You Do When Someone Dies

IN THIS CHAPTER, YOU WILL LEARN:

- Obituaries are a chance to celebrate a person's life.
- Obituary writing is changing, concentrating more on life stories.
- Better journalists resist formula.
- Great obituaries require unearthing telling moments.
- Obituaries become part of the public record and a trusted history lesson.

I feel like . . . I'm doing a service to the community by preserving contemporary history.
Alana Baranick, *The* (Cleveland) *Plain Dealer*

AS A FREE-LANCE WRITER AND REPORTER, Jim Sheeler has met a host of fascinating folks.

There was the former monk so brilliant he could sing in fluent Latin and explain how a carburetor worked—but was so irascible people could hardly stand him. He was kicked out of his religious order.

There was a woman who ran her own letterpress. There was the shoeshine man by day who was a jazz connoisseur by night.

And there was the wife who had just learned she had cancer. She was reading a story about a petty political squabble in her hometown, Boulder, Colo., when she looked up at her husband nearby.

"You know, these people need cancer. Not enough to kill them. But just enough to make them realize what's important," she told her husband.

The woman eventually died. Sheeler interviewed her husband later.

"It's not that there's too much cancer in the world," the distraught husband told Sheeler. "It's just that it's poorly distributed."

Sheeler says he met these people and many others through writing their obituaries, and their lives made him reconsider how he should conduct his own.

"They really teach you so much about life in a lot of these interviews where you'll be sitting in the interview and just learn these amazing things," says Sheeler, now a *Rocky Mountain News* staff reporter and winner of the Pulitzer Prize for feature writing. He says he will remember the rest of his life the words from the couple dealing with cancer.

"And I hope everybody else does," he says.

Though they have the grim task to report about people who have died—sometimes tragically—those who write obituaries don't see their jobs as tragic or grim. They call their work "life stories." They say they are fulfilling one of journalism's most important callings: information that not only tells readers what they need to know but also helps them understand their moment in history.

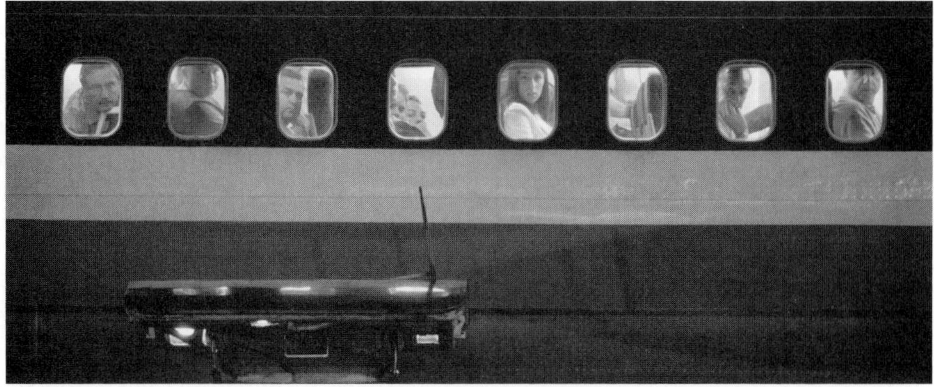

Passengers stare at military caskets as they are wheeled off their airplane. The photo is from "Final Salute," which won twin Pulitzer Prizes for photographer Todd Heisler and reporter Jim Sheeler of the *Rocky Mountain News*.

Most mainstream news publications and broadcasts routinely report the deaths of the celebrated. At many newspapers and online sites, obituaries are a staple of their daily or weekly news reports. Their stories become instruments of history, and the unofficial recordings of lives past.

WHY OBITUARIES MATTER

At *Entertainment Weekly*, David Hajdu wrote obituaries about several musicians, both prominent and obscure. Once, he was interviewing an entertainer's reluctant relative.

I just want to know the truth about this person, Hajdu told him.

"Be careful what you say," the relative replied. "What you say will become the truth."

Obituaries have been called the most enduring of stories. That's because relatives often will keep them for several years. Historians and genealogists rely on the news accounts to validate their research. A death can become a milestone, symbolizing more than the end of someone's life, but the passing of eras and legacies. Telling those stories matters to readers. Here's why:

- Obituaries can form a special bond with readers. "You know that these stories are going to be saved and cherished and put in scrapbooks a lot of the time," Sheeler says. "You can work for days on a front-page investigative piece and it's gone with a few days, but these pieces really are saved."
- Obituaries have a responsibility to get it right. "They're valuable in many ways," says Chris Calhoun, a literary agent and the editor of '*52 McGs.*', a book that reprinted obituaries from noted *The New York Times* writer Robert McG. Thomas. "They're an important part of the public record. . . . Everyone should have at least a notice, not exactly an obituary, but it's an important social marking."
- Obituaries are the shorthand of a community's past. "I feel like . . . I'm doing a service to the community by preserving contemporary history," says Alana Baranick, a national award-winning obituary writer for *The* (Cleveland) *Plain Dealer*. "I'm informing readers that maybe somebody they know has passed."
- Obituaries are history lessons in real time. They teach readers the significance of a life, even if the audience knows little or nothing of the person. Reading about their accomplishments lends insights into the eras they lived.
- Obituaries can console those closest to the subjects and those who barely knew them. "An obituary is kind of like therapy," says Claire Martin of *The Denver Post*. "And

ADVANCED TIP
The Past Is Prologue

"The truth is the past doesn't really exist. It's always being remade by the way we see the present. . . . Had I written [Frank Sinatra's] obituary in 1975 or 1985 or 1995, it would have been completely different because he meant something different in each of those eras. An obituary ultimately is not about what a person did, but about what the person meant."

—David Hajdu, author, columnist, Columbia University professor

David Hajdu's obituary on Frank Sinatra would have changed depending on the context and the era when Sinatra had died.

it's not just written for the family and the reader who is curious about a life, but for other people whose relatives maybe had similar lives or deaths."

Obituaries put lives in context. When the singer Frank Sinatra died in 1998, Hajdu wrote the story for *Entertainment Weekly*. How he cast Sinatra's life at that time would have changed had the singer died earlier, or later.

"History is a fluid thing," says Hajdu, the author of three books and now a professor at Columbia University. "The truth is the past doesn't really exist. It's always being remade by the way we see the present.

". . . Had I written that obituary in 1975 or 1985 or 1995, it would have been completely different because he meant something different in each of those eras. An obituary ultimately is not about what a person did, but about what the person meant."

LIFE STORIES VS. PAID OBITS

Just a generation ago, most newspapers ran standard obituaries written primarily through formula: A person died, he worked at this place and belonged to this club, he was survived by these people, and funeral services and burial were scheduled for here at this time.

More and more, papers now run paid obituaries, meaning family or friends write their own and pay the newspaper to print them. Often a distinctive typeface separates the paid obits from other news stories. Should someone with notoriety die, most news outlets usually run a story reported by their staffs or wire services.

Many papers, though, have also found an audience for a different type of obit. Readers are seeing what some call life stories, or feature obits. These stories profile a person who might not be well known but who lived a meaningful life. In fact, some writers take pride in chronicling the more obscure, letting their work state that all lives have meaning, well known or not.

Inspired in part by Jim Nicholson, retired from the *Philadelphia Daily News*, and the late Robert McG. Thomas of *The New York Times*, these writers don't use fame as a qualifier. They look for a common thread of humanity.

The art of writing about the unknown with whimsy and grace came to full flower with Nicholson in Philadelphia in the mid-1980s. In her book *The Dead Beat*, Marilyn Johnson says editors put Nicholson on the obituary desk as punishment, but he soon made the most of his new assignment, turning his daily stories into an art form. He even won an award from the American Society of Newspaper Editors in 1987 for his obituary work.

"He figured out a way to make the obit porous and let some of the real world leach into the strict borders of the form," Johnson writes, noting that Nicholson slipped details about his subjects' ordinary lives into his stories to make them approachable for readers.

The Art of Storytelling

Few stories in journalism are as shackled by formula as obituaries. For years, a traveler could read obituaries in newspapers across the country and find little difference. Though invaluable to a community's rhythm, these obituaries did little more than notify readers of who died, what they did, who survived and what time were the services. Editors usually assigned the task to beginning reporters.

Now many daily newspapers sell their obituary space to readers. Family members or funeral directors write the notices and memorials. That has left reporters unburdened from past practices when they write about those who have died. Journalists now have the chance to use storytelling techniques to tell life stories.

Jim Sheeler, a Pulitzer Prize-winning obituary writer for the *Rocky Mountain News*, says he resists writing with formula and welcomes all chances to use scenes and chronology with his stories.

"I find that obits have been written by a formula for so long that I think that it's good to try and break it in as many places as you can," he says.

Sheeler once wrote a life story about a man who had the shortest obituary in the newspaper. He decided to begin his story defying convention and formula. He described the scene at the cemetery:

> Section 37, block 7, lot 22, grave 9.
>
> The cemetery worker bends down and finds a cement number in the ground near a headstone, then stands up and begins to count.
>
> "Six, seven, eight, nine," he says, pointing to plots. "There it is."
>
> The gravesite is virtually impossible to find without help. There is no headstone, no marker of any kind. A browning patch of sod is the only indication of a recent burial.
>
> On one side of gravesite No. 9 is smooth, untouched lawn. On another side, a dead, brown bouquet on another unmarked grave.
>
> The man in the new gravesite spent the bulk of his life working in the reflection of some of the city's most powerful people, in a job where he had to look up

Nicholson's appeal—showing a person's humanity—is the cornerstone of great obituaries. To Martin of *The Denver Post*, that means finding stories that reveal a person's character and explain who they were when the camera was turned off. Martin hunts for what might surprise even those close to her subject. She says she enjoys telling her readers about the sinner as well as the saint.

to meet their eyes. He spent much of his spare time in the background, at night, listening.

Thousands of people knew his face. Few knew him.

Writing with scenes and anecdotes add interest to these stories. Anecdotes are the stories within the larger story. They have a point and a beginning, middle and end. They are the moments that reveal a person's character or wisdom. Readers find them irresistible. They help stories breathe with life and movement.

But unearthing those moments is difficult. Sheeler says he spends as much time as he can with families and those familiar with his subject to capture those revealing anecdotes. He combs through photo albums and personal effects to discover the stories that make his subjects have character and feeling.

"Part of it is just trying to get into the space where they live," he says. "I try to do all my interviews in person and place where I can actually pick up the books that they read and look for the dog-eared pages.

"Sit in their chair and go through all the photo albums and find out what's behind the pictures, what's in the margins of the pictures we don't see. Try and get the real stories of what's left behind."

Because anecdotes demand narrative writing, they elevate a story. A routine obituary can become an engrossing tale. Anecdotes strengthen pieces with their evocative and engaging styles. Journalists who use them can't help but tell stories.

"I try to interview people in the space where the person lived," he says. "If he was a mechanic, I'd want to go do the interview in a shop. You look for scenes. Even in death, you look for the scenes of life."

Sheeler once wrote an obituary on a woman who ran a small letterpress. To find a scene for his story, Sheeler talked to a former student. He asked him what his plans were for the next day.

"Well actually I'm going to be in my shop printing up her funeral brochure on her old letterpress," he told Sheeler.

"So of course that's where I interviewed him," Sheeler says, "printing up her funeral brochure on her old letterpress."

"We tend to get all reverent about our dead as soon as they expire," she says. "What you ought to get out of an obituary is the same thing that you get out of a good Irish wake."

Once, Martin was writing about a woman who was a pillar in her church, well respected by her congregation and in a position of spiritual authority. Martin asked

ADVANCED TIP
Celebrate a Life

"We tend to get all reverent about our dead as soon as they expire. What you ought to get out of an obituary is the same thing that you get out of a good Irish wake."

—Claire Martin, staff writer, The *Denver Post*

the woman's daughter what would surprise people about her mother.

"Her daughter said, 'Well, I don't know if I should tell you this, but . . .' and then that's when you know you've got something good coming. And it was actually tame."

The daughter said her mother liked risqué romance novels. But she always hid them inside her Bible so it wouldn't appear she was reading something untoward. Martin loved it.

"I think that's brilliant," she says. "I love finding out stuff like that. And it also makes people more human because the real danger, I think, isn't so much about what you have to put into obituaries but what you should not succumb to, which is don't make them into a eulogy."

The appeal of life stories starts, Hajdu argues, with the tacit agreement that the well-known are not the only ones whose lives deserve discussion.

"We care about famous people because we know that they matter, that they've had an impact on the world," Hajdu says. "We'd like to think that all people matter in some way. Obituaries are the rare opportunities to prove that there are . . . many, many people who left a mark. It could be a little pellet, to use a cliché, in the ripple of the water."

HOW TO WRITE LIFE STORIES

Those who write life stories feel free to resist the formulas that harnessed earlier obituaries. The writers' advice: write in scenes and with an insight into the subjects' lives.

Life stories should start by capturing the essence of the person. These leads could range from a poignant moment in the subject's life, or with a sweeping wrap-up of the subject's significance.

Perhaps a master at writing the sweeping lead was *The New York Times* Thomas.

"I think there was something particularly warm about them, eccentric and really joyous," says Calhoun, the literary agent who published a collection of Thomas's obituaries, calling them "McGs.," because of the unusual byline: Robert McG. Thomas, Jr., the middle abbreviated for "McGill."

"That's the great thing about reading a McG. And now some of the obits at the *Times*, that they're really a celebration of a life, and there's nothing sad about them. I think that sort of tone has gone all through the paper, especially in the obituary section."

In this lead, Thomas announces the death of one of Hollywood's top hair stylists during its golden age

> Sydney Guilaroff, who gave Claudette Colbert her bangs, made Lucille Ball a redhead, gave Judy Garland her "Wizard of Oz" braids and cut, curled, coiffed and

> cosseted virtually every other MGM star in a 40-year reign as Hollywood's most creative and celebrated hairdresser, died on Wednesday in a nursing home in Beverly Hills, Calif. He was 89.

"I think they had a humanity to them that not only other obituaries lacked but the rest of *The New York Times* lacked, and that's no slight against *The Times*—any American newspaper lacked to my knowledge," Calhoun says.

By the end of most leads, obituary writers must tell the readers when and where the subject died, their age and cause of death, if available. But even more important is to say why the person's life mattered.

One of Calhoun's favorite McGs. was the Goat Man, or Charles McCartney, who traveled mainly in the rural South after the Depression with a wagon and herd of goats, attracting great attention in a simpler era. He died in a nursing home at 97. This is how Thomas put McCartney's life in context.

> As many who grew up in the South in the 1940's, 50's and 60's could attest, when the Goat Man came to town it was an event, one that inevitably produced a story and a photograph in the local paper.
>
> Someone would spot him and his 30 or so goats coming down the highway, his wagon piled high with interesting junk, word would get around and pretty soon parents would be driving their children out to meet him, those familiar with the drill taking the precaution of staying upwind of the Goat Man.
>
> As Mr. McCartney, who never took a bath or washed his clothes, once boasted, nobody but his goats could stand the smell of him.

Thomas's particular strength was his ability to set out a person's background while making a point. In this obituary about Judge J. K. Stout, Thomas makes a statement while detailing her accomplishments: especially that she was the first black judge in Pennsylvania.

> It may not say much about Pennsylvania that the first black woman to gain a seat on a state bench was born in Wewoka, Okla., received a bachelor's degree from the University of Iowa and studied law at Indiana University, but it is to the state's credit that once Judge Stout established a practice in Philadelphia in 1954, it did not take the local legal community long to recognize that it had gained a treasure.

Thomas died from abdominal cancer in 2000. By the time of his death, Calhoun saw McGs. exert a subtle and lasting influence on the newspaper. Twenty months later, terrorists flew airplanes into the World Trade Center. As part of its Pulitzer-winning

HOW TO
Write Life Stories

- **Resist Formula:** Obituaries traditionally have followed formulaic writing. Use storytelling techniques, such as scenes, dialogue, chronology.
- **Capture a Person's Essence:** All lives have meaning. A writer needs to look to find a person's accomplishments and personality.
- **Make the Story a Celebration:** Life stories adopt the tone of celebration rather than sadness, even though death can be a sad event.
- **Write with Anecdotes:** Everyone has stories to tell. Find the special moments that reveal a subject's personality.

Talent Showcase

ALANA BARANICK

The* (Cleveland) *Plain Dealer

Alana Baranick began her obituary of Josephine Milbrandt describing a simple box on Milbrandt's back porch.

The container, a recycled candy box, contained a precise amount of change. Customers buying eggs from Milbrandt were on their honor, taking the eggs they wanted, leaving the correct amount of money, making their own change, if needed.

For Baranick, the box meant much more than just a tiller of money.

"It spoke to a different time to say that someone would [put] a box on the back porch and trust people to leave the money for the eggs and stuff," Baranick says. "I thought that was a great statement.

"Then I thought, well she really trusted people and she kept the trust in the box."

So Baranick, an obituary writer with *The* (Cleveland) *Plain Dealer,* given the job of summing up the essence of a person's life, understood that starting her obituary by describing the box was "a no-brainer."

"She had a specific amount she left and she trusted everything would work out all right," Baranick says.

This was Baranick's lead:

> Avon Lake—Josephine Milbrandt kept three quarters, four dimes, two nickels and scads of trust in a Whitman Sampler candy box on her back porch.
>
> Alongside the box were dozens of fresh eggs.
>
> Milbrandt, who died June 27 at age 93, sold eggs from the enclosed porch of her Avon Lake home for more than 40 years. She banked on people putting money in the box and taking only the change they were due—and, of course, their eggs.
>
> "She had the honor system," said her neighbor and customer, Mary Mackin. "If you didn't have the money, you put an IOU in the box. . . ."

This type of obituary and layered writing style won Baranick a national award from the American Society of Newspaper Editors (ASNE) for obituary writing in 2005. She also co-authored a book, *Life on the Dead Beat*, a handbook for obituary writers.

For Baranick, her leads must capture a person and be so true to her subjects' characters that people who knew them would recognize them.

"I want to give the reader an idea of who the person was, some kind of identifying item on it, but at the

coverage, *The New York Times* devoted a full page each day to "Portraits of Grief," which were moving and poignant obituaries of those who died from the attacks. Calhoun sees a direct link between McGs. and the portraits.

"And because of McG., the *Times* covered the victims of 9/11 in a way they wouldn't have done without the model of McG. celebrating ordinary lives. They won a Pulitzer for that, all because of the model that Robert McG. Thomas set," he said.

same time want them to read on. I want to grab them," she says.

"And with the life stories, the particular kind of feature that got me the ASNE award, I try to start with a lively image and then after getting into all that, then go into the chronology of the life.

"And then I try to bring it back at the end with something that either makes it come full circle or might touch your heart or make you go, 'Yeah that makes sense.' "

Baranick started reporting at a small newspaper west of Cleveland before moving to *The Plain Dealer,* where she began writing feature obits, or life stories. These require more information than news organizations—mostly newspapers—usually receive from funeral directors, relatives or coworkers.

"I start with basic information that maybe the family provided or the funeral home or the company they worked for or all of that, and I interview people from all over the place, getting different views. I try to hit on as much as I can. I always end up with much more information than I can use," she says.

Once she has talked to as many as possible, she uses a device many other experienced journalists find helpful: chronology. Setting out the major moments in a person's life lets Baranick organize her thoughts.

"I may not know what I'm starting with. I might have an idea of what I want to go with and often times it's like, well, this could be the lead or this could be the walk off at the end," she says.

Even seasoned journalists get stumped sometimes. When Baranick finds herself at a loss, she resorts to her timeline and starts writing.

"So I just do a 'He was born' and go all the way down to this is what he did last week. And then pull out from that the cool images or the profound statements that people make, whatever.

"So I'm a big proponent of making the story flow so it's just not a laundry list of information."

The stories and insights she gathers, no matter how colorful or witty, never trump the need for accuracy. She checks even the most basic facts to ensure that her stories not only read well but are true.

"The first rule of obituaries is make sure they're dead," she says. "That's a big issue for me. Make sure they're dead. Make sure they really did serve in the military. Make sure they really are married to that person they listed as their wife."

And like all journalists at one time or another, Baranick must write a controversial story. She doesn't look forward to it, but knows her obligation to the truth. Sometimes, she discovers the unpleasant in a person's life. As a reporter, she's obligated to include the bad news in the obituary if it is relevant.

"I hate it when I have to do that. People have this perception that obituaries are supposed to be these tributes. Even people who have never met the deceased don't understand they're not tributes. I get calls from people who never met the deceased complaining how come I mentioned their jail time."

HOW TO TALK TO THE BEREAVED

Everybody has interesting moments happen in their lives.

"The trick is to get people to tell you about it and to ask the right questions," Martin says.

To write strong life stories, you need just that: stories. Journalists across the board hunt for those moments to elevate their obituaries. But those stories aren't always easy to discover.

The Plain Dealer's Baranick never relies solely on the funeral home because "most of the time, they're just filling in blanks." She also knows she has to let the family talk about the person in ways that help them grieve, but don't necessarily show human qualities.

"So you don't even get how anybody is going to identify him. With an obit, one of the first things you've got to figure is you need to tell people who is this person. How would you know him?" she says.

Obit writers rely on these habits to find the stuff of interesting reading:

- Have good questions that encourage acquaintances to open up. Baranick's favorite question is: What set them apart from the rest of the crowd? She and Sheeler also ask: What have you learned from this person?
- Generalities weaken stories. Specific information adds spark. Obituary writers let families talk in general terms but follow up with specific questions. "If the person says, 'Her smile lit up a room' or 'She never met a stranger' or 'He'd give you the shirt off his back,' then I'll wait a beat and say, 'Really. Can you give me an example of when he was particularly generous?' or 'What kind of thing made her smile?' " Martin says.
- Sometimes obvious questions yield insights. Martin usually asks if the family is burying anything special with someone. "Sometimes it's family photographs. With children, it's often a toy." Those answers reveal what was important or meaningful to the person.
- Interview people in places that remind them of their loss. Sheeler tries to sit in their chairs and look at photo albums to discover what's behind the pictures. He once interviewed a piano teacher's student at her piano, and had him play songs that reminded him of his teacher. He finds that just showing those close to the subject that he cares and wants to listen opens the door to let people talk.
- Be respectful, but not shy about approaching people. Unless it is a breaking news story where someone died tragically or controversially, obit writers find that families don't mind talking. "People want to tell the stories," Sheeler says. "It's a time when so many things are awkward. People don't know what to say. They'll come up and they feel awkward around somebody who's just lost somebody. As a reporter, that notebook is a pretty amazing passport into this place where all you're doing is you're asking the questions they want to answer."
- Do the legwork. Sheeler follows two rules. He looks for scenes of the person's life. And he never leaves an interview without a strong sense of his lead and ending. "It's so much easier to spend the extra half-hour there than to find yourself back at your desk struggling to figure out what the beginning or the end is going to be. But if you just make the effort to ask to see inside one more box or ask to talk to one more person, it almost always pays off," he says.

DEVELOP AN EYE FOR THE COMMON

Martin's search for stories that show a person's humanity led to Jade Greene, a 23-year-old woman who had taken a new name and hoped to remake her body. She weighed at least 400 pounds and underwent gastric bypass surgery. She died when one of the staples worked loose, spewing infection into her system.

To write about her, Martin learned she had kept a blog.

"I've often got calls from people whose niece or nephew under age 18 has died and they want to know how to write about this person's life, which hasn't lasted that long, but a lot of people keep life journal pages."

Martin used the entries to write a moving obituary.

> "It is my only chance for a normal life," she wrote in July 2002 on her Web log.
>
> Shy in person, she was forthcoming, articulate and candid when she posted her thoughts on ObesityHelp.com, an online message board, and on other newsgroups frequented by people considering weight-loss options.
>
> She turned to surgery after unsuccessfully trying diets, once losing 50 pounds through Weight Watchers before gaining it all back.
>
> In October, when Greene met with her surgeon and finalized arrangements for the operation, she was upbeat.
>
> "I have been overweight all my life, and so in a way this will mark the beginning for me to start to live instead of just exist," she wrote.
>
> A few days later, she expressed misgivings.
>
> "I feel like I am on an emotional roller coaster," she wrote.
>
> "There are so many unknowns here. I have never been healthy, thin and fit, which are my goals, and I have no idea what I am going to look like after the surgery. I look at food when I eat, and realize that after the surgery, I will never be eating this again—or I will not be eating it like I am—and there is a bit of sadness."
>
> She made a list of post-surgery life as she envisioned it:
>
> "People not looking at me like I am going to break their furniture when I sit down.
>
> "Not feeling like Rudolph—you know, left out of all the reindeer games.
>
> "Taking baths and not sticking to the tub.
>
> "Wearing jeans—something I have not done since I was 16.
>
> "Dancing with people and not feeling like everyone is looking at me.
>
> "Being the me [that] I am inside but can't get out because of all the weight."

Martin found the candor in Greene's blog extraordinary. It let her show Greene's fear and bravery. She was uneasy with her size but faced the possibility of dying calmly.

"It never occurred to me that for someone who was so overweight it was difficult to walk," Martin says. "I began to appreciate that at the end of [my] pregnancies when I was toting around a pretty large load . . . and I never got over 150 or 155, but for someone who got into the 300s and 400s, think about getting stuck in a bathtub, that blew me away."

Martin found a reference to Greene's death in a note she wrote as she prepared her will.

> A second operation found that one of the stomach pouch staples had worked loose, leaking septic fluid that caused an infection. The fever persisted, and a few days later, she was declared brain-dead.
>
> She stopped breathing at 4:16 p.m. on Jan. 30, a week after the operation.
>
> "If you are reading this, then chances are that I did not make it through the surgery, or I died of complications afterwards," she had written when she arranged her will.
>
> "I know this is hard, but I am OK with it. Remember what you do will return to you. The energy you send out, whether it be good or bad, will come back. That is one lesson I have learned in my life. When you see the moon rising in a dark sky, think of me."

ALWAYS CHECK

Baranick of *The Plain Dealer* confesses that she nearly made a disastrous mistake early in her career. Working in Ohio, she wrote an obituary with information that came from a funeral home in Florida. The woman's name failed to register, but an alert editor caught the obit before it ran. The woman had been married to the man who invented a certain faucet. A plant for the faucet employed many in her town. Never write an obituary without checking the files, her editor scolded her.

She says she learned the lesson. A few weeks later, a rural funeral home in her county sent her information about a man in his 40s. The funeral director said he doubted if the man was notable. You won't find anything on him, he said. Still, Baranick checked the files.

She discovered he had run for president of the United States.

"Three times," Baranick says. "All he did was take out the petitions. He never got enough signatures, obviously. But each time he was interviewed about it because it was weird, you know.

"It was one of my first really good obit stories. . . . And that was a great moment of revelation for me about obits. Just the fact that the information that comes to you isn't necessarily what the story is."

Baranick since moved to *The Plain Dealer* and later won a national writing award for her obituaries. Her stories were reprinted in the *Best American Newspaper Writing* book edited by the Poynter Institute. One story told of an unusual woman who cooked for priests at a nearby parish.

> Clementine Werfel blessed priests at St. Joseph Catholic Church in Strongsville with heavenly desserts, memorable meals and seemingly miraculous coffee.
>
> The retired parish housekeeper, who died Aug. 2 at age 96, routinely walked around the dining table in the rectory, offering coffee to each priest.
>
> "Would Father like regular or decaf?" the 4-foot-something Werfel asked them one by one.
>
> Regardless of the priests' individual preferences, she filled all their cups with coffee from the same pot. The coffee drinkers silently accepted what they got, as

> though Werfel really could turn regular coffee into decaffeinated, much the way that the biblical Jesus turned water into wine.

"A couple of different priests told me about the coffee thing, and I thought it was hilarious," Baranick says. "And it went with that image of the feisty little woman. She was a tiny little gal. When I'm writing a story that's got something to do with religion, I like to use religious-type words. With her in particular, it was just so obvious. Jesus turned the water into wine. Clemmie turned the caffeinated into decaf."

Baranick also had heard from the priests that the woman didn't like to cook. That led to the discovery of this exchange:

> But she didn't treat her charges with kid gloves. When a priest told her that he liked his beef "a little red," the diminutive Werfel handed him a bottle of ketchup and said, "Here. You can make it red."

LOOK FOR THE UNUSUAL

Sheeler realized the value of writing about the lesser known when he discovered Severin Foley.

"It was one of those guys you might walk past every single day pushing a shopping cart," he says. ". . . He ended up being, as so many people are, not who you would think."

Foley died penniless, but he had been an ordained priest, educator and prolific letter writer. Most described him as brilliant.

"He was very off-putting and very anti-social," Sheeler says. Still, he could be friendly at times. He also rebelled against authority in a way that inspired others.

> He moved to San Francisco and lived on the streets and in subsidized housing thanks to help from his brother and a welfare check. He proceeded to antagonize every landlord he met, piling his homes full of magazines, newspapers and various trinkets and junk, sometimes all the way to the ceiling.
>
> He relished the inevitable trials that would come after each eviction notice. It didn't matter that he lost every case, and was often thrown out of court. He was also tossed from government aid offices and several nursing homes. He chalked the evictions to victories since he refused to cave in on his principles. Whenever someone tried to have him tested for mental problems, he reverted to his knowledge of psychiatry and faked his way through the interview.

On another occasion, when Sheeler read Johnny Richardson's obituary in *The Denver Post*, the sparse six lines used this lone descriptor: He shined shoes and liked jazz.

Sheeler, who at that time free-lanced for the *Post*, decided he would write a feature obit on Richardson, the person with the least amount written in a traditional obituary format.

So Sheeler found out that Richardson lived alone in his apartment. He had no survivors. Everything he owned was in a shoebox outside a lawyer's office, waiting for someone to claim it. Sheeler hung out in jazz clubs where Richardson frequented. He found a letter from an ex-girlfriend that explained more of who he was.

> If anyone asked—if they really seemed interested—Johnny Richardson would tell them he was a man in an honorable trade, and a dying one.
>
> If anyone asked, really asked, he would hold up his shoe polish-stained hands and show them the intricacies of the craft. He would show them how to the snap the towel, how to rub with the right touch, how to give good spit shine.

"It ended up being one of the longest obituaries I've ever written. . . . I'm just as proud of that story, of Johnny Richardson, as any other," Sheeler says.

IN CONCLUSION

Obituaries, a staple in the life of any news organization, fulfill the important role of telling readers and viewers who has died. In the past, obituaries usually followed a strict formula. The more in-depth obituaries were reserved for those well known.

Recently, though, news organizations have begun writing about those whose lives were interesting but obscure to all but their inner circle of families, friends and contacts. These stories celebrate life, no matter if the person was a celebrity or commoner.

Obituaries matter to readers. Martin of *The Denver Post* first discovered this several years ago when she and her 1-year-old daughter visited relatives.

"Two weeks after we came back to Colorado, one of my cousins ran over another cousin's child, who was the same age as my daughter, and he died. It was one of those driveway accidents that you don't hear much about," she says.

What hurt the child's mother was the newspaper ran a story about the accident but not about the child. Martin knew more could be said.

"You don't say much about kids because what do you say about a 1-year-old? But because I had a 1-year-old myself, I thought, you know, I know that my daughter taught Noah how to go up and down the stairs and he taught her how to manage walking along this balance beam kind of thing, and there are things you can say.

"I knew from being in that experience myself that obituaries were really important."

TOOL KIT

Some books you might want to consider:

52 McGs., The Best Obituaries from Legendary New York Times Reporter Robert McG. Thomas, Scribner, New York, Edited by Chris Calhoun, 2001.

Life on the Death Beat, by Alana Baranick, Jim Sheeler and Stephen Miller, Marion Street Press Inc., Oak Park, IL., 2005.

The Dead Beat, by Marilyn Johnson, HarperCollins Publishers, New York, 2006.

EXERCISE 1

Write an obituary from the following:

"He used to stand right there on that corner," said Daynel White. "Every day except on Sunday he would put his barbeque stand up and serve ribs, and sausage, and uh, oh yeah, beef. Everything he cooked was really good. But his sauce. Oh, that man sold sauce made in heaven. It was the thickest, richest, best-tasting sauce in four counties."

She's talking about Darnell Smithson. Smithson died Monday. He had just finished serving his last lunch customer when he fell over. He died of a heart attack. His age was 76.

His barbeque stand was known as Double D's. He worked six days a week. He also was a deacon in the Colvin Street Baptist Church. His wife is still living. Her name is Mary. He had three children, Martin, Marshall and Malcolm.

Smithson's funeral will be Wednesday at the church at 10 a.m. He will be buried in Hawley Memorial Gardens right after the service.

His barbeque was named best in Ohio by *Modern Cuisine Magazine* in 1997. He had been at the same spot, the corner of South Salina Street and the Seneca Turnpike for about 40 years. He had grown up in Georgia but moved to Henrietta when he was a boy, about 12 years old.

His sons went to Henrietta College. Marshall played basketball for a while. The other two now work in New York City, one as a broker on Wall Street and the other as a police officer. Malcolm is the cop. Martin is on Wall Street. Marshall is a musician in Los Angeles.

"I loved his barbeque," said James Alistair, Henrietta's basketball coach. "I knew about his stand when I was a student. I didn't know he had a kid who could play basketball until one day I stopped by for lunch and DD was talking his usual stuff, you know. Then he just grabs me and says he has a feeling about his son playing basketball for me. Well, you know about DD and his feelings. So I don't even eat. I walk right over to where Marshall is playing. I realize DD is right. Marshall's at our school after he graduates."

"We learned how to cook our barbeque from him," said John Troutman, owner of Big J's Barbeque Express in Henrietta. "I was just a biker eating lunch one day and I couldn't help thinking how good it was tasting. I started talking to him and he tells me that one day I'm going to own my own place. I thought he was crazy. A few years later, I started working at a place in Tennessee and got to thinking I should start my own. Then I remembered what he said. I quit that day and got on my bike and rode to Henrietta. When I got here, I drove right to DD and told him I wanted to work. That's how I learned, and he helped get Big J's going. I owe him everything."

"What I loved about picking up barbeque was the scriptures," said Saundra Hassell. "He was a religious man and every time he gave you a plate, he would quote a scripture. Everyone got a different scripture. He knew the Bible."

Smithson lived at 358 Clark Road in Henrietta. He started working in restaurants. He cooked at The Eatery, considered one of Ohio's finest restaurants until he saved enough money to open his stand.

An article in the *Henrietta Daily News* 10 years ago said he never wanted to expand because it gave him time to close after lunch and work at the Southwest Community Center. There he worked with early teenagers, usually between 13–15 years olds. They called him Mr. DD. He had no assigned job but was there for the teens to talk to.

"I had somebody help me when I was younger. That was my father. If I could be half the man he was, I'd go out of this world knowing I had left my mark. He taught me to give and encouraged me to go to church," the article quotes Smithson.

The article says his feelings helped him locate the corner for his first business. When he first saw his wife in church, he says he knew he was going to marry her.

The Henrietta Chamber of Commerce named him Outstanding Citizen in 1985, the first African American to win that honor.

EXERCISE 2

Analyze the following story:

Jerry Thompson spent much of his life cleaning up after students and faculty at Pamona County Community College. A thankless job for some. But for Thompson, an honest day's labor.

"He loved going to work," said his mother, Elizabeth Thompson, president of Pamona. "I never heard Jerry complain that it was too early or he was too tired. I think it gave him a purpose, you know, to be able to do something for a living."

Thompson, 35, died Wednesday from a rare bacterial infection. Doctors believe he contracted the illness during his daily handling of trash at the school. Health officials believe no student or faculty face the risk of contracting the same illness.

Thompson had worked at Pamona for 15 years. He started almost by accident. Diagnosed autistic, he would follow his mother to work some days. Elizabeth Thompson then was dean of academic affairs. To occupy her son, she sent him to each room and office to take care of the trash.

"Once I sent him off, I knew I had an hour free. Then one day, the head of janitorial services was in my office wanting to hire Jerry. He said he had never seen a worker as conscientious as Jerry. He's been working here since."

Thompson was born about the time autism was being recognized by doctors. By the time he was 6, Elizabeth Thompson said she knew he was different. He was diagnosed when he was 10 but attended mainstream schools throughout his life, even graduating from high school.

"As a parent of an autistic child, you often wonder what will happen to them as they age. We worried about where Jerry would work, if he even could work. But once he found this job, his outlook changed. He felt part of a larger community. He felt important, and necessary."

Students might know Jerry as the unofficial greeter at Towson Hall. Thompson stood near the front door each morning he worked, greeting those who came through with a loud, "Welcome to Pamona Community College, home of the fighting Panthers." He usually stretched out the word "fighting" to several syllables.

"I'll miss that guy," said Aaron Weiss, a second-year student. "Even if you were in a bad mood, or you were worried about a test or paper or something, one 'fiiiiiiiiiiight-ing Panthers' from JT would change that."

Answer the following:

1. Why does this story begin contrasting menial with meaningful work?
2. Why not play up the irony of a job he loved actually causing his death?
3. How is the obituary organized?
4. What benefit is the final quote?

CHAPTER 15

Writing Profiles

IN THIS CHAPTER, YOU LEARN:

- Who makes a good profile subject.
- The importance of tying the subject to a current event.
- How to write about your subjects honestly.
- How to begin your stories.
- How you should organize your profile.
- How to find the moments that make profiles compelling.

Silence is the greatest reporting tool you can have.
Katherine Boo,
The New Yorker

JIM MURRAY, A PULITZER PRIZE–WINNING SPORTSWRITER FOR THE *LOS ANGELES TIMES*, ONCE told a television interviewer his secret to writing interesting stories.

People.

In a business of games, statistics and events, Murray said few had ever asked him to recount any of the great moments in sports. When Hank Aaron's home run broke Babe Ruth's career record, for example, he said he found no one who wanted him to describe how the ball sailed over the fence.

What people did ask him was this:

Hank Aaron, what's he really like?

The lesson every journalist should learn from Murray is one sometimes forgotten. Readers want to know who people are.

At some point, nearly all journalists write stories about the people they cover. Profiles are excellent tools for explaining how people behave when the camera is turned off. They can show readers a person who is living a fascinating life, or they can tell a moving tale about how people have overcome the curves life throws at them.

People lie at the heart of interesting reading. They create more interest than issues.

CHOOSING THE RIGHT PERSON

Few Central New Yorkers knew Dee Barney. She lived without notoriety in a small town, her life focused on her family, church and clients at a heart center where she worked.

Then she discovered her right breast inflamed. A visit to the doctor told her she had an aggressive form of breast cancer. She would need the full treatment: chemotherapy, radiation, surgery.

Reporter Janet Gramza painted the toes of her profile subject, Dee Barney. Painting the toes bright red before surgery is a family tradition in Gramza's household. It gives the person something bright to look at in a drab hospital room.

She decided to share her story with the public. A reporter at *The* (Syracuse) *Post-Standard*, Janet Gramza, profiled Barney and her ordeal in a series of stories that ran periodically over a year. *The Post-Standard* readers responded with waves of sympathy and help.

The story of a woman fighting breast cancer had been done before. Why did this story stand out from the rest? Gramza's series read fresh and carried emotional power because she wrote about Barney honestly. Gramza's stories didn't mask the pain and fear Barney felt, but also showed her humor and bravery fueled by an unwavering religious faith.

Typical of the stories was this exchange between Barney and her 8-year-old son, Cassidy, as she was leaving for the hospital to undergo a mastectomy.

The day before surgery, Dee felt keyed up, like she was "leaving on a vacation." She packed a bag, ironed Cassidy's school clothes and prayed with friends on the phone. In bed, she woke at 2 a.m. and couldn't sleep. She opened her Bible for two hours and closed it filled with peace.

That Thursday morning, she took Cassidy in her arms. "Good luck, Mom," he said.

"Buddy, I don't need luck, I've got God," she said.

He burst into tears.

"Feeling scared?" she asked.

"Yeah," he said.

Minutes later, he confessed, "I'm afraid it's your time and God wants you to go to heaven."

"I don't think it is," she said. "I think everything's going to be OK."

Great profiles need great subjects. Not everyone a journalist meets demands his own story. Most seasoned journalists can recognize someone their readers would find interesting. The fastest giveaway is a person's notoriety. But other people less known can intrigue readers just as easily:

- A person with an interesting job.
- A relatively unknown person who has suddenly become well known.
- An unknown person who has done something unusual.
- An unknown person who through unusual circumstances is thrust into the limelight.
- A person who departs from typical behavior.
- A person who has an interesting life history.

WELL-KNOWN VS. THE UNKNOWN

The famous usually make the first targets to profile, but they also can be the most difficult. Their notoriety means they have been written about before. The greater their fame, the more daunting the task to write a fresh story.

Profiles about the unknown offer different challenges. Journalists must make the reader care about the person profiled. They must find nuggets of detail that will interest the reader.

The unknown person who has suddenly become well known carries strong appeal. David Kaczynski lived in relative obscurity until the mid-1990s. He had begun suspecting his brother, Ted, was a person the FBI called, "The Unabomber," so called because a killer was mailing booby-trapped packages to universities, among others. When opened, the packages would explode, usually killing those within a few feet.

ADVANCED TIP
Who Makes a Good Profile Subject

Beginning journalists sometimes choose to profile people who might seem interesting but their lives don't translate well in a story. Look for these points:

- **Conflicts:** Did the subject have to overcome a difficulty or setback?
- **Moments:** Does the subject have special times that turned their lives or professions?
- **History:** Do the subjects' pasts answer why they act as they do today?
- **Relevance:** Do the subjects' situations or actions still provoke interest with people who have little in common with them?

WIRED AND WIRELESS | WEB

Marcus Hayes of the *Philadelphia Daily News* says he looks at all previous stories and press releases—everything possible—even if he believes he knows a person thoroughly.

"I read as much about the person as I can find, no matter how well I know them," said Hayes, who has covered both professional football and baseball in Philadelphia—the Eagles and the Phillies.

"There's always something new, even with guys you see every day. If they are interested in something odd—interior decorating, producing rap records, wearing shoes made of the hides of endangered species—I research that to some degree, too, so I can speak about it with some degree of expertise."

One great strength of the Internet is its repository of knowledge. The Internet offers a host of information in a few hours that used to take days to track down. Research through online sources has become a great tool for journalists. Databases such as Lexis/Nexis and ProQuest that house newspaper and magazine articles and news show transcripts can yield a variety of stories.

These search engines can find you more specific stories than search engines that look for information through subjects, such as Google. Google has its use, and sometimes can find an obscure source, but it often aims too wide.

One warning: not all websites are reliable. Just because a site has information doesn't mean the information is accurate or true. Journalists should always recheck their sources for accuracy, and that includes websites that seem reliable. Usually a journalist can take information posted on web pages maintained by the government, traditional mainstream media and many corporations and professional associations as a beginning to their reporting. But they should follow the mantra of the Reagan administration: trust, but verify. The mainstream media sources sometimes have published erroneous stories. Government documents could have typos. Circumstances or facts might have changed since the last posting.

A journalist should always question websites with political leanings or causes. Call the group and go over the facts. Then recheck those facts with groups that espouse neutrality and objectivity or, best of all, trace the information to the original source.

David Kaczynski read the Unabomber's manifesto in *The Washington Post* and believed his brother wrote it. He and his wife contacted the FBI. His brother was arrested, ending an exhaustive 17-year manhunt.

David Kaczynski and his family found themselves thrust into the international spotlight. Many wanted to know: Who was the man who would do the right thing and turn in his own brother, even if his brother would serve life in prison?

This newness to the spotlight awakens a natural curiosity: the entertainer who has just landed a plum role, the newly appointed superintendent, the athlete who has just had a breakout game, the challenger who has just upset the incumbent office holder.

Sometimes, a person's behavior doesn't follow typical patterns, or their creativity gives them skills few possess. *The Wall Street Journal* once found that some artists had begun drawing pictures using the toy, Etch A Sketch. The undisputed king was Steve Hanks, who lived in Albuquerque, N.M. Hanks discovered that he could twist the knobs on the toy and draw life-like portraits and landscapes. Of course, Etch A Sketch let him draw only one continuous line, and he had to think of ways to preserve his art (one good shake and they were lost forever). Yet Hanks' story was unusual, and worth writing about.

Sometimes a person has such a compelling life that even though much of it is in the past, it still makes an interesting tale. That's why survivors of the Holocaust can command their own stories. Who could not read about a young Jewish woman who, with every Jew in her village, was stripped naked and lined up to be shot. As Nazi soldiers fired and killed all her family and villagers, the bullets somehow missed her. She fell back anyway, and lay still among the slain, faking her own death until night. Then, still naked, she went to a Gentile doctor sympathetic to Jews. As she reached the door, she realized the doctor lived next door to a Nazi party member. Doubt clutched her. Did she have the right house? The wrong knock, and she would be dead. She took a chance, and knocked. She made the right choice, and lived to escape to America. That story—all true—never tires.

NEWS PEG

Hidden in the discussion about choosing a subject to profile is the need for timeliness. Other than writing about a person who simply has an interesting background, such as the Holocaust survivor, most profile subjects should be part of a recent event to give the writer a reason for the story.

This is called a news peg. A news peg makes the person more interesting to readers. Readers need to know why they should invest their own time in the story. Timeliness gives journalists the open door to profile a subject.

A news peg can be:

- An anniversary of a memorable event. The 20-year anniversary of the space shuttle *Challenger* disaster prompted a fresh round of stories about New Hampshire school teacher Christa McAuliffe, who died in the explosion.
- A news event that sheds new light on a familiar face. Stephen Colbert of the television comedy show, *The Colbert Report*, won acclaim for coining the word "truthiness." When it was selected as the best new word of 2005, stories about Colbert ran throughout the country, including *Time* magazine.
- A news event that elevates a relative unknown to the spotlight. When Ben Bernanke was appointed as the Federal Reserve's new chairman, replacing Alan Greenspan, few had ever heard of the Princeton economics professor. Just after President Bush named him the Fed's next leader, journalists profiled him in newspapers and newsmagazines. Among the nuggets: He scored nearly perfect on his SATs (1590 of 1600), he hesitated buying a house near Stanford in 1979 because he thought prices had hit their peak (they've quadrupled since) and he needed to know calculus to get into Harvard, so he taught himself. None of that is remarkable alone. But because Bernanke had just become one of the more powerful people in the world, those facts had grown important to explain the person running the United States' central bank.

The Art of Storytelling

Julie Sullivan-Springhetti fills her profiles with dramatic conflict, with vexing problems that defy solutions, with scenes that show the human condition.

She was told the secret, she says, early in her career: to attract readers, her profiles must crackle with tension.

Julie Sullivan-Springhetti, reporter for *The* (Portland) *Oregonian*.

She first drew national notice with a series of short profiles on residents of a low-income apartment house in downtown Spokane, Wash. Those evocative stories—written on deadline in just a few days for *The Spokesman-Review*—showed these residents living just above the breaking point of society. The series won a national writing award from the American Society of Newspaper Editors.

After she moved to Portland to join *The Oregonian* staff, she wrote another award-winning profile of a mother whose round-the-clock care of her autistic twin daughters was destroying her marriage and her family's core. The story showed the frenzy the mother endured trying to keep pace with two young daughters who were nearly out of control and incapable of knowing how to behave.

Sullivan-Springhetti, who uses her maiden name "Sullivan" for her byline, said an editor once told her that "a profile rose and fell not over whether somebody had to be particularly interesting or outrageous. There had to be a tension to make a profile work."

Sullivan-Springhetti carried that lesson to a story that, in 2001, helped *The Oregonian* win the Pulitzer Prize for public service, the highest award in journalism. As part of a team reporting on the federal government's questionable immigration practices, she coaxed the reluctant government official at the center of the controversy to talk to her for a story.

"The tension was obvious in that case in that he was the most unpopular type, he was totally under siege and nobody knew anything about him," said Sullivan-Springhetti.

"And he was totally under siege because he had so much control over so many people, and he was really interfering in business practices at a time when Oregon was really trying to develop."

Those weren't the only conflicts she found. Her subject, David Beebe, ran the Immigration and Naturalization Service in Portland by the book. He followed the rules meticulously, which led to awkward decisions and created the controversy. Sullivan-Springhetti wanted to explain why Beebe followed the rules so carefully.

"What made it interesting is, why was someone so rigid. From the outside, I think that everybody is motivated by their personal needs. I think people really do act very personal. They do things to benefit or meet whatever it is they need. For some people that's money. For some people that's power."

For Beebe, it was all about control, which began with his upbringing, Sullivan-Springhetti discovered. She told readers about his strict childhood. He was raised on a farm. One of her favorite quotes explained a lot: "I came from dirt," he told her.

That unlocked the key to his personality. It played out not only in his decisions at his job but other parts of his life. Sullivan-Springhetti wrote about his precise nature, that his neighbors trusted him completely, that he returned everything borrowed in better condition.

"I had to understand what it was that made him so rigid," she said.

She wrote the story in just a few days. *The Oregonian* published many other stories that explained the controversy and dug into the fallout of the INS's policies enforced by Beebe and his staff.

Beebe eventually was forced to retire from the INS. Afterward, Sullivan-Springhetti ran into him during a legal proceeding.

"We were in this incredibly adversarial relationship with the agency that went on for years, and I remember Mr. Beebe at one point said, 'It was a pleasure.'

"I felt like that even though I put very personal things that he might have later bitten his tongue off for having told me, I do think his story was important and he believed it needed to be told," she said.

Profiles complement and round out the day's coverage of the news, Sullivan-Springhetti believes. They show the human side of authority figures previously known to readers only by their official actions. When readers see a well-known person's behavior in private, they better understand his actions in public.

"I want to do the profiles on the people that everybody is wondering about and sort of gossiping about or probably doesn't want to talk to the media," she said.

"And those are kind of natural profiles because I think that our job is to go places that other people can't go, and that includes profiles."

- A situation that places a person at the forefront, such as a minority or woman who breaks through into a profession or office dominated by the majority or males.

All these examples carry immediacy. That urgency translates to your story, giving it energy and interest.

CAPTURING THE ESSENCE

Roy Peter Clark, a pre-eminent writing teacher at the Poynter Institute, once was asked to spend some time helping reporters at the *St. Petersburg Times* in Florida. In the newsroom, he ran into reporter Howell Raines. Raines had just published two books, and recently written a series about the lieutenant governor's race. Other reporters so admired the series that they could quote from it.

Clark was just beginning as a writing coach. He realized offering Raines advice was beyond him. Instead, Clark turned reporter and interviewed Raines about how he wrote such a compelling series.

Raines told Clark that when he had worked at a previous newspaper, he heard many stories about local politicians from reporters. They were great stories, the kind that could entertain a crowd and reveal a candid side of the politician.

But when Raines read these same reporters' news stories, he found the copy void of those tales they told around the table at the local bars. Raines soon left to report for the *St. Petersburg Times*, vowing that every time he heard a great story about a local politician he would somehow try to confirm it and publish it.

His series on the politicians worked, he said, because he filled the stories with those great tales that many journalists knew about but few had the vision to use them in the newspaper.

Raines eventually rose to win a Pulitzer Prize and serve a controversial stint as executive editor of *The New York Times*. His lesson at St. Petersburg, though, is clear: A great profile draws an honest portrait of a person. The story tells readers what the person is really like.

- The writer must avoid making the subject extreme, meaning either unrealistically good or bad. We all have inconsistencies. Even the best people's behavior, at times, embarrasses them. Even the worst people do something redeemable.
- The writer should portray the subject as three-dimensional. Every human feels emotions: fear, joy, sadness, elation, anger. The writer should show the subject's emotions to tap into an experience shared by all.
- It's important for journalists to paint an accurate picture of the subject. Journalists can't say everything about a person, but they shouldn't leave out important parts of a subject's life because they might be controversial.
- Don't fear an honest, frank portrayal. Beginning journalists sometimes cringe at writing profiles that don't lionize a subject. They don't want to criticize. But they often confuse criticism with honesty. Being honest adds humanity without judgment. Showing a person who has just noble feelings or only exemplary reactions rings hollow with readers. They simply won't believe it.

AN EXAMPLE OF CAPTURING THE ESSENCE

When Julie Sullivan-Springhetti reported for the *Spokesman-Review* in Spokane, Wash., she wrote a series of unblinking profiles on people who lived in a low-income hotel in Spokane. The hotel, called The Merlin, was one of a few vanishing low-income buildings in Spokane's downtown landscape. The newspaper wanted to write about the people who lived in these spots. Sullivan-Springhetti, who uses "Sullivan" for her byline, was sent to The Merlin.

She wrote several profiles—all short and moody—that told the subject's stories in just a few paragraphs. The stories won a distinguished writing award from the American Society of Newspaper Editors and were selected to appear in the *Best Newspaper Writing 1991* book published by The Poynter Institute. So evocative was Sullivan's portrayals that the organization created a category just to accommodate her entries.

> Krystal Wilhelm crouches on the seventh stair of the Merlin Apartments, thin knees pulled against her 16-year-old stomach, insides cramping.
>
> She's dope sick. Not from withdrawal, but from injecting cocaine she suspects was cut with lidocaine, a local anesthetic.
>
> Living in the Merlin, one cracked cement step from the street, the Coeur d'Alene girl knows impure drugs are an occupational hazard.
>
> She rocks with cramps. But she needs $2 for a pack of cigarettes and that means going upstairs, finding her shoes, and heading out in the cold for a "date."
>
> She'll make $100 a day getting into cars with strangers, but she can spend twice that much on cocaine. Her last meal was a box of macaroni and cheese, made with water, no butter, no milk.
>
> "I like the high," she says softly. "It keeps me from being depressed all the time."
>
> At 5-foot-1 and 100 pounds, Wilhelm says she's been running away since she walked to Rathdrum at age 9. She married at 14, had a baby at 15, and watched the state of Washington take the child after a boyfriend snuffed out a cigarette on her son's tiny 2-month-old fist.
>
> None of it shows. Wilhelm's face is an expanse of unlined innocence. She says she loves her parents, but couldn't care less what they think. She'd die if her son ever used drugs, but her arms are so scarred by needles it looks like razors have been used to slice her skin.
>
> Traveling with a hairbrush and a short, tight black skirt, Wilhelm puts on her third borrowed coat of the week. Renting rooms by the night, she shares bed, board, and clothes, but not needles. Fear of AIDS also keeps a condom in her pocket.
>
> She wants to quit drugs, she says over and over.
>
> Maybe on March 4, after spending her last $100 on two "8-balls" of cocaine. One last blowout, the day she will turn 17.

This story runs just 11 paragraphs, but with a frank and simple style, Sullivan-Springhetti writes a stark account of a prostitute who at 16 has experienced as much as people twice her age. The honest writing creates sympathy and invites suspicion. Though readers understand the cycle that traps the 16-year-old, they also don't believe her when she claims she wants out.

CONFLICT

Few skate through life. Challenges, hurdles and troubles afflict everyone. Nothing goes as smoothly as we would hope. Everyone errs at some point.

Writers should include these universal parts of life in profiles. These experiences make the profiles not only more believable but also more readable. Solving problems, overcoming challenges, dealing with adversity, changing the status quo—all very human circumstances—create intrigue for readers and spur them to the finish line.

Looking again at the profile of the breast cancer patient, Dee Barney, the writer, Janet Gramza, shows unflinchingly the struggles Barney faces as she recovers from chemotherapy and surgery.

This part of the series is just after Barney underwent a mastectomy. Notice the conflict, especially the first time the doctor removes her bandages and she can see that her breast is gone. Her honesty, and Gramza's honest writing, give this story great insight into the human condition and great emotional appeal to the reader.

> She looked down. Her chest was slightly sunken where the breast used to be, and a line of black sutures ran across her right chest and down under her arm.
>
> "My ribs always did stick out further anyway," Dee joked.
>
> The incision looked clean and neat. Diane blurted, "It looks great!" Dr. Rogers agreed. So did Dee. It would take her a few days to cry.

Gramza adds many conflicts to this excerpt. Barney had to face looking at the incision following surgery. The reader knows her surgery will take awhile to heal. She is upset, but tries not to reveal her emotions. But the writer knows, and lets the readers in on the secret, that in a few days, Barney will display her vulnerability.

Profiles without conflict might inform readers, but they fail to intrigue them. The subjects must experience the same issues the rest of us face. How they overcome those issues is the stuff of great reading.

CHANGE

How people change piques readers' interest. This change might happen in a moment, or it might take years. Follow the arc of people growing and their lives evolving. You will write a stronger profile.

Journalists should never ignore how events and challenges shape or influence a person. The past hides clues to the present. Readers like to see how people have grown from their experiences.

Rick Lyman wrote in *The New York Times* about comedian and television actor Jerry Seinfeld's return to stand-up comedy. Seinfeld's television show had one of the most successful runs ever. When this story ran, Seinfeld was 48 and had little left to prove. Yet Seinfeld had written a new comedy act.

> Shortly after new episodes of "Seinfeld" stopped running on NBC in 1998, Mr. Seinfeld announced that not only was he returning to stand-up but that he was also

ADVANCED TIP

Before You Write a Profile, Answer These Questions

- Have you interviewed enough?
- What is your best beginning?
- Have you justified why you should write the profile?
- When should you go into the person's background?
- Do you have some telling moments?
- Do you have an ending?

going to retire all his old material and build a new act from scratch. Mr. Seinfeld says he always felt that the best comics—Richard Pryor, George Carlin and, above all, Bill Cosby—were those who were capable of creating new acts with entirely new material on a regular basis. Mr. Seinfeld wanted to prove to himself that he could do that, too—that his name belonged alongside theirs.

"I'll tell you how this started," he says. "I was working Boston or someplace. Adam Sandler was opening for me. It was 1993 or so, and I started to do this bit and someone out in the audience went, 'Heard it!' It was like someone throwing a spear in the balcony and it went right through my chest. Because you're presenting your material like it's all fresh and new and clever, and here's his guy going, 'Heard it!' That was a moment of such intense pain. Just to avoid that ever happening again. I went through all of this."

The story of why Seinfeld returned to comedy and wrote all new jokes becomes clear after he tells the story. The comment from the audience influenced the comic. He learned from the incident. He changed.

Chronicling those changes gives the journalist added benefits. Since change means starting from one point and moving to another, then following that change puts the reader on the story arc. The profile has movement.

WRITING THE PROFILE

Before you begin to write your story, ask yourself a list of questions. Being able to answer will help you focus your story and understand what will make it as intriguing as possible to readers.

Answer these questions:

- Have you interviewed enough?
- What is your best beginning?
- Have you justified why you should write the profile?
- When should you go into the person's background?
- Do you have some telling moments?
- Do you have an ending?

HAVE YOU INTERVIEWED ENOUGH?

Gathering the information needed for great profiles requires the writer to interview as many as possible. To get a full picture of the subject, talk to those who surround the subject: friends, immediate family, spouses, bosses, employees, enemies.

Talent Showcase

KATHERINE BOO ▶

The New Yorker, The Washington Post

Katherine Boo has written a Pulitzer Prize-winning story for *The Washington Post* and a national magazine award-winning profile for *The New Yorker*. In between, she was awarded a MacArthur Foundation fellowship.

When did she discover that journalism could have an impact, could really make a difference?

"When I got kicked out of a strip club in Washington, D.C., when I was working at the alternative newspaper," she says.

"I think I had an idea that I would review the food at these strip clubs where you could go for lunch and naked dancing, and I was impressed about what the food was like there. I went into one of them and promptly got kicked out. And they wouldn't let me sit there, and I said 'Well, why not?' And it was because they thought I was a prostitute looking for men. They had a policy of no unaccompanied females."

So Boo did the sensible thing and wrote the story. A city official joined her cause. Soon, the wrong was righted.

"Now the strip clubs of Washington can't discriminate against a woman who comes in and wants to watch by herself. So I thought 'Aha. Sometimes you can make a difference.'

"I'm not sure positive or negative."

She can be assured of her work and awards. The American Society of Magazine Editors named her story in 2004 the best feature story in magazines that year. For *The Washington Post*, her story in 2000 won the Pulitzer Gold Medal for Public Service category—the highest newspaper award possible.

What does she know now that she wishes she had known when she started writing and reporting?

"I wish I'd known that silence is the greatest reporting tool you can have," Boo says. "We as reporters barge into people's lives and say 'This, and this, and I want to know this, and I want to know this.' I think that I'm less interested in what people say about their lives and what governments say about what they do than what governments actually do and what people actually do. I think that it's not in expression, but in the choices that people make in living their lives and that governments make in enacting their policies where the truth of things is.

"It sounds crazy but if we just shut up and listen and watch, if I hadn't felt the need to direct the conversations as a young reporter, I think I would have learned a lot more about what was going on in the world."

Boo's stories drill deep into the heart of her subjects' lives. The story that won her the national magazine award followed two women in Oklahoma trying to get out of poverty through a government-sponsored program on marriage.

Boo's story "The Marriage Cure" painted a rich and dark portrait of the difficult struggle. What helped her to understand these women's plights, and many others' she has chronicled, was not her own agenda, she says. It's a lesson she learned the hard way—through trial and error.

"I think it was in trying to interview very poor people with very chaotic and busy, difficult lives, and they didn't have time to answer my questions," she says. "I realized my questions weren't the things that were really central to their lives.

"I think sometimes you get an idea and you go and you sort of prosecute it in communities or whatever, and often it's the wrong idea. Often there's something that's far more important to be asking about and thinking about but you're never going to find out what that is unless you give up control and start listening and watching and not trying to set the agenda as strenuously as we usually do as journalists."

Boo says even after her experience and accolades she still works at her writing. She rewrites her stories several times before turning them into her editors at *The New Yorker*. She's picked up some valuable advice along the way. A former editor used to "circle something and say 'That's my get-a-beer line.' It's that soft, silly sentence that's 'Ah, I'll read this later' and they'll get up and go get a beer. So you have to look at every sentence as if it's essential. You have to be ruthless in thinking, 'What am I including here?' "

She also faces every writer's daunting task: finding her lead.

"That's the very hardest part of the story," she says. "A friend of mine likened it to walking around with an oil drill on your back and you're coming to a spot and you're putting it in. . . . It's often almost experimental. In that case I might try 10 different ways of starting and see where it takes me. Often I'll be wedded to a certain image or I'll just have to accept the fact that as good as the image is, it doesn't actually reflect, it doesn't actually set me up for where I'm going in the rest of the story."

Despite the struggles, Boo says she sometimes stumbles across a story where the lead is easy to find. That happened to her when she wrote about the women from Oklahoma, the story that won her the national features award.

"Sometimes the lead is just there. Sometimes you just see someone. . . . [In Oklahoma] it was so clear to me that the lead was about a girl getting dressed and putting her jeans over her gold lame thong and going off to church. That was her outfit. Going to church, that seemed to me where it begins. So the clash between street and church cultures seemed to me that was captured in this moment."

She spends so much time on her leads because they draw readers into her stories. She knows she has just a few moments to entice them to stay with her story.

"It has to get you past the I-don't-want-to-read-this. . . . It has to get you past 'Do you want to read about marriage promotion classes in a church in a ghetto of northeast Oklahoma City?' I mean, probably not. If I give you Kimberly, and meeting Corine in their battered car that is smoking out, maybe you'll follow them along."

She also rewrites to make her prose as concise as possible and lets her facts rule the story.

"One of the things that I notice between my first drafts and my last drafts is that I begin strident, I begin harsh. I begin with overstatement. By the last draft, I've learned you have to let the facts, let the information come out and take away your own outrage.

"The less of me in a story, the more room there is for everyone else. I do it by narrowing in on what the important facts are. Ten fuzzy, mediocre facts are not half as good as two earned facts. So the better your reporting, the tighter your sentences."

Her story about strip clubs aside, she's written seriously about conditions of the impoverished and defenseless. What sustains her drive to write is the notion that if she tells enough people, something will change.

"I used to think that people didn't care. And now I think that people didn't know. I think that there is an impulse in this country, there is a desire for things to be more just. But if people don't have a clear sense of where the Catch-22s are in society . . . if the public doesn't know, there's no way to begin to address these kinds of problems."

- Don't confine your interviewing to the main subject. The writer will get a more accurate portrait though multiple sources. Either the subject doesn't tell the journalist the entire truth or is too humble to reveal challenges she has overcome.
- If the profile is controversial, the journalist must quote sources who agree and others who disagree with the subject. The writer has to go to both friends and enemies.
- The journalist should look for an independent third party, one who has no investment in the outcome of the profile or no emotional tie to the profile's subject. Interviewing this disinterested source gives enormous credibility to the story.
- All profiles need telling moments about the subject. These anecdotes—stories within stories—are important to show the reader how the subject acts in real situations, not just in a face-to-face interview.

WHAT IS YOUR BEST BEGINNING?

Leads for profiles should reflect the core point of the story. Just as a profile captures the essence of the subject, the lead must capture this essence as well.

The obvious point here is one made in previous chapters. The writer must know the story's core. The journalist needs to have figured out what makes the person interesting, what makes the subject worthy of a profile. The beginning, then, shows that thinking. The story starts with what lies at its heart.

The writer should also remember that leads can't be stale. Journalists almost always have but one crack at catching the reader's fancy. It's important to start strong before the reader decides to move elsewhere. A weak beginning is not a luxury a writer can afford.

Leads can be anecdotal. They can start with a memorable story that snares the turning point in a person's life. They can be scene setting, describing a setting that reveals the subject's personality.

Remember the earlier story about the Etch A Sketch artist from New Mexico. This is the way the writer, Alix M. Freedman, started that story:

> ALBUQUERQUE, N.M.—Many a night, Steve Hanks sits in some corner of a hazy bar, sipping 7Up and manipulating the two white knobs of a red-framed toy that looks like a miniature television screen. You might not think so, but an artist is at work.
>
> In one tavern, a lanky urban cowboy discovers the same thing that amazes everyone else about the 36-year-old Mr. Hanks' skill with the toy: His portraits are as accurate as pencil sketches.
>
> "It's good. Damn good," the cowboy stammers, pointing to his own likeness. "I've never looked better."
>
> Mr. Hanks is the Toulouse-Lautrec of the Etch A sketch.

Profile leads also can run as a series of sentences that, strung together, make up a person's personality. This lead is by a legendary *Associated Press* feature writer, the late Saul Pett. Pett had to profile then–New York City mayor Ed Koch. At the time of this profile, Koch was in top form as mayor, having stabilized the huge New York City bureaucracy. He also sported a flair for the dramatic. Pett's lead tried to put his arms around the force of nature that was Ed Koch.

> He is the freshest thing to blossom in New York since chopped liver, a mixed metaphor of a politician, the antithesis of the packaged leader, irrepressible, candid, impolitic, spontaneous, funny, feisty, independent, uncowed by voter blocs, unsexy, unhandsome, unfashionable and altogether charismatic, a man oddly at peace with himself in an unpeaceful place, a mayor who presides over the country's largest Babel with unseemly joy.
>
> Clearly, an original. Asked once what he thought his weaknesses were, Ed Koch said that for the life of him he couldn't think of any. "I like myself," he said.
>
> The streets are still dirty. The subways are still unsafe. The specter of bankruptcy is never farther away than next year's loan. But Edward Irving Koch, who runs the place like a solicitous Jewish mother with no fear of the rich relatives, appears to be the most popular mayor of this implausible town since Fiorello LaGuardia more than a generation ago.

Pett's lead gains momentum and creates interest by using opposites to describe Koch: unsexy yet charismatic, peaceful in an unpeaceful place. These observations came after Pett conducted an intense round of interviewing subordinates, enemies, allies and the mayor himself.

HAVE YOU JUSTIFIED WHY YOU SHOULD WRITE THIS PROFILE?

One of the most important parts of profile writing that often goes overlooked is justifying why readers should dive into the story. Readers need to sense that they will spend their time wisely. Seasoned writers understand the need to be clear about why their subject is interesting.

Writers justify their profiles in many ways:

- They can tell readers why a person is important or interesting now. They are at the top of their field or on the edge of a current trend.
- They can offer a news peg to heighten a story's relevance.
- They can show the reader the conflict the subject has faced or overcome.
- They can tell readers that this person might influence them sometime in the future.

These justifications resemble the nut graph mentioned in earlier chapters. The best profiles use them to hook the reader into the main body of the story.

Here is the way Janet Gramza justified to her readers why reading about Dee Barney's struggle with cancer would be worth their while. Treatments were making Barney's hair fall out. So she decided to cut it instead of wait. She enlisted the help of a friend, Betty Berkley.

> Overnight, she was swept into a whirlwind of medical visits, rearranged plans and worrisome phone calls. Overnight, she had to give up home-schooling her 8-year-old son to make time for her treatment. Overnight, the woman who helps heart patients maintain their health had lost control of hers.
>
> Now she was going to lose her hair. But she could decide when and how.
>
> "This is a lot better than sitting around feeling sorry for yourself as your hair falls out," Barney said as her friend shaved off her short, dark hair.
>
> An hour later, Berkley spiked the Mohawk and sprayed it pink. Barney giggled and ran upstairs to show her husband, Neil.
>
> "You look like some freak in London," he joked, adding, "It really doesn't look bad!" . . .
>
> When Cassidy glimpsed her, he jumped up and squealed. "Oh my goodness! You look SO COOL."
>
> Moments like that—when she turned a loss into a party—are what Dee Barney is striving for as she embarks on a fight for her life.

WHEN DO YOU GIVE THE PERSON'S BACKGROUND?

One obvious mistake beginning writers sometimes make is jumping to the past too quickly. The reader needs to appreciate what the subject is doing in the present before learning about the past. Even if the story is all about a person's remarkable life, the reader still must have a sense that the present is important.

Profiles should contain basic biographical facts: age, residence, where subjects were born, where they grew up. Add them to the story when it makes sense, that is, when the information is relevant or necessary to explain a part of their lives.

HAVE YOU IDENTIFIED THE BEST MOMENTS?

In a profile, the best writing usually occurs when the author has found the key moments in a person's life. Those moments are:

- What are the events that influenced the subject?
- What were the times that showed the subject's personality?
- What were the amusing or entertaining experiences?

In the Saul Pett profile of former New York City Mayor Ed Koch, Pett peppers the story with many such moments. Together they paint a portrait of the mayor just by showing him at work.

> In his third month in office, Koch went to a large meeting of white, middle-class constituents at a Catholic high school in Queens, where his administration was to

be put on "trial." Koch asked if he could have two minutes for opening remarks. The presiding priest said he could have one minute. Koch said in that case, he was leaving, and left.

"Now, nobody walks out on 1,100 Irish and Italian Catholics in a church setting," the mayor recalled. "Somebody asked me, how can you do this? I said, you don't treat me with respect, I walk out. They've got a kangaroo court in there and I don't happen to be a kangaroo."

DO YOU HAVE AN ENDING?

In all profiles, the story must end with distinction. That is, readers should have no doubt the story is over. The writer should reward readers with an ending that wraps up the story or ties back to the lead. Good endings do both.

In the profile of Jerry Seinfeld's return to stand-up comedy, the writer began the piece with Seinfeld going to typical places in his neighborhood in Manhattan, such as a Starbucks, looking for material for his act. Seinfeld, as part of the story, wrote jokes from what he saw in one afternoon, then tried them out that night, just a few hours later. They worked.

The writer, Rick Lyman, ends the story as Seinfeld is leaving the small comedy club where he has just performed his new material.

> "Not bad for an hour's work," he says. "I'll take it."
>
> He smiles broadly and begins for the door, then stops abruptly and turns back.
>
> "You know, I want to reassure you that this was honest," he says. "I could have taken something and pretended. I could have used material that I'd come up with before. But I really did do this. I could easily have cheated, but I didn't."
>
> His driver pulls up at the curb outside.
>
> "I didn't think it would work," Mr. Seinfeld says. "But I thought it would be just as interesting if it didn't. But it happened to work. Amazing. That was really fun."

IN CONCLUSION

People always are the most interesting parts of stories, and journalists who write about them have a built-in advantage to engage an audience. The good profiles take a lot of work. The secret to making them good lies in the reporting. The journalist has to get beyond the surface and dig deeper for the details that make subjects three-dimensional with feelings and experiences that show their personalities. Writers have a limitless store to shop from to find just the right ingredients to make profiles memorable. Once they've found the right person, the justification, the telling moments in that person's life, the way to begin and the way to end, the rest is memorable reading.

TOOL KIT

Some books you might wish to consider:

Life Stories: Profiles from The New Yorkers, edited by David Remnick, Random House, New York, 2000.
NewsTalk I, by Shirley Biagi, Wadsworth Publishing Co., Belmont, Calif., 1987.
Bird by Bird: Some Instructions on Writing and Life, by Anne Lamott, Anchor Books, New York, 1994.
Best Newspaper Writing 1981, edited by Roy Peter Clark, Modern Media Institute, St. Petersburg, Fla., 1981.

To read about Dee Barney:
www.syracuse.com/news/godsbasket/

EXERCISE

Write a profile from the following:

Alicia Flores:

"I grew up in San Antonio, and I always wanted to be an athlete like Jackie Joyner-Kersee. When I was in high school, I realized I wasn't that good, so I decided to concentrate on doing good for others. I decided if it was within my power, I would never let another person go hungry. I think that comes from a time when I was in middle school, about the eighth grade, and we didn't have that much to eat. There were seven kids in our family, and we were close, but sometimes it got tough. So my mom called some agency, and a church gave our family some food. I'll never forget the day they arrived. All these white kids with nice clothes and all this food and so smug. I mean they were polite and everything, and I was grateful to eat but you could tell they thought this was beneath them and I was so angry that we had to get food from them. I can still remember just staring at them. I wouldn't even talk to them when they tried to talk to me. So now that I'm in college here at Trinity I know that all white kids are not like that. When I started "Food U," I had as many white kids as Latino. In fact, my vice president is Heather Tidwell. She's white and she and I are best friends now. She's even learning Spanish. Our group takes food to families that need it. When I show up I know how they're feeling. Grateful to eat. Angry that we have to be there. So I always tell them about my experience when I was younger. Just the other day, I went to this family of nine. The dad was there, and it was hard for him because he was proud. But he had gotten hurt and wasn't working his normal three jobs. So when we arrived, I went straight to him and asked his permission to come in. I let him order things about and tell his children what to take. You could tell he appreciated being treated with dignity. He told me, "You have made my family's Christmas." When I left I felt great. Then three days later, I got a card from every one of his children wishing me a Merry Christmas. I'm majoring now in political science. I hope to someday run for political office and help those who need it the most."

Heather Tidwell:

"When I first heard that this group was forming, I thought it would be cool. What I didn't realize was the extent of the problem. It's a large void that we're trying to fill a little bit at a time. I now lie awake at night worrying about the family we visited that day. I credit Alicia with opening my eyes to that. Without her leadership, I think I would have traveled blithely through life not really knowing what was going on. I remember the first time we took food to a family. We had been chatting in a van on the way over, except for Alicia. Then when we got there and saw how these people had to live, we all stopped talking immediately. So Alicia looked at me and said, "You're up." That meant I had to take the lead on talking with the family. Sometimes I couldn't understand them, and they couldn't understand me, you know, because of the language thing. That's when I knew I had to learn Spanish. The next day I changed my major to both Spanish and social work. Alicia did that."

Raymond Russell, professor, Trinity College:

"The sky's the limit for someone like Alicia. I don't think she'll graduate at the top of her class. In fact, I'm sure of that. But her work is something you can't teach in a classroom. She'll certainly be the person the chancellor talks about at the end of the year."

Nora Pena:

"We grew up two houses down. Childhood was hard on Alicia. She was the oldest, and spent most summers babysitting her brothers and sisters while her parents worked. We were the same age and all she talked about was how different it was going to be when she got older. There was this time when people had to bring food for the family. For weeks later, she would talk about it. "This will never happen to me. This will never happen to me." She would just keep saying that. She's a strong person and I think that time is what made her who she is today."

CHAPTER 16

Features

IN THIS CHAPTER, YOU'LL LEARN:

- What is a feature and how it differs from breaking news.
- Features give readers a respite from breaking news.
- Features are organized by a beginning, middle and end.
- Feature leads are nontraditional.
- Features use chronology or "present, past, future."
- Endings play an important role in features.

I was first a reporter. And what I've learned is that you can't be a good writer unless you're a good reporter.
Tom Hallman, Pulitzer Prize-winner, *The Oregonian*

THE WALL STREET JOURNAL **ONCE RAN A STORY** about a campus craze at Harvard: videotaping lectures to show them on the university's website. Through the Internet, students who missed class could watch the tape and easily catch up.

The problem? Students were skipping entire weeks, then cramming all their lectures into a few days just before finals. Some early classes had become empty rooms that yawned at professors and a handful of students.

This story, called "Skipping Class 101," broke little news but was highly entertaining and informative. At one glance, the story took an amusing look at a new twist on campus. On another level, it discussed an issue deeper than just sleeping late: Was this the best way for students to learn?

Most editors call that story a feature. Features give readers a break from the steady drumbeat of stories tied to events. They are free from news cycles and don't have to run at the next deadline. They can cover the same subjects as hard news, but tell their stories differently, taking an unusual or offbeat angle. Reporters can use a freer or more overt writing style.

Feature stories run throughout print and digital media. They have grown into a necessary part of daily and periodic journalism. Most magazines fill their pages with nothing but features. Newspaper sections—including the front page—run more and more of these stories. Younger readers especially prefer them. National Public Radio has made a career of airing intriguing reports on trends and issues across the world. Even the time-starved network evening news shows use these stories.

WHAT IS A FEATURE?

Some have defined features as any story that's not breaking news. Though inadequate, that definition shows the wide range of stories that fall into this category. Features differ from breaking news stories chiefly in their timeliness and approach.

Breaking news stories must run as soon as the next news cycle allows. A feature doesn't. Journalists historically call many features "evergreens" because their vitality endures beyond several news cycles. But the best features usually are so attractive that editors want to get them in print or online as soon as possible. Their urgency lies in their strong writing and reader appeal. They are interesting to read, sometimes fun, often useful and informative.

Feature stories come in all varieties. Some are serious. After Hurricane Katrina leveled most buildings and homes along Mississippi's Gulf Coast, a journalist followed a mother trying to find safe water for her children. The story showed readers how difficult life had grown for survivors.

Some features are called "how to's," or service stories. They tell readers how to paint rooms, download software, apply makeup,

ADVANCED TIP

What Is a Feature?

Editors across journalism disciplines use the term "feature" to describe many story forms. Essentially, though, they call a story a feature if it covers an angle other than the immediate breaking news. Features can be profiles, lists, analyses, trends, humor, among other stories. A feature's common characteristic is that although it might be tied to an event, it takes such an angle that it can last through several news cycles.

balance budgets. They usually display light, straightforward writing styles. Magazines and lifestyle sections in newspapers are filled with these.

Some features report on trends—social, leisure, sports, medicine, education, business. Some features are profiles of newsworthy or interesting people. Other features explain the background of a recent news event, or reveal the inner workings of important decisions. These stories try to answer: "What really happened?"

TIME ELEMENT

A feature's delayed timeliness sometimes tempts writers to avoid including a time element in their stories. Because features can last through a news cycle, connecting them to a current event or breaking news story at first might seem less critical. The best feature writers know that the more timely their stories, the more interesting. In the right hands, history can come alive. But reading stories with little connection to today's news grows old quickly. The best features carry an obvious peg to current events or trends.

To some, features might seem optional reads. You don't have to plow through them to keep up on what's happening today. But they can educate the reader sometimes better than breaking news. A story that ran in *The Washington Post* Sunday magazine took readers into a home to understand just how much television has become part of the American familial landscape. The story, written by Pulitzer Prize-winner David Finkel, made no overt judgments. But Finkel's reporting let readers see that televisions were on and watched during the family's nearly every waking moment. By the article's end, the reader understands profoundly that this family shares the same habits of many across the country. The need to watch television at all hours has crept into the American social fabric. Few have considered the consequences.

Features are so agreeable to readers that a story's worth is measured in audience appeal. Editors might hold a feature for another news cycle. But once it runs or airs, it often can become the day's best story.

ORGANIZATION

Features also differ from hard news in their approach. The guidelines about leads and organization that govern breaking news stories fade with features. They aren't written with the five W's and H crammed into the first paragraph. Their leads take an indirect path. They must reveal to readers the point of the story, and usually early on, but that has no specific place. The story isn't told with the most important information first. The story's merit depends on its writing style, its vivid characters, its ability to keep readers intrigued. Creativity rules. What matters is a well-told tale.

Unlike breaking news, features follow no set organization. Writers usually divide them into three parts: beginning, middle, end. The distinction between features and breaking news stories comes in the weight attached to each part. In breaking news, the story unfolds in descending order of importance. In theory, editors could cut these stories from the bottom without losing their point or essence.

In features, that mindset changes. Each part—the beginning, middle and end—plays an indispensable role. An editor looking to cut can't just prowl near the story's end to find an extra quote to lift. To trim the story, editors—and preferably, the writer—must cut from throughout the piece.

FEATURE LEADS

Features give writers as much freedom as needed to lure the reader into the story. Nontraditional leads usually work best. Many begin with anecdotes or stories, or describe a scene. The most effective leads stay true to the story's main point. Feature stories, like news stories, need a central theme: there must be a reason for writing the story. The reader needs to understand that reason. The writer may never stray from it. All sentences, all paragraphs should lead the reader directly to the point.

Working as a washerwoman, Oseola McCarty saved $150,000 and gave it to the University of Southern Mississippi in her hometown, Hattiesburg, Miss. *The New York Times* writer Rick Bragg told her life in an evocative story.

In the mid-1990s, Rick Bragg was in the midst of a marvelous run in daily journalism and won a Pulitzer Prize. He had come into his own as a writer at the *St. Petersburg Times* in Florida, then moved to *The New York Times.*

By the time he wrote the following story, Bragg was considered one of the better feature writers in America. His Southern literary voice conveyed edge and grace.

In the lead to this story, Bragg shows his style: subtle and distinct. He also leads the reader directly to the story's point, which carries strong news value.

> HATTIESBURG, Miss.—Oseola McCarty spent a lifetime making other people look nice. Day after day, for most of her 87 years, she took in bundles of dirty clothes, and made them clean and neat for parties she never attended, weddings to which she was never invited, graduations she never saw.
>
> She had quit school in the sixth grade to go to work, never married, never had children and never learned to drive because there was never anyplace in particular she wanted to go. All she ever had was the work, which she saw as a blessing. Too many other black people in rural Mississippi did not have even that.
>
> She spent almost nothing, living in her old family home, cutting the toes out of

Talent Showcase

TOM HALLMAN ▶

Pulitzer Prize winner, *The* (Portland) *Oregonian*

Tom Hallman won two prestigious national writing awards in 2001 for his series on Sam Lightner, a boy with such a debilitating disease that his face swelled to grotesque proportions.

The boy's disease was similar to the one depicted in the 1980s movie, *Mask*. Hallman's story shows the boy's family deciding to undergo risky surgery, and then chronicles the story from Portland across the United States to Boston, where Sam submitted to the procedure.

Hallman's account, full of detail and adorned with sparse prose, put the reader at Sam's side throughout the ordeal. Hallman's story won the American Society of Newspaper Editors award for nondeadline writing and then the 2001 Pulitzer Prize for feature writing. A few years later, Hallman turned the story into a book *Sam: The Story Behind the Mask*.

Comments on the series usually focus on Hallman's clear and vivid writing style. Hallman credits that style to his days as a hard-news reporter. He says he still considers himself a reporter first, and a writer second. He says great writing builds on great reporting.

"I grew up in the tradition of . . . a hard news reporter, being a police reporter for 10 years. The writing part came later," Hallman says. "So I was first a reporter. And what I've learned is that you can't be a good writer unless you're a good reporter. You have to love reporting. If someone, especially a young person, starts to consider themselves a writer, it takes them away from the business of reporting.

"It's in the reporting that you find the story, that you find the elements needed for the story to make it powerful."

The story about Sam Lightner is full of scenes from the boy's life. It often reads like a short story or novel: fictional techniques used in a nonfiction setting that give Hallman's writing unusual power. Once during the story, Hallman described something as simple as Sam's family walking to an open house at Portland's Grant High School.

> Soon the streets fill with teen-agers on their way to Grant. Sam recognizes a girl who goes to his school, Gregory Heights Middle School. Sam has a secret crush on her. She has brown hair, wavy, and a smile that makes his hands sweat and his heart race when he sees her in class.
>
> "Hi, Sam," she says.
>
> He nods.
>
> "Hi," he says.
>
> The boy's parents fall behind, allowing their son and the girl to walk side by side. She does most of the talking.
>
> He's spent a lifetime trying to make himself understood, and he's found alternatives to the words that are so hard for him to

shape. He uses his good eye and hand gestures to get his point across.

Two blocks from Grant, kids jam the streets. The wavy-haired girl subtly, discreetly, falls behind. When the boy slows to match her step, she hurries ahead. Sam lets her go and walks alone.

Hallman wrote the story pledging never to call anything a quote unless he observed it himself or he took it from a document. That careful reporting, Hallman says, improved the story.

"If you look at the Sam story, it was all based on reporting, basically police reporting—what's happening, what are the significant details. It wasn't somebody thinking, 'Now's my chance to be a writer,' and go sit at the computer and impress people with the language. For me, it's always been a reporting-driven process and the writing comes next," Hallman says.

Once he has reported the story, though, Hallman says he must approach the writing differently than if he was writing a breaking news story. He must consider what Hallman calls "story elements," that is, what makes narrative writing distinct from straight news reporting.

"A character, something going on, movement in the story," Hallman says. "Not a little vignette, then a little bullet, and then you go back to a hard news kind of story [but] where the tone, the pace, the narration stays the same throughout the whole piece, where you feel like you're reading a story.

"And when you're done . . . what you remember is the story, not necessarily the facts of the story."

Though he values his start as a breaking news reporter, Hallman says he worked hard on his writing. He had to work through what he calls "the process of becoming a writer." Because a feature writer has more freedom, that often means the writer struggles, he says.

"It's difficult. You have false starts. You have stories that don't work, because there's no template to work from like there is when you can go out and cover Iraq, go cover a fire, go cover the budget hearing at city council. Once you've done enough of those, you kind of know how to do them. But for feature stories, and the narrative stories, there is no template."

Still, Hallman says he believes that feature writers should work at writing breaking news stories first. That experience helped him win awards. He strongly suggests beginning reporters wait until they are seasoned before paddling out into the uncharted feature waters.

"You don't want to be brand new, being in the business for a year thinking, 'Well, I'd like to do a three-part series on something.' More than likely, you're going to fail."

To balance reporting and writing, Hallman suggests tackling the toughest reporting beats at publications that help new writers learn basic reporting techniques.

"If you're a young person, do reporting, do lots of different kinds of reporting: city hall, police, learn how to get a city councilman not to overwhelm the interview, you learn how to control the interview. If you can get a cop to talk to you, you learn how to get people who have no benefit from talking to you to open up.

"In the middle stages of your career, it's important you decide which path you're going to take. Not everybody is going to want to be a feature writer. Not everybody should be one.

"But if you want to, it's in the middle stages of your career that you begin to find your voice, and find the kind of stories you're good at."

For Tom Hallman, that's a career path that has paid dividends, including a Pulitzer Prize.

shoes if they did not fit right and binding her ragged Bible with Scotch tape to keep *Corinthians* from falling out. Over the decades, her pay—mostly dollar bills and change—grew to more than $150,000.

"More than I could ever use," Miss McCarty said the other day without a trace of self-pity. So she is giving her money away, to finance scholarships for black students at the University of Southern Mississippi here in her hometown, where tuition is $2,400 a year.

This lead gains strength when Bragg over and over writes "never" or "nothing," showing the reader McCarty's simple life and the barriers she faced as a black woman in the segregated South.

Bragg also uses vivid examples: cutting the toes from shoes, ironing and cleaning, binding her Bible together with tape. These form pictures in the readers' minds and keep them engaged in the story.

Ultimately readers sense the lead is taking them somewhere. Bragg creates tension as he pulls out thread after thread of a poor woman's life. Then he ends his lead with a powerful twist: the poor woman actually has plenty of money, and instead of spending it on herself, she will give it all away.

In features, the lead must take readers to the place where the story's point becomes clear. They should then see why they should continue reading. Sometimes this occurs in the first paragraph. Sometimes, as in Bragg's piece, the hook comes several paragraphs later. But it does occur, and the clever writer leads readers to where they can decide to stop reading or plunge forward. Good writers push readers to the end of the diving board and then make the water look so inviting that there's little question the reader will jump in.

RECONSTRUCTION LEADS

Some features reconstruct what has happened before. Through memories and emotions, writers can take readers inside their subjects' minds. Writers also can use sentence construction to imitate the story's action, as in this story from *ESPN: The Magazine* about Ken Griffey Jr.

Injuries often had kept Griffey, one of the best baseball players ever, from playing for several years. Fans in Cincinnati had grown impatient. Griffey received ugly phone calls and even threats to himself and his family.

He is being followed. He is sure of it. Why? Who knows. But Ken Griffey Jr. is absolutely, 100 percent sure that right now, on this dark, rainy afternoon in late February, as he pulls his midnight-blue Mercedes sedan out of the parking lot of Ed Smith Stadium and onto the streets of Sarasota, Fla., he is being tailed by someone in a little

ADVANCED TIP
Features vs. Breaking News

In breaking news, the story unfolds in descending order of importance. In theory, editors could cut these stories from the bottom without losing their point or essence. In features, that mindset changes. Each part—the beginning, middle and end—plays an indispensable role. An editor looking to cut can't just prowl near the story's end to find an extra quote to lift. To trim the story, editors—and preferably, the writer—must cut from throughout the piece.

black car. To prove to himself that he's not crazy, not making this up, Griffey drives like a confused, lost tourist. Blinker on. Blinker off. Lane change right. Lane change left. Speed up. Slow down. The black car mimics the Mercedes' every move. Griffey's seen enough. He signals for a left turn and begins to fade in the direction of the left-turn lane, then suddenly zips to the right, across two lanes, to make a right. He is in the clear. For now, anyway.

"You too can have this lifestyle," Griffey says the next day, shaking his head.

The writing mimics what Griffey had to do to rid himself of the car following him. The sentences grow short, almost jerky. That is the movement of Griffey's car changing lanes and abruptly switching sides of the road.

The story also puts you inside Griffey's mind, one of print journalism's greatest strengths. The reader can understand what Griffey is thinking. Griffey's emotions are just at the surface, and the reader can sense Griffey's feelings. Once readers go inside Griffey's mind, they concentrate on the action. They are hooked, and their own mind's eye plays the scene for them.

Lastly, the quote that ends the anecdote sums up the action. Griffey's comment shows he has tried to rise above these incidents by light joking. But the quote also drives home the point that Griffey can't disguise his feelings of disgust.

INTRIGUING STATEMENT

The Wall Street Journal, long regarded as one of the better-written publications in the United States, has perfected the two-paragraph intriguing statement. The *Journal* usually showcases three front-page stories each day it publishes. Sometimes these are tied to immediate events. Almost each day, one story is a feature, usually led by this type of lead:

> HENDRICKSVILLE, IND.—When sports statistician Jeff Sagarin arrives at the two-room Rose's Diner here most Monday mornings at 7 a.m., his watch reads 6:14 a.m.
>
> That's perfectly logical, he says. But convincing the rest of Indiana he's right is proving a challenge.

The story tackles Indiana's circumspect dance with Daylight Savings Time. It's the only state that until 2006 didn't require counties to adopt the practice. Notice the lead immediately sets up a conflict and obstacle to overcome. The outcome is in doubt, which lets the writer promise implicitly that the reader will discover whether Indiana will change its ways and follow the suggestions of math whiz Sagarin.

These shorter leads have grown important because space in many newspapers and magazines has shrunk, and online stories demand a quick payoff at the beginning. The trend throughout journalism is to write shorter stories. These leads fit this style. They get to the point in lightning speed and take up little space.

A writer may use other leads we have introduced in other parts of this book. The important point to remember is feature writers have enormous freedom to lure readers into their stories, but they must follow the guidelines of great writing: they can't waste the readers' time or make them work. This is especially true when writ-

The Art of Storytelling

Feature writers follow the adage of great storytelling: Show, don't tell. What that means is the writer avoids reciting information that readers could understand better if they could see it.

Beginning writers sometimes want to tell readers more than they need. They tell them the crowd appreciated a musician instead of showing them the five-minute standing ovation. The reader easily could have sensed the crowd's overwhelming reaction.

In this story from *The New York Times Sunday Magazine*, writer Alex Witchel clearly wants her readers to know that the actor Nathan Lane is in a morose mood. When the story appeared, Lane was in the midst of a triumphant run on Broadway. He and his co-star, Matthew Broderick, were playing in *The Producers*. The show was a runaway hit, and Lane eventually won a Tony award for best actor.

Still, the success wasn't making Lane happy. Witchel could have said that outright. Instead she shows the reader a scene in a New York City store where Lane, Broderick and the show's creator, Mel Brooks, were signing the first CDs of their Broadway hit.

> Lane kept signing, fast, his name increasingly illegible. "Have you ever heard 'the bigger the star, the worse the penmanship?' " he was asking Broderick, when another man confronted Lane.
>
> "Are you signing Playbills at the matinee?" he demanded. "I went there, and you weren't signing."
>
> "Well," Lane countered, "some days are good days and some days are long days. Daddy has to go home and rest."
>
> "Don't try matinee days," Broderick offered, trying to be helpful.
>
> The man walked off.
>
> "They all hate me," Lane wailed. "They're all afraid of me. They go right to you. Right to Ferris."
>
> "That's not true," Broderick said, laughing.
>
> The air was filled with a dizzying odor of ammonia from the thick black markers they were using to sign the CD's, and the lights overhead were hot.

"Feel like Santa a little?" Broderick asked. Lane pointed up to the speakers. "It's a loop of the overture," he said. "That's hell, isn't it? Over and over?"

A teenage girl presented Lane with a handmade photomontage that featured the actor in a variety of roles. Her hands trembled. "From Meghan, your No. 1 fan," the cover said.

Lane surveyed the photos, oblivious to the teenager awaiting his approval. "See how my weight fluctuates?" he asked Broderick. When he finally looked up, she burst into tears. Lane grew red-faced and shook her hand.

"Thank you very much," he said courteously as she kept on crying. He looked away, left, right, anywhere else. The moment seemed to last forever. Finally, she was gone.

"You once sat next to me on the PATH train," a man exclaimed.

"How about that?" Lane answered. "Nice to see you again."

"Does it feel nice to be back on top?" another man asked and moved on. Lane looked chagrined. "When did I hit bottom?" He moaned to Broderick, who was sympathetic. "That's OK. People say to me, 'Are you still making movies?' "

A woman planted herself in front of Lane and put her hands on her hips.

"I want a smile," she commanded, unsmiling. Lane sat still a minute. "This is it," he blasted, "as happy as I get, baby." She looked startled, but he went on. "Thirty therapists couldn't do it, so why should you?" She froze. He reached over and shook her hand.

This piece of writing shows Lane's mood more convincingly than if the author had merely written "Lane was disagreeable that night, sulked to Broderick, all but ignored an adoring teenage fan and flat out refused a woman's demand that he smile, for once." The author's recording of Lane's interaction with his fans reveals his personality. He can't hide it. The person he is becomes obvious to the reader.

Witchell also organizes her lead around chronology. She lets the important events unfold as they happened in real time. In that way, the interactions build to a climax. One after another, Lane's fans try to communicate with him. When the woman demands that Lane smile, his comment sums up the attitude he displayed throughout. The woman's reaction also symbolizes what many of Lane's fans must have experienced.

The lead's strength lies in classic storytelling. Witchel masterfully shows Lane's personality through his own actions. His behavior spoke volumes. Witchel had the awareness to recognize that this scene would say it all.

ers are given great freedom. The temptation to lapse into self-indulgence grows when writers mistakenly believe they can throw off disciplined sentences and careful word choice. Writing that holds up over generations avoids saying "Look at me," but counters with "Look at my content."

THE MIDDLE

After readers understand the story's point and choose to keep reading, the writer must take great care to keep the readers' interest. The middle of the story embellishes its content. It has the story's point clearly in mind. It keeps that point fresh in the reader's attention.

The story must promise readers that if they continue, they'll find the reading worthwhile. This part of the feature story has many names: nut graph, billboarding, theme statement. Whatever the name, this part tells the reader there's a story here that's worth the investment. This is the bridge from the lead to the middle. It is necessary to quality feature writing.

This example ran in *Esquire* magazine. The paragraph comes at the end of a long introduction where the writer merely observes Hillary Clinton as she speaks to a breakfast group outside Rochester, N.Y. Magazine writers are allowed more freedom in their analysis, but the observations are rooted in fact and obvious research.

> But at Laborers' Hall, Hillary Clinton looks different. As the speeches end, people touch her shoulder and ask for autographs and pull her close to whisper secrets. She leans into everyone, taking their hands and hearing their thoughts, and for a minute, the sight doesn't sync; it won't connect to years of images of a steely woman who stared back at interrogators and enemies and America with eyes like sewn-in marbles that warned, Back off. She tells these people, one after another, "Thank you for coming to see me," and her voice is different, too; it lacks policy and planning and barbed-wire fencing, and when she disappears for a moment into the push of people and all that is left is her voice, you hear a young woman speaking; you hear Hillary Clinton as she must have sounded all those years ago, when anything was possible for her. "Thank you for coming to see me," she says. It sounds like a genuine thank-you, not a politician's thank-you and in that moment it occurs to you that Hillary Clinton might be thanking these people for more than just coming to see her, that with her new book and new job and a life separate from Bill Clinton for the first time in nearly thirty years, Hillary Clinton might be thanking them for taking part in her liberation.

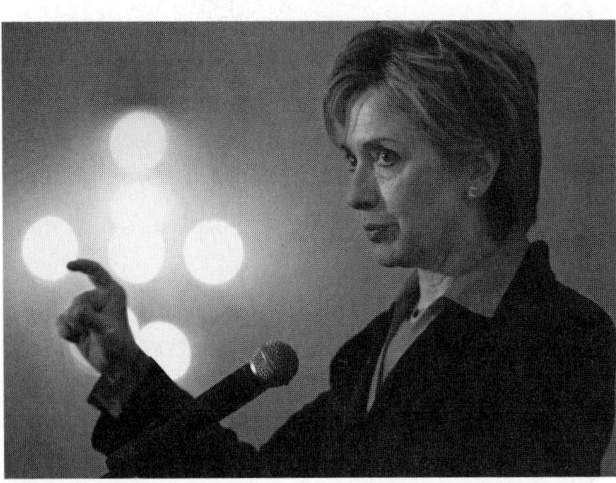

Many stories have chronicled the life of Hillary Rodham Clinton. But *Esquire* magazine wrote a story offering a fresh look. An effective nut graph promised readers that something new was coming later in the piece.

This paragraph promises fresh information about a woman whose life has been under public scrutiny for decades. Despite what you might think you know, the authors implies, I have new reporting that will show you Clinton is walking a different path. Despite the reader's political ideology or knowledge about the Clinton family, the promise of a change in direction compels the reader to plunge forward.

CHRONOLOGY

Feature writers can organize their stories' middles in many ways. Two popular and workable ways focus on either chronology or what's known as "present, past, future."

Organizing by chronology means the writer introduces a moment of time, then lets the events unfold as they happened. This natural plot line leads the reader through the story.

Chronology works well when the writer recounts a significant event. If an athlete has been injured and is making a comeback, a journalist might follow the athlete's progress throughout the game. The writer weaves pertinent information in and out of the athlete's performance. She lets the natural flow of events lead the reader through the story until the game's end.

Chronology gives nonfiction writing power because it pushes the story forward on its own. The reader naturally follows the story's action. The most experienced feature writers use chronology as often as their stories permit.

HOW TO USE CHRONOLOGY

Chronology means action. The main subjects must move through the story through scenes and narration, but they need to act. After the writer introduces a situation to readers, the story's natural flow travels along time. Characters act in real time.

After bomber Timothy McVeigh blew up the federal courthouse in Oklahoma City in 1994, a team of reporters from *The Philadelphia Inquirer* produced an exhaustive story. Their lead showed one victim who did nothing extraordinary that day but follow her morning routine. By the time the bomb finally explodes, the tension is as tight as a noose.

> Prisilla Salyers was having an off morning. She looked in her closet and couldn't decide what to wear. Finally she picked the hot pink blouse. It had a spot on it, but she didn't care because her black jacket would cover it up. She put on a flowered skirt and black shoes that she didn't really like because the heels were too high.
>
> Salyers, a blond-haired woman of 44, was supposed to stop at a friend's house on

ADVANCED TIP
Chronology Is Your Friend

Veteran writers know a great secret to compelling features: use chronology as often as the story allows. Chronology lets the reader float along time with the story. It is a common way to recount events. Readers are used to hearing stories told this way. Writers who let their stories follow timelines help readers organize their thoughts. Following the chronology of an event gives stories a natural plotline. Readers win in the end.

the way to work at the federal building, but she felt out of sorts and skipped it. She parked in the bottom level of the underground parking garage and took the elevator to the Customs Service office on the fifth floor. She used her special code to unlock the door and turn off the alarm, flicked on the copy machine and made coffee.

It was just after eight when she fetched the mail. She was sorting it when agent Paul Ice, 42, arrived. They were exchanging small talk when agent Claude Medearis, 41, arrived a few minutes later, waved hello and went straight to his desk to make phone calls.

Shortly before nine she was back at her cubicle, sipping coffee and arranging the files she'd be reviewing that morning. Her back was to the northside windows. Medearis was on the phone at his desk behind her, facing the same way. Ice had just stepped up to her desk, just a foot away, when he gestured to something on her desk and asked the question.

She looked up. She saw Ice. She started to say "What?" and everything went black.

"Then I saw white flashes and I heard a loud wind noise going past my ears."

She thought she was having a seizure. She felt her head being pushed down, down, she thought, toward her desk. A seizure would be embarrassing. What would people think?

"I thought Paul was going to grab me. I thought, 'What is he thinking?' "

WIRED AND WIRELESS | WEB

Though they can be long or short, features often run longer than breaking news stories. In print, writers, editors and layout artists negotiate length. They can accommodate an excellent but long feature, as long as the story reads compellingly.

On the Internet, space is limitless, but not so readers' attention. Those who oversee websites say that longer stories may have joined the endangered species list.

Charles Madigan, who until recently ran the website for the *Chicago Tribune*, saw website visitors shy away from any story of real length. So is long-form journalism near death?

"There may be a limited place for it but it's [the Internet] such a new phenomenon that those things have not really been clarified," Madigan says. "What we know right now is that people who use the Internet for news use it for breaking news stories that are short and constantly updated."

Madigan has seen website visitors click on interesting and long stories, but he finds that the exception rather than the rule.

"It used to be that when we started a long time ago, what was happening is that content was being created for the newspapers in terms of traditional long newspaper stories. Then it was being processed through technology and presented on the Internet in the same version that it was in when it appeared in the newspaper. And that was like the entry-level kind of get-the-news-onto-the-Internet thing."

But that's changed radically. Larger newspapers translate the longer stories into more usable, smaller chunks.

"They're still repurposing newspaper copy. But what they're coming out with is a much more abbreviated version of what goes on than what you'd read in the actual papers," Madigan says.

> It stopped. Everything stopped. Salyers was lying face down, her right arm under her stomach. She was unable to move. She realized, slowly, that she was covered with debris.

This recounting of Salyers' experiences after the Oklahoma City bombing follows the natural plot line of time, or chronology. Since readers know through a headline and photos that the story recounts the terrorist attack, Salyers' mundane actions only add to the intrigue. The more routine and insignificant her actions, the more important they grow.

PRESENT, PAST, FUTURE

Some stories don't allow a natural chronological flow. Sometimes, they simply need to convey information. A more common way to organize features is what's called "present, past, future." In that way, writers tell the readers what the issue or trend or point of the story is at the moment. Then once the reader understands the story fully, the writer gives them background, or the past. Afterwards, the writer looks to the future, telling the reader what's likely to happen.

This organization works for many reasons. Chief among them: It mirrors the way we discover information. When you first move into a new town or apartment, or begin a new school or job, you are immediately struck by what is new, what is in front of you. That is the "present" in the stories.

After you've grown used to your new surroundings, you begin to question why something has occurred. What's gone before? That is the "past" or background. After a while, newcomers begin to care about where they are. They have a stake in the future.

Readers approach a story much the same way. They learn the information before them, begin to wonder how it came to be, and then are intrigued by what soon will happen. Present, past, future.

Looking at Rick Bragg's story on Oseola McCarty, he takes great care to explain to his readers why the story is so powerful. After his lead, the story continues a few paragraphs later:

> People in Hattiesburg call her donation the Gift. She made it, in part, in anticipation of her death.
>
> As she sat in her warm, dark living room, she talked of that death matter-of-factly, the same way she talked about the possibility of an afternoon thundershower. To her, the Gift was a preparation, like closing the bedroom windows to keep the rain from blowing in on the bedspread.
>
> "I know it won't be too many years before I pass on," she said, "and I just figured the money would do them a lot more good than it would me."
>
> Her donation has piqued interest around the nation. In a few short days, Oseola McCarty, the washerwoman, has risen from obscurity to a notice she does not understand. She sits in her little frame house, just blocks from the university, and patiently greets the reporters, business leaders and others who line up outside her door.

> "I live where I want to live, and I live the way I want to live," she said. "I couldn't drive a car if I had one. I'm too old to go to college. So I planned to do this. I planned it myself."
>
> It has been only three decades since the university integrated. "My race used to not get to go to that college," she said. "But now they can."
>
> When asked why she had picked this university instead of a predominantly black institution, she said, "Because it's here; it's close."
>
> While Miss McCarty does not want a building named for her or a statue in her honor, she would like one thing in return: to attend the graduation of a student who made it through college because of her gift. "I'd like to see it," she said.

Notice how Bragg makes sure the reader knows the story's point and significance. He tells them why they should read the story now, or the "present": it's interested the nation, it's at her hometown university. Bragg has purposely told his reader why the story is important now. Later, he will give McCarty's background, where she was born, what her life was like until now. Then at the end, he talks about what will happen with her gift and who received the first scholarship. His story followed the present, past, future pattern.

ENDINGS

Endings are especially important to feature stories. Most breaking news stories end when the information dries up. The best features have endings written on purpose. They tie up loose ends. They reflect the lead. They leave the reader with a sense of completion. Written well, these endings are difficult to trim, and impossible to omit without doing the story irreparable harm.

The best endings usually refer back to the lead. That echo might be faint, but it is obvious. Endings that reflect the lead often leave the reader with a feeling of completion. It's as if the story has gone full circle. This sometimes is called "the 360 effect," referring to the geometric degrees in a circle.

These endings reward readers who stayed with the entire story. They give them a send-off, usually memorable. They leave the story with a strong feeling and a sense of accomplishment.

In Rick Bragg's story about Oseola McCarty, he led by saying she had cleaned clothes for "graduations she never saw." In the story's middle, he mentions that the only thing she wanted in return for her donation was to see a student helped by her money graduate.

So Bragg concludes the story by introducing the scholarship's first recipient, saying she felt some pressure to graduate:

"She counts on Miss McCarty being there four years from now, when she graduates."

The ending echoes slightly what Bragg wrote in his lead.

In *The Wall Street Journal* story about skipping class at Harvard, which began this chapter, the writer led with a student, Katrien Naessens, who was missing physics to row in the morning on the nearby Charles River. She wasn't worried, because she could watch the taped lectures on a private website. Her actions typified the story's point.

To end the piece, the writer returns to Naessens:

> Consider Ms. Naessens the day before her physics final last spring. Motionless at her desk in days-old pajamas, unbrushed hair tied up in a pony tail, Ms. Naessens took in 16 hours of tapes over two days. While sitting there bleary eyed, she says she had moments of regret about skipping six weeks of class.
>
> But now, when she recalls those crisp mornings on the Charles, she says it was definitely worth it. "Even though my mom would be furious if she found out I had been rowing, for me personally, it was wonderful to do a team sport, to be out on the water and have a really positive start to the day."
>
> Beside, Ms. Naessens adds, she slipped by with a B.

The writer did a 360. She echoed the lead by returning to the student, referring to the rowing and reflecting the action: all solid techniques to make a solid ending.

IN CONCLUSION

Features give readers a respite from breaking news. Features can cover the same topics, but take a different approach. They don't need to run at the next news cycle. Writers organize them independent of news stories. Their leads, middles and ends set them apart from the routine. Their popularity has made them necessary, and they take many forms. But they always return to the core of great journalism: intriguing information that entertains and informs.

TOOL KIT

Some books you might wish to consider:

The Art of Fact: A Historical Anthology of Literary Journalism, edited by Kevin Kerrane and Ben Yagoda, Touchtone, New York, 1997.

The Art of Writing Nonfiction, by Andre Fontaine and William A. Glavin, Jr., Syracuse University Press, Syracuse, N.Y., 1987.

Writing for Story, by Jon Franklin, Plume, New York, 1986.

EXERCISE 1

Write a feature story from the following information:

You are a reporter for your student newspaper and its website. The Bravo Inn is closing. The Bravo Inn is just off the campus at Atwater University. It's housed students and their families for as long as Atwater has been around. It's interesting because the inn and the university started exactly the same time, 100 years ago this year. You run over to the inn and find the owner—well known to those on campus—just locking the door. Her name is Susan Hopkins. "I'm closing the door to a lot of great memories. My grandfather built this whole building. I don't know what he would think now. We've housed three presidents here—Lyndon Johnson, Harry Truman and Woodrow Wilson. We've had parties and celebrations. When Atwater won the national championship in basketball 40 years ago—I had just graduated and joined my dad in running the place—you couldn't have found a seat in here. We didn't have big-screen TV back then, so we just set up all these televisions with rabbit ear antennas. It was great. But right after that, when the university needed to integrate, it still had blacks in separate dorms from whites. And so the kids met at this one special table—it was so touching. White kids and black kids decided the university was moving too slow so they decided to hold this protest. After two weeks, the whole campus joined them, and I mean everybody, black and white and the university changed its policy. Right in there at the corner table is where it started. The Atwater Eight. But there were really nine students, but no one knows that. That marker right past the administration building is still there for the Atwater Eight. And I'll never forget how it started. Bill Lucas was this football player, the captain that year, 1969, and he walks over to this table of other football players, all black players, and he says to Jeremy Lovit, he was the leader of the black players, "It's not right." And Lovit just looks at him. And Lucas says it again. So Lovit stands up, and I thought there was going to be this fight so I go over. But Lovit says, "So what are you going to do about it?" And Lucas says, "Change it." So they don't fight but sit down and that's how it started. And then the protests, and within a month, everything changed. Well, a lot of good memories. Especially the one my grandfather told about meeting my grandmother here. She came in for a job, and no girls hardly went to college then. My grandfather didn't need any help and he was about to turn her away when he asked what she was doing at college. She said she was there because her father told her she couldn't go to college. So she and mother schemed together and got her in and she ran away from her father and enrolled. So my grandfather was so smitten that he hired and later married her. Their reception was right inside. Well, we're closing because I'm 65 and can't run it anymore and the university has bought the building. They're going to tear it down and build their own hotel. We could only hold 10 guests, but the new hotel will be 200 at least. I guess it's progress, but to me it seems like getting rid of something that doesn't need it."

EXERCISE 2

Go to a website, magazine or newspaper and select a feature story. Answer the following about features in general and your story in particular:

1. What are the differences between features and breaking news?
2. Could this story have been a breaking news story at some point?
3. How do leads differ between features and breaking news?
4. Does the lead in your feature pull the reader inside the story?
5. What purpose do nut graphs serve?
6. Where is the nut graph in your story?
7. What are the two common ways writers can organize the middle of features?
8. How is the middle organized in your feature?
9. How do endings help a feature?
10. Is the ending in your feature effective?

CHAPTER 17

Ending Stories Well

IN THIS CHAPTER, YOU'LL LEARN:

- Endings, often overlooked in daily journalism, improve stories.
- The best writers see endings as vital to their stories' structure.
- Endings are important because they leave the final impression on the reader.
- As with leads, there is more than one way to end your stories.

You discover sometimes what your story is about while you're writing it.
Barry Siegel,
Pulizer Prize-winner

MARCUS HAYES HAS SIMPLE ADVICE for any writer hunting the end to their story. Write two leads, the sports writer from the *Philadelphia Daily News* says.

"Then use the better one as the ending."

Hayes' suggestion, delivered half-seriously, reflects an understanding shared among the best writers. How they leave their readers is almost as important as how they greet them.

Perhaps the most overlooked parts of stories, endings rarely dominate newsroom debates. Reporters and editors usually spend more time discussing leads. But leads, no matter their importance, shouldn't overshadow the value of a great ending.

A strong ending rewards someone who has read to the story's end. A well-constructed ending confirms the story's point, signals that the story is done and sends readers off with an emotional investment. An ending often echoes the beginning, which puts readers in a satisfying spot: back where they started.

On any story other than those with inverted-pyramid structure, endings should be a necessary part of the story's organization. The best writers use them. The best stories have them.

WHY ENDINGS MATTER

Some journalists, especially newspaper reporters, spend their careers never worrying about where they will stop writing. Some write to a determined length and just quit. Others, if they need an ending, look for a catchy quote. These kickers, as they are called, can work in many stories. For some reporters, kickers are the only ending they write. But journalists have overused them.

The better writers try to end their stories with purpose. They want to wrap things up, and give their readers a bonus for staying with them. They hope to leave their readers wanting more.

Endings have many functions. These guidelines will help reporters find their endings:

- Endings should be memorable. Endings are the last words a journalist has to impress the reader. These final thoughts should leave the reader with a strong feeling about the story.
- Endings conclude the story in a way that satisfies the reader, no matter the emotion. A satisfied reader understands the writer has finished the story at the appropriate spot, not just because space ran out.
- Endings are part of a story's structure. Many writing coaches preach that stories should have beginnings, middles and ends. Each plays its part, meaning that you can't neglect one for the other. A strong ending balances the piece.

ADVANCED TIPS

Characteristics of Strong Endings:

- **Reader Satisfaction:** Good endings leave the reader feeling rewarded for reading the story completely.
- **Memorable:** Good endings make the story last beyond the first read.
- **Structure:** Good endings are part of a well-organized story.
- **Pace:** Good endings slow as they approach the finish.

- Good endings slow as they approach the final sentence. Journalists generally try to write leads that read quickly and get the reader into the story with little effort. Ends should read effortlessly as well, but don't have to be in such a hurry to finish. Readers usually don't mind a leisurely paced ending. It's like parking a car: The driver must slow down before coming to a complete stop.
- An ending can take many forms. It can echo the lead by recalling a similar phrase or returning to the same person or theme. It can be a kicker quote. Or it can end with a description or decisive scene that represents an emotion.

ECHO THE LEAD

To write memorable endings, start at the beginning. Take readers back to where the story opened. Thus the story runs full circle, a fulfilling way for readers to finish.

Some beginning writers mistake this technique and repeat a large part of the lead. Readers usually remember your lead and don't need a replay. Echoing doesn't need to fully mimic the lead.

An echo ending can take many forms:

- Writers can just borrow a phrase from the lead and use the phrase with a twist to give the sense that the story has circled back. If the lead is *Lamar Nichols never knew his mother*, the writer can end: *Nichols believes he now knows* or *She became the mother Nichols never knew*. Just a whisper of the beginning works well.
- End the story with the same person who is in the lead. Many writers begin by showing a subject's situation that represents the story's point. These subjects might never appear in the story again until the end. That circle takes the reader back to reintroduce the person whose situation started it all.
- Writers can end at the same geographic spot. If a story begins at a gym, restaurant, office or home, a writer can end the story back at the same sites.
- The ending can be thematic. A story about a family that lost all in a fire might start with the parents asking why. The story can end with the family still wondering and no closer to answers.

HOW TO Echo the Lead:

- **Start over:** Think back to the beginning. How did you begin your story? Is there something with your lead that will let you circle to your ending?
- **People:** If you began your story with a person, does it make sense to bring this person back into the story as your ending?
- **Location:** Often you can return to the same location where you began.
- **Thematic:** Revisit the same issue, even if the people or location have changed.

AN EXAMPLE OF AN ECHO

Julie Sullivan-Springhetti, a Pulitzer Prize-winning reporter at *The* (Portland) *Oregonian*, once chronicled the life of a couple who had autistic twins. The two girls spent most of their days running amok, wrecking their house, sapping their mother of emotional energy.

The Art of Storytelling

Purposeful endings are integral to great stories. Narratives have a point, work to a point and eventually arrive at a point. That arrival is the ending, often ignored by daily journalists but treasured by those who understand the power of leaving a story at just the right moment with just the right touch.

Narrative writing can't survive without endings. They belong to the narrative structure of beginning, middle and end. Traditionally, great stories find a character. The author endears the character to readers. The character then faces a major conflict, and works through several minor conflicts to a climax. Then the author sends the reader and the character off.

At the story's close, the ending leaves the reader wishing for more, or thinking of what the character will face in the next chapter. To those who teach narrative nonfiction, the ending should be as much a part of the journey as the start and the middle.

"The key thing about endings, particularly for this kind of narrative nonfiction, literary journalism, whatever you want to call it, is you have to have a sense that what you're doing is unfolding a nonfiction short story," says Barry Siegel, who won the Pulitzer Prize for feature writing and now teaches literary journalism at the University of California–Irvine.

"And in that story, the story has to arrive someplace."

Narrative writing lets journalists tell stories in new ways. Writers limit themselves only by their imagination. They have the freedom to take the most mundane fact and, through great reporting and great vision, turn it into a moving piece that evokes a reader to feel deeply and consider new viewpoints.

Sullivan-Springhetti led the story with the mother driving her twins in Portland. One twin decided to get out of her seatbelt, strip off her clothes and jump into the back of the car. Her mother had to find a way to pull to the curb and deal with her daughter at the side of the road. The description leaves readers exhausted.

Sullivan-Springhetti decided to end the story echoing the beginning. She shows the mother, Donna, picking up her two daughters from school, the ARC. The mother has been granted a brief respite from the constant energy of her two daughters. There's no end to the motion, and no solution to her problems.

In the mid-1980s, Adrian Peracchio wrote a story that did just that. Working for *Newsday*, the newspaper based in Long Island, Peracchio took a routine circumstance—an aging man caring for his debilitated wife—and made it anything but routine. The story lacked the conventional writing normally seen in newspapers. The reader doesn't even know the names of the two main characters. There are no street addresses, or identifying characteristics of a nursing home, where the story is set.

The intriguing point about this story is how Peracchio builds to the end. The author follows his own interaction with the couple. He starts the story with his own visit to the nursing home. He then listens to the husband's tale. At the end, he closes when he finally meets the woman. The reader learns the story as the author does.

Peracchio closes the story with a quote from the husband talking to his ill wife.

> "She's not looking her best today," he said softly, turning aside from her. "Sometimes she can't sleep, you know, so they give her drugs." He looked at her again. "She's a little uneasy with strangers," he told his visitor, "so, if you don't mind . . ." His eyes were beginning to brim with tears, but his voice was steady and cheerful, as he turned to her and said, "Dear, you'll love this. I found this new detective novel by that English fellow, the one you've always liked. It's a long one, so let me start reading . . ."

Endings finish stories with purpose. They can't be left out of the planning or execution.

"But above all, the idea in narrative is that you are actually moving toward something," Siegel says. "And the end is the point of arrival of something. This is a very different concept from a news story."

Tomorrow when the twins wake up, they'll have autism.

She says this aloud. She loves them, will care for them as long as she can. She cannot cure them.

She sits in the car outside the ARC, allowing herself, for the first time, to imagine a way through this grief, imagining what she might do to make a living, how she might help others, who she might yet be. She smiles.

She walks into the center, where the waiting twins are agitated. The picture book Renee wears around her neck to communicate is missing. Rachel pulls Donna

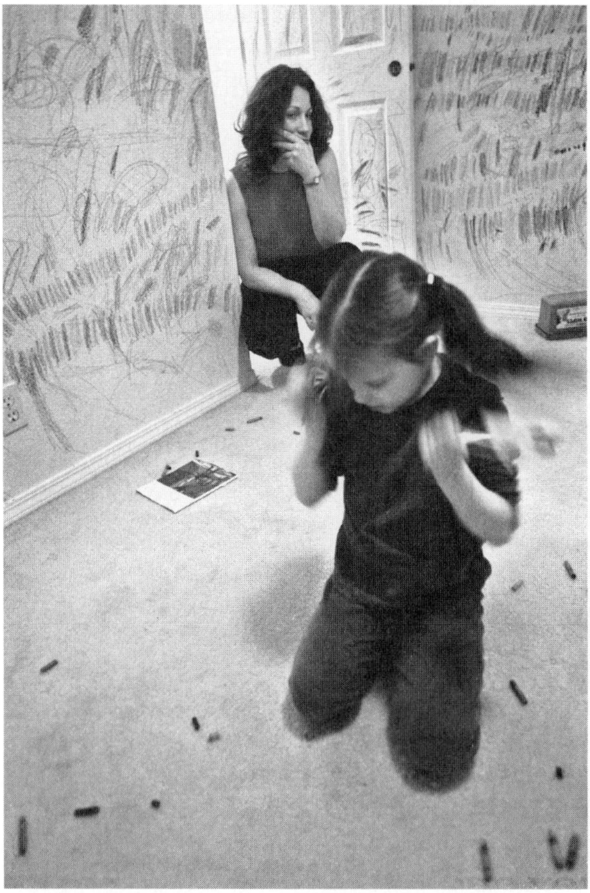

Pulitzer Prize-winner Julie Sullivan-Springhetti captured a mother coping with the chaos of raising autistic twin daughters. Sullivan-Springhetti starts the story in a hectic van ride, then ends with the mother once again driving, resigned to help her daughters any way she can.

toward the center's sink for a drink; her sister drops to the ground screaming in protest. Donna gets Rachel water, which she dumps on the floor.

A look falls over Donna's face. She gets more water, finds the book, slings a backpack over each shoulder, then takes both girls' hands firmly, walks to the car and buckles them into their seats.

She stares straight ahead, starts the car and drives.

Sullivan-Springhetti said she chose to start the story in the car and end in the car almost by instinct. She understood on a deep level that the car symbolized more than just driving.

"That was the motif in all of the story," Sullivan-Springhetti said. "And it was because I spent so much time in the car with her. Part of it was she was constantly driving somewhere looking for help. I actually think the car was sane, the car represented some sort of sane island for her and that she could actually see the kids, control them most of the time in a place where she was directed with her kids and not having to deal with all their craziness. So the car motif was a natural."

The mother and father in the story had separated, but during the reporting, they reunited. Sullivan-Springhetti thought that might be her ending, because she was waiting for the mother to "light some place" and "it was such a hopeless story in so many ways."

So how did Sullivan-Springhetti know she made the right choice of endings?

"It was the ending because the fact is it's such an active motherhood. So many suburban, urban, rural mothers everywhere: Anybody who has a child knows that life is driving. They shouldn't give you a bassinet or stroller when you have a baby. They should give you a car."

Sullivan-Springhetti also sensed the mother would never actually get off that road or out of that car.

"She was going to be doing that probably for all her life," she said. "For me it symbolized a lot of different things and I just knew it was just forever."

OTHER EXAMPLES OF ECHOES

Echoes can simply reintroduce the person who was the main character in the lead. This doesn't need elaboration. The mention can be just a flicker. But that's enough to bring the reader back to the start.

In this story that won the Pulitzer Prize in 2004 for explanatory journalism, Thomas M. Burton of *The Wall Street Journal* began the piece citing an incident involving a woman from Virginia.

> Jo-Anne Coe took every medical test recommended by doctors and was determined to stay healthy. At 69 years old, she was working as an aide to former Sen. Bob Dole while remodeling a Virginia farmhouse.
>
> But on Sept. 27, while shopping for kitchen cabinets, Ms. Coe felt an intense pain in her back and went to an emergency room. Unlike chest pain, back pain often isn't regarded as urgent, so she waited 90 minutes to see a doctor. After finding that blood was pouring into her body from a leaking aneurysm—a ballooned section of a blood vessel—alarmed doctors rushed her into surgery. During the operation, on her torn aorta, she died.
>
> The popular impression is that aneurysms are like lightning: striking rarely, suddenly and unpredictably. In fact, the most lethal aneurysms, those on the aorta, develop slowly, are often easy to diagnose with an inexpensive ultrasound test, and can usually be treated.

To end the long story, Burton introduces new information but briefly returns to Jo-Anne Coe to refer to the lead.

> A large new study is being organized in the U.S. by the medical schools of Dartmouth, the University of Pennsylvania and the University of Pittsburgh. Initially it will measure the prevalence of aneurysms; a later phase will check for a mortality benefit from screening.
>
> "There is reasonable emerging evidence suggesting that it's reasonable to screen men over 60" for abdominal aortic aneurysm, "particularly if they have a history of smoking, and anyone with a first-degree relative with an aneurysm," says Jack L. Cronenwett, a study organizer and chief of vascular surgery at Dartmouth. That would have included Ms. Coe in Virginia: Her mother, too, had an aortic aneurysm.

Marjie Lundstrom, a writing coach and reporter for *The Sacramento Bee*, says she likes to "bookend," meaning she looks at "how I started, and how I grabbed them. And I bring it back full circle. That works very well in a column and in news stories."

When she wrote a series with her husband, fellow *Sacramento Bee* reporter, Sam Stanton, endings became important. The series tells the random murder of a police officer and ran for five days. Each ending left the reader hanging each day, looking to the next day's story.

Their first story uses Lundstrom's bookend method. They led the series with this:

> He crouched in the shadows behind a metal bin, waiting to kill. He had passed on earlier targets—two uniformed sheriff's deputies who had stopped by the dimly lit gas station on the edge of Red Bluff to refuel their patrol car.
>
> But the man in the shadows had a plan.

Stanton and Lundstrom ended their story by referring to their lead and using the brief mention of a plan. The police investigating the shooting thought their suspect was traveling south, instead of north.

> They were looking in the wrong direction. The man they wanted was halfway to Oregon, and everything was going exactly to plan.

THE KICKER QUOTE

Despite their overuse, kicker quotes still can end a story well. Sometimes, kickers are the best endings. As their name implies, they can punch the last paragraph, leaving readers with a memorable jolt.

Don't confuse a kicker with just a routine quote. Journalists are in the habit of ending many stories, including breaking news, with quotes. A random look at a newspaper will show that often as many as two of every three stories end with a quote.

These aren't kickers, which require more planning and forethought. They are just quotes that come at the end of a story, long or short, breaking news or features.

Kickers let journalists restate—through a character—the story's point in a subtle way. The subject's own words lend credibility to the final conclusion.

But before using a kicker quote, consider:

- The pet peeve of *The Sacramento Bee*'s Lundstrom is writers who always end on a quote. "As a writing coach, I challenge people: Why am I abdicating the last word to someone else?"
- If the story covers a controversial subject, ending with a quote sometimes implies the journalist favors one side—the side of the person who had the last word.
- Tina Griego, a columnist for the *Rocky Mountain News*, says it's OK to use a kicker "if it's a punchy quote that sums it up." She sometimes ends her columns with kickers because the quote "says it better, and wraps it up better than anything I could say."
- Griego does not rely on quotes to end many of her news stories, takeouts or projects. "I'm the one telling the story. When my muse is with me, I know what the ending is. The ending is not someone else's voice. I'm telling someone else's story, but I'm still the narrator. I'm the one who is going to organize it, structure it and find the ending."

ADVANCED TIP
Don't Overuse Kicker Quotes

"I'm the one telling the story. When my muse is with me, I know what the ending is. The ending is not someone else's voice. I'm telling someone else's story, but I'm still the narrator. I'm the one who is going to organize it, structure it and find the ending."

—Tina Griego, *Rocky Mountain News*

SOME KICKERS THAT WORK

Despite the caution from writing teachers and seasoned journalists, a quote at the end of a story can display remarkable power. That's why journalists use them so much.

In this story, Laura M. Holson of *The New York Times* writes about the failing of a new Hollywood studio. She begins:

> For more than a year, Joe Roth has been hearing the Hollywood gossips predict the demise of his six-year-old movie studio, Revolution Studios. Now that they are right, he wants to set the record straight.

Holson ends with a nod to the beginning, but finds a quote that says her point poignantly.

> Last week, as Mr. Roth mulled his new venture at Sony, he was introspective. He talked about the movies that he had made that other studios would not. "I love orphans," he said. One of those is "Rocky Balboa," the sixth film in a 30-year-old franchise, which is to be released in the fall. In it, a 59-year-old Sylvester Stallone stars as a boxer past his prime who returns to the ring for one last shot at being the champ.
>
> "This is our story," Mr. Roth said he told a friend. "Everyone is entitled to a third act."

This ending plays on the notion in drama that stories conclude, or reach their dramatic tension, in the third act. The ending paints Roth's hope that he will rebound. Had the reporter written in her own words what she quoted Roth as saying, the ending would have seemed contrived or, some could argue, biased. Though it's a cliché, that Roth believes in the hope of a third act makes the words read fresh.

In *The Wall Street Journal*, Philip Shishkin wrote a story from Baghdad about a doctor who ran a hospital and made his staffers sign an agreement that the hospital was not responsible should the staffers be "kidnapped, injured or killed." A protest broke out, but most signed. The life of the doctor, Mr. Mustafa, hadn't been the same. Shishkin ends the story with this quote:

> Since that day, the local police have no particular affection for Mr. Mustafa and his staff. When the clinic managers asked the police to beef up security around the hospital, the cops turned a deaf ear, Mr. Mustafa says.
>
> Meanwhile, he has grown so tense from all the stress that he now sleeps with two automatic weapons, a pistol, two flashlights and a hammer next to his bed. "I'm so paranoid that whenever I hear a noise at night, I pick up a gun," he says.

Just like the earlier quote, the last sentence would grow less potent without the subject's emotional investment. Quoting Mustafa gives the ending more punch than if the reporter had written the same words.

In a *USA Today* story on immigration, an Arizona sheriff dealing with the illegal immigrants who stream across the national border and into his county criticized the government's efforts. The story ends quoting the sheriff, Larry Dever.

Talent Showcase

BARRY SIEGEL ▸

former *Los Angeles Times* reporter

All writers approach their story endings differently. Some know from the start where they will wind up. Some write their ending first, then circle back to start their lead. Still others just start writing knowing they eventually will reach a logical stop.

Barry Siegel, a former *Los Angeles Times* reporter, who won a Pulitzer Prize for feature writing in 2002, counts himself among those who need to see their destinations before they start.

"I certainly would like to know where I'm going," Siegel says. "I would probably put myself in the camp of saying that I do kind of want to have an idea of a narrative arc and direction I'm going in.

"It doesn't always mean that by the time I get there that my original plan is going to stay in place. Because you discover sometimes what your story is about while you're writing it."

Siegel spent several years as the national correspondent for the *Los Angeles Times*. He now teaches students at the University of California–Irvine how to write narrative journalism. Endings are an important part of those stories, if sometimes elusive to define.

"But what the ending is, and this is what I keep trying to emphasize to the students so much, that ending does not always have to be a major climactic event," says Spiegel, who directs the university's literary journalism program. "The guns don't have to go off. Somebody doesn't have to fall over dead. Or somebody doesn't have to break the net at the finish line, either.

"It can be much more subtle than that. It can be a point of insight. An epiphany. An acceptance of something."

Siegel follows his own advice. To end his story that won the Pulitzer, Siegel set his sights on the judicial relationship between two men: a judge and a man accused of causing his son's unintentional death. The judge, Robert Hilder, struggled throughout the story with how he should punish the man, Paul Wayment. Wayment's son, Gage, was 2 and wandered into the woods while his father thought he was sleeping in their truck. Hilder decided to sentence Wayment to 30 days. The day before he was to begin his sentence, Wayment committed suicide.

The reason? The story began quoting Dever, who opposes letting the 12 million illegal immigrants have a free pass. His quote says with emotion what the neutral writer should not say.

> As for recent immigrant rallies in the USA, the sheriff grinds his teeth. "That just makes my blood boil. Can you imagine 100,000 or 10,000 of us . . . marching down there?"

BEING CAREFUL, FAIR

Many journalists avoid ending with kickers from a sense of fairness. The reporters don't want to appear that they favor a side on a controversial story.

This is how Siegel chose to end the story:

Soon enough, there came an even greater wave of support for Hilder from lawyers, pundits, hundreds of citizens and—over and over—Wayment's sister, Valerie Burke. "I don't believe the 30-day sentence caused Paul to kill himself," she told reporters. "I think the judge was compassionate. Our family understands where the judge was coming from, and we don't blame him at all. He had to do what he felt was right."

Hilder can only shake his head at that phrase, "what he felt was right." He takes comfort from all the support but is no more certain now than before of making correct decisions. This latest experience, above all, has made him look even harder at the role of the judge.

He reflects on what the law accomplishes, what the law can't accomplish. He loves the law but does not worship it. He believes it does not have the answer to everything. In matters full of ambiguity, he suggests, there may be no good solution. "Black and white answers are not always what's needed," he says. "But sometimes they're the only answer."

He says something else as well: "It's not a bad thing to have Paul Wayment's face forever part of my life."

During his reporting, Siegel learned much that he had to leave out. To keep the story sharp and readable, he kept the rope of dramatic tension pulled tight between his two principals. As he approached his end, he slowed his pace, and eased the tension.

"I didn't want any high drama or high speed. What I was getting at really was a moment of I don't know if it's epiphany but of acceptance, a recognition by Judge Hilder.

"The structure of the story that finally came to me was really the story of Judge Hilder watching this case come towards him, watching it come towards him knowing that he was going to have to make a decision and decide about it. And this giving him the occasion, and us the occasion, to visit as he meditates on all the things that bother him: his own doubts about being a judge, about making black-and-white decisions in shades-of-gray world, his doubts about the Mormon church, which is also a black-and-white, yes-or-no thing. His doubts about God.

"And here he was knowing he was going to have to make a black-and-white, yes-or-no decision in a shade area. And it's not just this case that made him full of questions about that, but it sure highlighted it.

"That's where I was trying to drive at the end."

"Usually the quote is a point of view," *The Sacramento Bee*'s Lundstrom says. "You end up tipping the story. You're letting someone summarize your story. And you're inclined to conclude with someone you agree with. So you may be tipping the story in a biased fashion."

That is especially true when reporting on political races or contested public policies. Ending with a quote leaves the journalist open to criticism, the *Rocky Mountain News*' Griego says.

"If writing a story about a political campaign, or an adversarial relationship, the person who gets the last word—especially if it's the last paragraph—it's an implied favor," she says.

Once, she wrote about a controversy in a Denver suburb. But one side refused to talk to her.

Former *Los Angeles Times* reporter Barry Siegel won the Pulitzer prize for his sensitive story on Utah judge Robert Hilder. The judge struggled to find a fair sentence for a man who briefly left his son sleeping in his truck. The son woke up, wandered in the woods and later died from exposure.

"There was a family who didn't like kids riding bikes in the street, playing street hockey—the things that kids do. So they started calling police, citing an ordinance about blocking traffic."

But the story's adversarial nature sent up red flags. She knew she had to take great care to present a fair discussion. Griego had to use court documents and police reports to balance the story. She quoted from the documents.

"That was the only place I could get their voice. I was very conscious about getting their side. And very conscious that I wasn't going to end the story with a quote from one side," she says.

WRAP-UP SCENE

Journalists' stories often take them to emotional scenes. They see their subjects in situations that evoke a range of feelings, whether the joy of athletes winning titles or the sadness of parents burying their children.

Ending stories with these scenes lets readers experience the same emotions. The journalist refrains from passing judgment, but simply describes the action and puts the reader in the jury box. The result can be surprising and powerful.

Anthony Shadid, a *Washington Post* writer, reported on deadline during the first week of the Iraq war. His Pulitzer Prize-winning stories for international reporting told of the war's early days when Iraqis watched Saddam Hussein's rule crumble. But they also had to wait for American-led soldiers to capture Baghdad.

Shadid spent an afternoon with a family. They spoke openly that they hoped Americans would free them. But then they heard the sound of airplanes and knew that more bombs would fall. They were on edge. The smallest sound made them jump. Shadid ended his story this way:

> Outside, the sounds of ordinary life came from the street. A cart passed the house, its horn blowing. It had come to collect trash and refill kerosene tanks for cooking. As the cart passed, the routine it evoked seemed to anger the son.
>
> "I should be able to live like other people are living," he said glumly. "I shouldn't fear bombs falling on my head, I shouldn't be hearing sirens. Why should I have to like this? Why should this be normal?"
>
> Everyone looked to the floor, no one saying a word.

The ending tells the reader that the family is frustrated and afraid but no one has the answer to the son's piercing questions. From the family's reaction—looking to the floor, saying nothing—it's obvious that they are asking themselves the same question.

Hayes, the *Philadelphia Daily News* sports writer, wrote a story about the boxing condition known as *dementia pugilistica*, commonly called punch drunk. His story, which was honored by *The Associated Press* sports editors, told of boxers who clearly were struggling with slurred speech and lost trains of thought.

Hayes focused on Jimmy Young, a Philadelphia native who once was a heavyweight title contender. But several years later, when Hayes found him again in north Philadelphia, Young was showing signs that he had taken too many hits to his head.

This is how Hayes began the piece:

> You have heard Jimmy Young is punch-drunk, but you don't want to believe it.
>
> And Jimmy Young looks good from a distance. He emerges from his home on Seybert Street with a wide smile. He walks erect, head high, with the rhythmic bounce of an athlete. He's maybe a tiny bit pot-bellied, but appears in remarkably good shape for a 47-year-old former heavyweight contender.
>
> He looks worse as he gets closer.
>
> He wears no socks in his filthy sneakers. A tattered shirt covers a ratty undershirt. Blue work pants sag under the belly. They are stained with grease and dirt. The pants are unzipped.
>
> And just when you think the picture can get no worse, he speaks.
>
> "I'm, you know, damn, thinking I could come back," Young says with a slur. "I think I can do it. I was lying there thinking, this morning, I swear I could do it. Hey, uh, what time is it?'"
>
> It's 8:30.
>
> "I gotta work at 9:30.
>
> "You know," he continues, smiling slyly, "we all think we can do it. Come back.
>
> "My birthday was Tuesday," he interjects, proud, like a child. "I turned a 4. And a 7. Hey, man, what time is it?"
>
> It's 8:32.
>
> "You know, I gotta work at, ah, 9:30."

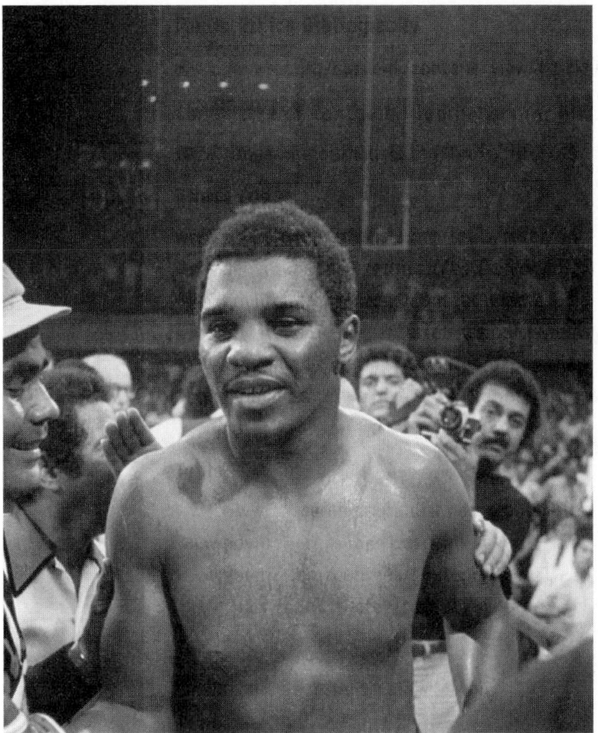

Jimmy Young, once a heavyweight contender, was suffering from dementia pugilistica, or punch drunk, when *Philadelphia Daily News* sportswriter Marcus Hayes interviewed him. Hayes' story comes to an uncomfortable climax, sympathetic to Young's plight, but an honest appraisal of his condition.

Hayes' story showed boxers, some as young as 30, who speak in halting slurs. Many lose their focus in conversation. He returned to Young at the story's end. Notice how he closes by referring briefly to the lead, but with a memorable nod to Young's life at that time.

> And sometimes, boxers can't even count on loved ones to keep them from tragedy.
>
> Jimmy Young's mother, Ruth Harris, denies to this day that anything is wrong with her son.
>
> But his wife, Barbara, says she noticed Jimmy slipping 25 years ago. She heard the slurred speech. For a while, she endured the mood swings he still exhibits—from gaiety to sadness to indignation.
>
> But Barbara, who works at Temple University Hospital as a medical technician, didn't encourage Jimmy to quit. She doesn't regret her silence.
>
> "Boxing was something he loved," Barbara says. "It was part of him. That would have been robbing him of his dreams."
>
> And so today, Jimmy Young walks the streets of North Philly, wondering what time it is, dreaming his dreams.

Hayes says he prefers this ending because "it reflected what Jimmy's day was: clouded, deluded, in contrast to those, like Barbara, who let him slip away like that."

Hayes' ending also leaves the reader with a strong emotion connected to Young's life, and a strong notion that he will continue to grow worse.

IN CONCLUSION

Though journalists might not discuss endings as much as leads, all writers should add purposeful endings to their repertoire. They leave readers with an impression. The best endings wrap up by underscoring the story's main point. Writers can use many devices: echoes, kickers, scenes. But they should avoid ending their stories just because they have used up all their space.

All stories end, but the best stories have endings.

EXERCISE 1

Go to a website, newspaper or magazine and select several stories.

Answer the following questions:

1. How do these stories end?
2. Do these stories have endings that the author wrote with a purpose, or do you sense the author just stopped writing?
3. Pick one story that has a purposed ending. What are its characteristics? Does it end with the reader feeling satisfied?
4. Pick a story without a purposed ending. How could you write an ending that would improve this story?

EXERCISE 2

Here are samples of leads. Read them and identify elements in the leads that could be used later when the writer is ready to end the story:

1. Casper Ellington sat on the hard turf at Manlius Stadium. He and his Manlius Wildcats had just lost the state championship. Ellington himself had fumbled in the closing minute just as the Wildcats were about to score and tie the game. Ellington's head was bowed. His hands held his helmet.

   "I know I should feel bad, but the sun will rise tomorrow," he said quietly. "I just hope that I look back on this in 20 years and be pleased with my behavior."
2. The wind blew wicked through the canyons of downtown Flanners on Saturday, tossing the balloons at the annual St. Patrick's Day parade against buildings and into the crowds.

   But despite the gusts of nearly 50 mph, the parade went on. Gaelic dancers pranced down Congress Avenue. Children dressed in green cheered from the sidewalks. And green beer was offered to all those old enough to drink.

   "It's just a gentle breeze," shouted Patrick Kearn, the parade's grand marshal. "Soon no one will feel it."
3. "He's upstairs on the roof," a worker told a visitor, pointing to the top of the church. And sure enough, there stood Charles Billings, former heavyweight champion turned Southern Baptist preacher, hands on his hips, 50 pounds more than his last title fight, and a smile that would melt the heart of any sinner.

   "If you come here," he told the visitor, "you can see all of downtown Houston, and be closer to the Lord."

CHAPTER 18

Writing and Reporting Online

IN THIS CHAPTER, YOU WILL LEARN:

- Writing for the Web and for newspapers is similar.
- Reporting for the Web has deadlines reminiscent of wire services.
- A big difference with Web presentations is thinking visually.
- Daily news websites show off their talent when news is breaking.
- Web editors encourage budding reporters to master traditional journalistic values.

The web can accommodate a level of detail that the newspaper can't.
Jim Amoss, editor,
The Times-Picayune

MARY FLOOD STARTED IN JOURNALISM when Jimmy Carter was president, chasing police stories, sitting through trials, covering natural disasters—her editors found it amusing that when rivers overflowed they sent a reporter named "Flood."

She later earned a law degree from Harvard, and practiced in Washington, D.C. She returned to journalism to cover courts for the *Houston Chronicle*, eventually writing about one of the most scandalous corporate collapses in American history: the giant utility Enron.

Yet when Flood covered the last of the Enron trials—where a jury found CEO Kenneth Lay guilty—she says she learned something new about journalism.

Flood realized fully the depth, power and pitfalls of reporting online.

Because Enron's headquarters were in Houston, Lay's trial gripped the Houston area. *Chronicle* editors assigned a reporter to write a blog updated throughout the day. Flood often contributed, meeting with the paper's team of reporters during breaks. She did morning interviews for National Public Radio and evening interviews for a sister Houston television station. Mostly on the weekends, she answered questions online about the trial that readers sent through the *Chronicle*'s website.

She also wrote a daily trial story for the newspaper's print version. But even that was different. Working the story through so many media platforms—especially the Internet—improved her print story: It was more in-depth, more analytical, more complete, she says.

"I think we just changed journalism," she says. "I'm not sure anybody noticed. . . . My dailies were these hybrids. When I would sit down—I've been doing this for a long time—I could tell the difference. I wasn't writing a wire news story. I wasn't writing a feature. I wasn't writing an analysis.

"I was writing all three because we put so much on the blog."

Flood also saw errors. Often reporters were working too fast, and they reported wrong information in their blogs. These mistakes ran on major newspapers' Websites.

What Flood discovered—the power and depth of the Web—has been known to many who work on websites for daily news organizations. They understand the Web gives them more tools to tell a story:

- No longer confined to text and photos appearing once a day, journalists use video, audio, text, photo galleries and links to related stories to give readers and viewers a depth of information and knowledge never before available.
- Journalists now update as often as the story demands, no longer forced to wait until the next news cycle, press deadline or broadcast. Updates can be microscopic or monumental, depending on the new information, but all are instantaneous.
- Websites post information from readers who have extensive knowledge of a subject or who have arrived first at a breaking news scene.
- They prompt feedback from the community they cover, setting up cyber conversations between journalists and residents or simply among residents themselves.

- They link to other websites that give readers information as critical as how to survive natural disasters or as routine as how to contact public officials to voice opinions.
- They store full texts of speeches, policies, reports or statistics. Especially for investigative pieces, readers peruse these details at their own pace and according to interests.
- They provide vast photo galleries of both breaking news and regular features. Editors and photographers used to make sometimes painful decisions about which photograph they should run to illustrate a story. They now offer readers all the out takes they consider worthy.
- Video and live camera shots show critical moments of a story.

Like Flood, editors and reporters at newspapers, television stations, radio networks and websites are seeing the rules of daily journalism rewritten faster than veterans have ever experienced. Speed, always a virtue, now is a prerequisite.

Though exciting, the pace of change has caused some to worry about traditional journalistic values: accuracy, honesty, fairness, balance, error-free reporting. They worry these hallmarks of journalism will be lost amid the seduction of the 24-hour news cycle, the ability to measure precisely a story's popularity, the sassy writing style of blogs.

What does this mean for the journalists of tomorrow? Will they be required to shoot video, do stand-ups, update constantly and write in-depth analyses—all on the same story and in one day? Will they change the definition of news to what's hot rather than what's important? And will the delivery system of the Internet so alter the content that the valuable job of journalists asking tough questions for society's benefit fade into a cyber black hole?

LIKE A WIRE SERVICE

Vlae Kershner worked at newspapers up and down the West Coast before settling at the *San Francisco Chronicle*. He now runs his paper's Web operation. He and his coworkers update constantly as news rolls in from both nearby and around the world.

He uses a familiar phrase to describe the fast pace and the constant updates.

"Obviously working for the Web is a lot like working for an old-fashioned p.m. or like for a wire service," he says. ". . . Speed is the primary consideration so you don't wait until you have the full story. You just, you know, write it and put it up."

Those who share Kershner's title at other daily news sites websites also share his assessment of how new journalists will contribute to the Web. Those in charge say reporting and writing a story as fast as possible define the product. Updating constantly keeps the website fresh and makes it essential for viewers.

The hourly drumbeat for more information and newer stories marks the chief difference between working for the Web and working for newspapers, says Mark Micheli, the news editor for boston.com, the online version of *The Boston Globe*.

"Reporting online is different than reporting for a newspaper because you are constantly under deadline," he says. "A newspaper has one deadline each day or maybe as many as four, depending on how many editions they put out.

"But online we're updating and publishing constantly to bring readers the latest news. News is often written on the fly—similar to wire services that are constantly filing updates to stories."

Working for the Web and the wire services such as *The Associated Press* requires a disciplined approach to both reporting and writing. Breaking news in wire stories usually is written in an inverted-pyramid style. That means, of course, that the most important news content is in the first paragraph and answers the basic questions of who, what, when, where, why and how.

Reporters for *The Associated Press* carry the reputation for accuracy. They write quickly, and file breaking news stories for the wire service throughout the day. But they don't let speed hurt their reporting. Being right beats being fast.

In much the same way, Web reporters must file stories quickly but never sacrifice accuracy for haste. It's better to be correct and a bit late than post incorrect and sometimes embarrassing stories.

Writing for the Web also requires brevity. Stories are shorter than what appears in newspapers or on television. They get to the core quickly. Don't look for that to change soon, says Charles M. Madigan, a columnist, senior editor and senior writer for the *Chicago Tribune* and former editor of the paper's website.

"It's very much the same as working for a wire service," he says. ". . . The objective was to feed the wire, make the stories move all the time, keep them pithy and tight, inverted pyramids and things like that and stay away from expanded anything.

"And that's a hard message to deliver, but anybody who comes into the Internet, into Internet news thinking that they're going to write long tome poems explaining the varieties of life is setting in the wrong direction."

THINK WITH VISUALS

The Web promises a dizzying array of ways to tell a story. Text is important, says Jim Brady, the executive editor for *The Washington Post's* website, washingtonpost.com. But so are sight and sound and movement.

In a traditional newspaper, the reporter has words, graphics and photos. On the Web, a reporter writing about a new singer could write a story, videotape a performance, have audio of the singer, link to an mp3 download, run part of the interview that appears in print. Editors and reporters are freed from the limits of the printing press.

"The big difference between newspapers and the Web is not the writing. . . . I think the big difference is the varieties of storytelling devices at your disposal," he says.

Once, a *Post* reporter in Baghdad was embedded with troops on patrol when they came under fire. He had a video camera and shot several minutes of footage. He also wrote a story. Brady says the words were less compelling than the video.

The Art of Storytelling

Just nine months out of graduate school and into her first job in journalism, Barbra Hernandez was taught how to use a video camera.

Here, her editors at the *Ocala Star-Banner* in Florida told her, you now have a new way of telling stories to our readers. The publisher had told the staff "eventually we would end up carrying our own video cameras. We would shoot our own video and we would produce our own online, video content," she said.

Despite earning a master's degree from a top journalism school, Hernandez joined reporters at newspapers and television newsrooms across the country who are learning a new lesson: in the digital age, there's more than one way to tell your audience the news.

Once confined to mere text, print journalists can thank the Web for letting them step into a new era. Journalists now use video, sound, still photography, podcasts as well as text. They produce slide shows. They narrate. They let subjects in their stories do their own narration. They run video of subjects telling their stories.

In short, using the Web opens the door for journalists to tell stories in many forms through many media.

Look no further than *The Washington Post* for innovation. A few years ago, the newspaper examined the role of black men at the 50th anniversary of the seminal work, *The Invisible Man.*

The newspaper wrote traditional stories explaining the issues. But its website, washingtonpost.com, offered video narratives of what it meant to be black and male in America. Hearing and seeing the subjects were compelling pieces of the story. The paper ran photo galleries, released a poll and received a host of reader submissions, said Jim Brady, the website's executive editor.

The series, "Being a Black Man," was "very well received," Brady said. It attracted millions of page views during the year and won a Peabody Award, the most prestigious honor in broadcasting. The series also won two Emmys.

Leonard Downie, executive editor of *The Washington Post*, told the *Columbia Journalism Review* that he and others in the newsroom at one time "worried about the competition from the Web, and its effect on the journalism. We were wrong. The Web is not the distraction we feared it would be, and all the feedback improves the journalism."

Some reporters who work for companies that own television stations, newspapers and websites file stories for television, newspapers and the Web. They work on one story but tell it three ways, depending on the platform.

Reporters in Lawrence, Kan., for years have worked in multiple media. The World Co. owns the newspaper, the *Journal-World*, the cable system, Sunflower Broadband, several weekly papers between Lawrence and Kansas City and a television station in Topeka. The company, taking advantage of its shared properties, was one of the first to combine broadcast, print and online storytelling.

Often, reporters for the newspaper and cable news program will jump to other platforms to deliver different versions of the same story, usually on the same day. Awkward at first, those who work in Lawrence now say that's just part of the job.

Yet at the core of the journalism lies the ability of reporters to tell a story. How they deliver the story, and which method they choose, takes a back seat to knowing what intrigues readers, visitors or viewers.

Pulitzer Prize-winning reporter Tom Hallman of *The* (Portland) *Oregonian* argues that point in an essay for *The Quill* magazine, published by the Society of Professional Journalists. Yes, new reporters will be asked to learn other methods of journalism. Knowing their way around multimedia will even help them land their first job.

But they still must be able to identify why a story is worth telling.

"The word 'narrative' can be tossed around so casually that the meaning can be diluted," Hallman writes. "Reporters say they want to write 'narrative' but upon questioning can't explain what that means. Narrative isn't a label slapped on a standard feature that simply opens with a scene-setting lead.

"A story takes readers on a journey. The mysteries, questions and answers are revealed throughout that journey. Putting it together requires in-depth thinking at each stage of the process: reporting, structuring and writing. The story doesn't rise and fall on the writing, although that's obviously important, but with the thought behind the story."

Once journalists understand their core points, they can then pick the best platform or platforms for telling their stories. Is it text only? A photo gallery? A slide show with narration? A video with many parts? An interactive component? Or the obvious: a combination of some or all, depending on the narrative.

For storytellers, the Web offers new tablets upon which they can scrawl.

Figure 18.1 **Yahoo News Is the 2006 Online Traffic Winner**

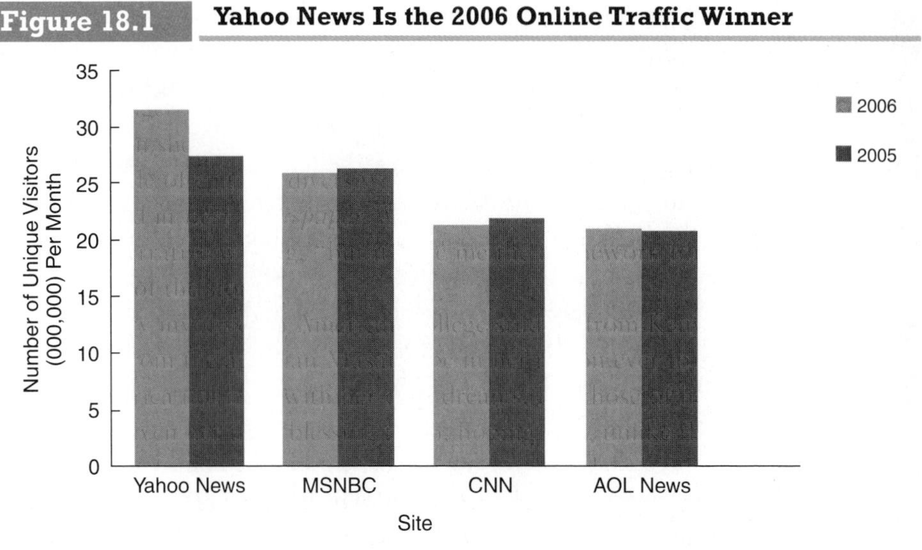

Source: (Statistics) Year-end report from comScore Media Metrix, http://www.journalism.org/node/3737.

"If you had to choose one of the two ways to experience the story, there would be no contest," he says.

The video wins every time.

At boston.com, the staff covered a story about a girl who had a brain tumor removed when she was 6. Doctors gave her perhaps six months to live. Fourteen years later, she entered Harvard University as a freshman, majoring in math.

Defying traditional storytelling techniques, boston.com staffers and *Boston Globe* reporters put together three slide shows, narrated by a reporter but with sound bites from the woman, her parents, her doctors. Each ran between five and six minutes, the last showing her friendship with the country music singer, Garth Brooks.

"Boston.com and others are trying to push the boundaries of online storytelling by creating content specifically for the Web," says Micheli, the site's news editor. "This content takes advantage of what the online medium offers, keeping in mind users' habits and preferences. The Web is a much more visual medium than print. It also has no limit in the amount of information it can present. And the Web also allows the reader to participate or interact with the content."

BREAKING NEWS

If any traditional journalist wondered whether the Web would ever grow into an essential reporting tool, Hurricane Katrina removed that doubt. The storm that

Louisiana Gov. Kathleen Blanco speaks to reporters at a service held a month after Hurricane Katrina flooded New Orleans and devastated the Mississippi coast. The newspapers—*The Times-Picayune* in New Orleans and the Biloxi *Sun Herald* both won Pulitzer Prizes for their reporting in the days following the storm. *The Times-Picayune* relied especially on its website to publish stories vital to the New Orleans area.

flooded New Orleans and ruined blocks of homes also revealed that readers would go to the Web for information.

The (New Orleans) *Times-Picayune* and the *Sun Herald* both won Pulitzer Prizes for their coverage. Each relied on the Web when their presses were shackled by the hurricane's aftermath.

"There wouldn't have been a trip to Columbia [University] to collect the Pulitzer if Nola hadn't been there," says Jon Donley, editor of nola.com.

Those two papers weren't the only ones that saw their website traffic increase. In Chicago for instance, those seeking more information flocked to the *Chicago Tribune*'s website. Despite being thousands of miles away, tribune.com posted photo galleries and ran personal accounts from *Tribune* reporters. Editors produced two special sections of Katrina coverage.

Web editors have discovered that nothing shows off the Internet's talents like breaking news. Editors not only can update immediately but also are not limited by their own staff's reporting. They can use information, photographs, first-person accounts and dialogue from residents.

At sfgate.com in San Francisco, editors put this in practice once when a mudslide hit the area.

"You can get, you know, just the combination of instant stories, photos, videos and even having a blog and having readers submit photos or say what's going on in their area," the *Chronicle*'s Kershner says. "It can really work well on something like that, just as you saw with the Katrina thing. The information can really come from the reader base where it couldn't really before."

Using what's known as user-generated content marks a vast departure from most newsrooms, which pride themselves on doing their own reporting. Many editors still feel uncomfortable using content not vetted by their staff. However, the Internet lets photos shot by readers and information they know become part of the presentation.

"We sort of have a three-concentric-ring theory, which we really haven't executed," Kershner says. "The center ring is our own staff, sort of the authoritative voice. The second ring is sort of like affiliates, you know, other wire content, other content. And then the final ring is like the citizen community."

For major stories such as the mudslide, all three rings would be in play.

Longer stories are seeking a home on the Web. Editors still insist on shorter reads. But long stories still can work, the *Chicago Tribune*'s Madigan says.

Talent Showcase

JIM AMOSS ▸

Editor, *The Times-Picayune*

WHAT NEW ORLEANS LEARNED FROM THE WEB

When the waters of Hurricane Katrina washed over the levees and into New Orleans, *The Times-Picayune* witnessed its own sea change. Its press shut down, and editors were forced to rely on its website to inform the community.

Now that, according to nola.com editor Jon Donley, "*The Times-Picayune* is the poster child for what could happen," the lessons are flowing nearly as rapidly as the flood waters:

The Community Depends More on www.nola.com

After the initial spike in page views, traffic has settled at about twice the pre-Katrina levels. The website is profitable for the first time.

The Community Depends More on *The Times-Picayune*

Even before Katrina, the printed *Times-Picayune* reached the highest percentage of homes in its market of all major city newspapers in America. But its post-storm coverage, still the No. 1 story in town a year later, has earned it unaccustomed endearment. Citizens recognize their dependency more than ever.

"The interest from readers is just astounding," Jim Amoss, *The Times-Picayune* editor, said in an interview with the Dart Center for Journalism & Trauma eight months after Katrina. "Not a day goes by that we don't get flooded with e-mails. Or just running into people we don't know, who when they learn we're from *The Times-Picayune*, they just can't stop talking about how much the paper has meant to them, how intensely they're interested in it. Many times they will also say, 'You know, I really didn't like you all that much before, but now it's my vital link to this community.' "

Journalists and the Community Are Embracing www.nola.com as Their Communication Tool

Donley ticks off the ways *Times-Picayune* print journalists are experimenting with the Web: "The entertainment editor has recorded his first weekly column, "Hot Picks." Tomorrow he will post it as his very first podcast. The photo department has just discovered flash multimedia slide shows. Cooperation has not dropped off at all since Katrina.

Meanwhile, Donley is nola.com's evangelist in the community. "We'll start with trusted bloggers. We're holding Journalism 101 classes for people in the community. I've been teaching copy editors coming out of universities who don't know a thing. And I'm targeting pastors personally, to evangelize them."

"The *Tribune* had a series that it did a while ago on heroin use in the suburbs. And that's like Katie-bar-the-doors as far as readership interest is concerned. Heroin, suburbs, that's all you need to hear about that. That was very heavily read on the Internet even though it was a long, long piece.

"But that's rare. Most long foreign exposés, most long foreign news stories, most long national news stories, most long political stories don't get much viewership on the Internet."

The Website Is Exploring New Journalistic Techniques

After the water had receded, nola.com featured an interactive, animated graphic that shows how New Orleans flooded. Click on any area of the city, or click on "Start" and watch the flow of water, while reading a text description of the sequence and the effect. "The effect is 'Ah, that's how it happened,' " Donley explained.

As this book was going to press, Amoss told the authors that he was looking forward to allowing online readers to customize their use of other graphics.

"Right now we're putting together this mega-graphic that seeks to delineate how New Orleans residents are returning and where they are settling," Amoss said.

Flooding patterns shown in the graphic will help readers decide whether to locate in a place that flooded first or that had 12 feet of water.

"Or it can tell you things about how your block is being settled," Amoss added. "It will show the electrical permits by block. You may have a pressing concern: 'I'm thinking of staying or not staying. I'd like to know if I'm the only person on my block who is going to renovate and I'll be in this semi-blighted area.' "

Amoss envisions this guiding public policy as well. "You can juxtapose the depth of water at which a neighborhood flooded with the number of building permits."

That would inform public officials and help prioritize their efforts.

The Horizon of Journalism's Future Seems Nearer

"We can combine the unlimited space of the website and the assets of the newspaper—the resources to deploy reporters with the knowledge of our back yard that only newspapers have," Amoss said. "The Web can accommodate a level of detail that the newspaper can't. We can give people information about their own back yards. We can serve more people with the lowest tier of information that you can possibly provide."

The website "is going to become second nature to a huge number of people for their daily news needs," Amoss forecasted. "At the same time, though, it's going to drive people into the arms of newspapers—maybe not print editions of newspapers. For our readers, it's opened a lot of people's eyes about what they can get from the newspaper through this medium.

"For our newsroom, it's opened our eyes in the ways it can be a medium for what we do and enhance what we do, as opposed to regarding it as a looming monster that we have to be wary of."

On that last score, nola.com's role in Katrina "has brought about a cultural change in our newsroom that no amount of sermonizing on my part could have produced," Amoss said.

In turn, nola.com has become more news-oriented.

Donley estimates that *The Times-Picayune*'s dependence on nola.com during and after Katrina "probably took three to five years off the process" of developing the Web's news potential in New Orleans. "And you know how long that is on the Internet."

In turn, he suspects that *The Times-Picayune*—and newspapers everywhere—can recapture some of their past.

"For a long time, newspapers have been the soul of a community, the social center of the community. With the Internet, we have a chance to capture that part of the community that is slipping away from newspapers."

WHAT ABOUT VOICE?

Traditionally, journalists learned to write with a neutral voice. Not that editors haven't encouraged writers to experiment with words, but daily journalists chiefly have adopted a muted tone when writing news. That gives their writing the credibility of presenting factual information. It also lets them write with an understated authority.

But to some on the Web, neutrality and nuance translate to boring. Bloggers with attitude attract visitors. The style is freer, looser. That sends shivers through many traditionalists who have spent their careers writing stories that take great pains to avoid bias and sass.

Brady, the executive editor of washingtonpost.com, believes those are big differences between writing for the Web and for traditional newspapers: voice and opinion.

"In terms of blogs and alternative media, voice is becoming something readers like. That's a difficult thing for journalists."

Brady says the question swirling in newsrooms is how to give voice to a story on the Web without conflicting with a prime core value of journalism: delivering news fairly, with no bias.

"How do you walk that line?" Brady asks.

Voice is still the big issue, not so much for columnists but for reporters. Readers like voice. Brady's website features a blog from the bureau that covers Fairfax County. It's updated but not with any style.

"Part of the reason it doesn't have a lot of volume" he says is the lack of voice. "That's a case where a little more voice would be nice."

He doesn't advocate injecting opinion into stories. He never wants to lose journalistic integrity and overwhelm the journalism with bias. But he does want more personality for his Web product.

"That's the line we're all trying to figure out: voice vs. opinion," he says.

Editors and reporters at *The Washington Post* are still debating the point. They are not alone. Newsrooms throughout the country have accepted blogs as part of their Web product. But many quickly point out the differences to readers: blogs based in opinion are obvious.

Madigan compares blogs to pamphlets in the 19th century. Writers could express any opinion as long as they had the money to print and circulate their work.

"The thing now is that it doesn't cost any money," he says. "You can get it circulated instantaneously all over the place. But that's led to a culture in which people think the important thing is being able to gas on stuff. And there's a place for that. I mean gassing on is hilarious and great fun. I love it just as much as anybody else, but I don't make this mistake of thinking that it's news. It's just talk."

Madigan fears blogging will smother stories difficult to read but important to society. He sees those stories being "devalued on grounds that what people want to read, basically what you hear on talk radio, you know, people screaming at each other except they're typing."

Still, as a journalist, Madigan believes in free expression. The Internet and blogs are great for that. The difference between opinion and journalism should follow the same separation of church and state.

"This is a wonderful medium for expression and I've always believed that in this culture, you're better if you talk about something than if you sit there and stew. So that part's good. If it invites you to participate, then that's good, too.

"But the distinction between opinion and news has to be maintained somehow," he says.

ADVANCED TIPS

Top Newspaper Websites (unique visitors in millions) as of November 2006.

1. *The New York Times* (13.2)
2. The *Washington Post* (10.6)
3. *USA Today* (10.3)
4. *The Wall Street Journal* (6.3)
5. *Los Angeles Times* (4.5)
6. *The Boston Globe* (3.7)
7. *San Francisco Chronicle* (3.5)
8. *Seattle Post-Intelligencer* (3.2)
9. *Chicago Tribune* (2.9)
10. *New York Post* (2.7)

Source: Newspaper Association of America.

Some bloggers do original reporting, rather than read what others have written and then turn around their own blogs. Those should be commended, says the *Houston Chronicle*'s Flood. Journalism is reporting, and then putting that information in a digestible form.

"I think it's going to be an easy way to think you're a journalist just like all sorts of people who read what's in the newspaper, write their opinion about it and think they're competing with us," Flood says. "I mean I've had bloggers who don't do any original reporting, don't care whether it's accurate, are just putting their opinion out, think they're doing journalism. I think there's something really dangerous there."

DRIVEN BY NUMBERS

Reporters historically find themselves ranked next to politicians in popularity polls. Those who go into the business gradually come to accept that often their publication will print a highly unpopular story.

When *The New York Times* decided to run a story about the United States government tracking the movements of terrorists by monitoring their banking, some conservative pundits questioned *The Times*' loyalty and patriotism. A conservative talk show host in California actually said *The Times* editor, Bill Keller, should be executed for treason.

Although that example is severe, newspapers across the country routinely irk politicians and those in power with stories they print. They print them anyway.

The Web offers measurements of who has visited the page and read the stories. That's now a powerful tool for marketers. Should editors begin making decisions based on a story's popularity, that also could be a dangerous precedent.

"One of the mythologies is that the Internet is boundless and endless as far as the amount of space that it contains," says the *Chicago Tribune*'s Madigan. "And that's technically true. But it's also the most severely market-driven of all the media. And what that means is that it creates itself anew every day based on the metrics of use on the part of the people who are actually making the page use. And that's a huge difference in what happens in the Internet and what happens in the newspaper."

Does that mean that stories will go soft because readers find them easier and more fun to read?

"If you believe in the historic importance of what journalists do—we've never been liked, it's not a question of being liked—but it's like what is your role in a free society in informing people? And it's never been dictated by telling people what they wanted to hear. And the problem now is that we're on the verge of moving into a culture where that's how things are going to be done. Basically we're on the verge of turning media into local television, in which everything was done on the basis of these metrics and Nielson reports. The same thing is happening here."

WHAT BEGINNING JOURNALISTS SHOULD KNOW

Those who run the most popular websites for news agree: if you want to succeed at online journalism, learn the basics. The foundations of journalism—accurate reporting, lively writing—are just as important for the Web as for newspapers, television broadcasts and radio shows.

Those traditional core values are essential to websites. The stories might be shorter or have video with them, but websites demand content that informs viewers as well as entertains them.

There's no shortcut to quality. It comes from the hard task of digging for a story and then writing it as compellingly as possible. Here the basics of sound journalism come into play.

"You know great painters learn the basics before they learn their own style," says the *Houston Chronicle*'s Flood. "I can't imagine that this is going to change that, that the journalists are still going to need to know how to do the basics, the need to know how to put in the who, what, when, where, why to be able to do any of this.

"Even though in some ways blogging is easier because it's frequently morsels instead of the whole meal. You can blog about one little event."

Those who run websites suggest the following:

- Understand the core values of journalism. Learn to write and report: "It goes without saying," Brady of the *Washington Post* says.
- The essentials of Journalism 101 are just as valuable in Internet writing and reporting. "You need who, what, when, where, why," Madigan of the *Chicago Tribune* says. "You need a story that's clearly written and quickly delivered. It's very easy to get swept up in blogging and a whole bunch of other things that are not really about journalism and think that you're doing journalism and doing that but you aren't. The journalism rules are still the journalism rules and the journalism values are still journalism values."
- Journalism is still the key to a successful website. "The key to the whole thing is being able to, you know, find out what's going on and communicate it clearly," Kershner of the *San Francisco Chronicle* says. "I remember . . . Bill Keller of *The New York Times*, when I was at *The Oregonian* many, many years ago, he was the Washington correspondent. And I remember somebody said, 'He's really the best writer we've got.' And somebody else said, 'All he is is clear.' And I really thought that was a really good statement. It wasn't flashy at all, but he was clear. That skill will always be in demand, I hope."

- "Journalism students need to learn what they've always learned as far as news gathering and reporting is concerned," Micheli of *The Boston Globe* says. "In addition, they need to develop a new way of thinking regarding how stories can be told and they need to develop some technical skills. This new way of thinking involves using the benefits of the online medium (its strong visual orientation; its immediacy; its database capabilities; and its interactive components) to improve storytelling. It is imperative that young journalism students learn to think imaginatively and have an outlet for experimentation because they will be the ones that shape this new form of storytelling."

IN CONCLUSION

Despite their call to honor traditional journalism values, these top Web editors also believe emerging journalists should throw out the clamps on creativity. Remember the roots of truth, fairness, accuracy. But also use the power of the Web to tell stories in new ways, with new tools. The Internet lets these journalists of tomorrow create content in exciting and interactive ways. The daily Web is at its best when news is breaking. It attracts citizens to join in the production of news coverage.

Though many traditional journalists feel threatened by the Web's ability to deliver information in a flash and with a punch, others believe the Web has strengthened the news media, especially newspapers.

"The immediacy of online journalism," *The Boston Globe*'s Micheli says, "has made newspapers play up their strengths: thoughtful in-depth reporting and analysis. . . . Because the website is used for breaking news, it is critical that newspapers continue to do what they do best.

"Newspapers have been through this before with television news and are learning to tweak their offerings, again, in response to online news."

EXERCISE 1

Read the following story:

Smooth Williams is alone on a tiny stage at Rockports just off downtown Portsmith. Only two people sit in the coffeehouse audience. They have turned their backs to him. Their voices compete with his music.

Williams doesn't seem to notice.

He rocks back on his stool and tilts up his saxophone. He is playing to a crowd only he can see. The music fills the room. He changes notes, grows louder, softens his tone, whispers his next riff.

The two stop talking and turn their chairs around.

Williams won't stop for another hour. By the time he's finished, the crowd has grown to 20. They break into hearty applause. He nods, puts down his sax and walks to an empty table. He's in no hurry.

"One at a time," he tells a visitor, speaking slowly, "I win them over one at a time."

Williams has been trying to win them over for 40 years. He only recently has seen signs of success.

Rockports is his coffeehouse, and he is its lone star. He's become what many in Portsmith call the key to resurrecting the once live-music area known as Alley's Gate.

"He's the most important part of the puzzle over there," said Ariana Place, chair of the Alley's Gate Renewal Group. "If he hadn't reopened Rockports, this area would never have made a comeback."

On the afternoon before his recent performance, Williams showed off the area many jazz and rock stars credit with their first starts. Williams stopped first at the Mills and Wall intersection.

"I began myself on the corner right here," Williams said, laughing. "I needed the money so bad, I would play in the winter as long as I could stand it. I only came in if it snowed or a woman offered me a drink."

He walked down Mills Street, and pointed to a bar.

"That's where Jazz Turner started," he said. "Next to that is where the Haley Brothers played for free, just to get people in."

He paused, looking into a storefront long empty.

"And that was the first Rockports," he said softly, almost as soft as his sax on a low note. "Of course, Shirley sang, and I played, and nobody could find a seat."

Shirley was his only wife, Shirley Hayes, who died 35 years ago in a car accident. Williams played for a few more years in Rockports, but his heart wasn't in it.

"The crowds could tell," he said, his voice still soft. "They could tell."

It wasn't long until Rockports closed, and Alley's Gate began its long decline. One after one, the famous bars closed and aspiring jazz and rock musicians sought their fame elsewhere. Williams himself drifted, moving to Los Angeles, then Las Vegas, then Houston, then to farm in southern Alabama. He even quit playing for 10 years.

"Then one day, I decided I was going to sell my instrument. Just like that. I decided to get rid of it. If I could get rid of it, maybe I'd feel better.

"I found it in my closet. I opened the case. I picked it up like this, and I don't know why but for some reason I just blew into it. It was a sound I hadn't heard in a long while. It was a good sound. It made me feel good.

"So right there I played for an hour, never stopping. I didn't think I could go that long. If just for me, and Shirley, and the crowds I remembered at Rockports."

Williams then called a friend, who got him a job. Within a month, he was playing steady. Within three months, he had decided to move back to Portsmith and reopen Rockports.

His announcement breathed new life into Alley's Gate. Five bars have opened in the last six months. Two more should open within three weeks. Crowds have begun to find their way to this part of downtown Portsmith.

"I'm now into this for the music, not the money," he said. "I believe in the music. I believe in what I can do with the music."

Back in Rockports, Williams has finished his break. He rises slowly from the table. the crowd is standing room only now, close to 50. Faces hover outside the door.

Smooth Williams doesn't seem to notice. The stool rocks back. The saxophone tilts. The music starts. All chairs are turned. All eyes focus on him.

1. Rewrite the story to make it more appealing on a website.
2. What visuals would make this story more appealing to Internet readers?
3. What graphics could be used?
4. What sounds could a journalist add for the Internet?
5. What are the links the editors could use to give readers a way to find more information?

EXERCISE 2

Pick up the front page of your local or student newspaper. Look at all the stories. Answer the following questions.

1. How could editors make these more appealing to readers on the paper's websites?
2. What visuals could the editors use?
3. What audio could reporters record to make these stories more appealing?
4. What are the journalistic values that the reporters used for the print stories that they must duplicate for the Web stories?

EXERCISE 3

Go to a news website. Answer these questions.

1. How do the stories differ from stories you would find during a television broadcast or on the front page of a newspaper?
2. What are the visual components that help some of the stories?
3. Do any of the stories have audio? How does that enhance the stories?
4. What sorts of news judgments come into play? How are these similar or different from those used at newspapers or television stations?

C H A P T E R 19

An Ethical Approach to Journalism

IN THIS CHAPTER, YOU WILL LEARN:

- Ethical behavior helps build credibility and preserve journalistic independence.
- The six leading principles of ethical behavior:
  - Don't accept anything of value from anybody.
  - Resist alliances that suggest conflicts of interest.
  - Do your own work.
  - Don't deceive your audience or your sources.
  - When in doubt, ask.
  - Disclosure is preventive medicine.

It's better to have an ethics policy and to have it in writing and damn what might happen in court.
Greg Moore, editor,
The Denver Post

FLAMBOYANT BOXING PROMOTER DON KING was facing tougher questions from reporters than he was accustomed, and he didn't like it. He rose and began to lecture his Atlantic City audience. How dare you bite the hand that feeds you? You owe it to me that you get to travel the world to cover championship fights. You ride on my airplanes, eat my food, stay in nice hotels. All because of me. Just where is your loyalty?

King's counter-punching left some of those reporters cold. In those moments, reporters who had long argued that their independence could not be bought by freebies came to understand that is what the people they covered *believed* they were buying. Sources see freeloading journalists as weak and pliable. They expect favors in return—if not now, then down the road.

This makes abundant sense: If today's cost-conscious corporations did not think they benefit from sending gifts and hosting journalists, why would they go to the expense? Do you think you would receive the same privileges if you were not part of a news organization? This is business, not friendship.

Journalistic independence costs money—for tickets, meals, airfare and more that influence-peddlers would gladly buy. And the love of money, as the Bible says, is the root of all evil. No wonder there are so many ethical dilemmas.

A thorough discussion of journalism ethics could fill a book of this length and consume an entire semester's work—or more. *The New York Times*' ethics policy is nearly 50 pages. "The ways a newspaper can discredit itself are beyond calculation," the *Los Angeles Times*' ethics policy notes.

Amid high-profile embarrassments—and firings—over fabrications, plagiarism, anonymous sources and other journalism scandals, focus on professional standards and conduct is expanding. Thousands of industry articles have appeared about the concerns in these specific cases and in general. At least nine of The Poynter Institute's consulting staff list expertise in ethics. In the last decade, news organizations that long resisted putting their ethics policies in writing have not only done so, but have made them public.

Ethics policies vary in content and tone. Some are more far-reaching. Even the lengthiest policies acknowledge that none can envision all potential matters of concern. Still, the general principles of journalistic independence and professional conduct can be summarized in a few simple sentences. Your integrity and your career are on the line, so understand them well.

- Don't accept anything of value from anybody.
- Resist alliances that suggest conflicts of interest.
- Do your own work.
- Don't deceive your audience or your sources.
- When in doubt, ask.
- Disclosure is preventive medicine.

ADVANCED TIP

Principles of Journalistic Independence and Professional Conduct:

- Don't accept anything of value from anybody.
- Resist alliances that suggest conflicts of interest.
- Do your own work.
- Don't deceive your audience or your sources.
- When in doubt, ask.
- Disclosure is preventive medicine.

DON'T ACCEPT ANYTHING OF VALUE FROM ANYBODY

This includes freebies, discounts and special favors not available to the rest of the public.

Journalists performing the government-watchdog role expose undue influence achieved by major political donors, lobbyists, vendors and suppliers making kick-back payments in return for government contracts.

Similarly, journalistic integrity depends upon avoiding the perception that some receive favorable treatment in the news because they buy ads, host lavish media parties or send gifts to news organizations and their journalists.

This is a bedrock principle. Others should not feel they have to be equally generous to compete for space in news columns. Others should not feel excluded from fair treatment because they can't offer free trips or refuse to provide complimentary tickets to games and stage events.

Shun the argument that "I can't be bought for [fill in the blank]." At that point, the conversation is only about price.

It is never appropriate to invoke your employment in private disputes, such as when you have a consumer complaint with an airline or car repair shop, or in seeking service as a citizen, such as to get favored status from officials at your child's school. Such behavior will be interpreted as an offer of reward or a threat of retribution. Both tell readers that your work and your organization's news report are untrustworthy—the work of manipulative people who are susceptible to influence-peddling.

RESIST ALLIANCES THAT SUGGEST CONFLICTS OF INTEREST

Once focused on social and professional relationships with sources, this area has expanded rapidly in recent years. If readers believe journalists are too cozy with sources or too devoted to causes, either because of their own involvement or that of their families, then readers distrust the news. They don't think they are getting an unbiased account. In the same way that readers discount opinions from those whose self-interest is too strong (e.g., a gun-store owner on the issue of gun-control), they suspect the motives of journalists whose independence may be compromised by personal or economic relationships.

The New York Times, which has taken a leadership role in allowing its policy to be posted on industry training websites, summarizes conflicts of interest this way:

"Conflicts of interest, real or apparent, may come up in many areas. They may involve the relationships of staff members with readers, news sources, advocacy groups, advertisers, or competitors; with one another, or with the newspaper or its parent company. And at a time when two-career families are the norm, the civic and professional activities of spouses, family and companions can create conflicts or the appearance of conflicts."

ADVANCED TIP

Should Sports Reporters Vote for the Heisman?

The *Los Angeles Times* policy states:

"The *Times*, like many newspapers, for years has allowed its sports writers to participate in voting for baseball's Hall of Fame, college football's Heisman Trophy and national rankings in college sports, among other areas. Participation in these polls creates possibilities for conflicts of interest. Similar issues arise in the arts when journalists are invited to vote for awards and prizes in film, literature and other fields."

Note that conflicts of interest can be "real or apparent."

The common phrase, "Perception is reality," is as true in ethics as it is in counterintelligence. People act on what they believe is true. If your alliances and conduct convince others you have a conflict, then it can be an insurmountable task to persuade them otherwise.

When *The Denver Post* reconsidered its ethics policy in 2005, its committee found that guidelines on conflicts of interest needed to cover more ground.

"There was a tremendous amount of confusion about what was acceptable and what was not," Editor Greg Moore said. "People thought it was OK to serve on the library board in a community they covered. They thought it was OK to host political fund-raisers that their spouses were having for people they [the journalists] cover."

Other journalists have risked their independence by co-authoring books or hosting radio and TV shows with the people they cover. In each case, the journalist became a business partner with a subject the journalist covered. Similarly, writers, photographers and artists are forbidden to freelance for, accept speaking honoraria from or otherwise get on the payroll of organizations they cover. For editors, the prohibition extends to organizations that are affected by the editors' news judgments.

Typically, news organizations forbid their staffs to participate in political partisanship—either on behalf of candidates or causes. Increasingly, news organizations forbid their business-news staffs to invest in locally covered companies. The *Los Angeles Times* is on the leading edge of news organizations restricting sports and arts writers' involvement in awards-voting.

Jayson Blair, former reporter for *The New York Times*, who resigned from the newspaper in May 2003 after being caught for blatant plagiarism and fabrication of facts.

"The *Times*, like many newspapers, for years has allowed its sports writers to participate in voting for baseball's Hall of Fame, college football's Heisman Trophy and national rankings in college sports, among other areas. Participation in these polls creates possibilities for conflicts of interest. Similar issues arise in the arts when journalists are invited to vote for awards and prizes in film, literature and other fields."

The *Times* policy then instructs: "In general, it is inappropriate for reporters to vote for awards and rankings; doing so could reasonably be seen as compromising their objectivity." And: "No staff member who votes for an award—whether in sports, the arts or any other area—may be part of the paper's news coverage of that award."

The economic fortunes of athletes, performers and their teams can rest on such voting. Perception-wise, journalist-voters are in a no-

The Art of Storytelling

Excellent storytelling requires a level of descriptive detail that can only be obtained by diligent reporting. Taking shortcuts on the reporting can lead to omissions in the storytelling. Omissions can distort the truth.

We think of ethical transgressions as overt acts. But if, by omission, we permit readers to believe something we know is not true, that is deceitful.

Among countless possibilities, here are some all-too-common distortions. Some reflect a reporter's lack of sophistication. Others reflect lazy reporting. Worse yet, others omit inconvenient truths, where facts are not permitted to get in the way of a good story—or a reporter's predisposition.

Show a True Picture

We've all seen the close-up photos and TV frames full of animated picketers demonstrating loudly for political or workplace justice. Sometimes, the tired and bored demonstrators are quiet until the cameras arrive. Then, the picketers jump into action. In words and pictures, don't permit readers or viewers to believe it's an angry throng unless it really is.

Early and often in a reporter's career, stories arrive that summon outrage from readers. A consumer is cheated. A citizen is victimized by unthinking government bureaucracy. An innocent person is wounded, or falsely accused. Too often, these stories of injustice are presented one-dimensionally. They may be accurate as far as they go, but the truth requires more depth. For the better story, find this out: Is this misfortune something that happens all the time? Or is it almost unprecedented? Either way, this is a good story: in the first case, a broad warning to others; in the second, showing just how bad things can get because of lax enforcement. The extra reporting gives deeper understanding, permitting viewers and readers to assign proper weight to the facts. It also adds drama to narrative.

Take care to consider the difference between parallel events (e.g., coincidence) and true cause-and-effect. A study released in April 2007 concluded that left-handed women are more likely to live shorter lives. Various scientists scoffed at the research, but even if the math and science were meticulous, the research did not show that being left-handed caused women to die sooner. Research undoubtedly would show that the football teams whose quarterbacks most often "took a knee" (deliberately put themselves down untouched so as not to risk a fumble at the end of games when their teams are safely ahead) won nearly 100 percent of their games. Obviously, that does not mean taking a knee at end of games would turn a losing team into a dominant winner.

Truth often is elusive. Facts have to suffice for now. There is no shame in telling our audiences both what we know and what questions remain unanswered. Mystery is a fine element in storytelling, yet many reporters lack the humility or the courage to explain what they do not know. They would rather write around these gaps of knowledge, muddying their prose and the audience's comprehension.

Use Voices of True Authority

Exaggerating the number of sources can mislead readers or viewers by suggesting the information is worth more confidence than it deserves. Don't write "sources" when you have only one—a common practice among some journalists. Similarly, don't allow yourself to be misled. Is that second source in the police department someone who has direct knowledge or someone just repeating what that officer has heard in the hall?

Similarly, reporters too often rely on experts with titles, but no direct experience in the matter being investigated. It's easy to find a psychiatrist, academic or financial analyst both studious and eager to be quoted. But if they haven't actually been working on the issue at hand, their quotes are theoretical. In theory, anything is possible, so they are liable to say anything that fits the story's thesis. Their quotes can sound full of meaning, yet be meaningless.

When a student gunman killed 32 people and then committed suicide at Virginia Tech University in April 2007, media everywhere sought experts to explain why anyone would do this. Consider the difference in authority among these sources:

- A psychiatrist.
- A psychiatrist considered by peers to have done the most thorough studies of mass murderers.
- A psychiatrist who examined the killer, Cho Seung-Hui.

Watch your language when citing polls and studies. All polls have a margin of error, often plus or minus 4 percent. This means every number in the poll could be 4 percentage points higher or lower than it really should be. Thus, a poll showing a 54–46 advantage for a candidate or a preferred product may actually be showing no advantage at all, because the true numbers could be 50–50. This is why so-called horse-race polls offer little more than entertainment value and so often prove to be off the mark on Election Day. When quoting a poll, be sure to include the margin of error.

Stories on academic and scientific studies require another disclosure: Who fi-

(continued)

nanced the study? In a study of the addictive effects of cigarettes, readers would assign different weights to the study sponsored by the American Heart Association and the study sponsored by the tobacco industry. Privately financed studies, such as those released by commercial interests, deserve an additional layer of skepticism. Even when the science is not in question, recognize that only those studies showing desirable results are made public.

Writers striving for balance can inadvertently distort reality by failing to report that one speaker represents the view held by the vast majority and another represents the view of a tiny minority. We have achieved balance, of sorts, by giving each side equal time, but have failed to give our audience the context. In 2007, this distortion was occurring most often in reporting on such issues as global warming, stem-cell research and the debate over teaching evolution and creationism in science classes. But it happens much more often than that. Ask about the predominant view, and whether the minority view is gaining converts. That natural tension is a fine element of storytelling.

win situation. If they vote for the local team or player, they are homers. If not, they are traitors.

When Stephen Glass was fired from *The New Republic* for fabricating parts of stories, it helped focus the news industry's attention on authenticating sources.

DO YOUR OWN WORK

Most of the early 21st century journalistic felonies occurred in the related crimes of fabrication, plagiarism and failure to attribute others' reporting and writing.

The Jayson Blair scandal that also cost *The New York Times*' editor and managing editor their jobs left many news people aghast because of its audacity—an ongoing campaign of outright fabrication. The departures of Stephen Glass from *The New Republic* and Jack Kelley of *USA Today* followed investigations that found frequent fabrication in their work. Their cases were as spectacularly tragic as earlier scandals at *The Washington Post* and *The Boston Globe*. Other cases at *The Sacramento Bee* and elsewhere convinced journalists that the disasters could happen anywhere if they could occur at America's leading newspapers.

Plagiarism is a journalistic felony second only to outright fabrication. The plagiarist steals the words or reporting of others and claims it as his own.

News organizations became much more active in writing and distributing ethics policies after plagiarism and fabrication scandals cost jobs of such prominent journalists as *USA Today*'s Jack Kelley.

"Acts of plagiarism or fabrication announce to the world that the writer did not have the honesty, skill, savvy or energy to do the work that someone else performed," *The Denver Post* ethics policy scolds.

DON'T DECEIVE YOUR AUDIENCE OR YOUR SOURCES

As *New York Times* reporter Judith Miller spent 85 days in jail while concealing the name of her source (for a story she never wrote), many journalists suffered. Empathy turned to outrage, however, when Miller herself later revealed what else she had been willing to do to keep secret the identity of Vice President Dick Cheney's chief of staff, I. Lewis "Scooter" Libby.

Once Libby released Miller from her oath of secrecy, she testified before a grand jury investigating who leaked the identity of CIA operative Valerie Plame. Plame's husband, Joseph Wilson, had earned the enmity of the Bush Administration for undercutting the administration's claim that Iraq sought weapons of mass destruction.

Then, for the Oct. 16, 2005, *Times*, Miller wrote this in a long account of her testimony under questioning by special prosecutor Patrick Fitzgerald.

> My recollection, I told him, was that Mr. Libby wanted to modify our prior understanding that I would attribute information from him to a senior administration official. When the subject turned to Mr. Wilson, Mr. Libby requested that he be identified only as a former hill staffer. I agreed to the new ground rules because I knew that Mr. Libby had once worked on Capitol Hill.
>
> Did Mr. Libby explain this request? Mr. Fitzgerald asked. No, I don't recall, I replied. But I said I assume Mr. Libby did not want the White House to be seen as attacking Mr. Wilson.

Miller had been willing to deceive her readers about the White House's aggression, perhaps even willing to abet the White House tactics. Soon after, Miller negotiated her departure from *The Times*.

Bob Steele, director of the Ethics Program at The Poynter Institute for Media Studies, reacted to this in the larger context of journalistic ethics: "There is not nearly enough emphasis on this matter of independence. The Plame case may reveal to us how often we get suckered into making deals with the powerful—granting confidentiality to power-brokers who are dropping dimes and throwing brickbats, not legitimate whistle-blowers."

Much more often than fabrication, journalists deceive readers through conscious omission.

Like many other people in our society, some journalists begin with a preconceived notion of the truth, then exclude contrary information. They have failed to keep an open mind and their reports distort reality.

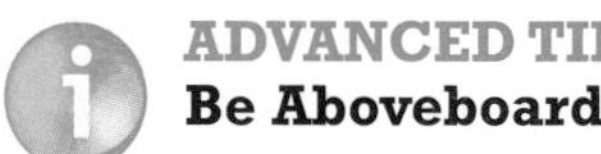

ADVANCED TIP
Be Aboveboard

"We should clearly identify ourselves to inexperienced sources, such as crime victims, children and others, and be willing to explain to them the context of their portrayal in stories. Such disclosure respects the victim's dignity. It also builds trust."

—*The Denver Post* ethics policy

Some fail to adequately identify sources, denying readers the opportunity to judge whether the source is unduly biased.

Some exaggerate the authority in their stories with phrases like "police sources" when referring to information from a single officer.

Some use photographs without disclosing to readers that the image has been posed or digitally altered.

In misguided attempts to present a balanced story, they get it decisively out of balance by giving each side of the story equal weight, then failing to reveal that one side is the minority view.

In all these instances and more, the news report is factual, but does not paint an accurate picture. It is deceptive.

> *"It is no longer enough to report the fact truthfully. It is now necessary to report the truth about the facts."*

That pearl of wisdom, pregnant with contemporary value, dates to the 1947 Hutchins Commission report on press freedom.

Journalists also are expected to be honest and fair in their dealings with the people they interview and cover.

Do not misrepresent yourself. Those you interview ought to know that they are speaking to a news reporter and that you are working on a story.

This is especially important when talking to people unaccustomed to the media spotlight.

"We should clearly identify ourselves to inexperienced sources, such as crime victims, children and others, and be willing to explain to them the context of their portrayal in stories," *The Denver Post* policy states. "Such disclosure respects the victim's dignity. It also builds trust."

Reporters ought to make sure that even their media-savvy sources understand the terms and limits of confidentiality. Not for attribution, off the record and background mean different things to different people. In some newsrooms, confidentiality may be forfeited if the source is untruthful, reveals the information publicly, or if a court demands disclosure.

WHEN IN DOUBT, ASK

What you don't know can hurt you. No matter who else is at fault, your ethical lapse can cost you dearly. If you have any question about what you should do next, pose that question to a supervisor.

Want to freelance for a magazine? Don't assume that magazine is not in competition with another entity in your news organization's corporate empire. Ask.

WIRED AND WIRELESS | WEB

Ethics and the Internet

Veteran and rookie journalists recently fired or suspended for plagiarism have brought reporting through the Internet into sharp focus.

A wonderful research tool, the Internet's cut-and-paste convenience makes it too easy for short-cutting journalists to lift the work of others without attribution or verification. Conversely, the multitude's access to the Internet makes it relatively easy for someone in the public to expose the plagiarist. In short, the Internet inspired more plagiarists and also made it more likely they would be caught.

In other cases, material lifted from Internet sources turned out to be false as originally reported. Accepting the unverified accounts as fact spread and perpetuated the errors.

In a late-2005 memorandum to his staff, *San Francisco Chronicle* editor Phil Bronstein cautioned: "Every time you copy anything from the web (or anywhere else), you need to clearly state the source of that information in your notes and maintain that sourcing identification throughout whatever process you use to cull/edit/merge/however those notes evolve, right through to publication."

Humility is a virtue here. There is not a thing wrong with disclosing to readers that you obtained information from a variety of sources. That's what good reporters do.

Want to grant absolute anonymity to a source? Don't assume that your editors will agree that anonymity is necessary, or that they will defend your inclination to defy a subsequent court order to reveal the source. Ask.

Want to write a book or appear on TV to advance your expertise on a big story? Don't assume it's your prerogative to withhold information from your own news organization's audience to use it first elsewhere. Ask.

Want to run for a position on the local school board? Even if your job doesn't include covering education stories, don't assume that you can hold office and keep your job as a journalist. Ask.

DISCLOSURE IS PREVENTIVE MEDICINE

Asking is a form of disclosure—alerting your boss that there's an issue before it becomes a problem. Increasingly, newsroom leaders are demanding disclosure to readers, too, as a form of transparency on how news is collected and presented.

ADVANCED TIP
Facts or Truth?

"It is no longer enough to report the fact truthfully. It is now necessary to report the truth about the facts."

—The Hutchins Commission report on press freedom, 1947

In this environment, news reports disclose what they know, and what remains unanswered or unconfirmed. They disclose how they know it (e.g., documents and identified sources) and what effort was made to learn what is not yet known. *The Denver Post* ethics policy, which uses the words "disclose" and "disclosure" 18 times, requires that read-

Talent Showcase

GREG MOORE ▸
editor, *The Denver Post*

As the story-fabrication cases of *The New York Times'* Jayson Blair, *USA Today's* Jack Kelley and others cost reporters and even their top editors their jobs, many news organizations decided they needed to be clearer about their professional standards. Instead of assuming that their newsroom staffs were soundly grounded in journalistic ethics, more editors put their policies in writing and initiated more regular conversations about them.

A few pioneering editors took the bolder step of sharing those standards with the public. In the process, they began tackling broader public skepticism about journalistic independence and credibility.

The Denver Post took months to rewrite and expand its ethics policy, then posted it online with a link from its home page. *The Post*, Poynter Institute Ethics Program Director Bob Steele said, is among the first "handful, maybe a double handful" to do so.

"We wanted to be fully transparent," *Post* editor Greg Moore said. "The key to having a good ethics policy is for the people you deal with understand what it is.

"For instance, we wanted politicians and others to know we can't accept gifts. To avoid awkward situations we can cite the policy online.

"We also wanted accountability—anyone who is unsatisfied and has questions can see our policy."

Steele, who consulted with *The Post* on this, said the newspaper's transparency can only help.

"We can hope that as a result, the public would have greater appreciation for, and support of, what we do—journalism," Steele said.

"This may translate into concrete results. Perhaps more members of juries will have heightened respect for the roles of journalists, appropriately scrutinized. We should be kicked in the shins when we fail, but journalists do certain things on behalf of the public: investigative journalism; using graphic images to tell a story; using confidential sources.

"In making our standards public, we should be using the word independence, which I think is a lynchpin word in journalism that we don't use often enough."

Active in industry circles, Moore knows that *The Post's* example is recent and atypical, but gradually more news organizations are posting their policies.

"Ten to 15 years ago, it used to be: Never put any-

ers be told whenever a photo is altered or its content has been posed. Such disclosure to readers builds confidence in the information and trust in the news organization.

A legendary story in the world of public relations involves Bill Newkirk, a veteran wire-service reporter who became the ranking public relations executive for Goodyear. Hearing other company executives grouse about negative news coverage, he shot back, "If you don't want to read bad news, stop making it."

The corollary for journalists—for anyone wrestling with a decision—is articulated in the *Los Angeles Times* ethics policy: "We do nothing while gathering the thing in writing. Lots of ethics issues blew up. They blew up in Boston. I was there [as managing editor]. I never saw an ethics policy. Now the thinking is that it's better to have an ethics policy and to have it in writing and damn what might happen in court. New employees get it. Every year we circulate it."

Steele agrees strongly that newsrooms need guidelines—"guidelines more than rules, because rules are restrictive"—communicated clearly.

"Journalists appropriately scrutinize many other institutions for their ethical behavior. Their standards, policies, decision-making. It is not only disingenuous, but hypocritical to say, 'But we're not going to have them because it may hurt us in court.' "

Both Steele and Moore also see clear communication as a matter of fairness to newsroom staffs.

"It's unfair to employees not to be clear about standards and expectations," Steele said. "If we're not clear about the expectations, we send them out onto a lake with very thin ice.

"We live in an atmosphere of zero tolerance," Moore said. "In the past, something you might have given the person a warning for or suspended him, now people lose their jobs. It's all the more important to have an ethics policy that everyone understands. The consequences are really dire.

"Is this a good thing? No. We're all human beings. We all make unintentional mistakes. Now, as editor, I feel that I have to lower the boom on anyone who violates any of the principal tenets. In the past, people tended not to pay attention to yellow lights, caution lights. I understand why we're in an era of zero tolerance, but it doesn't make me feel any better."

Modern technology makes accountability inevitable.

"A lot more people will hold you accountable, not just me," Moore counsels his staff. "Online, they can check your words against the words of others. They can see what's on TV and compare it to what you put in the paper. I tell people, I might not know that you're sitting in that box at the game, but someone else in the box knows. And if he ever gets angry at you, he's going to call me."

So far, Moore said, making the ethics policy public has had the desired effects.

Externally, "We've gotten notes [from the public] saying your person violated your ethics policy. But mostly, people were really pleased."

Internally, "There is more disclosure and conversation. There is more conversation on the floor. 'Should I do this?'

"We want people to disclose—come talk to us. And they are."

There is one more benefit, Moore admitted. The editor's anxiety level has gone down a little bit.

"The Jayson Blair thing scared the shit out of me. You have a big enough ethical lapse, it can wipe out a lot of people—the editor, the managing editor. We are operating in a much more ethical environment. I feel more confident that I don't have a ticking time bomb."

news that we would be ashamed to see in print or on television. We do not let the behavior of the pack set standards for us."

If you could *assume* that your behavior would be on Page One tomorrow, what would you decide?

That's not a wild assumption. If not on Page One, then spread throughout the world via Internet blogs and radio/TV talk shows.

Steele of The Poynter Institute said he believes that more ethics policies are being written and revised because of "increasing scrutiny by the public of not just what is published, but how the journalists behave. The concern and criticism of citizens and readers is that journalists fail in their reporting process, which leads to errors in what ends up in the newspapers. These are issues regarding fairness and accuracy, and concerns over invasion of privacy."

Steele cites another reason: Recent lawsuits against journalists focus less often on what was published than how the information was gathered. Reporters and photographers—especially in broadcast news, but also in newspapers—have been sued for invading privacy, trespassing on private property and obtaining information only after improperly falsifying their identity.

WHAT JOURNALISTS CAN DO

Issues involving journalistic ethics cover a vast landscape. Consider the topics above to be ethical guideposts. Then, when wrestling with questions of objectivity and bias, or whether to publish or withhold sensitive material, these principles can help you decide and act.

Still, most of the topics above are presented as cautions and prohibitions. Journalists also need guidance on what they *should do*.

Some advice:

- Master your organization's ethics policy. Also read others. The policies at *The Denver Post*, the *Los Angeles Times, The New York Times* and *The Associated Press* (among others) are thoughtful and eloquently crafted. The URLs are in the Toolkit on page 333.
- Remember that many of the best policies are written as guidelines, intended to give staff an ethical foundation and a general sense of how to resolve doubt.
- When in doubt, ask. Make disclosure an instinct—your default option.
- Rely on verification to overcome assumption, temptation and charges of bias.
- Remember a lesson from the Committee of Concerned Journalists: Journalists are not objective; their processes are. We all have biases. Professional standards and sound ethics help keep us neutral and our stories even-handed.
- Adopt an attitude that it is never too late to do the right thing; never too late to get it right. "Readers and staff members who bring mistakes to our attention deserve our gratitude," the *Los Angeles Times* ethics policy states.
- Encourage vigorous debate about professional standards. "A robust, ongoing discussion of ethics at all levels of the newsroom is essential to producing a first-rate newspaper," the LA *Times* policy asserts. Even where consensus is elusive, journalists made aware that their behavior might be frowned on by others will think twice the next time.
- Above all, take this advice from the LA *Times* policy: "Listen carefully to [your] individual sense of right and wrong."

The *Times* takes it further: "If you know of anything that might cast a shadow on the paper's reputation, you are expected to inform a supervising editor.

"This can be an uncomfortable duty; under some circumstances, it can do harm to one's relationships with others in the newsroom. It is a duty nevertheless. Credibility, a newspaper's most precious asset, is arduously acquired and easily squandered. It can be maintained only if each of us accepts responsibility for it."

IN CONCLUSION

Ethical behavior is an essential part of journalistic credibility.

Although organizations can and should provide guidelines, ultimately, individual journalists are responsible for their ethical conduct. They can ensure that their behavior is sound by disclosing potential conflicts to their supervisors and asking when in doubt.

In general, resist behavior and alliances that compromise your independence. Don't deceive your audience or your sources. And always do your own work: neither inexperience nor a long track record of success is a mitigating factor for plagiarism.

TOOL KIT

Media Ethics Bibliography

www.poynter.org/content/content_view.asp?id=1208&sid=32

Committee of Concerned Journalists re: Bias and Objectivity

www.concernedjournalists.org/tools/filter/49

Ethics codes

www.concernedjournalists.org/tools/filter/64
www.denverpost.com/ethics (*The Denver Post*)
www.poynter.org/content/content_view.asp?id=91088 (*Los Angeles Times*)
www.poynterextra.org/extra/ethics.pdf (*The New York Times*)
www2.mysanantonio.com/aboutus/expressnews/ethics.cfm (*San Antonio Express-News*)
http://poynteronline.org/content/content_view.asp?id=5522&sid=32 (Bob Steele's sampling of clauses in ethics codes)

Tools

www.www.concernedjournalists.org/tools/filter/41
www.poynter.org/subject.asp?id=32
www.poynter.org/content/content_view.asp?id=42476&sid=32
The Ethics Tool (10-step): www.poynter.org/ethics/Default.asp

For TV

www.rtnda.org/ethics/balance.html

For Online

www.concernedjournalists.org/tools/filter/64

More from Bob Steele:
Ask 10 Questions to Make Good Ethical Decisions

http://www.poynter.org/column.asp?id=36&aid=4346

Guiding Principles for the Journalist

www.poynter.org/column.asp?id=36&aid=4349

EXERCISE 1

Explain what you would do with the following story:

A student at your university has been found dead in her dorm room. Both local police, medical examiners and university officials say the cause of death was a suicide. You are writing a story on this person's life, so you interview her roommates, students on the same floor and those in the elite a cappella group where she sang soprano. Her fellow singers in the choir all report that she was intense but apparently happy. They saw nothing that would cause her to take her own life. You get the same reports from the students up and down her floor at the dorm: no problems, no issues, no clues to the tragedy. Then her roommates tell you a different story. They say she was taking drugs frequently. One time, they almost called in the residential adviser because they were afraid she would harm herself. Your story is slated to run the same day as her memorial, so her parents and family will be in town and probably read it.

1. Under what circumstances would you print what you've found out from her roommates?
2. What are the guidelines you would use if you decided to publish the information you have received?
3. Who else would you consult to confirm what the roommates told you?
4. What reactions would you expect from the family and university officials? Would that make you not print the information?
5. What are your obligations to your readers? Do they have a right to know what happened with this student's death?

EXERCISE 2

Explain what you would do with the following story:

A reporter for a daily newspaper and website has heard from the county that it is losing money on its recycling program. The problem? People are going around at night when residents have put their recyclables out for pickup and stealing the bottles and cans worth five cents each. Officials then suspect those taking the bottles are redeeming them for cash. The law says that once residents put out the recyclables at the curb, they belong to the county. Anyone taking them for resale is violating the law. The reporter talks to all those in charge to determine how much the county is losing. Then he goes with police on a stakeout at several spots where thieves have been known to take the bottles. The police catch many that night, but the people surprise the reporter. These folks, he discovered, are mostly fathers and mothers who are poor and use the money to feed their children. Police charge the parents with misdemeanor theft and say they have to appear in court and perhaps pay a fine. The reporter interviews several parents. Independently they all say the same story: The money they make selling the bottles helps them keep their household going. Their stories are moving and sum up the heart of the issue.

1. The parents' names and charges are a matter of public record. Do you use them as the lead to your story?
2. Do you use the parents' names and their tales at all in your story?

3. Argue for how your readers are better served by having a full and complete record of what is happening in this story. Taxpayers are losing money. Why not tell your readers who is causing this?
4. Argue against running the names and the parents' stories. Are readers really that poorly served by not embarrassing these impoverished families?
5. How could you achieve both ends, that is, how could you use their plights and yet treat them with sensitivity?

EXERCISE 3

Explain how you would handle the following stories:

1. A female athlete in a minor sport claims a high-profile basketball player didn't stop when they were back at her room late one night. She says it was date-rape. He says the sex was consensual. Police did not charge the player but simply asked the district attorney to determine if there was enough evidence to arrest the player. You have the female athlete's interview on tape and on the record. Would you run the player's name?
2. A student who died in a car accident two years ago had her identity stolen by a current student. Police have arrested the current student and charged her with felony identity theft. You are going to run the story until the mother of the student who died calls you. She says run the story, fine, but don't run the name. "I don't want to open that wound again," the mother says. "If you run the story, people will come up and want to talk to me and I will hurt all over again. If you run the story, you will cause me so much pain that I don't know if I can recover from this a second time." Do you run the name of the deceased student whose identity was stolen?
3. A beloved patron of your university has given the school several million dollars over the past 30 years. The patron also is considered a saint by the townspeople in the city where your university is located. She founded, ran and helped pay for one of the leading centers for autism in the country. Hundreds of children have led improved lives because of her. The patron dies at age 88. Her will is public record, as are all wills. Your student newspaper easily obtains a copy of the will, as any citizen has a right. In the will, you find the patron gave most of her money to her family, the university and her center for autistic children. She also gave money to a white-supremacist group. Do you print that information?
4. The president of your university has had an affair with his administrative assistant for as long as any student can remember. It is an open secret across campus, although the two have never acknowledged it and both are married to others. The two even appear at some public functions, but are always distant with one another. The president abruptly resigns, and files for divorce. Do you pursue the angle that his affair might have led to his divorce and resignation from the university?
5. You attend a state university. You ask to see the salaries of all the administrators and the faculty for the university, which are paid through taxes. The information is public record but you discover many of the professors receive low salaries. You know once you publish this, you will embarrass many of your favorite professors. Do you publish the salaries anyway?

CHAPTER 20

Diversity as Ethics

IN THIS CHAPTER, YOU WILL LEARN:

- When newsrooms are blind to diversity issues, their ethics may be challenged.
- Diversity is a matter of race, ethnicity and gender, but also of age, family, beliefs, geography and talent.
- A diverse newsroom should be more adept at finding a wide range of stories throughout the community, with a deeper array of sources.
- Young journalists can help their newsrooms become more diverse.

Set aside expectations and stereotypes and find the authentic story.
Marjie Lundstrom

AS FLOOD WATERS FROM HURRICANE KATRINA RAVAGED NEW ORLEANS, two similar photos with different captions set off a storm of controversy.

An *Associated Press* photo showed a dark-skinned survivor in deep water, carrying a shoe box and a large bag. The next day, an *Agence France-Presse* photo showed a white man and a white woman in deep water, carrying backpacks. She also has packages of food.

The *AP* caption:

> A young man walks through chest-deep water after looting a grocery store in New Orleans on Tuesday, Aug. 30, 2005. Flood waters continue to rise in New Orleans after Hurricane Katrina did extensive damage. . . .

The *AFP* caption:

> Two residents wade through chest-deep water after finding bread and soda from a local grocery store after Hurricane Katrina came through the area in New Orleans, Louisiana.

Within hours of both photos appearing, bloggers, media commentators and talk-show callers seized on the words "looting" and "finding." Some saw racism: black people loot, white people find. Some saw a nation preoccupied with race. All saw the news media's ethics in the center of the storm.

It mattered little that the cross-fire commentary was largely unsupported by independent reporting or verification. It just multiplied until the controversy had a life of its own.

As it turns out, *AP* said that its photographer, Dave Martin, "saw the person go into the shop and take the goods," while *AFP* photographer Chris Graythen volunteered this explanation:

"There were a million items floating in the water—we were right near a grocery store that had 5-plus feet of water in it. It had no doors. The water was moving, and the stuff was floating away. These people were not ducking into a store and busting down windows to get electronics. They picked up bread and cokes that were floating in the water. They would have floated away anyhow."

These accounts were available on Sept. 1, 2005—one day after the second photo appeared—in well-reported summaries on salon.com and on the Urban Legends reference pages on Snopes.com. But even that quick work was too late to prevent a figurative flood of controversy.

The experience offered several questions that pose as lessons for contemporary journalists:

- Were newsrooms insensitive about word choice and/or blind to the likelihood of controversy? If so, could that have been averted in a diverse newsroom where

ADVANCED TIP

What about the Photographs?

The Associated Press and *Agence France-Presse* photographs of Hurricane Katrina victims getting food during the New Orleans flood can be found at these websites. The sites also offer solid explanations of both photographs and how the photographers wrote their captions.

www.snopes.com/katrina/photos/looters.asp
www.salon.com/news/feature/2005/09/01/photo_controversy/

Controversy about media bias escalated after captions accompanying this *Associated Press* photo reported that a dark-skinned man had *looted* a grocery store in New Orleans after Hurricane Katrina struck.

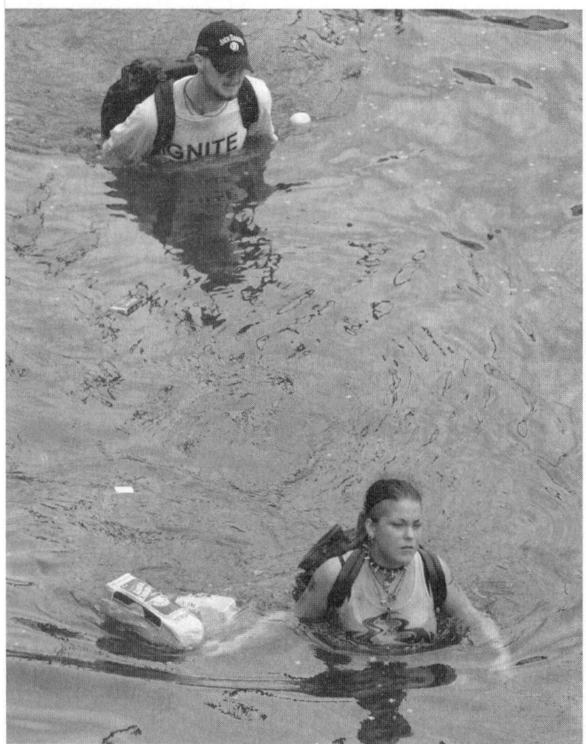

The caption that accompanied this *Agence France-Presse* photo didn't accuse two white survivors of Hurricane Katrina of looting, but reported they *found* bread and soda near a New Orleans grocery store.

content routinely passes through the hands of people with different backgrounds and sensibilities?

- If aware that controversy was inevitable, could newsrooms have offered the eyewitness "testimony" of the photographers with the photos to help inform readers and subdue outrage?
- With many hundreds dying around you, is it looting if you are taking survival items like food and clothing that are going to perish soon in floodwaters anyway?
- Would any or all of these points have surfaced in a newsroom that not only has a diverse makeup, but a culture that encourages its people to share their points of view openly?

TRUE NEWSROOM DIVERSITY

Like other fine writers, Keith Woods is concerned about voice. Like others who choose journalism as a calling, Woods is concerned about voices, particularly those of the voiceless. Woods, dean of The Poynter Institute for Media Studies, speaks of newsroom diversity and diversity in news coverage as ethics issues.

"To deny a person his voice, is to deny his truth," Woods counsels. "Exclude the individuals and you exclude their truth."

The voices Woods champions are those of sources too often missing from the news report and those of diverse journalists too often missing or silent in the newsroom.

To achieve the benefits of diversity, a newsroom must have the disparate experience of people with disparate backgrounds and points of view. These backgrounds are determined by who raised you, where you went to school, where you grew up, where you have worked and more. Stories and

ADVANCED TIP
The Voice of Diversity

"To deny a person his voice, is to deny his truth. Exclude the individuals and you exclude their truth."

—Keith Woods, dean of The Poynter Institute for Media Studies

photographs will occur to some reporters that do not occur to others, solely because of experience. Editors will notice perfect or flawed phrases and pictures solely because of experience.

It is never enough merely to hire such a workforce. The newsroom culture must encourage openness and mutual respect—the atmosphere that lets each person benefit from the experience of others. Leaders must share information for a news staff to see how their unique knowledge fits into the bigger picture. Then, leaders must *encourage* informed dissent in order to make fully informed decisions. In the end, an alternate point of view may not carry the day, but decisions can be made weighing and accounting for possible consequences.

The American Society of Newspaper Editors has authored newsroom census reports since 1978. It tracks minority representation on professional staffs by race, ethnicity and gender. The latest (www.asne.org/index.cfm?id=1138) shows that a bit fewer than 14 percent are people of color, a bit fewer than 38 percent are female. While this represents gradual progress, most newsrooms fall short of reflecting the diversity in their communities. Remarkably in the 21st century, nearly 40 percent of daily-newspaper newsrooms have no minority staff at all.

Even if newspapers achieve the Society's goal of racial, ethnic and gender parity by 2025, diversity does not end there. Even if the faces in the staff photo look different, a newsroom struggles to reflect its community unless there is:

- **Age Diversity:** As it is, few newsrooms employ teens or 70-year-olds. But in the search for more young readers, newsrooms need writers and editors who can relate. And as the huge Baby Boom generation retires, full-time beats devoted to aging and to society's pursuit of so many older consumers are not luxuries. Society's accommodation of a generation that large changes life for all generations. That is an underreported story.
- **Family Diversity:** News organizations often assign their youngest, single reporters to the suburbs, whose homes are disproportionately filled with married couples and children. The fragmenting family structure—more unmarried parents, more homes with no children, more gay and lesbian couples—is among the ways American society has diversified most in the last generation. The consequent challenges and controversies are ripe for the understanding that journalism can offer.
- **Belief Diversity:** Religious and political views polarize America most of all. The dividing lines are clearest here. A staff able to recognize the emotional trigger points will do a superior job of covering the biggest stories of our time. Elections turn on such matters. The book *What's the Matter with Kansas?* explains seemingly counterintuitive American attitudes in ways that election coverage has typically been unable to grasp. In the 21st century alone, Muslim belief and the Catholic Church priest-molestation cases have made the religion beat

Figure 20.1 **Newsroom Minority Growth Slow Since 1995**

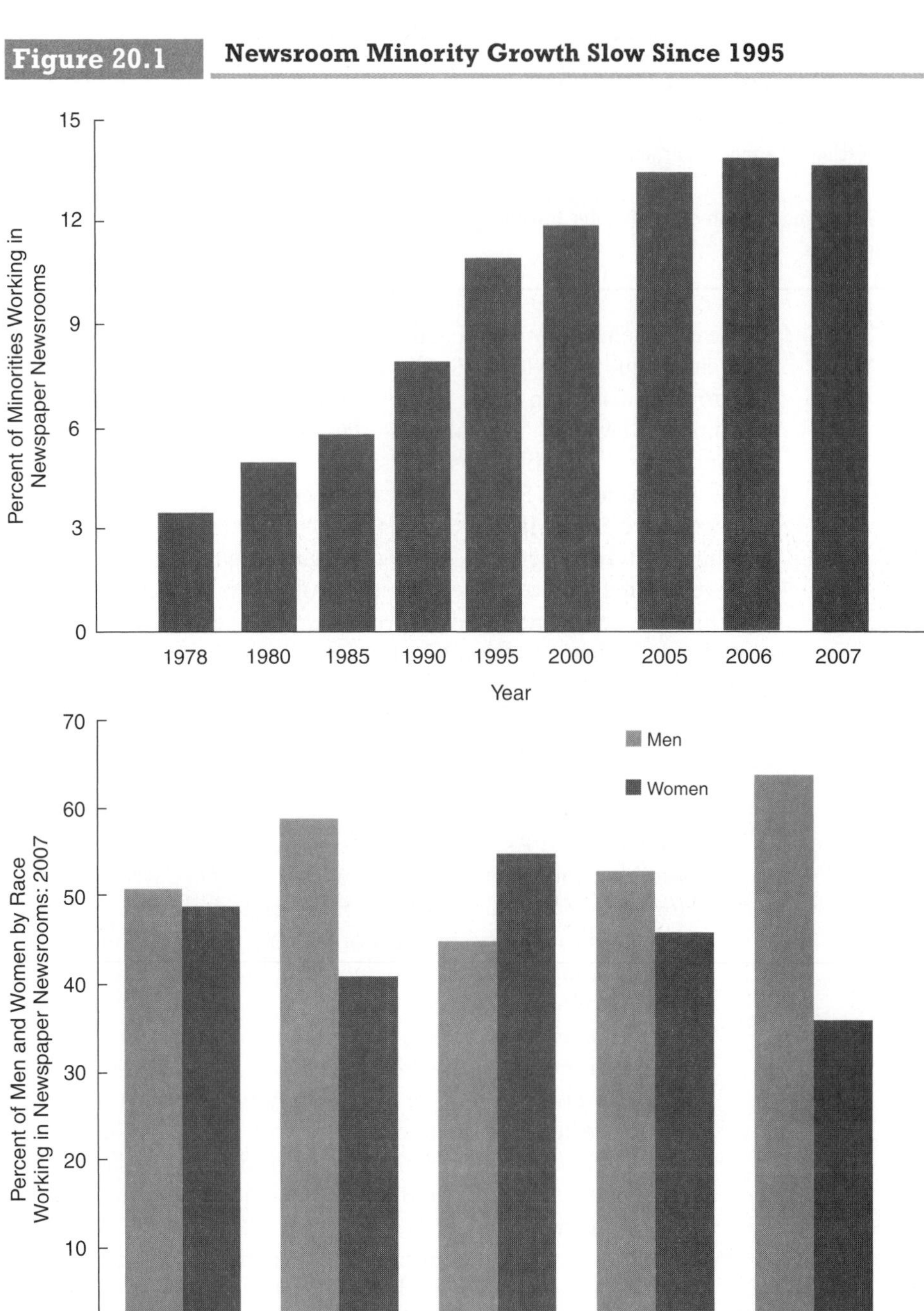

Source: American Society of Newspaper Editors

among the most important. Abortion, stem-cell research and school prayer persist as divisive issues that can decide who becomes the next Supreme Court justice. They can influence elections as surely as such issues as taxes, peace and prosperity.

- **Cultural Diversity:** At a record pace, American communities are diversifying with influxes of Hispanic, Asian and African populations large enough to form their own communities within communities. Citizens' ability to coexist in a thriving democracy may depend on the light and education that comes from good journalism. "I need to know that community before I vote on that tax," Woods says.
- **Geographic Diversity:** A newsroom benefits from a mix of people who have seen things done differently (sometimes better) elsewhere. This is true of journalistic practices and also such content matters as social programs, election systems, law enforcement, education and more. On a micro level, perhaps nothing has challenged news media more than urban sprawl. Reaching further-flung readers with news close enough to home requires more reporters, news space and air time than one-size-fits-all news reports can offer. The crisis becomes more acute when, as typical, most of the news staff lives in the city, close to the office, while two-thirds of the potential audience lives elsewhere.
- **Interest Diversity:** Americans have diversified most of all by communities of interest. The exploding expansion of lifestyle choices offers a huge opportunity for mass media to overcome steep geographic hurdles. Interests in occupations, hobbies, families and beliefs cross geographic borders. This is the lure of the Internet. Mass media can use both the Internet and its core news reports to remain vital to wide swaths of population.
- **Talent Diversity:** Last on this list, but far from least, newsrooms depend upon having the right people for the right stories. Some reporters are more gifted in narrative writing than investigative reporting. Some are better at unearthing crucial documents than interviewing. Some are better at beat reporting than writing profiles. Some know civics better than science. A newsroom needs all these skills and many more. It needs expertise in many subjects.

DIVERSITY IMPROVES CONTENT

In these ways, we see that diversity is, at its core, a content issue. If diversity is to have meaning beyond honorable intentions, then the benefits of hiring, development and diverse points of view in the newsroom ought to show up in the news report.

Conversely, if the ingredients in truth—accuracy, fairness, thoroughness and all sides of the story—are to be upheld as principles fundamental to independent journalism, newsrooms must have the staff capable of finding truth while diversity in the United States grows at historic rates.

The task is tall and news organizations have barely begun to climb. But reporters and editors can take many steps even in their earliest years as professionals.

The Art of Storytelling

Amy Argetsinger was a beat reporter covering higher education for *The Washington Post* when she discovered that narrative storytelling was the best way to tell a fascinating tale of cultural diversity.

As related in *Best Newspaper Writing 2004*, Argetsinger said this was her first attempt at narrative writing, "but it gave me the framework for working through the elements of the story."

That story involved an American college student from Kenya: a woman, the first female from the agrarian Masai tribe in her region ever to attend college. She went to America not only with her own dreams, but those of her village. The villagers have given her their blessing to go, hoping that, unlike the boys who made this journey before her, a woman would return. And then become the leader who would change all their lives for the better.

In a story about Kakenya Ntaiya's hopes and burdens, Argetsinger describes a young woman alternately buoyant and weary, both ambitious for the world and lonely for home.

> Four years ago, she sat in her family's living room with two letters of admission, one from Randolph-Macon, the other from a teachers' academy in Kiambu, seven hours from home. If she had gone to Kiambu, she wouldn't have received a university education. But she would have earned her teaching credentials, and she would have finished a couple of years ago. She would be working and making money by now. And she would be home.
>
> Instead, she picked Randolph-Macon. She had wept for days; still, it was always the choice of her heart—the U.S. college, and all the big things it could bring her way.
>
> And so she had made the deal. If she had to leave so many responsibilities behind, then she could not go just for herself.
>
> Times like these, she thinks ahead. About all the things she has to do when she gets back to Enoosaen. The things her community needs. The things she promised.
>
> Like a boarding school for girls.
>
> And a maternity clinic.
>
> And a way to improve the drinking water, which comes up on the backs of donkeys from the river at the bottom of the cow pastures, sometimes carrying disease. And better roads, and maybe electricity. And some positive leadership from an educated woman who can demonstrate on a daily basis that schooling is important, that feminism is good.
>
> These are ambitious things, she knows. "It's gonna work," she says on another, sunnier day. "It's gonna take some time."

In Argetsinger's narrative, at times Ntaiya is the typical college student. But mostly, she is not. That is the story.

Argetsinger said she had expected to find Ntaiya to be part of a different article about international students in America. But in Argetsinger's choice to focus on Ntaiya alone, we can see the reasons why cultural-diversity stories lend themselves so well to narrative storytelling.

Obviously, distant cultures are not well understood. Showing the ways they are different from, and similar to, our own is often the best way to explain them.

The histories of foreign cultures, especially like that of the nearly illiterate Masai, are not recorded. They must be recounted orally. Given that recorded history most often is written, interpreted and published by those in authority, oral histories also are essential to telling the story of any American underclass. The stories of Civil War–era slaves, for instance, and those of Negro Leagues baseball players, have been told in more depth via interviews rather than the spotty written accounts of their day.

The cultural storyteller has special challenges. Fewer written sources of verification exist. Often, the reporter must overcome language barriers. The risk of seeing and hearing, but not understanding, is constant.

The resourceful storyteller, however, has other techniques used infrequently by other news reporters. Cultural fashion and artifacts have their own revealing stories. Customs and legends are fascinating to repeat. Indeed, that is how they have been passed between generations.

Why make so much effort for stories about little-seen corners of our vast society?

That question is more easily answered after Sept. 11, 2001. Suddenly, Americans had great need to understand about different cultures and attitudes, not only in remote corners of Afghanistan and the Middle East, but in pockets of countless American communities, where immigrants worshipped in mosques and carried out the customs of their upbringing, while struggling to cope with the more privileged natives surrounding them.

In the weeks after the son of an immigrant Korean family shot and killed 32 students and professors at Virginia Tech University, news consumers heard a timeless lesson: Families who devote so much time to work that they have scant moments left for their children, may be raising maladjusted sons and daughters. That story, told in spring 2007 through the lens of Asian-immigrant aspiration, shows how unfamiliar cultures may be similar to the ones we know best.

Even without these life-altering events, America's heritage of welcoming people from everywhere changes communities over time as surely as oceans change shorelines.

Ironically, as news organizations redevote themselves to local news, we are in the era when local politics, the local economy, even the local weather, are influenced more than ever by global factors.

Journalists shrink the world, making it more familiar, through *stories* close to home.

Content improves when newsroom staffs represent a wide array of backgrounds, professional experience and interests.

DEVELOP SOURCES. Insist that beats and individual stories breathe with the lives of diverse sources. Yes, there is only one president of the United States. There may be only one local university president, one head football coach and one chamber of commerce president, and they may all be 50-something white males. But if stories are audience-driven, they begin with the citizens, fans and consumers. They show readers their stake in the outcome. By dwelling on the outcomes, journalists find many more story angles and help readers/viewers make informed decisions. The voices in these stories are fresh with variety and relevance. Regard official sources as desirable at times, even necessary at times, but supplemental, not primary.

TEST YOUR ASSUMPTIONS. We are all limited by our experience. That experience gives us unique value. But it also blinds us to truths we have never known. "Test your assumptions" is the affirmative version of a universal truth in journalistic integrity: Don't assume.

Test your assumption that people of one minority group are essentially like the others. In all groups, there is wide disparity in economic class, behavior, outlook and political choice (among many other differences).

Test your assumption about historical wisdom. *The Associated Press'* landmark series, "Torn from the Land," documented hundreds of cases where land was stolen from Southern blacks via intimidation, including murder. It exposed that while the Ku Klux Klan may have been motivated by hate (the historical wisdom), it had a more practical motive—its members wanted the land.

Testing assumptions requires commitment. This does not come naturally. In "See No Bias" (www.washingtonpost.com/wp-dyn/articles/A27067-2005Jan21.html), *Washington Post* reporter Shankar Vedantam showcased a psychological test that demonstrated just how unnatural it is to reverse prejudice, because most of us are unaware of it.

Vedantam focused on the research of Mahzarin Banaji, a native of India and a Yale scholar.

> The research has also upset notions of how prejudice can best be addressed. Through much of the 20th century, activists believed that biases were merely errors of conscious thought that could be corrected through education. This hopeful idea is behind the popularity of diversity training. But Banaji suggests such training relies on the wrong idea of how people form biases.
>
> There is likely a biological reason people so quickly make assumptions—good or bad—about others, Banaji says. The implicit system is likely a part of the "primi-

tive" brain, designed to be reactive rather than reasoned. It specializes in quick generalizations, not subtle distinctions. Such mental shortcuts probably helped our ancestors survive. It was more important when they encountered a snake in the jungle to leap back swiftly than to deduce whether the snake belonged to a poisonous species. The same mental shortcuts in the urban jungles of the 21st century are what cause people to form unwelcome stereotypes about other people, Banaji says. People revert to the shortcuts simply because they require less effort. But powerful as such assumptions are, they are far from permanent, she says. The latest research, in fact, suggests these attitudes are highly malleable.

Woods wrote a particularly clever and creative column for The Poynter Institute that addresses one of these blind spots. In "Harry Potter And The Imbalance of Race" (www.poynter.org/column.asp?id=58&aid=85445), Woods shows how author J. K. Rowling offers scant description of people of color, as if a single characteristic, such as skin color or hair style, is enough to distinguish them. Meanwhile, she writes richly detailed physical and personality descriptions of whites.

GAIN PROXIMITY. Gain new sources and test assumptions by spending your time in the places where people live. News organizations have the bad habit of assigning beats by building. That leads to covering institutions rather than people and their concerns. Instead, go to the neighborhoods where the stories begin, and where they play out after government action. Here, you can be an eyewitness.

Minority communities have a common complaint—common because it is so often true—that they don't see reporters unless something spectacularly bad is happening in their neighborhoods. Regular presence permits reporters to report on problems before they erupt into crisis. This is part of the equation in giving voice to the voiceless. Presence also permits finding success stories and profiling the people who are making a difference. These are not puff stories. They are primers for other communities facing similar problems. Reporters who do these stories gain sources and trust. Then, when something awful happens, they have enough credibility to learn the truth from the right sources on those stories, too.

Reporters can volunteer for neighborhood beats, even if they do not yet exist. If the news organization is not ready to create such a beat, reporters and editors will learn much by spending a week or more immersed in a neighborhood.

After 9/11, news organizations were much more likely to immerse themselves in Muslim communities. Americans everywhere needed understanding about that faith and why some Muslims overseas hated America so. But other minorities are not so easily found in a mosque.

Accordingly, alert news organizations have created Indian Affairs beats and immigration beats. Native Americans are unique minorities. Their reservations are independent nations with their own land and governance. Elsewhere, Indians are not as likely to be concentrated in specific neighborhoods. Thus, coverage may be more focused on communities of interest (employment, elections, parenting, hobbies, etc.) rather than geographic communities.

ADVANCED TIP

Not Just Race and Gender

News staffs should express diversity in many forms—not just the important categories of race and gender. To achieve well-rounded diversity, news staff should consider these categories as well:

- age
- family
- belief
- culture
- geography
- interest
- talent

So, too, with immigration. Fundamental to the historical growth of America as a diverse country, immigration is a hot-button topic now. The focus on immigration has magnified since 9/11. Controversy over border security is part of Homeland Security coverage. That focus also magnified how the hotel, resort and agriculture industries, among others, have depended on immigrant labor—often, *illegal* immigrant labor—to keep its jobs filled at low cost. In these ways, immigration goes far beyond being a social issue.

WRITE FOR, NOT ABOUT. Job One for any communicator: understand your audience. As a suburban journalist, are you writing for a suburban audience or a city audience? Perhaps both. As a business writer, are you writing for those in the know or for everyone? Presumably, both need to know. Content and tone depend upon your answers. Great journalism often involves shining light in one remote area (of geography, culture or knowledge) so that others may learn from it. But take care not to present your story subjects as objects of amusement and condescension. The circumstances may be odd. Behavior may be startling. Outcomes may be ironic. But unless the intent is humor in a clearly humorous situation, careless journalists risk lasting damage to their credibility.

Marjie Lundstrom, who cautions about geographic stereotyping (see the Lundstrom Talent Showcase), urges that this conscientiousness goes beyond the duty of reporters.

"For students who go down the editing path, they need to encourage a newsroom where employees are able to challenge a story and, most importantly, listen to many voices," Lundstrom says. "That doesn't mean the masses run the newsroom, but ask for those views. This is essential for a newsroom with a strong ethical core."

She says she'll never forget an incident soon after she had won a Pulitzer Prize and soon thereafter had become the first female city editor in the history of *The Sacramento Bee*.

"We'd get news tips from a local wire service. One day, we received an item about a domestic violence case we hadn't covered. A Vietnamese couple. The woman had been beaten. In the last paragraph, it said she'd been beaten with a frozen squirrel. All the male editors wanted to run this story. I was just furious: 'Domestic violence is not entertainment.' They dug their heels in. I dug in my heels and we ended up with an all-out war."

The story did not run, but Lundstrom did not feel victorious.

"I realized subsequently that there was a hell of a story in between. We may have tripped across some very important information about immigrants and lack of access to services. Journalists always have to ask themselves, 'What are my alternatives?' The choices are not just publish-or-not-publish. That goes for photos, too. We can crop it [rather than kill it]."

Talent Showcase

MARJIE LUNDSTROM ▶

Senior Editor, Columnist and Writing Coach, *The Sacramento Bee*

Probably sooner than later, a young reporter will be sent to a foreign place and get lost. Trained on a pastoral college campus, the reporter will go to work in the heart of the big city and find it decayed, congested and impersonal. Another, single and restless for action, will be dispatched to suburbs full of church-going families and will write about manicured lawns and quiet towns invariably shocked by any crime. And still another, who has known only urban life, will be sent to seek a story in rural America. And will step in it.

In the span of two paragraphs, it's almost guaranteed, these writers will commit multiple journalistic sins: using clichés to stereotype, writing about their audience rather than for it, and providing both superficial and misleading images while missing more revealing stories.

As a Pulitzer Prize-winning reporter, a columnist, a city editor, a writing coach, and an ethics fellow for The Poynter Institute, Marjie Lundstrom has done a lot, seen more. She has seen more than she wants of geographic clichés, but she's pessimistic that she's seen anywhere near the last of them. Even veteran reporters parachuting into unfamiliar regions of America, or overseas, succumb to first impressions. If they don't take the time to seek understanding through research and reporting to test their assumptions, their work is doomed to repeat some ugly journalistic history.

Worse than superficial—bad enough—these stories are inaccurate. That's an instant credibility problem to the many who know better. An industry fighting to reclaim higher credibility can scarcely afford this evidence of bias. Anything that puts journalistic integrity at risk is an ethics problem. Lundstrom has taken the lead on this one.

"If you have a limited amount of time, say what you know," she counsels. "You don't have to reach for those great conclusions about what the place is all about."

In "Farm-Fresh Clichés," a column for Poynter, Lundstrom targeted one of the more persistent cases of geographic stereotyping.

> I grew up in the Cornhusker state, but I don't always recognize the place non-native journalists see on the rare occasions they visit.
>
> To them, Nebraska is amusing, a simple and quaint spot where men sport seed caps 24/7 and women wear floral dresses and sensible shoes, their upper arms jiggling like blocks of Jell-O.
>
> This, they pronounce solemnly, is the "heartland," though few who live there would ever call it that.
>
> Visiting journalists tell folksy stories about the good settlers—solid, law-abiding, church-going stock—as though killer Charles Starkweather never existed and the Nebraska state prisons sit empty on the plains.
>
> News stories in the two largest cities are generally what bring them, but they are more likely to shoot a silo than the architecturally unique state capitol in Lincoln.

(continued)

Talent Showcase *(continued)*

Then they pack up and leave until the next time around, when news happens to find the "heartland" again.

As a journalist, I often find myself wondering: Why do we do this? Why do we wedge people's complex lives into neat little geographic boxes with nice little labels? Why is it that the less we know about a people or place, the more we tend to say? Does our very "outsider-ness" somehow give us license to be that much more authoritative, as though ignorance is synonymous with being "fresh"?

I am guilty, too.

When I was a national writer, I traveled to Florida—practically a foreign country to me—to cover the 1989 execution of serial killer Ted Bundy. The party and carnival-like atmosphere outside the Florida State Prison near Starke was so astonishing I felt compelled to write an op-ed piece.

Mercifully, it was never published.

"It was a community affair," I wrote, "a celebration of sorts for the people of Starke and the whole state of Florida, who gussied up and turned out en masse for the death of Ted Bundy. Young mothers brought their children and retired couples lugged lawn chairs and coolers and teen-agers posed in homemade T-shirts for pocket Instamatics."

Why I decided to speak for the "whole state of Florida" in the top of the story remains a mystery to me, since the bottom of the piece was loaded with people who spoke just fine for themselves—and made the point I was trying to make. One young mother had taken her 6-year-old twin daughters out of school and, along with an infant, driven up from Orlando for what she called an educational "field trip." In the pre-dawn darkness, there were her adorable twins, dressed in matching lavender jackets, chanting, "Fry Bundy, fry Bundy," before the television cameras.

In a complex world, it is often tempting to view people and places as one-dimensional, especially when their lives are so different from our own. In the Midwest, the journalistic declaration that "life is simpler here" is so predictable it is cliché, and each time I hear it or read it, I want to shout:

"Simpler than what?"

Today I live in California, but roots run deep. A few years back, a *Sacramento Bee* sports writer wrote a feature about the die-hard Nebraska fans who had traveled to Berkeley for a football match-up between the Huskers and Cal.

"It wasn't the strangest thing the Nebraska faithful had ever seen," the lede began. "After all, earlier in the day they had stood with their jaws in vapor lock on Telegraph Avenue."

The message was unmistakable: Hicksville meets the City.

HELP YOUR NEWS ORGANIZATION RECRUIT. You encounter other journalists and their work. You will sense when their experience, skill and work habits can complement your staff's. If diversity is to be achieved sooner than later, it is everyone's job.

READ THE BEST WORK. The most enjoyable and instructive continuing education is through reading successful stories—our craft's best practice. Much of it resides

> Yet in the same way not all Floridians celebrate the death penalty, it is also true that not all Nebraskans lead sheltered lives devoid of skylines, water and pretty bridges. Nebraskans have these things, too. (And, anyway, they do let us out sometimes.)

After this diagnosis, Lundstrom turns prescriptive:

- "Set aside expectations and stereotypes and find the authentic story."
- If time is too short for that, "begin to think more in snapshots than in sweeping images." Write "about the three or four Husker fans who stood in awe on Telegraph Avenue instead of the 'Nebraska faithful.' Describe in detail the mother of the 6-year-old twins, not the 'whole state of Florida.' "
- "When in doubt, ask a native."

Lundstrom notes that "the heartland" is hardly alone. Every region of the country is susceptible. Journalists are taught early about the perils of having a preconceived view in advance of reporting facts. But when they start with stereotypes about California, Texas, the South, Washington, D.C., New England—any and every place, really—they have committed equivalent sins. When editors see these flaws and fail to ask, "Do we really want to say this?" they have denied their news organizations the opportunity to save itself, or at least to benefit from important debate.

Provide valuable context about a place that might be foreign to many of your readers, without extending the life of clichés, Lundstrom challenges. It doesn't help that political candidates, setting up photo ops and playing the lead roles in ads, use stereotypical backdrops.

The key, as the Committee of Concerned Journalists advises, rests in being humble about what you know and don't know. When Americans suddenly had a powerful need to know about Afghanistan and Pakistan after the Sept. 11 terrorist attacks, news reports benefited from geographic humility that came honestly: few journalists knew much about these seldom-discussed places, either. With few prejudicial assumptions, stories were freshly informative.

Times change. Just think: Until the 21st century, the newspaper term for an obscure editorial was "Afghanistanism."

* * *

Stereotypes are staples of stand-up comedy, which takes a nugget of truth and exaggerates for effect. News stories are not supposed to exaggerate. The solitary "throw-away line" (so-named because it's expendable) attempt at humor in an otherwise-serious story often seems much funnier to the writer than to readers. That one line can turn the tables on a news story. Instead of being taken seriously for the other good work within, it is ridiculed mercilessly because of one quip that was unnecessary to the story in the first place.

There's a place for humor in a news report. A daily dose would help more than hurt—as long as the humor in a piece is its clearly understood intent. Then, the execution on a humor article needs to be as effective as it is on news stories.

among the award winners presented annually at Columbia University's "Let's Do it Better!" workshop.

Aside from issues of diversity, the works are splendid examples of investigative journalism, explanatory journalism, narrative journalism, trend stories, profile writing and more. Find the award winners from 1999 to the present at www.jrn.columbia.edu/events/race/honorees/.

Also see the book and DVD, *The Authentic Voice: The Best Reporting on Race and Ethnicity*, which showcases and deconstructs 13 of these stories, including interviews with the authors.

Coauthor Arlene Morgan is Associate Dean of Prizes and Programs and the Director of Workshops in Journalism, Race and Ethnicity at Columbia.

She said the story topics in the book range from searching for identity, searching for equality, and finding untold stories to cultural competency: "Understanding about a culture, what about the Somali religion makes the Somali Muslim different from a Saudi Arabian Muslim."

They have in common the three things that the "Let's-Do-It-Better!" judges look for: voice, context and complexity.

"You want to be a journalist?" Morgan challenges. "Don't tell me you like to write. Go write books. Tell me about journalism. Tell me about the profiles you are going to do, the context. So that I know what is going on when the story is over."

She offers this counsel:

- **Start out with the small story:** Morgan cites how Ted Koppel's team at *Nightline* got started on exemplary work: "Talking to the cops in this suburb, talking to the people in the bar, talking to people in the neighborhood. But the more you cover race, or, for that matter, education—understanding the culture of any community—the more you become an authority, the easier it is to do the stories," Morgan encourages. "Get away from the structure of institutional journalism. It's better to do storytelling. The real stories come from people, not the spokespeople of government."
- **Fight your own preconceived assumptions:** As above, she cited the assumptions about the KKK that were challenged in the AP's "Torn from the Land" series.
- **What was in it for your sources?** Here, Morgan is talking about the story's "Voice" (capital V) again. "Voice. Whatever voice you pick—let it come out, let them tell the story," Morgan says. "And if *you* are going to tell the story, you have to be the authority."

Aside from matters of race, she invoked the names of the famed investigative reporting team, Don Barlett and Jim Steele.

"The details in their stories and the voice allowed their stories to be told in the most authoritative way."

IN CONCLUSION

Newsrooms have much to gain from a diverse staff—a staff that can relate to the different cultures, ages, communities and interests of its readers. Such a diverse staff finds more stories and more sources. It builds credibility by its presence throughout its community and by how accurately it handles stories that understand different cultures.

Young journalists can help their newsrooms become more diverse. They find stories of interest to younger readers. They develop sources in new places. And they help the newsroom recruit a diverse pool of top talent.

TOOL KIT

Let's Do It Better! award winners:

www.jrn.columbia.edu/events/race/honorees/

The Authentic Voice: The Best Reporting on Race and Ethnicity by Arlene Notoro Morgan, Alice Irene Pifer and Keith Woods; Columbia University Press, New York, 2006.

Numerous columns, tip sheets and more from various Poynter Institute authors:

www.poynter.org/subject.asp?id=5

"Farm-fresh cliches" on geographical bias: www.poynter.org/content/content_view.asp?id=4685

"Parchute Journalism" re geographic bias: www.poynter.org/content/content_view.asp?id=4682

Nieman Reports article on covering California recall election: www.nieman.harvard.edu/reports/03-4NRwinter/53-56V57N4.pdf

Some among various organizations of minority journalists:

Asian American Journalists Association: www.aaja.org/

Native American Journalists Association: www.naja.com/

National Association of Black Journalists: www.nabj.org/

National Association of Hispanic Journalists: www.nahj.org/

National Lesbian & Gay Journalists Association: www.nlgja.org/

EXERCISE 1

Discuss the following questions:

1. Reporters often must refer to race when writing stories. They have several words they can use. When are some uses more appropriate than others? What are ways you refer to these ethnic groups? What descriptors would you avoid?
   a. White/Anglo/Caucasian
   b. Black/African American/Negro
   c. Hispanic/Latino/Latina/Mexican American/Cuban American/Dominican/Haitian/Columbian
   d. Asian/Oriental/Chinese/Asian Indian/Korean/Japanese
   e. Native Americans/Indians
2. When is race appropriate to use in a news story? When is it inappropriate?
3. If an ethnic group asks journalists to change how the journalists refer to them, are the journalists obligated?
4. How should groups categorized through sexual orientation receive the same sensitivity afforded groups of ethnic minorities?

EXERCISE 2

Find a story where the principal subject belongs to a minority group. Answer the following questions:

1. How did the news medium where the story ran handle the person's ethnicity or sexual orientation?
2. Was it necessary to identify the subject through ethnicity or sexual orientation?
3. Did readers benefit from the diverse nature of this story?
4. How could readers benefit even further? Did the story leave out information or fail to discuss issues that would have furthered the understanding of a diverse culture?
5. Imagine the principal subject as a member of a different minority group. How would the story have changed? Would the story be different if the principal subject were part of the majority?

EXERCISE 3

In this chapter, Keith Woods of The Poynter Institute says that we should look at diversity in news coverage as an ethics issue. That is, journalists should approach diversity more seriously than just following the correct guidelines offered in stylebooks.

"To deny a person his voice, is to deny his truth," Woods counsels. "Exclude the individual and you exclude their truth."

1. What does Woods mean by denying "a person his voice, is to deny his truth"?
2. How can journalists better show diversity in their reporting?
3. How do readers benefit when journalists are able to report fairly and truthfully about ethnicity and avoid stereotypes of race?
4. In the controversial photographs following Hurricane Katrina, how could those writing the captions for the photographs have improved the understanding of diversity?
5. What are the impact and message that photojournalists give when they publish images depicting racial diversity?

CHAPTER 21

Libel: What Journalists Need to Know about the Law

IN THIS CHAPTER, YOU WILL LEARN:

- What are the limits of free speech and a free press.
- What libel is, and why journalists need to understand it.
- How journalists can defend themselves against libel suits.
- Who public figures are and why they are in a special category.
- When journalists have to respect a person's privacy.
- What a journalist is allowed to print.

(Richard) Jewell's libel case, one of the more noted in the past decade, illustrates how libel laws work in the United States.

On a hot night in Atlanta in 1996, revelers had crowded Centennial Olympic Park to celebrate the summer Olympic Games. A pipe bomb filled with nails exploded, killing one and injuring 111. After a few days, the FBI began to suspect a security guard named Richard Jewell.

Jewell earlier had discovered the suspicious backpack under a park bench. He alerted law enforcement officials and had begun to clear the area. Jewell's actions no doubt saved lives. He was hailed as a hero. He freely gave interviews to television and print reporters.

But Jewell fit the FBI's profile of a bomber. He quickly became the FBI's chief suspect. News media, overflowing in Atlanta because of the Olympics, turned their focus on him. Both CNN and NBC ran reports mentioning Jewell. The *Atlanta Journal-Constitution* printed an extra edition saying the FBI suspected he sought acclaim by saving lives.

Three months later, federal law enforcement officials decided Jewell had nothing to do with the explosion, and apologized. Another man, who hid in the North Carolina wilderness, later confessed to the crime.

What happened to Jewell? The security man sued NBC, CNN and the *Journal-Constitution* for what is known as libel—that these media had reported false information linking him to a felony crime. Those accusations, he said, hurt his reputation.

Jewell settled with CNN and NBC out of court. But in court, he and the newspaper battled for 10 years. Jewell died a few months before this book went to press. A Georgia judge later dismissed the last claim of his suit.

Jewell's libel case, one of the more noted in the past decade, illustrates how libel laws work in the United States.

News subjects have limited ways to defend themselves against false information reported by media. Outside of the courts, these subjects can push the media to run corrections, write follow-up stories and print rebutting guest columns or letters to the editor. Some news subjects tell their stories to competing media to set the record straight. Groups and corporations can mount public relations campaigns.

In the courts, libel and privacy laws govern the media. The courts have consistently ruled that the media play an important role in telling citizens how their government and society are behaving. Other than extremely rare cases, the courts never tell the news media beforehand what they can publish or broadcast. But when the media run false information that hurts reputations, those injured can sue the media for money.

Journalists must know what boundaries they can't cross when reporting for their publications or websites or when editing their news shows. All journalists should have a working knowledge of what makes a news report libelous.

LIMITS OF SPEECH AND PRINT

Americans are justifiably proud of their rights to free speech and a free press. Some of the most important movements in history—abolishing slavery, women's suffrage, protecting civil rights—were possible because the First Amendment to the U.S. Constitution lets us challenge government and openly follow our conscience.

The First Amendment sounds absolute: "Congress shall make *no law* . . . abridging the freedom of speech, or of the press. . . ." But, in many ways, laws and court cases over the years have limited what we can say or publish. For example:

- Threatening to hurt someone physically can get you arrested.
- The government classifies information that might imperil our national security.
- Through copyrights, you can't use another's intellectual property unless through payment or permission.
- Tobacco companies can't advertise cigarettes on television.

Journalists themselves have imposed limits on what they print. Editors usually decline to print profanity. They edit out speech that might offend certain groups—many newspapers and television stations recently declined to show a cartoon depicting the prophet Muhammad. In some states, the names of juvenile crime offenders and sexual assault victims are available to anyone who bothers to read the police reports. However, most television stations and newspapers decline to air or print those names to protect the juvenile and victim. Only when rape victims give their permission will many daily news organizations run the names.

These are voluntary. Editors try to judge their communities' sensibilities and report what they believe readers or viewers will tolerate. They will hold back or edit what they believe will offend, such as sexually explicit photos. Other publications—special-interest magazines, for example—print profanity and photos without worry of reader backlash. It's legal in most cases, and their niche audiences tolerate the words and content.

All this lies outside the law. Some limits to a free press, however, are imposed through laws. Journalism falls under what are known as libel laws. These laws, which differ from state to state, lay the ground rules journalists should follow to avoid losing lawsuits and paying damages.

WHAT IS LIBEL

Journalists in the United States are not licensed as doctors and lawyers are. There is no approval process or state board that decides who can practice journalism. Anyone with the money to print a newspaper or magazine can become a print journalist. The freedom bloggers enjoy on the Internet flows directly from this constitutional right of free expression, although most bloggers may not be considered journalists.

In the United States, libel is one of the more prominent legal tools used to curb journalists. Understanding how the courts define libel is important to reporters of all experience levels.

Libel is publishing a false statement that hurts a person's reputation within society. It can also mean printing false information that holds a person up to ridicule within society. From that simple definition grows a list of complex shadings.

ADVANCED TIP
What Is Libel?

Libel is publishing a false statement that hurts a person's reputation within society. It can also mean printing false information that holds a person up to ridicule among those acquaintances.

To prove libel, a person claiming injury has to show four key points, sometimes known as the plaintiff's burdens of proof:

- That the information in the story (or broadcast, advertisement, public relations release, pamphlet, newsletter, website) was wrong. The information might be a direct statement or what readers might infer from the information.
- The information was published or aired.
- Those suing have to show the published or broadcast error was about them and not about someone else.
- The injured parties have to show that the false information damaged their reputations or held them up to public ridicule and that they suffered as a result.

All states have libel laws, although the definitions of libel and protections for journalists vary from state to state. Judges' decisions have helped form definitions. Although journalists can err in many ways, some common areas that can hurt a person and get journalists in trouble are:

CRIMINAL ACTIVITY. When journalists falsely report that someone has committed a crime, especially a felony, they are open to libel suits. Much of the Richard Jewell case in Atlanta was based on the implication that the FBI suspected Jewell had set and ignited the deadly bomb in Centennial Olympic Park. Agents never charged Jewell with a crime. His lawyers argued that Jewell's reputation was damaged through media reports that quoted sources saying Jewell was the chief suspect, thereby linking him to the killing.

In many states, journalists are protected if they get the information from police reports or are told by the district attorney and police that a person has been charged with a crime. In Jewell's case, the bombing investigators were the sources for the news reports, but because no law enforcement agency filed a charge against him, he argued that journalists acted outside that protection.

INCOMPETENCE IN BUSINESS. A few years back, a *New York Times* business reporter wrote a book about the television personality and businessman, Donald Trump. In the book, the reporter, Timothy O'Brien, put Trump's wealth in the millions. The statement upset Trump. He claimed that he was worth billions, and that O'Brien's reporting had hurt his reputation because he would be perceived in a less favorable light as an entrepreneur. Trump later dropped the suit. Regardless of who's right in this instance, it shows that people are sensitive to criticism of their business. Journalists must take care

ADVANCED TIP
What the Plaintiff Must Prove in Libel Cases?

1. The information was false.
2. The information was about you.
3. The information was published.
4. The information was damaging.

that information critical of a business is strongly supported by credible interviews and documents.

LOATHSOME DISEASE: In general, if a journalist reports someone has venereal disease, HIV/AIDS or other unsociable disease, it implies that the person can transmit the illness and should be avoided. That hurts their reputation. If false, that meets a standard for libel.

DISHONESTY OR IMMORALITY: Journalists who report about a person's dishonesty or sexual morality run the risk of libel if the information is false. *The Philadelphia Inquirer* once settled a libel suit with a former assistant district attorney it had accused of helping to thwart the prosecution of a friend's son for murder. After 23 years, the newspaper and the former assistant district attorney settled out of court. Two trials had found the newspaper had not knowingly printed falsehoods but had made several errors and quoted sources out of context.

Libel falls under civil laws, meaning the only recourse. Some states have criminal libel laws still on their books, but prosecution for criminal libel is rare. The only recourse in the justice system for people who feel they've been libeled is to sue.

The sister offense to libel is slander. Libel is written, slander spoken. In all but four states, television and radio journalists are subject to libel laws even though they speak their reports. That's because they usually read from scripts and their broadcasts are taped as opposed to passing conversation, and therefore have a degree of permanence. Only two states make the distinction of reading from a script and ad lib comments. Libel laws conveniently have put most journalists—print or electronic—under the same umbrella.

DEFENSES

Facing a libel suit, journalists and media companies counter using several defenses. Some defenses are as easy as answering this question: Was the information true? Other key questions that may influence how a libel case is defended include: Was the publication an opinion, not a fact? Was the story's subject a prominent person or government official? Finally, when does the law excuse a mistake?

TRUTH: The obvious solution to avoiding libel suits is never print false information or make mistakes reporting. Libel requires published statements that are false. Take away that element and journalists neutralize the complaint. That won't prevent someone from suing, but truth traditionally is the best defense for libel.

Most journalists work their entire careers without ever being sued for libel. Most seasoned reporters avoid writing or airing information if they doubt its veracity. Information can damage someone's reputation. But if the information is true, it's not libelous.

ADVANCED TIP
Defending Libel

Here are the common defenses against libel:

- Truth
- Opinion or fair comment
- Privilege

OPINION OR FAIR COMMENT. As part of the courts' desire to see a robust public debate, judges have let columnists and critics express their opinions or comment on people's actions. But the courts hold opinion writing to two standards.

First, the courts don't give columnists carte blanche to hide false statements under the cloak of opinion. No courts protect *I think Bill Smith is a murderer* if Bill Smith can prove he's no murderer.

Second, you know it's opinion when it's difficult to prove or disprove. That is, a sports columnist can say a coach made the wrong tactical decision. No one could prove the statement right or wrong because who could show what would have happened had the coach made a different choice? *I think Austin is the best city* can't be proven or discredited.

Political columnists can question a governor's actions, movie reviewers can label a film thumbs up or down, a metro columnist can call a blighted area in the city deplorable: All fall under opinion because none are provable facts.

PRIVILEGE. The usual rule in libel is that journalists are legally responsible for whatever they publish, even if they're merely quoting someone else. However, you can sometimes quote people or documents without worrying about a libel risk—even when you know what you're quoting isn't true. The clearest examples are when we quote what lawyers and witnesses say in court or in the documents they file in court, what police and witnesses are quoted as saying in official police reports and what members of Congress or a city council say during official meetings.

The reason? The courts want trials to be a search for the truth, without putting everything everyone says under the threat of libel or slander suits. The same goes for public debates by elected officials. And if those in public life get such protection, then our reporting on such statements—as long as it's accurate—should also be protected.

Be careful, though. Laws vary from state to state, so this protection isn't guaranteed. Plus, it may not be fair or wise to publish falsehoods just because you are immune from a libel suit. And once you interview someone outside the courtroom or off the Legislature floor, the privilege no longer applies.

PUBLIC OFFICIAL, PUBLIC FIGURE

Until 40 years ago, defending libel suits was more difficult for the news media. The rules were strict: No matter how you made a fact error, and no matter whom you were writing about, any mistake could mean that you lost. And once you were accused of libel, then it was up to you to prove your report was true—or lose the case.

That changed in 1964 when a landmark case, *The New York Times v. Sullivan*, rewrote the way American courts decide libel.

Since then, the burden of proving a story's accuracy has switched from the news media to the person filing the suit. The U.S. Supreme Court created the standard

Figure 21.1 **Number of Libel Trials**

From 1980 to 2006, the media faced fewer trials for libel, privacy and related claims, and won a higher percentage of these cases, according to the Media Law Resource Center.

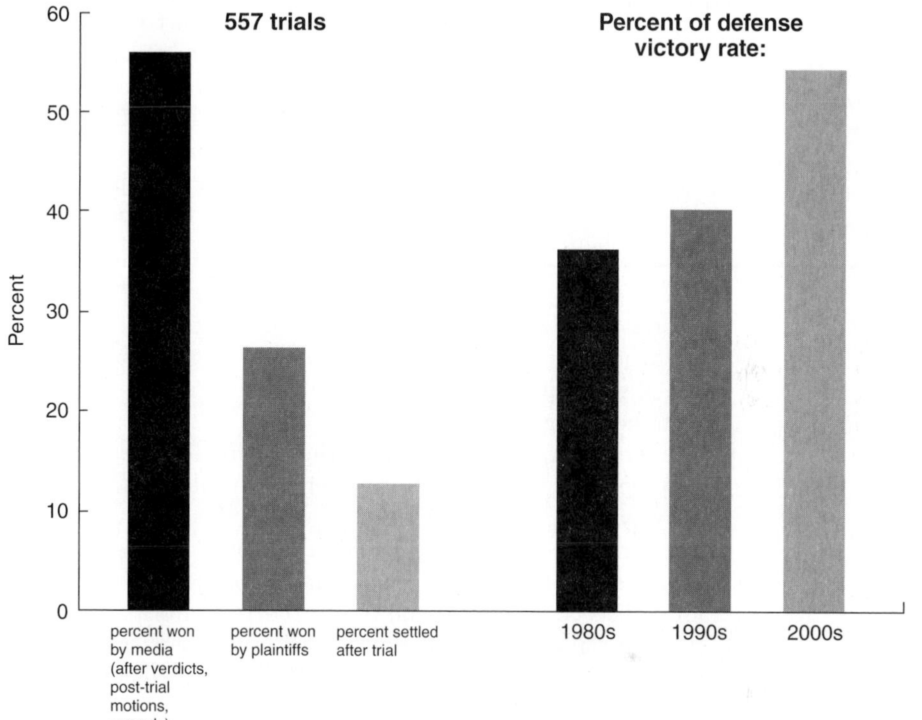

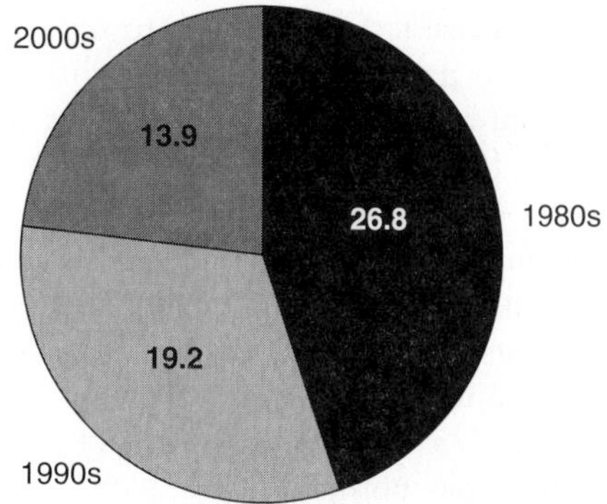

Source: Media Law Resource Center

ADVANCED TIP
Landmark Case

The landmark Supreme Court case, *The New York Times v. Sullivan*, rewrote the way libel is judged in the United States. The case makes it difficult for public officials and figures—that is, politicians and celebrities—to win libel cases. They must prove that the journalists knowingly published false information. In general, the courts have favored robust debate on public issues. To ensure spirited discussion, the courts often let journalists err as long as they are not doing so to hurt a well-known person's reputation.

"actual malice" for the truth when deciding libel. Now, those in the public eye face a steep hurdle to win lawsuits, even when the information about them is false.

The landmark case, decided by the Supreme Court over a civil rights advertisement, said a critical fact in deciding libel is whether the person making the libel claim is a public official. Later cases expanded public official to public figure, meaning a person of notoriety. Being a public official or public figure puts that person in a special category.

- Public officials usually mean elected or appointed members of government. Public figures can be entertainers, celebrities or athletes. They also can be a private person who has joined the public debate or sought publicity on an issue. Richard Jewell was a private figure until he volunteered for interviews in the 1996 Atlanta bombing case.
- The term "actual malice" means those suing for libel have to show that editors and reporters knew the information was probably false but printed or aired it anyway.
- The term "reckless disregard for the truth" means editors or reporters purposely failed to follow the ways most journalists check out information and journalists could have found out the correct information.
- If those claiming libel are considered private citizens, they need only to show careless reporting in checking out the false statement. The actual malice standard does not apply in their cases.

The courts have ruled that journalism plays a significant part in strengthening democracy. Journalism informs the electorate, spurs robust debates on issues and adds another check and balance to the three branches of government. Therefore the courts cut journalists a wide path to report aggressively on people in the spotlight.

The courts understand that journalists sometimes will make mistakes. But when writing about public figures, if journalists erred unknowingly and clearly tried to get at the truth, the courts often have given them a pass. An aggressive press outweighs the errors journalists sometimes will make in the normal course of reporting.

In the mid-1990s, a jury decided that the news show *20/20* had libeled a Florida businessman, Alan Levan. The show's report had accused Levan of shady practices with investors in his savings and loan. The jury awarded Levan $8.5 million, and his business another $1.25 million.

On appeal, a higher court reversed the decision and said ABC, which produces *20/20*, had to pay nothing. The reason? The panel of judges decided that Levan was a public figure and had failed to show that *20/20* knew some information was false but aired it anyway. In other words, the judges believed ABC acted without actual malice.

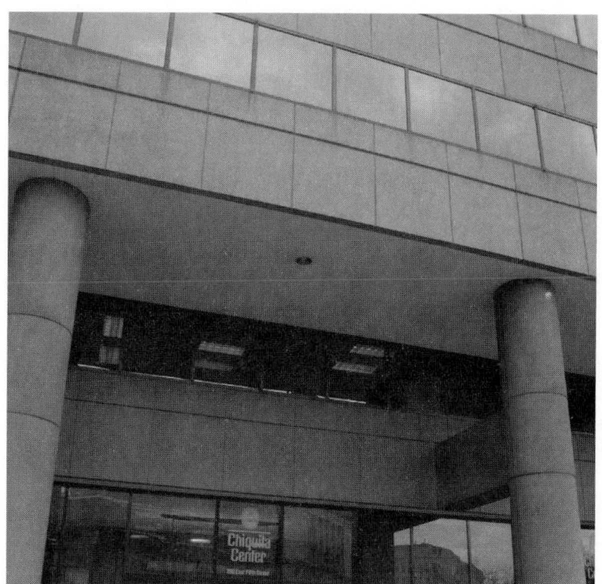

The *Cincinnati Enquirer* wrote an exposé about Chiquita Brands International Inc., whose headquarters are in Cincinnati. But because a reporter admitted he accessed company voice mails—a violation of privacy law—the newspaper had to apologize to the company and pay it $10 million.

In a nutshell, the more public a person is, the more difficult to win a libel lawsuit. The more private a person is, the lower the standards for proving libel. All libel involves a false statement, so journalists learn early that truth is their best defense. The lesson from most libel cases is to avoid sloppy and unfair reporting, especially when stories stray into the areas that qualify as libelous.

THE CHIQUITA CASE

In the late 1990s, the *Cincinnati Enquirer* ran an 18-page special section accusing Chiquita Brands International Inc. of questionable business practices in Central America. The giant banana company, headquartered in Cincinnati, called the accusations unfair.

The *Enquirer* used Chiquita company voice mails as part of its investigation. Many of those voice mails seemed to support the newspaper's findings. The newspaper said it had secured the internal communication from a company source.

After protests from the company, the *Enquirer* investigated further. Its reporter, Michael Gallagher, later admitted he had accessed the voice mails. A former Chiquita employee had given Gallagher confidential access codes to the voice mail system. Gallagher often tapped into the voice-mail system, which is illegal, to find support for his story's accusations. In all, Gallagher had listened to about 2,000 voice mails.

Gallagher violated privacy laws. Two months after the story ran, the *Enquirer* ran a front-page apology, retracted the entire story, fired Gallagher and paid Chiquita $10 million.

Gallagher was charged with crimes. He faced a possible two-and-one-half-year prison term but struck a plea bargain with prosecutors. He was sentenced to five years probation and 200 hours of community service.

As part of his plea agreement, Gallagher also told prosecutors who gave him the access codes. That person, a former Chiquita lawyer, pled guilty to four misdemeanor charges and received two years probation and 40 hours of community service.

The Chiquita case points out an area where journalists receive no special protection from the law. If journalists break laws to gather news, they face the same punishment as any other citizen. Many of these laws fall under the area known as privacy.

WEN HO LEE

In 1999, the United States government accused a scientist at the Los Alamos National Laboratory of spying for China. Government sources leaked the story and information about the scientist's background to five media companies: *The Associated Press*, *The New York Times*, *The Washington Post*, the *Los Angeles Times* and CNN. All ran stories mentioning the scientist by name.

Wen Ho Lee smiles after giving a brief statement to the press upon his release outside the United States Courthouse in Albuquerque, N.M., on Sept. 13, 2000.

The scientist, Wen Ho Lee, originally from Taiwan, was jailed in solitary confinement for nine months while the government worked his case. At the end, the FBI dropped 58 of 59 charges against him. Lee pled guilty to a charge of mishandling information.

Lee sued the government for invasion of privacy. His lawyers wanted the five reporters in the case to reveal the confidential sources who leaked the misinformation. A judge held the five reporters in contempt when they refused to divulge their sources. They faced fines and jail if they refused to reveal the confidential sources.

Lee, the United States government and the five media companies settled the suit out of court in 2006. Lee received $895,000 from the government and $750,000 from the five media companies who paid $150,000 each. The media companies, who were not part of the privacy suit, helped the government settle the case to avoid contempt charges against the reporters.

The Lee case points out even though the reporters were not part of the invasion-of-privacy suit, they were instruments for spreading the information about Lee. In an editorial in *The Boston Globe*, the newspaper criticized the reporters for relying on untrustworthy sources. *The New York Times* said in an editor's note a year after Lee's arrest that it wishes it had done things differently to give Lee more "benefit of the doubt."

PRIVACY

About 100 years ago, the thought that citizens have a right to privacy was introduced into the law. Though a newer concept than libel, privacy laws now are on the books in all states. Journalists must understand that they receive no special protection when dealing with privacy and need to know the boundaries of privacy when gathering information.

Invasion of privacy can be criminal, as the Chiquita case demonstrated, and journalists could go to jail for violating privacy laws. Privacy can also be civil, as

WIRED AND WIRELESS | WEB

In the world of freewheeling blogging and website linking, journalists must ask this question: Do the libel laws of print and broadcast apply the same online?

The general answer: yes. The courts consider posting a message online the same as circulating it through print or sending it over airways. A libelous statement in the old media is still a libelous statement in the new.

That means that those who run websites and those who blog must adhere to the laws that regulate defamatory statements.

Congress, though, has given a special protection to those who run websites. To encourage the public to engage in robust discussions, lawmakers have said if someone posts libelous statements to a site during a chat room, the site's owner is not responsible.

According to Prof. Mark Obbie, who runs a legal reporting program at Syracuse University's Newhouse School, this was Congress' way of fostering greater use of the Internet by the public. This exception lets commercial website publishers relax and allow freewheeling commentary by the public, he says.

Bloggers are protected from libelous suits if a third party sends them libelous material, even if it's posted on their blog or website. But according to the Electronic Frontier Foundation, bloggers must take care. Should bloggers use the libelous material in their own postings, they would fall under the same guidelines and possibly lose their protection.

No court cases have tested that yet, the foundation's website says. But the provision in the federal law says it plainly.

The rule of thumb: Follow the same guidelines online as you would if you were printing a newspaper or magazine or airing a report on television or the radio. In that way you fall under the protections for traditional media that the courts have upheld for years.

the Lee case shows. Lee said the government jailed him illegally and invaded his privacy by leaking his personal information to journalists. Thus, the news organizations became involved tangentially, and later paid to settle the suit.

Journalists also must know that truth, the ultimate defense for libel, will not always get them off the hook when dealing with privacy. Those who sue claiming violation of privacy are saying they have been embarrassed unduly. The facts that were published were true, but they were so revealing that the person has been humiliated. They are not suing because of reputation, which is at the heart of libel suits.

The courts have outlined several standards that qualify for privacy:

- Publishing an embarrassing fact. When writing about people, journalists must be certain incidents are relevant to their stories. Sometimes a stray fact, though intriguing and true, might upset the story's subject. Depending on how private the person is, the fact might fall under privacy laws.
- Trespassing to get a story. Journalists have to obey the same trespassing laws as any citizen. They are allowed to report on what can be seen or heard from the street or public places. But they are not allowed to trespass on private property—or electronically trespass in voice mail—to get a story or take a picture.

- Unapproved use of someone's image. This applies more to advertisements, but a person's photo can't run in a commercial use without permission. Editors can run photos taken in public to accompany news stories. But one area of editorial use of photos or quotes where journalists should be careful is in depicting or naming children. It's much safer, and fairer, to get permission from a responsible adult before using a child's name or image in a news report.

In general, be cautious about publicizing an embarrassing incident that happened in the past and has little bearing on today's events. And, when dealing with private property or sensitive personal topics—such as medical, income tax or academic records—keep in mind that there are many laws protecting people's privacy and putting journalists at legal risk.

WHAT JOURNALISTS ARE ALLOWED TO PRINT

Despite legal and self-imposed limits, American journalists enjoy vast freedoms to report newsworthy information unfettered from government interference. When revealing the actions of government, its office holders and its citizens, American journalists work in the wide latitude given them by judges and legislators.

Journalists are allowed to report on many controversial and mundane issues. Essentially, all government meetings or court proceedings that let the public watch also are open to journalists.

That means anytime a majority of an elected body, such as a quorum of city council members, gathers, journalists can report on their actions. Meetings of government are open except those discussing ongoing personnel issues, legal matters or real estate transactions.

Stories on governments are not limited to meetings. With few exceptions, journalists can report on most reports, memos and e-mail written by elected officials and public servants.

Journalists also have the freedom to tell their readers or viewers about their public officials' conduct outside government's offices. Courts generally have allowed reporters to reveal freely how their officials behave. Reporters even can look through their officials' garbage.

Journalists aren't limited to official government actions and proceedings. Again, what the public can view, journalists can report. They can observe people in public places, such as parks, beaches and streets. They can review movies, plays and music. They can report on sporting events.

They are free to report on a private citizen who becomes part of a newsworthy event. The courts have ruled that informing the public trumps a person's privacy in these matters.

The freer a society, the freer its press. The notion of what is news has changed over generations. But the notion that government would stop the news from reaching its free citizens has not been tolerated.

IN CONCLUSION

Journalists must have a strong working knowledge of libel laws so they know the boundaries of what they should print. The courts have usually ruled in favor of an aggressive press, especially when the media and government officials have clashed. The courts have encouraged robust debate spurred by journalists' reporting, despite recognizing that the media sometimes will err.

EXERCISE 1

Rewrite the following sentences to remove libel or add balance:

1. James Fields' neighbor, Bonnie Hunt, says she often heard the animals crying from Fields' yard. She says she believes Fields ignored his pets and was starving them.
2. The fatal accident occurred at the corner of Velasko and Cherry streets. The van, driven by Tom Wellington, caused the accident by running the stop sign at Cherry and hitting the other car crossing through the intersection.
3. Police are interviewing Harold Plamet about his killing the two women on Thursday.
4. Police charged the three teenager boys with felony possession of cocaine. They have yet to charge the other two, Jewel Spence and Jessica Abrams, with felony drug possession.
5. Salinity Corp. leaked toxic chemicals into the lake. Company officials say it never happened. State environmental investigators looking into the cause of the dying fish will issue their report in a month.

EXERCISE 2

What does this item do correctly when dealing with libel? Where does it need editing to eliminate the libel and add balance?

Student Stole Roommate's Credit Cards to Buy TV, Phones

Bardwell police have charged a Bardwell College student with stealing his roommates' credit cards and buying a television set and top-of-the line cell phones.

The student, Josh Hayes, racked up more than $1,500 in charges on his roommates' credit cards. He stole them while his roommate, Jaime Chavez, was sleeping with his girlfriend, Belinda Ashloff, in her room.

Students who live on the same floor as Hayes say he has taken other items from dorm rooms, but no one has been able to catch him until now.

"He's as cunning as anyone you'll ever meet," said one student who declined to give his name or dorm room number. "I'm just glad they caught the thief."

Police say they are holding Hayes on $1,000 bail. They said they have located the merchandise and will return the stolen items after they close the case.

1. Is the headline fair to the student who was charged with the crime?
2. Should the reporter attribute the information in the second paragraph?

3. Should the reporter include the detailed information of where Chavez was when his cards were stolen?
4. Should the reporter identify Chavez' girlfriend by name?
5. What is wrong with the student's statement that accuses Hayes of more crimes?
6. Should the reporter rewrite the paragraph or leave it out?
7. Should the reporter quote an anonymous source? What are the issues associated with nameless sources?
8. Should the reporter leave the quote in the fourth paragraph in the story?
9. Why does attributing the information to police in the fifth paragraph add authority and fairness to the information?
10. Should the words "stolen items" be left in the story?

EXERCISE 3

Discuss the following:

1. Should people running for elected office have their personal relationships exposed to the public?
2. When is a person's sexual orientation OK to use in a story?
3. When is it permissible for a journalist to trespass to get a story?
4. Should a journalist be allowed to listen to voice mail and read e-mail to expose corruption in the government? Does this also apply to private businesses?
5. When the news media print false information about someone, should running a correction be enough to satisfy the injured party?

CHAPTER 22

How to Land Your First Job (and Your First Promotion)

IN THIS CHAPTER, YOU WILL LEARN:

- How to search for a job as a journalist.
- Effective techniques for your cover letter, résumé, and work samples.
- How to prepare for and conduct a job interview.
- Advice for succeeding on the job.

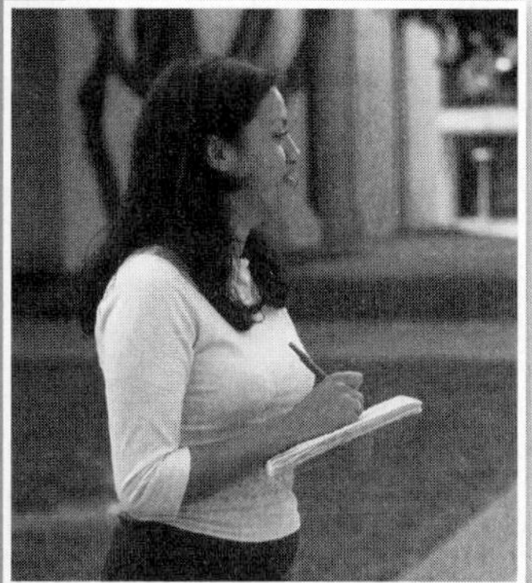

Your first job is not about money. It's about gaining experience.
Advice from the authors, who have hired hundreds of journalists

Most of this book focuses on developing your skills in this craft so that you can excel throughout your career. Now, having hired hundreds of journalists, the authors of this book offer a few tips on finding your first job—and earning your second.

YOUR SEARCH

Cast Your Net Wide

It's simple math: The more places you are willing to work, the more likely one of them will have an opening that suits you and will be willing to hire you.

You are the best judge of your needs, but confining your search to narrow geography, to a certain size of newspaper or website or to a specialized role (environmental reporter, religion writer) restricts your chances. That's self-defeating, because experience breeds opportunity. Early on, you need as much experience as you can get to attract as many good employers as possible.

More than 1,400 newspapers publish daily in the United States. Most of these have websites. In addition, many more weeklies—both community weeklies in suburban and rural towns as well as big-city alternative weeklies—need writers, editors and graphic designers. You may be very happy at a smaller operation, where you can enjoy being closer to your audience, connected in your community and able to do a wide range of journalism. As long as you are at a place that prizes good work and offers the chance to improve (through solid editing, for instance), size is secondary.

SET REALISTIC EXPECTATIONS

It's always been true that entry-level jobs in journalism don't pay recent college graduates as well as some other careers. But remember:

Your first job is not about money. It's about gaining experience. You have to have experience to get the better jobs. If you excel in the job you have, raises and promotions will follow. Each new job will pay more than the last one. If working for a larger daily newspaper appeals to you, keep this in mind: pay scales at larger newspapers generally are defined by years of experience at daily newspapers, whatever the size. The pay scale doesn't distinguish between whether that first two years of experience was at a 20,000 circulation newspaper or a 100,000 circulation newspaper.

Appreciate any opportunity to advance your skills, knowledge and qualifications. Initially, a general-assignments reporting job or a police beat might fill that description. Perhaps you have your sights set on something more glamorous. Perhaps you've already been a columnist for your college newspaper and already have a popular blog. Keep things in perspective: Chances are, freshmen were not given those column-writing jobs. Your "freshman" professional job is not likely to be at the column-writing level.

WIRED AND WIRELESS | WEB

Job Searches and the Internet

Facebook and Myspace provide countless hours of entertainment, communication, cyber-stalking and amusement for college students. These websites also can be the demise of job searches.

More and more companies are using Facebook and Myspace to recruit potential employees. Even political campaigns are contacting students through these websites to promote their candidates. Such promotions are facts of life in the 21st century.

But the downside to this trend is that many companies are combing the Web to see if their future employees have posted anything that could embarrass the employees or the company. An innocent but untoward comment here or there or an item posted purely in jest could hurt your chances to land the job.

The rule of thumb is this: Don't put anything online that you wouldn't show an employer during an interview. That means embarrassing or suggestive photos, insensitive comments, derisive remarks, jokes that in the moment sound too hilarious but later prove in poor taste: all might find their way to the organization where you most want to work.

Much of the Internet is permanent and leaves cyber footprints. That goes for e-mails as well. Even though sending messages through cyberspace feels like the same conversation you would have on the phone, it's not. Those messages can be retrieved and questioned later.

Again the rule of thumb: Don't put anything in an e-mail that you wouldn't in a formal letter. Don't write anything down now that would embarrass you later during an interview.

YOUR APPLICATION

These are the three basic elements of your application: a cover letter, a resume and examples of your published work.

Cover Letter

The best cover letters are brief, preferably less than one page. Your resume and published work will do the other speaking for you. The cover letter establishes your interest in whatever job you seek and how soon you can be available for an interview.

Glenn Guzzo, coauthor of this book, likes to tell others about the best cover letter he received from a job applicant. In its entirety, it read:

"Rumor has it that you have openings. Please let it be true."

In 12 words, the applicant expressed her interest and showed she doesn't overwrite. She demonstrated a light touch. Her interview and her clips supported that perception. She was hired.

Your letter does not need to be that brief. It is fine to describe what job you seek (e.g., generally, a reporting job, or specifically, a job that you know is open). Better yet, leave some wiggle room. You might know the news organization is looking for someone to cover education. You can express interest in that, but add that you would be interested in any reporting job.

Caution: Getting just any job does not necessarily lead to the one you really want. If you are sure you want to write, for instance, don't assume that a job on the copy desk will get you in line to be a reporter. At some newspapers, it never does. If in doubt, ask.

Résumé

Your résumé should be concise, though not necessarily brief. Others may advise you to keep it to one page. That has never been our requirement as hiring editors. But we do want to know that you think clearly: Stick to what is relevant. Work experience and education are relevant. So are community work and hobbies, because they show your range of interests and might suggest your qualifications for current or future roles in the news organization. Your religion, personal relationships and pets are not likely to be relevant to your qualifications.

Never exaggerate your experience. That's a lie, and it's lethal. It's tough living up to something you pretended to be. A prospective employer is likely to view your dishonesty as an indication of what your work will be like. You can be fired for misrepresenting yourself on a job application.

Include references, by name and with contact information—mailing address, phone and e-mail. Advice to defer references with a line such as "References will be provided upon request," may work to your extreme disadvantage.

Hiring editors are busy, and they receive many more applications than they have jobs to offer. Frankly, they are looking for reasons to disqualify applicants. Talent equal, the applicants who make it easier for the hiring editor to proceed have an edge. Why make work for hiring editors by demanding that they ask for your references? Why cost them time by waiting for the references to arrive? Impatient hiring editors are going to find references of their own—you would rather they be contacting people you know will say complimentary things. *Do* call those references first, get their permission and find out what they will say about you if contacted.

Published Work

You must include quality examples of your experience. This is why internships, work for your college newspaper and other experience are so valuable.

If you don't have these things, perhaps you have been writing a blog, or you have written some excellent, unpublished essays. These can demonstrate your talent, too. However, the best experience is relevant experience. For writers, that's a writing role where you were edited and had to meet deadlines. That also provides relevant references.

How many clips should you send? We suggest that you ignore the common advice that you limit yourself to three, or 10. It's important that you send your best work. You have sent too many clips when you have included work that is not up to your highest standards. You have sent too few when the

ADVANCED TIP
Advice for Résumés

Stick to what is relevant. Work experience and education are relevant. So are community work and hobbies, because they show your range of interests and might suggest your qualifications for current or future roles in the news organization.

The Art of Storytelling

More than ever, hiring editors are looking for storytelling skills. They want to see good command of inverted-pyramid leads and hard-news stories, for that is basic training, and it is the currency of up-to-the-hour news online and in broadcast.

However, since the hard-news approach is so common, storytelling is a way of distinguishing one news organization from the rest. Not every news organization has the ability to put the reader at the scene, surrounded by telling detail, dialogue and action. If you can do that, your value as a job candidate is higher.

An ideal clip file to include with your resume would have all of these:

- Breaking news that demonstrates your ability to write clearly on deadline.
- Live-event coverage (e.g., meeting coverage if you are a news reporter, a ballgame if you are a sports writer, a concert if you are a lifestyles writer) that shows your ability to describe action and environment in context with the news.
- At least one nondeadline news feature that combines your ability to find and describe unique detail on a timely news topic. This should show how well you represent conflicting viewpoints.
- A well-reported, multisource profile of a newsworthy subject. Try to show, not tell, readers *what* they ought to remember about the person.
- A story with a lighter touch—a short bright or a longer piece that shows how well you capture irony and how well you juxtapose facts and quotes.
- Stories, including some of the above, with the key narrative elements—scene, motion, dialogue, complication, resolution—all producing a beginning, middle and end with character development and a payoff ending.

package understates the range of your ability—the subject matter and the writing styles you have mastered.

At that point, it's up to the recipient to read all of what you sent, or none of it. You have no entitlement. But you also do not want to disqualify yourself by failing to send the clip that would have convinced the hiring editor that you are just right for the job.

To make the best first impression, put your best clip first, and so on. Make sure these have strong leads. An impatient hiring editor who is not impressed immediately might not spend more time reading more deeply.

ADVANCED TIP
How Many Clips?

How many clips should you send? We suggest that you ignore the common advice that you limit yourself to three, or 10. It's important that you send your best work. You have sent too many clips when you have included work that is not up to your highest standards. You have sent too few when the package understates the range of your ability—the subject matter and the writing styles you have mastered.

Reread your clips occasionally. Talented writers get better every year. You should be able to look back on year-old clips—and cringe. You are better now, and you know why (sharper leads, more potent nut graphs, better use of quotes, tighter transitions, fewer digressions). On the other hand, superior work holds up over time. Learn by rereading the old clips. And keep your package fresh with your best work.

YOUR INTERVIEW

A wise hiring editor will want to make sure that you are a good fit for the organization, but also that the organization is a good fit for you.

Listen first, and answer all questions. Among other things, be prepared to answer these basic questions:

- Why you chose to be a journalist
- Why you want to work for this organization
- Your short-term and long-term ambition
- An honest, perceptive self-evaluation of your talent, pro and con
- What you think others who have worked with you (and in competition with you) would say about you
- How willing you are to accept difficult duty—odd hours, short-notice assignments, etc.
- Changes in your work experience: Why you left one organization for another

Then, be prepared to seek the answers you need, too. If it hasn't already been covered, you'll want to know at least this:

- What is expected of you in this job
- What the news organization's ambition/vision/mission is
- What opportunities exist to develop your talent (training, mentoring, etc.)
- What is the track record of advancement from the position you would be hired into?

Also prepare to express your ambition without being pushy or presumptuous.

There is no need to overdo this. Asking a few important questions is not overbearing—it's a sign of a good reporter.

Your demeanor is important. If your prior experience has earned you confidence that you are qualified for whatever opening there might be, then you are much more likely to be at ease.

YOUR JOB

Demands of the Job

Many newsrooms and websites are 24/7 operations, or nearly so. The biggest news can break at any hour. Journalists must prepare themselves and their families for the likelihood that they will work at night, on weekends and on short notice—at least some of the time.

News reporting also may require travel on short notice. If not overseas or cross country, then the travel may take you to remote parts of the state, where local news stories are developing. This can happen for many reasons: a manhunt for a dangerous fugitive, a business contemplating expansion to your area, a governor's campaign trail, a local sports team's big game on the road.

Versatility, always an asset, may be required, especially early in your career. A general-assignment reporter may be changing story topics and sources each day. A veteran journalist may be changing roles within the news organization every two or three years. If this variety sounds like fun, you have the right aptitude. If it sounds like chaos, try to turn this into a positive: You will learn so much, so soon, that you will accelerate your qualifications for more prestigious journalism jobs.

Working odd hours under deadline pressure and the pressure of public scrutiny, journalists can become consumed by their work. That admirable devotion can become overly stressful. The authors of this book encourage you to have hobbies and friends outside of journalism. These are healthy ways to balance the sometimes uncompromising demands of journalism. They also widen the knowledge you can share with readers.

Proving Yourself

We cannot emphasize this enough: Once you get the job, you have just begun to prove yourself. You must prove yourself constantly—to colleagues, sources, readers, and, ultimately, to yourself. You are always preparing yourself for the next employer—the new managing editor, the editor overseeing your next assignment, the next news organization. Journalism doesn't have to be a nomadic life, but it can be. Your next job may be elsewhere. Then, you have to prove yourself again.

The equation is simple: Positive Performance + Positive Attitude = Success.

Unfortunately, there is no shortage of professionals who have deluded themselves into a sense of entitlement that one of these is enough.

Superior talent does not entitle one to be unethical or disrespectful to colleagues, sources and readers. Outstanding work may get a journalist some slack for ill behavior, but it is not a job guarantee. And your reputation follows you. The best news organizations do not have to settle for talented jerks.

Conversely, perfect disposition doesn't entitle the kindest soul to half-hearted work and promotions just for marking time in the old job. The best treatment of your colleagues, sources and readers is your best effort and your best results, as often as you are capable of delivering them.

Performance

This is the most ambitious, most honest goal anyone can have: Do the best work of your life, now and always. It's a renewable goal, and it's something you can measure, both on the written page and in your heart. Exceeding your own past performance is the healthiest spirit of competition. When you succeed at that, you surely will be meeting or exceeding others' expectations of you.

One of the ways you reach this goal is through constant self-improvement. Make yours a career of life-long learning. Seek training that will improve your knowledge, skills and qualifications. Apply the training in ways where you can see the development. Learn from experienced colleagues, from others whose work you admire, from the best practices that work for counterparts. When the opportunity comes, accept more responsibility.

Attitude

A healthy attitude is confidence in your ability, mixed with humility about what you don't know. Learn from your sources and readers by listening well and keeping an open mind.

Be a skeptic, not a cynic. Journalists are supposed to investigate rather than accept things at face value. Skepticism is a virtue. Cynicism—expecting the worst—is not. It is, however, self-fulfilling.

A wonderful television commercial aired in early 2006 showed an assertive adult and the youth he is mentoring. Only the mentor speaks:

"The man who believes he can and the man who believes he can't are both right.

"Which are *you* going to be?"

This is what it means to have a can-do attitude. Confidence that you *can* find a way, that you *can* succeed. That confidence comes from experience.

IN CONCLUSION

Successful career progress starts with realistic expectations and a wide job search.

Hiring editors look for specific content in cover letters, résumés and work samples. Pay close attention to these, which speak for you. They often determine whether you will have the chance for a face-to-face interview.

Typical job interviews require you to know how you will answer standard questions about your work history, ambition and more. But capitalize on that chance to ask questions that are important to you, too.

Once on the job, both performance and attitude count. Both prepare and endorse you for your next promotion.

Index

A

"A Nation Challenged," 183
Aaron, Hank, 254
ABC, xvi, 360
Abraham, Lisa, 101
Abramoff, Jack, 226
Abu Ghraib prison, 14–15, 17
"Achieving True Diversity," 352
Action verbs, 56–59, 60
Active voice, 41, 57
Adam, Pegie Stark, 77
Afghanistan, 2, 10–11, 30–31,108, 343, 349
Agence France-Presse, 337–338
AIDS, 24, 90, 357
Al Qaeda, 181,
All the President's Men, 17
"America: What Went Wrong?" 21
American Association for the Advancement of Science, 196
American Automobile Association (AAA), 198
American Heart Association, 326
American Society of Magazine Editors (ASME), 49, 264
American Society of Newspaper Editors (ASNE) (asne.org), 8, 75, 81, 85, 91, 163, 174–175, 185, 221, 240, 244–245, 258, 261, 276, 339–340
Amoss, Jim, 304, 312–313
Anderson, Bruce, 101
Adjectives, 61
Adverbs, 61
Anecdotes, 223–226
Anglo-Saxon, 66–70
Anonymous sources, 109–110
Argetsinger, Amy, 342–343
Arizona Republic, 232
Armstrong, Lance, 20
Army, *See* U.S. Army
The Art of Fact: A Historical Anthology of Literary Journalism, 288
The Art of Writing Nonfiction, 288
Asian American Journalists Association, 352
The Associated Press (AP), 6, 31, 39–40, 45–46, 48–50, 52, 68, 134, 143, 170–171, 221–222, 226, 228–233, 267, 307, 332, 337–338, 344, 350, 362
Associated Press Sports Editors, 301
Atlanta Journal-Constitution, 138, 223, 226, 354
The Authentic Voice: The Best Reporting on Race and Ethnicity, 350, 352

Avery, Libby, 101

B

Baghdad, *See* Iraq
The Baltimore Sun, 19, 22, 28, 29, 49, 102, 137
Banaji, Mahzarin, 344–345
Baranick, Alana, 233, 236, 238, 244–246, 248–249, 252
Barlett, Don, 21, 110, 350
Barker, Brandee, 164
Barney, Dee, 254, 262, 268, 271
Bayh, Evan, 108
BBC Sport, 46
Beebe, David, 259
"Being a Black Man," 308
Berkley, Betty, 268
Bernanke, Ben, 257
Bernstein, Carl, 15, 17
Best Newspaper Writing, 130, 163, 248, 261, 271, 342
Biagi, Shirley, 71
Bible, 242, 278
Biloxi *SunHerald, See SunHerald*
Bird by Bird: Some Instructions on Writing and Life, 271
Bissinger, Buzz, 177
Blackberry, 215
Black Hawk Down, 81
Blair, Jayson, 78, 323, 326, 330–331
Blanco, Kathleen, 171, 311
Blogs, 8, 363
Bloomberg News, 45
Bolan, Michael, 133
Boo, Katherine, 49, 253, 264–265
Borisov, Denis, 166
The Boston Globe (and boston.com), 12–13, 15, 55, 75, 192, 195, 200–201, 306, 310, 315, 317, 326, 362
Boston Herald, 164
Boston Marathon, 28
Bowden, Mark, 81
Brady, Jim, 307, 314, 316
Bragg, Rick, 21, 275, 278, 285–286
Brevity, 69
Bringing Court Stories to Life, 149
Broadway, 280
Broderick, Matthew, 280–281
Bronstein, Phil, 329
Brooks, Garth, 310
Brooks, Mel, 280
Brown University, 67
BTK serial killer, 78
Buchanan, Edna, 220, 234
The Buffalo News, 229
Bundy, Ted, 348
Bunn, Timothy, 13, 22
Burton, Thomas M., 295
Bush, George W. (and Bush Administration), 5, 15, 64, 188, 195–196, 257, 327

C

Calhoun, Chris, 238, 242–243, 245, 252
California-Irvine, University of, 289, 292, 298
Campbell, James, 101
Canadian Broadcasting Company, 45
Capote, Truman, 80
Cappon, Rene, 52
Carlin, George, 67, 263
Carter, Hodding Jr., 8, 13
Carter, Hodding III, 8
Carter, Jimmy, 305
Catholic Church, 12–13, 15, 104, 339
CBS, 100, 149
Centers for Disease Control (CDC), 197
Centennial Olympic Park, 354, 356
Central African Republic, 31
Central India, 31
Challenger space shuttle, 39, 257

Character development, 96
Charles River, 286
Chechnya, 31
Cheney, Dick, 26, 327
Chicago Tribune, 51, 133, 150, 153–158, 163, 182, 284, 307, 311–312, 315–316
Chiquita Brands International Inc., 361–362
Christianity (and Christians), 67
Christie, Agatha, 129
Chronology, 11, 245, 281, 283–285
Churchill, Winston, 67–68
CIA, 15, 66
Cincinnati Enquirer, 361
Civil War, The, 343
Civil rights, 8
Clarity, 48, 207
Clark, Roy Peter, 46, 197, 260, 271
Cleveland *Plain Dealer*, 233, 238, 244–246, 248–249
Clinton, Bill, 39, 103, 233
Clinton, Chelsea, 26
Clinton, Hillary, 57, 108, 233, 282–283
The Closer (TV show), 129
The Closers (book), 140
CNN, 32, 46, 354, 362
Cochran, Mike, 134
Coe, Jo-Anne, 295
Colbert, Stephen (and *The Colbert Report*), 35, 257
Cold War, 28
Coll, Steve, 1, 10–12
Colombia, 31
Columbia Journalism Review, 308
Columbia Missourian, 123
Columbia space shuttle, 38
Columbia University, 238–239, 311, 349–350, 352
Committee of Concerned Journalists (and concernedjournalists.com), 99, 104–105, 114, 149, 332, 335, 349, 352
Concrete words, 49
Congo, 31
Congress, 2, 24, 189, 192, 355, 363
Connelly, Michael, vii, 128, 131, 133–135, 140–141, 147
Context, 27–28
Cosby, Bill, 263
Covering Crime and Justice, 149
Cox News Service, 38, 233
Cran, William, 67
Crews, Timothy, 101
Crime Beat, 134, 140–141
Crime stories
  avoid mistakes, 139
  accidents, 142–146
  identity, 138–142
  incident, 136–138
  narrative ,144–146
  popularity, 129
  reporting, 140–141
  timeline, 130
  terms, 135
  types of, 129–135
  writing, 132–134
Criminal Justice Journalists, 149
Cruise, Tom, 26
CSI, 129
Currency, 24

D

The Daily Show, 35
Dallas Morning News, 230–231
Darfur, 31
DART Center, 157–158, 162, 185, 312
Davis, Thomas Cullen, 134
Daylight Savings Time, 279
Daytona Beach News Journal, 140
The Dead Beat, 240, 252
Delta Democrat Times, 8, 13

The Denver Post, 21, 44, 46–47, 49, 109–110, 124–125, 160, 164, 238, 241, 247–250, 320, 323, 327–332, 335
Dever, Larry, 297
Dialogue, 116–118
Disaster coverage
  enterprise, 175–181
  eyewitnesses, 174–175
  Hurricane Katrina ,172–173
  leads, 169–174
  narrative writing, 176–177
  organization, 170
  public service, 182–183
  stakeholders, 181
Diversity
  age, 339
  assumptions, 344
  audience, 346
  beliefs, 339
  cultural, 341
  family, 339
  geographic, 341, 347–348
  improving content, 341–350
  interest, 341
  Katrina photographs, 337–338
  newsrooms, 340
  recruiting, 348
  sources, 344
  talent, 341
Dobbs, Maisie, 95
Doctors Without Borders, 31
Donley, Jon, 172–173, 311–312
Dow Jones, 86
Downie, Leonard, 17, 308
Duncan, Tim, 106
Dwyer, James, 176–177

E

Eddins, Bill, 177
Edwards, John, 27
Electoral College, 39
The Elements of Journalism, 4, 9, 17, 189
The Elements of Style, 62
The Emperor's New Clothes, 102
Enron, 6, 14, 25, 157, 305
Enser, Barbara, 196, 201
Entertainment Weekly, 238–239
Enzi, Mike, 196
Epstein, Mike, 197–198
Erie Times-News, 151, 158
ESPN: The Magazine, 278–279
Esquire magazine, 282
Etch A Sketch, 256–257, 266
Ethics
  accepting gifts, 322
  actions, 332
  conflicts of interest, 322–326
  deception, 327–328
  disclosure, 329
  policy, 330–331
  voting on Heisman, 323
Endings
  echo the lead, 291–296
  importance, 290–291
  kickers, 296–298
  profiles, 269
  features ,286
  wrap–up scene, 300–302
Enterprise
  disasters, 175–181
  stakeholders, 181
  stories, 134–35
Evasive sources, 97
Eversmann, Matt, 81
Extraneous information, 91
Eyes on the News, 77

F

Facebook, 164, 369
FBI, 131, 255–256, 354, 356, 362
"Farm Fresh Clichés," 347, 352

Features
definition, 273–274
intriguing statement, 279–282
leads, 275–282
reconstruction leads, 278–279
time element, 274
organization, 274–275
Federal Communications Commission, 99
Federal Drug Administration, 196, 200–201
Federal Reserve, 257
Feldman, Claudia, 221
52 McGs, 238, 252
"Final Salute," 237
Finkel, David, 274
Firestone, 14
First Amendment, 354–355
Fitzgerald, Patrick, 327
Flood, Mary, 25, 153, 157, 165, 305–306, 315–316
Flores, Ana, 156
Flores, Tom, 156
Foley, Severin, 249
Fontaine, Andre, 288
Ford Foundation, 149
Fort Worth Star-Telegram, 27–29, 70, 157
Fort Worth Weekly, 219, 230
Fortune magazine, 14
Ft. Lauderdale Sun-Sentinel (and sunsentinel.com) (also, South Florida Sun-Sentinel), 140
Franklin, Jon, 75, 78, 288
Freedman, Alix M., 266
Freedom of Information Act, 155
French, 67–68
Friday Night Lights, 177
Fujimori, Alberto, 189
Fuller, Jack, 189
Fuller, Nicole, 137

G

Gallagher, Michael, 361
Garcia, Mario, 77
Gaulden, Sid, 101
Geoghan, John, 13
Ghost Wars, 12
Gillette, John, 151
Glass, Stephen, 326
Glavin, William, 48, 288
Goode, Wilson, 102–103
Goodyear, 330
Google.com, 256
Gore, Al, 24, 39, 114
Government reporting, 205–211
Gramza, Janet, 254–255, 262, 268
Grand Forks Herald, 7, 183
Grant High School, 276
Graythen, Chris, 337
Great Pyramids, 42
Green, Mackenzie, 116–118
Greene, Jade, 247–248
Greenspan, Alan, 257
Grenada, 67
Griego, Tina, 77, 91, 113, 121–124, 160–162, 296, 299
Griffey Jr., Ken, 278–279
Ground Zero, 175
Gruley, Bryan, 168, 174–175, 180
Guzzo, Glenn, 109–110, 131, 369

H

Haiti, 31
Hajdu, David, 238–239, 242
Hall of Fame (baseball), 323
Hall, Sandra, 221
Hallman, Tom, 7, 272, 276–277, 309
Hamill, Pete, 9
Hanks, Steve, 256–257
Hargraves, Richard, 101
Hartford Courant, 44, 46–47
Harvard University, 257, 273, 286, 305, 310

Hassell, John, 44
Hayes, Marcus, 54, 59–60, 256, 290, 301–302
Heisler, Todd, 237
Heisman Trophy, 323
Henderson, Diedtra, 75–76, 91, 186, 192, 195–197, 200–201
Henry, Patrick, 123
Hernandez, Barbra, 308
Hersh, Seymour, 14–15
Hezbollah, 31
Hight, Joe, 185
Hilder, Robert, 298–300
HIV, 357
Hollywood, 243, 297
Holmes, Katie, 26
Holmes, Sherlock, 129
Holocaust, 257
Holson, Laura M., 297
Hopkins, Jim, 82
Houston Chronicle, 6, 25, 153, 157, 165, 220–221, 305, 315–316
Howell, Deborah, 177
Hubbard, J. T. W., 52, 228
Hull, Anne, 2
Hurricane Andrew, 183
Hurricane Ivan, 87
Hurricane George, 172
Hurricane Katrina, 5, 6, 17, 21, 50, 124, 169–176, 178–181, 197, 226–228, 233, 273, 310–313, 337–338
Hurricane Rita, 60, 220–221
Hussein, Sadam, 14, 31, 39, 300
Hutcheson, Ron, 8, 9, 69–70, 194–196
Hutchins Commission, 328–329

I

Identity
  race, 139
  suspects, 139
  victims, 138
In Cold Blood, 80
Indiana, University of, 243
Indianapolis Colts, 233
Indonesia, 39
Inside the Police Beat, 149
Internet
  approaching victims, 164
  audience measurement, 315–316
  breaking news, 32, 50, 310–312
  ethics, 329
  exchanges, 199
  Hurricane Katrina, 172–173, 312–313
  impact of, 6
  interviewing, 100
  libel, 363
  long stories, 284
  narrative stories, 81
  quotes, 123
  research profiles, 256
  speeches, 194
  storytelling, 305–306
  using websites, 196
Inverted pyramid, 42–47
Interviewing
  anonymous sources, 109–110
  answers, 106–107
  backup plan, 97–98
  dialogue, 116–118
  evasive sources, 97
  email, 99
  for jobs, 372
  integrity, 100–103
  preparation, 95, 97–98, 102–103
  profiles, 263–266
  rapport with sources, 98–100
  questions, 97, 104–107
  speakers, 189
  stakeholders, 181
  taking notes, 107–108
  victims, 163–165
Investigative Reporters and Editors, 13

The Invisible Man, 308
Iowa, University of, 243
Iraq (and Baghdad), 2, 5, 6, 14–16, 24–25, 30–31, 39–40, 51, 67, 108, 111, 192, 297, 300, 307
Islam (and Islamists), 31
Israel, 31

J

Jackson, Michael, 26, 29
Jargon, 55–60, 68, 214
Jeffcoats, Kathy, 138
Jesus Christ, 249
Jewell, Richard, 353–354, 356, 360
Jobs
  application, 369–370
  expectations, 368
  published work, 371
  résumé, 370
  search, 368
Johns Hopkins University, 192
Johnson, Marilyn, 240, 252
Johnstown flood, 169–170
Jolie, Angelina, 26,
Jones, Jim, 182
Jordan, Michael, 30, 64
Journalism
  changes lives, 15–16
  community impact, 7, 9
  exposes wrongs, 14–15
  fairness, 8–9
  online basics, 316–317
  public service, 182–183
  questions institutions, 12–13
  why it matters, 4–5
  why it's necessary, 10–12
Journalists
  acting ethically, 332
  killed in Iraq, 16
  role, 2–4
Journal-World (Lawrence, Kan.), 309
justicejournalism.org, 149

K

Kaczynski, David, 255–256
Kaczynski, Ted, 255–256
Kaiser, Robert G., 17
Karem, Brian, 101
Katrina, *See* Hurricane Katrina
Keller, Bill, 315–316
Kelley, Jack, 326–327, 330
Kennedy, John F. (and Kennedy assassination), 24, 188
Kenya, 342
Kerrane, Kevin, 288
Kerry, John, 5, 27
Kershner, Vlae, 306, 311, 316
Kever, Jeannie, 221
KHOU-Houston, 14
Kicker endings, 296–300
Kidwell, David, 101
Kiernan, Louise, 150, 152–156, 158, 163, 165
King, Don, 321
King, Martin Luther, 188
King, Peter H., 124
Knight Ridder, 27, 70
Koch, Ed, 267–269
Kopetman, Roxana, 101
Koppel, Ted, 350
Kovach, Bill, 4, 9, 17, 189
Kropf, Schuyler, 101
Ku Klux Klan, 8, 13, 344, 350

L

Lake Placid Winter Olympics, 28
Lamott, Anne, 271
Lane, Nathan, 280–281
LaPeter, Leonora, 75–76, 85, 134, 152, 162–163
Latin words, 67–68
Law, Bernard, 13
Law & Order, 129

Lay, Bernard, 13
Lay, Ken, 6, 25, 305
Leads
  5 W's and H, 38, 47
  anecdotal, 280–281
  disaster stories, 169–174
  features, 275–282
  historic, 39
  how to begin, 40
  meeting stories, 211–214
  narrative, 84–88
  non-traditional, 219–234
  profiles, 265, 266–267
  Pulitzer Prize, 43–45
  role of, 37
  steps in writing, 40
  traditional, 38, 50
  word length, 50–51
Lee, Wen Ho, 362–363
Leggett, Vanessa, 101
"Let's Do It Better" workshop and judges, 349–350
Leovy, Jill, 130, 133, 144–146
Levan, Alan, 360
Lewinsky, Monica, 103
Lewis, Ashley, 85, 134
Libby, Lewis I. "Scooter," 66, 327
Libel
  defenses, 357–358
  definition, 355–357
  Jewell case, 354
  online, 363
  public officials, 358–361
  trials, 359
Lichtblau, Eric, 15
Life on the Dead Beat, 244, 252
Life Stories: Profiles from The New Yorkers, 271
Lightner, Sam, 7, 276
The Lincoln Lawyer, 140
Lloyd, Bob, 157
Lohan, Lindsay, 26
Look magazine, 13
Lohr, Steve, 81
Lopez, Steve, 91, 177
Los Alamos National Laboratory, 362
The Los Angeles Herald Examiner, 160
Los Angeles Times, 11, 14, 23, 43, 91, 124, 130, 133, 140–141, 144, 177, 221, 254, 289, 298–299, 315, 321, 323, 330–332, 335, 362
Love Canal, 114
Lundstrom, Marjie, 23, 295–296, 299, 336, 346–349
Lundy, Walker, 27
Lyman, Rick, 262, 269

M

MacArthur Foundation, 264
MacNeil, Robert, 67
Madigan, Charles, 284, 307, 311–312, 314–316
Magazine Editing, 228
Malone, Karl, 26,
Malvo, John Boyd, 130
Marimow, Bill, 94, 97, 102–103
Martin, Claire, 49, 238–239, 241–242, 246–248, 250
Martin, Dave, 337
Martinez, Mel, 197–198
Masai tribe, 342–343
Mask, 7, 276
MCI Worldcom, 230
McAuliffe,Christa, 39, 257
McCartney, Charles, 243
McCarty, Oseola, 275, 278, 285–286
McClatchy newspapers, 8, 9, 69–70, 194–195
McCrum, Robert, 67

McHugh, John, 108
McLean, Bethany, 14
McLellan, Scott, 66, 199
McNabb, Donovan, 17
McNulty, Tim, 182
McVeigh, Timothy, 283
Media Law Resource Center, 359
Meeting stories
  avoid bureaucratic traps, 206
  follow issues, 206, 210–211
  leads, 211–214
  preparation, 206–207, 215
  roundup stories, 214–217
Mencher, Melvin, 24
The Merlin hotel, 261
Miami Dolphins, 234
The Miami Herald, 183, 197, 220
Micheli, Mark, 306, 310, 317
Microsoft, 215
Middle East, 343
Middle English, 67
Milbrandt, Josephine, 244
"Miller Chop," 220
Miller, Gene, 220
Miller, Judith, 101, 327
Miller, Stephen, 252
Mississippi House of Representatives, 8, 13
Missouri, University of, 123
Moore, Greg, 124–125, 320, 323, 330–331
Moore, Paul, 19, 28–29
Moose, Charles, 129
Morgan, Arlene, 350, 352
Morin, Monte, 43
"Mortal Wounds," 130
Muhammad, John Allen, 130
Murray, Donald, 52, 55, 70
Murray, Jim, 254
Myers, Linnet, 133
MySpace, 164, 369
Mystery Guild, 131

N

Narrative writing, 78–80, 81, 84–88, 116, 144–146, 155, 176–177, 190, 240–241, 277, 292, 298
The Narrows, 140
Nashville Tennessean, 224
Nassens, Katrien, 286–287
National Association of Black Journalists, 352
National Association of Hispanic Journalists, 352
The National Enquirer, 29
National Geographic, 91
National Guard, 32, 174
National Lesbian & Gay Journalists Association, 352
National Public Radio, 102, 273, 305
Native American Journalists Association, 352
Nazi, 257
NBC, 354
Negro Leagues, 343
New England Journal of Medicine, 200
New Orleans, 5, 61, 124–125, 170–174, 176, 178–181, 183, 197, 226–228, 311–313, 337–338
New Orleans Superdome, 17
The New Republic, 326
Newkirk, Bill, 330
The News About the News, 17
News is a Verb: Journalism at the End of the Twentieth Century, 9
News judgment
  against the tide, 21
  change, 24, 28
  conflict, 30
  crowd, 33–34
  guidelines, 20
  people, 26–27

ticket to the backstage, 24–25
timeliness, 32–33
weird, 33
News story
crime, 132–134
elements of victim's story, 159–162
speeches, 187–192
press conferences, 196–198
structure, 88
*Newsday,*293
newslab.org, 149
New Republic, 326
NewsTalk, 271
Newsweek, 46
Newsweekly magazines, 32
The New Yorker, 10, 12, 14–15, 49, 117–118, 220, 230, 234, 253, 264–265, 275
New York Post, 316
The New York Times, 5, 13, 15–16, 21, 38–39, 61, 65, 81–82, 85, 91, 170–171, 176, 178, 180–181, 183, 238–239, 242–245, 260, 262, 275, 280–281, 297, 315–316, 321–323, 326–327, 330, 332, 335, 356, 362
New York Times v. Sullivan, 358, 360
New York University, 7
Nichols, Lamar, 291
Nicholson, Jim, 239–241
Nielson (ratings), 316
9/11, *See* Sept. 11, 2001
Nixon, Richard (and Nixon Administration), 15, 187
nola.com, 6, 172–173, 311–313
Non-traditional leads
anecdotes, 223–226
change in direction, 232–233
entertaining, 220
humor, 223–234
intriguing statement, 229–232, 279–282
reconstruction, 278–279
roundup, 228–229
situationers, 226–228
storytelling, 221–226
Norals, Alexis, 138
Norman Conquest, 67
North Korea, 31
Ntaiya, Kakenya, 342–343
Nut graph
analytical, 84
bridge to middle, 282
counter intuitive, 83–84
counter trend, 83
effective writing, 83–84
role of, 77–82
timing, 83
trend ,83
NYPD Blue, 129

O

Obbie, Mark, 363
Obituaries
importance, 238–239
life stories, 237–242
reporting, 237, 244–245, 248–250
storytelling, 240–241
writing, 242–248
O'Brien, Timothy, 356
Obmascik, Mark, 44
Ocala Star-Banner, 308
O'Hare Airport, 154
Old English, 67
Olympic Games, 354
Omit needless words, 62
Online
audience measurement,315–316
breaking news, 310–312
Hurricane Katrina, 312–313
libel, 363
storytelling, 305–306, 308–309

traffic, 310
visuals, 307
voice, 313–315
wire service, 306–307
*The Oregonian (*Portland *Oregonian),* 7, 258–259, 272, 276, 291, 293–294, 309, 316,
Organizing stories, 75–77, 88, 170, 274–275, 283–286
Ostrow, Joanne, 164
Owens, Terrell, 17

P

Pace, 89–90
Palattella, Ed, 151, 153, 158–159, 162, 165–166
The Palm Beach Post, 197
Pascal, Blaise, 77
Passive voice, 41, 57
Peabody Award, 308
Pelosi, Nancy, 30
Pennsylvania Newspaper Association, 151
Pentagon, 6, 38, 99
People, writing about, 26–27, 254
Peoples Temple, 182
Peracchio, Adrian, 293
Peru, 189
Pett, Saul, 267–269
Pew Research Center, 31
Pfeiffer, Michelle, 86
Philadelphia Daily News, 54, 59, 239, 256, 290, 301–302
Philadelphia Eagles, 17, 256
The Philadelphia Inquirer, 8, 13, 21, 28–29, 81, 102, 131, 177, 215, 283–284, 357
Philadelphia Phillies, 256
Phillips, Warren, 86
Pifer, Alice Irene, 352
Pirro, Jeanine, 232–233
Pitt, Brad, 26
Plagiarism
quotes, 123
stories, 326–327
Plame, Valerie, 66, 199, 327
Pollak, Lisa, 22, 49
Pope John Paul II, 32
"Portraits of Grief," 245
Potter, Harry, 90, 345
The Poynter Institute (and poynter.org), 46, 104, 149, 163, 260–261, 321, 327, 330–331, 335, 338–339, 345, 347, 351–352
Prayer for the City, 177
Prepositions, 62–63
Press conferences
coverage, 192–194
how to cover, 194–196
writing, 196–198
Press releases, 198–202
Priest, Dana, 2, 15
Privacy, 361–364
The Producers, 280
Profiles
change, 262–263
choosing subjects, 254–257
conflict, 262
endings, 269
honest reporting, 260–261
justification, 267–268
leads, 265, 266–267
news peg, 257–260
moments, 268–269
storytelling, 258–259
writing, 263–269
Proper names usage, 64–65
Pryor, Richard, 263
Public Broadcasting System, 129
Pugmire, Lance, 43
Pulitzer Prize, 7, 12, 13, 14–16, 21, 23, 43, 45, 47, 49, 75, 78, 91, 100, 152, 154, 183, 230, 234, 237, 240, 244–245, 258, 260,

264, 272, 274–277, 291, 292, 295, 298, 300, 309, 311, 347

Q

The Quill magazine, 309
Quindlen, Anna, 91
Quotes
  dialogue, 116–118
  ethics, 124–125
  how to quote, 120–121
  whom to quote, 115
  structuring, 122–123
  usage, 115–120, 121–122

R

Raines, Howell, 260
Reagan, Ronald (and Reagan Administration), 21, 256
Reaves, Gayle, 219, 230–231
Red River, 7
Redford, Robert, 86
Redundancy, 90
Reed, Ralph, 223–226
Remnick, David, 271
Repetitive phrases, 66
Reporters Committee for Freedom of the Press, 101
Reporters jailed, 101
Richardson, Johnny, 249–250
Risen, James, 13, 15
Robert's Rules of Order, 207
Roberts, Eugene (Gene), 8, 13, 86
Roberts, John, 69
Roberts, Julia, 64
Roche, Tim, 101
Rocky Mountain News, 77, 91, 121–123, 160, 198, 237, 240–241, 296, 299
Roe v. Wade, 29, 69
Roman Catholic Church, *See* Catholic Church
Roosevelt, Franklin Delano, 188
Rose, Bill, 197
Rosen, Jay, 7, 17
Rosenstiel, Tom, 4, 9, 17, 189
Roth, Joe, 297
Rove, Karl, 5, 66
Rowling, J. K., 345
Rumsfeld, Donald, 31, 51, 192–193
Ruth, Babe, 254

S

The Sacramento Bee, 23, 295–296, 299, 326, 336, 346–347
Sagarin, Jeff, 279
Sago Mine, 182
salon.com, 337
Salyers, Prisilla, 283–285
Sam: The Story Behind the Mask, 276
San Antonio Express-News (and mysanantonio.com), 335
San Francisco Chronicle (and sfgate.com), 142, 306, 311, 315–316, 329
Sanchez, Felix, 101
Sandler, Adam, 263
Sands, Ken, 99
Savannah Morning News, 85, 134, 162
Schaefer, Rebecca, 160
Schulte, Henry, 55
Scoppe, Cindi, 101
Seattle Post-Intelligencer, 315
"See No Bias," 344
Seinfeld, Jerry, 262–263, 269
Sept. 11, 2001, 10, 16, 24, 38, 50, 52, 99, 168, 174–178, 180–181, 245, 343, 345–346, 349, *See also* 9/11
Seung-Hui, Cho, 325
Shadid, Anthony, 300
Shain, Andrew, 101
Sharpe, Shannon, 125

Sheeler, Jim, 237, 240–241, 246–247, 249–250, 252
Shiskin, Philip, 297
Show don't tell, 280
Siegel, Barry, 23, 289, 292–293, 298–300
Simple writing, 41, 55, 60, 68
Simpson, O.J., 29, 129
Sinatra, Frank, 238–239
60 Minutes, 100
slate.com, 144–145
Smyth, Frank, 185
snopes.com, 337
Social Security, 195
Somalia (and Somalis), 31, 81
Sources
  anonymous, 109–110
  diversity, 344
  evasive, 97
  preparation, 97
  rapport, 98–100
South Florida Sun-Sentinel, See Ft. Lauderdale Sun-Sentinel
Soviet Union, 28
Speeches, 187–192
  be an eyewitness, 188
  interview speaker, 188
  prepare, 188
  seek reaction, 189
*The Spokesman-Review (*Spokane *Spokesman-Review), 99,* 258, 261
Spradley, Jacobie, 152
Springer, John, 44
Sri Lanka, 31
St. Petersburg Times, 152, 227, 260, 275
Stanford University, 26, 257
Stanton, Sam, 295–296
Starkweather, Charles, 347
StarTribune The Star-Ledger (Newark Star-Ledger), 44, 46–47
State of the Union, 194
Steele, Bob, 327, 330–332, 335
Steele, James, 21, 110, 350
Stewart, Jon, 35
The Story of English, 67
Storytelling, 22, 37, 190, 208–210, 221–226, 240–241, 258–259, 280–281, 308–309, 324–325, 342–343, 371
Stone, Brad, 101
Stout, J. K., 243
Strunk, Will, 62, 66
Strunk and White's *Elements of Style*, 66
Sullivan-Springhetti, Julie, 258–259, 261, 291–294
Sun Herald (Biloxi *Sun Herald*), 169, 311
Sunflower Broadband, 309
Supreme Court, *See* U.S. Supreme Court
Support lead, 88–89
S-V-O, 48
Syracuse *Post-Standard,* 22, 36–37, 49, 224, 254–255, 271
Syracuse University, 48, 55, 224, 363

T

Taborda, Carmen, 156
Taking notes, 107–108
Tampa Bay Buccaneers, 227
Tampa Tribune, xviii, 197
Taricani, Jim, 101
Tewogbola, Tasneem Grace, 36–37, 49, 224–225
Texas Chainsaw Massacre, 132
Texas, University of, 70
Thames River, 32
This American Life, 49
Thomas Jr., Robert McG., 238–239, 242–245

Thoreau, Henry David, 77
3 Nights in August, 177
Tillman, Pat, 10–12
Time magazine, 25, 31–32, 46, 100, 257
*The Times-Picayune (*New Orleans *Times-Picayune),* 6, 171–173, 179, 183, 304, 311–313
Tiner, Stan, 169
"Torn from the Land," 344, 350
Tour de France, 20
Tower of Pisa, 221
Tragedies and Journalists: A Guide for More Effective Coverage, 185
Tribune Co., 189
Trillin, Calvin, 220, 234
Truman, Harry S., 287
Trump, Donald, 356
Twain, Mark, 61, 77
20/20, 360
The Tyndall Report, 31

U

Unabomber, *See* Ted Kaczynski
University of Missouri, 123
Up Close and Personal, 86
USA Today, 39, 41, 48, 52, 82, 232–233, 315, 326–327, 330
U.S. Army, 2, 10–12
U.S. Constitution, 187, 355
U.S. Department of Homeland Security, 346
U.S. House of Representatives, 99, 205
U.S. Immigration and Naturalization Services, 259
U.S. Olympic hockey team, 28
U.S. Senate, 39
U.S. Supreme Court, 24, 29, 39, 130, 341, 358, 360

V

VandeHei, Jim, 199
Van Derbeken, Jaxon, 142
Van Ness, Chris, 101
Vedantam, Shankar, 344–345
Victims
- connecting with, 160–162
- how to approach, 153–158
- how to interview, 163
- viewpoint, 162–163
- why interview them, 152–153, 159

Vietnam (and Vietnam War), 5, 67
Virginia Tech University, 6, 50, 164, 325, 343
Von Bergen, Jane, ix, 204, 215–216
Voter News Service, 25

W

The Wall Street Journal, 39, 66, 82, 164, 174–175, 180, 185, 232, 256, 273, 279, 286–287, 295, 297, 315
Wallace, Mike, 100
Walsh, Adam, 21
Walter Reed Army Medical Center, 2
Warhover, Thomas, 123
Warrick, Joby, 182
Washington, D.C. (and Washington press corps), 98
The Washington Post (and washingtonpost.com), 1–2, 10–12, 15, 32, 39, 87, 114, 134, 174, 182, 199, 222, 227, 256, 264, 274, 300, 307–308, 314–316, 342, 344, 362
Washington University, 200
Watergate, 15
Wayment, Gage, 298
Wayment, Paul, 298–299
Wendy's, 27
Wenzl, Roy V., 74–75, 78–80

Werfel, Clemmie, 249
West Nile Virus, 197
What are Journalists For?, 8, 17
What's the Matter with Kansas?, 339
Whelan, Jeff, 44
"Whippy Dip," 158–159
White, E. B., 62, 66
White House, 69, 174, 194–195, 327
White House coverage, 8
Whitiker, Angela, 88
The Wichita Eagle, 75, 78–80, 210–211
Wilkerson, Isabel, 85–88
Willamette Week, 14
Wilson, Janet, 43
Wilson, Joseph, 327
Winspear, Jacqueline, 95
Witchel, Alex, 280–281
Wolf, Joshua, 101
Wolfe, Tom, 75
Woods, Keith, 338–339, 345, 351–352
Woodward, Bob, 15, 17
The Word, 52
The World Co., 309
World Trade Center, 38, 99, 168, 174–177, 244
World War I, 67
World War II, 67
Wrap-up scenes, 300–302
Writing
  adjectives, use of, 61–62
  anecdotal leads, 223–226
  Anglo-Saxon, 66–70
  brevity, 69
  clear language, 23, 48
  connection with reporting, 2, 276–277
  narratives, 78–80, 81, 84–88, 116, 144–146, 155, 176–177, 190, 240–241, 277, 292, 298
  numbers, 63–64
  nut graph,77–84
  one idea per sentence, 55
  prepositions, 62–63
  proper names, 64–65
  repetitive phrases, 66
  simplicity, 60, 68, 69
  vigorous, 22–23
Writing a news story, 76, 196–202, 211–217, 242–248
Writer's Toolbox, 46
Writing for Story, 288
Writing for Your Readers, 52, 55
Writing Tools, 197

Y

Yagoda, Ben, 288
Yahoo News, 310
Yale University, 344
Young, Jimmy, 301–302

Photo Credits

Page 1, 10, © Lauren Shay Lavin/Courtesy of Penguin Press; 3, © Alex Wong/ Getty Images; 13, AP Photo; 14, © Getty Images; 19, 28, Courtesy of Paul Moore; 25, AP Photo; 27, © Stephen Crowley/The New York Times; 36, Courtesy of Tasneem Grace Tewogbola; 39 top left, AP Photo; 39 middle left, © Doug Mills/AP Photo; 39 bottom left, © Walter Michot/AP Photo; 39 top right, © Markus Matzel/Peter Arnold; 39 bottom right, © AFP/Getty Images; 54, 60, Courtesy of Marcus Hayes; 62, AP Photo; 69, Courtesy of Ron Hutcheson; 74, 78, The Wichita Eagle; 81, © David Keane; 86, © Photos 12/Alamy; 94, 102, Courtesy of Bill Marimow; 105, © Tom Carter/PhotoEdit; 108, © Chuck Kennedy/MCT/Newscom; 113, 160, © Ellen Jaskol/Rocky Mountain News; 128, 140, 141, Courtesy of Michael Connelly; 129, © Reuters/CORBIS; 144, Courtesy of Jill Leovy; 150, 154, The Chicago Tribune; 166, © Rich Forsgren/ Erie Times-News; 168, © Neville Elder/CORBIS SYGMA; 172, Courtesy of Jon Donley; 179, Courtesy of Times-Picayune and nola.com; 186, 200, The Boston Globe; 189, © Oscar Paredes/Reuters/CORBIS; 195, The McClatchy Newspapers; 204, 215, © I. George Bilyk; 219, 230, © Vishal Malhotra; 236, 244, © Allison Carey; 237, © Todd Heisler/Rocky Mountain News/Polaris; 239, © Ho/AP Photo; 253, 264, Courtesy of Katherine Boo; 254, The Post-Standard and photographer Michelle Gabel; 258, The Oregonian; 272, 276, Courtesy of Tom Hallman; 275, © Steve Coleman/AP Photo; 282, © Alex Wong/Getty Images; 289, 298, © Amanda Edwards/Getty Images; 294, © Motoya Nakamura/The Oregonian; 300, © Douglas C. Pizac/AP Photo; 301, © Phil Sandlin/AP Photo; 304. 312, Courtesy of Jim Amoss; 311, © Ethan Miller/ Getty Images; 320, 330, Courtesy of Greg Moore; 323, The New York Times; 326, © Neville Elder/CORBIS; 327, © USA Today/AP Photo; 336, 347, Courtesy of Marjie Lundstrom; 338 top, © Dave Martin/AP Photo; 338 bottom, © Chris Graythen/Getty Images; 344, © Li-Hua Lan/Syracuse Newspapers/ The Image Works; 353, © Hulton Archive/Getty Images; 261, © Tom Uhlman/ AP Photo; 362, © Jake Schoellkopf/AP Photo; 367, © Michael Newman/ PhotoEdit.